Achieving ISO 9000 Registration

A Process Management Approach to the Optimum Quality System

SPC Press, Inc.
Knoxville, Tennessee

Achieving ISO 9000 Registration

A Process Management Approach to the Optimum Quality System

Dr. Bryn Owen, *Quality Consultant*
Optimum Systems for Quality, Ltd.

Tom Cothran,
Cothran PR

Peter Malkovich, *Quality Consultant*
Process Management International, Inc.

Doug 6/94
Best to you & all your quality endeavors.
Pete Malkovich

Several quotations from the ISO 9001 Standard are found in the book.
They are taken from ANSI/ASQC Q91-1987 AND ANSI/ASQC Q9001-1994,
published in the U.S. by ASQC Quality Press.
These quotations are used with the permission of ASQC Quality Press.

SPC Press, Inc.
5908 Toole Drive, Suite C
Knoxville, Tennessee 37919 U.S.A.
(615) 584-5005

For a free catalog of books published by SPC Press, call 1-800-545-8602

ISBN 0-945320-41-8

1 2 3 4 5 6 7 8 9

Table of Contents

About the Authors...

The three authors, Bryn Owen, Tom Cothran, and Peter Malkovich, share a wide range of experience and specialized knowledge that makes them ideally suited to prepare this book. Their international work in management and engineering in many different industries, and the quality movement, provides a strong foundation for this book. They have a thorough understanding of the theoretical basis of the ISO 9000 Standard and wide experience in successfully preparing many companies for registration.

Dr. Bryn Owen developed the Process Management Model for the implementation of ISO 9000. The founder of Optimum Systems for Quality, Ltd., he has worked with over 100 clients who have successfully used this model to develop systems that meet the requirements of the Standard, while improving their internal operations. Clients have included a wide range of service and manufacturing industries and government departments.

Dr. Owen trained as Quality Systems Lead Auditor but he presently works as a consultant. His undergraduate degrees are in Industrial Engineering and Management Studies. He also has an MSc for studies related to Metrology and Quality Control. His doctoral work (studies in the implementation of ISO 9000 in manufacturing industries) was completed in 1991 at Salford University.

He has held management and quality system positions both in England and Nigeria. While Quality Manager at Leyland Vehicles, his responsibilities included quality planning for the manufacture of a new range of trucks (which was later given the European Truck of the Year Award).

At Salford University College, he served as the Principal Lecturer in Engineering, specifically responsible for the development of courses in quality and computer-aided engineering. He also became a consultant in the field of quality systems, preparing his first client for successful registration to BS 5750 (ISO 9000) in 1987.

Since 1987 he has worked as a Quality Consultant, specializing in quality systems and various aspects of quality training. His specialty, of course, is helping clients achieve ISO 9000 registration.

Tom Cothran brings more than 23 years experience in communications to the quality field. His Minnesota-based company, Cothran PR, specializes in consulting and assisting quality engineers and other professionals in articulating their ideas and experiences.

Cothran is the chief contributing editor to *Profiles in Quality,* a book by Louis E. Schultz, surveying and synthesizing the major quality theories and approaches. Mr. Cothran has also written numerous speeches and articles on quality issues such as introducing quality, systems thinking, leadership, and the Malcolm Baldrige National Quality Award. Cothran PR's clientele includes companies ranging from Fortune 500 corporations to small businesses.

Cothran is a graduate of Wofford College in Spartanburg, S.C. Prior to launching his own communications enterprise in 1985, Cothran spent 15 years in journalism, serving as a regional news editor for the Associated Press and, prior to that, covering a wide range of political, industrial and scientific issues. His work has taken him to four continents and has included sessions with some of the major business and political figures of the day.

Peter M. Malkovich leads the ISO 9000 consulting practice at Process Management International, Inc. (PMI), an international Total Quality consulting and training firm. He has assisted many organizations, including PMI, in achieving ISO 9000 registration.

Mr. Malkovich has over 30 years of business, industrial, and consulting experience. He has worked as an engineer, in engineering management, and in senior staff and management positions in both manufacturing and service organizations.

He holds a Bachelor of Mechanical Engineering (with honors) and an MBA. While working on a Ph.D. at the University of Minnesota, he taught statistics and operations courses.

His consulting assignments have been numerous and diverse including technical projects, strategic planning, and business acquisitions and divestitures. His work has taken him to Japan, Israel, Austria, the Netherlands, and the United Kingdom. Now working with Process Management International, he specializes in assisting clients to achieve ISO 9000 registration.

Foreword: A Registrar's View

Written by Steve Clark, Technical Director
National Quality Assurance,
A Registrar accredited in the U.K. and U.S.A.

The International Standard, ISO 9000: Quality Systems, does not define how an organization must manage its affairs, but sets a series of requirements for an efficient system of management. This management system is called the documented quality system as it is through this system that the organization meets the needs and expectations of its customers, and achieves quality.

Our role as Registrars is to assess the documented quality system. This assessment is based on the documentation of the system, but more importantly its relevance and efficient operation. Through documentation the system is communicated to the employees, and it is the work of the employees that achieves quality.

Registrars know the requirements of the Standard and their task is the assessment of an organization's operations and confirming they meet those requirements. When making this assessment, Registrars are interested in the processes of the organization—how it communicates with its customers, how it accepts and processes orders, how it develops new products and services, and how the customers' requirements are met. These are examples of the processes by which an organization functions; the processes that make up the quality system.

The Process Management approach addresses these processes and provides procedures that efficiently describe the quality system. These procedures enable the auditors to understand the operation of the company and allow for an easy assessment, but more importantly, they enable the employees to understand the system and to work to it.

This book describes the Process Management approach and addresses the issues associated with registration to ISO 9000 in a practical and authoritative way.

It includes procedure guides that provide a good insight into what is required to meet the Standard. The information within them, and in the commentaries following them, explains how to meet the requirements of the Standard and gives examples of the pitfalls to be avoided and the shortcuts that may be taken.

The relationship between an organization and its Registrar is an important one. It is like a marriage, easier to get into than out of. Harmony and mutual understanding is important if the relationship is to prosper. The chapter on choosing a Registrar provides much useful information that will allow organizations to make an informed choice of registrar. The information will certainly make Registrars work harder for a living, and should encourage them to provide a better service.

Over the last four years, NQA has assessed numerous organizations in many different industries who have used this Process Management approach in preparing for registration. We have found the documentation easy to follow and this has allowed registration to be achieved with few problems.

This is a very useful text on implementing ISO 9000 using the Process Management approach; an approach we attempt to instill into our auditors.

Preface

The International Organization for Standardization (ISO) has responsibility for the content of all ISO Standards. To ensure that they meet current needs, Standards are periodically reviewed and revised. This revision process requires agreement by representatives of all participating countries. It is a long, formal process.

The ISO 9000 series of Standards was first issued in 1987 with an update scheduled for 1992. This update was approved in September 1993 and comes into force in 1994. The changes are not of a significant nature.

This book incorporates the 1994 Standard. The Process Management Model defines the optimum route by which an organization can analyze, define, document, and control its quality system—the infrastructure of the organization that allows it to identify, define, document, and meet its customers' requirements. The Process Management Model ensures that the organization operates efficiently and meets the requirements of the Standard.

The total contents of this book, and the Process Management Model contained in it, have been fully reviewed against the contents of the 1994 Standard. The Authors were pleased to learn that all of the clarification changes to the 1987 Standards were already incorporated into the Process Management Model. Where quotations from the Standard are in the book, it is clearly indicated whether they are from the 1987 version or the 1994 version. Where appropriate, both sets of quotations are given so the reader can better understand the development of the Standard.

While there are some quotations from the Standard in this book, the reader is strongly recommended to obtain a copy of the current Standard in force.

This book introduces the Process Management approach to ISO 9000 registration and discusses why and how it is effective and efficient for achieving registration. Process Management is a systems approach to ISO 9000 registration.

Systems thinking has long been advocated by Dr. W. Edwards Deming, and his own words best describe systems thinking. The following paper is used with the permission of Dr. Deming.

What Is a System?

It is a series of functions or activities (subprocesses, stages—hereinafter, components) within an organization that work together for the aim of the organization. The mechanical and electrical parts that work together to make an automobile or a vacuum cleaner form a system.

There is in almost any system interdependence between the components thereof. The components need not all be clearly defined and documented; people may merely do what needs to be done. All the people that work within a system can contribute to improvement, and thus enhance their joy in work. Management of a system therefore requires knowledge of the interrelationships between all the components within the system and of the people that work in it.

The aim of the system must be stated by the management thereof. Without an aim, there is no system. The components of a system are necessary but not sufficient in themselves to accomplish the aim. They must be managed.

The aim proposed here for management is for everybody to gain—stockholders, employees, suppliers, customers, community, the environment—over the long term. For example, the aim might be to provide for employees good leadership, opportunities for training, education for further growth, and other contributors to joy in work.

The organization will require someone in the position of aid to the president to teach and facilitate profound knowledge.

The performance of any component is to be evaluated in terms of its contribution to the aim of the system, not for its individual production or profit, nor for any other competitive measure. Some components may operate at a loss to themselves, for optimization of the whole system, including the components that take a loss.

A flow diagram is helpful toward understanding a system. By understanding a system, one may be able to trace the consequences of a proposed change.

If the aim, size or boundary of the organization changes, then the functions of the components will for optimization of the new system change. Time will bring changes that must be managed to achieve optimization.

The greater the interdependence between components, the greater the need for communication and cooperation between them.

Optimization

Management's job is to optimize the system over time. Suboptimization causes loss to everybody in the system. An additional responsibility of management is to be ready to change the boundary of the system for better service and profit.

An example of a system, well optimized, is a good orchestra. The players are not there to play solos as prima donnas, to catch the ear of the listener. They are there to support each other. They need not be the best players in the country.

An automobile is not merely several thousand pieces and subassemblies, all individually of top quality. It is several thousand pieces and subassemblies that are designed to work together.

It would be poor management, for example, to purchase materials and service at lowest price, or to maximize sales, or to minimize cost of manufacture, or design of product or of service, or to minimize cost of incoming supplies, to the exclusion of the effect on other stages of production and sales. All these would be suboptimization, causing loss. All these activities should be coordinated to optimize the whole system.

Any system that results in a win–lose structure is suboptimized. Examples of suboptimization in the management of people: the destructive effect of grading in school, from toddlers on up through the university, gold stars and prizes in school, the destructive effect of the so-called merit system, incentive pay, M.B.O. (management by objective), or M.B.I.R. (management by imposition of results, quotas). Other examples of suboptimization, causes of loss:

- Competition for share of market
- Barrier to trade

Fortunately, precise optimization is not necessary. One need only to come close to optimization. As a matter of fact, a precise optimum would be difficult to define. The Taguchi loss function will apply. The loss function at the bottom (minimum loss) will be a parabola. One may move away a short distance along the curve in either direction from the optimum, but rise in the vertical only an imperceptible distance.

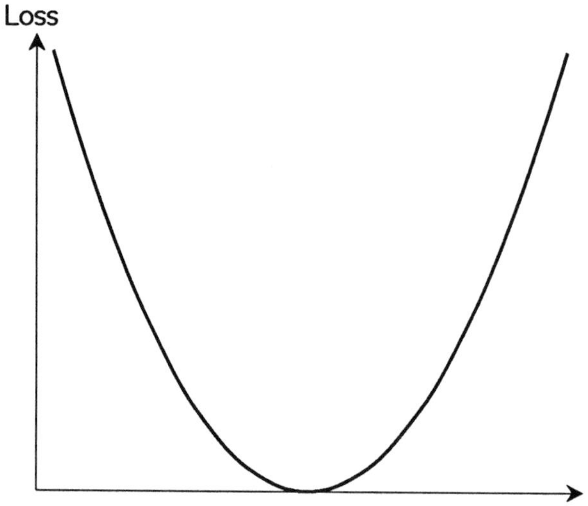

"Foundation for Management of Quality in the Western World"

By Dr. W. Edwards Deming

Delivered at a meeting of the Institute of Management Sciences in Osaka, Japan, July 24, 1989

An Overview...

This book is designed to guide an organization to ISO 9000 registration. The content comes from years of experience in assisting more than a hundred organizations, in both Europe and North America, achieve registration. These organizations include a wide range of manufacturing industries, service industries, and government agencies. Using this book as a guide, readers can learn to analyze and document their company's quality system to satisfy ISO 9000, implement it, and train the organization in continuing use of that defined system—all of which ensures registration to ISO 9000.

The quality system of an organization is a series of processes that impact the quality of goods or services the organization provides its customers. These processes include activities such as sales, purchasing, training, and manufacturing. Together they comprise an organization's means of satisfying its customers. The ISO 9000 Standards deal with how companies manage these processes.

Documentation and People are the two cornerstones of ISO 9000 registration. The Process Management Model was developed to guide organizations in designing and documenting their processes, and to ensure they will have a quality system that does more than merely meet the Standard. It provides an effective strategy and the necessary tools for documenting an organization's quality system. Based on work with more than 100 successfully registered organizations, it applies to all kinds of business—from service to manufacturing, from a few employees to thousands. Its 25 Procedure Guides cover all the processes necessary to comply with ISO 9000 Standards.

The book contains seven sections, each with several chapters. It takes the reader from conception to beyond registration, including all the issues and activities involved. Not everyone in the organization needs to know all of the details, but *those leading the implementation must be well informed.* Others may wish to review certain sections. The project manager should study it thoroughly to gain understanding and knowledge of how to prepare for registration and what the benefits are.

Getting Started:

Section I introduces ISO 9000 and the Process Management Model. The organization's executive management should understand this section thoroughly.

Design and Documentation of Your Quality System:

Section II is the bulk of the book. It contains the Process Management Model, a strategy that helps to analyze and document business processes while complying with the ISO 9000 requirements. The model is covered in Chapters 6–13, incorporating the ISO 9000 requirements in a way that allows the reader to use the model rather than study the Standard itself. The model covers all types of organizations. In modular form, it allows readers to select the parts that apply to their organizations. The applicable sections should be studied at length by those responsible for documenting the quality system.

ISO 9000 in 15 Different Business Sectors:

Section III supplements the Process Management Model by presenting issues and peculiarities of implementing the ISO 9000 Standards in fifteen different business sectors. It shows which sections of the model are likely to be required in a specific business sector. The chapter relating to your sector should be studied in conjunction with the model.

Implementing and Operating Your Quality System:

As you design and document your quality system, you will become ready for Section IV. In practice, much of the quality system will already be in place before this phase begins since implementation is concurrent with documentation. Implementation involves some new activities and processes such as internal audits, management review of the quality system, and formal corrective action.

Getting Registered:

Section V addresses the issues directly involved in the initial registration. Choosing the Registrar and arranging for a registration date should be done early in the project.

After Registration:

Section VI may be left until registration has been achieved—at least from a technical viewpoint. In practice, you may wish to read this section earlier since it provides the answers to many questions that may be raised during the preparation for registration. It points out the benefits an organization gains from registration to ISO 9000. Also discussed are surveillance audits and how suppliers fit into ISO 9000.

And Finally...

Section VII provides information needed to answer questions, communicate with employees, and stay motivated to keep moving ahead. In this section, some of the myths about ISO 9000 are discussed, and the relationship between ISO 9000 and Total Quality Management is addressed, as well as the future of ISO 9000.

The appendices provide examples of the various required documents, information on where to go for help, and a glossary of terms related to the ISO 9000 Standard.

You may want to read the Glossary before going on with the book. Although everyone uses a common Standard, terminology varies. In the glossary you will find definitions of selected terms that may have different meanings in some areas.

Good luck on your journey.
Let us be the first to congratulate you on
your successful ISO 9000 registration.

SECTION ONE

GETTING STARTED

Many companies pursue ISO 9000 registration to meet the needs and expectations of their customers. Some are required by their customers to do so; others do it because they believe it will give them a marketing advantage. Both are good reasons. However, there are other more subtle, and perhaps more compelling, reasons to seek registration.

ISO 9000 registration is a fine objective in itself, but our experience in assisting scores of organizations to become registered has revealed a host of other benefits. These experiences and benefits have been incorporated into *The Process Management Model* which will be unveiled in these pages. This model is a proven method for achieving registration efficiently and for making it a rewarding process.

Section One introduces *The Process Management Model*, looks at the Standards, and helps you plan the route ahead.

CONTENTS

Chapter 1 ◆ Introduction

Organizations exist to serve society by providing services and products. Each organization has its own methods for satisfying customers. However, a few fundamental elements are essential. These include:

- a clear vision
- a policy for quality
- a committed management

Policies are abstract. They require a system and a structure for successful implementation. The system, in turn, is made up of processes, methods, materials, and trained employees with clear instructions. The resulting infrastructure, optimized to identify and meet the customer needs and expectations, makes up an organization's quality system. The ISO 9000 Standard requires:

- a clear quality policy
- a firm managerial commitment
- an effective quality system

Quality Systems

All organizations have quality systems. We may not realize that the places where we spend our leisure time have systems for delivering customer satisfaction. In fact, churches and recreational clubs have quality systems just as other organizations do, although they may not be labeled as such. How well their systems work determines everything about the organization—customer satisfaction, employee morale, financial viability, and how well the organization serves its clientele.

The ISO 9000 Standard does not define quality. It requires an organization to develop and document systems designed to keep customer needs at the forefront of its effort. Quality will be the result if the organization does what it says it will do.

Under the ISO 9000 guidelines, the Quality System is very narrowly defined to be only the network of functions, processes, and activities that directly affect quality. For example, accounting activities, such as payroll processing, may have little influence on the quality of its goods or services. So ISO 9000 includes no clause on payroll. Training production workers, on the other hand, has an obvious impact on quality and is an element in the Standard.

A formal quality system is important to continuously produce dependable, pleasing goods and services—a requirement of most customers in today's competitive, global marketplace. Clear policies, strategies to implement the policies, and tactics to bring the elements together produce consistent performance and ongoing improvement.

The ISO 9000 Standard requires management to study and define the company's quality system. It does not tell them how to run the business. Instead, it requires definition, formalized documentation, and use of the defined quality system. The Process Management Approach *starts with the existing quality system*—only changing and/or expanding it when the current system does not comply with the ISO 9000 requirements—or where obvious improvements can be made.

Organizations are open systems in continuous interaction with their environment, each co-determining the other. The system consists of interdependent subsystems which similarly interact with their environment. This is illustrated in Figure 1.1 below.

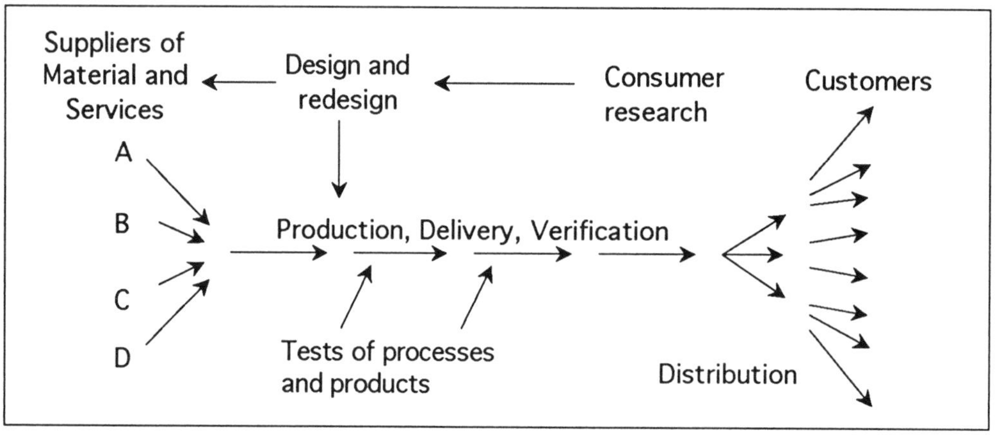

Figure 1.1 Systems View of the Organization

Viewing the organization as a system interacting with its environment leads to the holistic approach essential to a viable, prosperous business. Organizations must adapt to meet changes in the environment. They must understand the role of individuals and all other components in the system. Adaptation requires feedback and corrective actions. Feedback keeps the organization focused on its goal, or aim.

The quality system of an organization consists of:

- Processes
- Procedures
- Methods
- People

Without *people* there is no organization. The *procedures* and the *methods* describe the *processes* and support the people in achieving their objectives. They must provide a structure, not a stricture. The *people* use the *methods* and *procedures* to carry out the *processes*.

ISO 9000 requires an organization to document its quality system in such a way that management and employees can understand, accept, and use it. Documenting the system establishes both a foundation and a common language for quality improvement. Without such a structure, the organization risks functioning as a collection of individuals rather than a team. Well-maintained documentation keeps everyone informed of current policy, strategy, and tactics, and ensures that all are working toward the same goal.

The quality system could just as easily, and as accurately, be called the management system. There are two problems with this—both of them psychological. First, consider the employees. Announcing that "we are going to improve the management system" is unlikely to inspire them to participate. Ask them to work with you to improve the quality system and you get a different response. Everyone wants to improve quality; everyone wants to produce good work and meet their customers' requirements. It becomes a company-wide goal, and everyone buys in.

Second, consider the managers. They probably think they are doing a good job and do not need to improve. If you say we want to evaluate and improve the management system, they'll take it personally. Failure of a quality system audit is a reflection on the management, but somehow it is not as bad as failure of the management system. Tell managers that this is a program to improve the quality system, and just like the employees, they will respond positively.

Evolution of Quality Standards

The search for quality is as old as civilization. Plato observed that the customer, not the manufacturer, decides which requirements achieve quality.

In recent decades, various industries throughout the world developed standards intended to define the features and characteristics of systems that produce everything from automobile parts to food and drugs. The Standards aim to assure purchasers that the quality of the products and service meet their requirements.

Large purchasers of parts and materials wrote the first modern standards for their suppliers, often in contractual situations where the product was very specific to a particular industry. These purchasers developed many standards and visited the supplier to determine how well they met requirements. A company supplying several customers endured multiple assessments against various standards.

To create a uniform standard (which would make such multiple assessments unnecessary), the British Standards Institution (BSI) issued BS 5750 Quality Systems in 1979. BSI also offered an accompanying assessment service that would demonstrate compliance with the Standard. The BS 5750 Standard and assessment gradually gained acceptance and in 1987, the International Organization for Standardization (ISO) essentially adopted BS 5750:1979 as a worldwide Standard and designated it ISO 9000.

ISO 9000 slowly gained acceptance across the globe, largely replacing earlier industry-based standards. The European Community issued the Standard as EN 29000. In the United States, the American Society for Quality Control and the American National Standards Institute issued the Standards originally as Q90 and now as Q9000. By the end of 1993, over 70 countries had adopted the ISO 9000 Standard. Throughout this book, the Standard will be referred to as ISO 9000 rather than by any national designation. Each nation's equivalent standards are identical to ISO 9000.

National bodies throughout the world have responsibility for controlling the registration process. They accredit registrars who conduct audits and issue certificates to successfully audited companies. These certificates bear the logo or mark of the registrar and the accrediting body. Registered companies can use these marks on their documentation to indicate their registration. As the registration and the marks pertain to the quality system and not products, they may not be placed on the company's products. Lists of registered companies are maintained and issued by Registrars and national bodies.

Three factors propel the growing recognition of the ISO 9000 Standard:

1. Globalization and the increase in trading across national borders
2. Large manufacturers seeking efficiency in managing their supplier relationships
3. Operating and marketing benefits to organizations registered to the ISO 9000 Standard

By the end of 1993, there were over 2,000 North American organizations registered to ISO 9000, up 500 percent from the year before—with thousands more scrambling to get on board. The United Kingdom had some 25,000 registrations, from multinationals to small local businesses and local government agencies. The rate of growth of ISO 9000 registered organizations is so fast in the UK, that it is impossible to keep track of the number. There are thousands more in Europe and the rest of the world.

Chapter 2 ◆ The Process Management Approach

The approach in this book—*The Process Management Model*—is based on the premise that every organization is unique. It is a proven approach that facilitates ISO 9000 registration and more importantly, provides companies with an optimal quality system that leads to ongoing continual improvement. In fact, the model provides a quality improvement method so strong that registration to ISO 9000 becomes almost a byproduct of the effort.

There are, of course, many ways to approach ISO 9000 registration. Some of them are tortuous, or even impossible. In 1985, one of the authors made an attempt to develop a standard system to meet the needs of all types of manufacturers. The premise was that since all manufacturing companies sell, design, purchase, and deliver products in much the same way, a generic procedure should fit all of them.

Two years later the naiveté of this approach became apparent. *Organizations are too unique for generic procedures and documents to work.* The research focus changed, leading to the development of the Process Management Model.

This model applies to all types of business, having been tested and proven on more than 100 organizations, including manufacturing, process and service sectors, government, and health care. Before outlining the Process Management Model, however, we will discuss two common and less successful approaches to ISO 9000 registration. We call them *trying to implement a proven standard system* and *trying to implement the Standard.* These three approaches are illustrated in Figure 2.1 on page 8.

Trying to Implement a Proven System

This occurs when one organization tries to copy the solution already in use by another organization. The fallacy of this route is illustrated by two auto dealerships, owned by the same company, located about ten miles apart, and selling the same manufacturer's cars. The two dealerships had developed very different methods of control. They were quite different from each other, just as the people they employed were different from each other. The systems they had developed and evolved were different. The importation of a proven, *but foreign*, quality system to either one would disrupt the environment. It would not lead to successful registration and certainly not result in a continually improving management system.

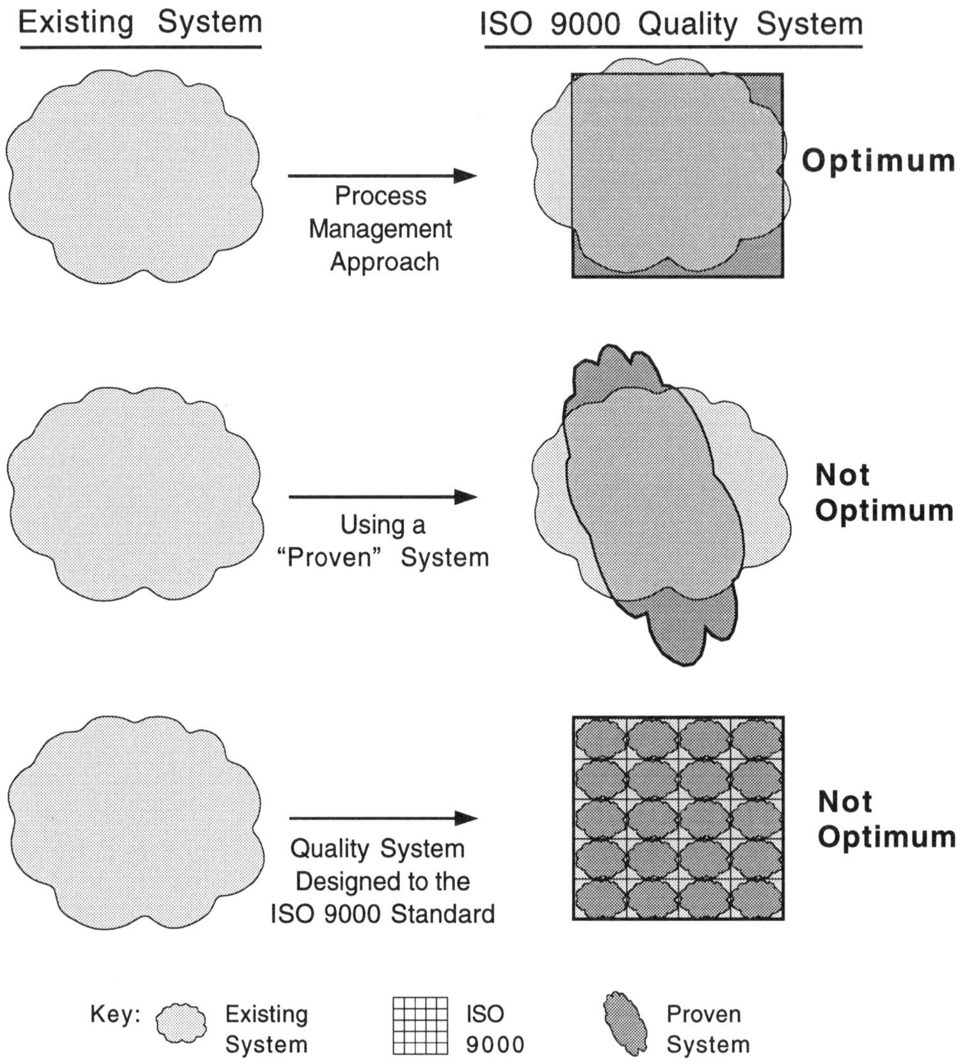

Figure 2.1 Approaches to ISO 9000 Registration

Individuals make up the organization. Imposing a "foreign system," no matter how good, alienates the employees and makes failure more likely. Nevertheless, there are manuals and software on the market, both in North America and in Europe, claiming to offer systems that are universally applicable to any organization. Some of them even claim that all the buyer has to do is insert an organizational name in the appropriate places in a generic manual. Purchased by the unwary, such manuals have taken some organizations as far as the ISO 9000 auditor's visit. But discussions with various ISO 9000 auditors indicate that companies' level of understanding soon becomes apparent and the audits may be aborted.

A variation of this theme is obtaining manuals from an ISO 9000-registered company; either a customer or other organization in a similar business. For example, one registered car dealership encouraged other dealers to visit, tour the system, and buy a copy of their manuals. Another organization, encouraged by a major customer to seek ISO 9000 registration, accepted their offer to use the customer's manuals. The client then spent months trying to prepare for registration. In frustration, they turned to the Process Management Model. When they achieved registration, less than eight months later, they said, "The Process Management Model really works."

Copying someone else's documents, or their final solution, is unsound. It is likely to disrupt the way the organization already operates, and it will most probably involve considerable work and expense.

Chain operations, such as fast food restaurants, are established, using a common system, with relatively unskilled employees disciplined to do things the same way, every time, in every franchise. The system is the basis for the product or service in question and ensures the same product or service everywhere. In that environment, a common, well-documented quality system is appropriate. Other than these special situations, a "cookbook approach" won't work very well.

Sample Quality Manuals, Procedures, Work Instructions, and other Documentation are included in the appendices. But these are *only* samples of documents used by successfully registered companies. They are not a starting point for documenting your system; they are someone else's end point. They may be used as examples and guides but not adopted as they stand.

To reiterate, every organization is unique, its quality system is unique, and its documentation must be unique.

Trying to Implement the Standard

The other fallacious notion is that you can implement the Standard itself. That is, you may study the Standard and then impose its features on the organization. This route may result in registration, but it will also result in a system that is hard to understand, maintain, and audit. Eventually, it will wear out the people who use it.

This route begins with selected employees studying the appropriate ISO 9000 Standard and planning how the organization intends to deal with each of its clauses. Companies using this approach usually have someone trained as a lead auditor who then knows how to interpret the Standard. Then the organization writes its procedures according to the Standard—not according to what its current processes are. Employees write the procedures using ISO 9000 clauses such as contract review, document control, process control, inspection, and test. They stick to clauses with application to the company, but make no attempt to cover a complete process with one procedure or to prevent overlap and duplication.

Sometimes the organization sets up committees for each clause, with the goal of allowing each one to determine how the company meets that clause. Inevitably the procedures written by these committees describe the parts of the processes which they believe pertain to the ISO 9000 clauses but not the whole process. These procedures then go into a manual containing a jumble of overlapping, disjointed information. The company may become registered on the strength of such a document, but it simultaneously hobbles itself with a meaningless set of procedures that have little relevance to its operations.

One of the authors ran into an example of this approach. Entering the offices of a new client, he found a room with twenty tables, each labeled with the title of an ISO 9000 clause. Each table contained a mass of paperwork and an assigned committee. The committee members asked, "What do we do next?" His answer: *"Go back to the beginning, and take the right route this time."*

Let's use a mail service as a hypothetical example to indicate what happens when you try to *implement the Standard.* The key process involves collecting and delivering mail. Identification and traceability is achieved through the address and return address on the letter or parcel. Using the approach described above, the organization would first address the Customer-Supplied Product clause of ISO 9000, describing the system for care and control of the mail. The customer purchases a pre-payment stamp, fixes it to an addressed envelope or package, and places it in a secure collection box. Periodically an authorized employee of the mail service opens the box, retrieves the mail, secures it in a bag, and transports it to a central collection facility. There employees sort the envelopes and packages and forward them to their destinations. An authorized person in that location takes all such mail and delivers it to the proper addresses.

Another procedure would be required to satisfy the identification and traceability clause of ISO 9000. This would describe the same process, stressing that the addresses on the letter provide identification. A third procedure, titled Process Control, would repeat the process description and a fourth titled, Inspection and Test, would add the verifications at the two sorting points. The overall manual, addressing all clauses of the Standard, would fully document the process but with extensive repetition and daunting language.

During the 1980s, a number of companies in the UK used this approach and wrote their documentation around BS 5750, the forerunner of ISO 9000. When BS 5750 changed, in 1987, they had to rewrite their documented quality systems to bring them into line with the new numbering and terminology. Their actual practices remained the same, but their documentation required a wholesale rewrite.

In contrast, we closely reviewed the contents of the Process Management Model after learning of the proposed changes in the 1994 draft of the ISO 9000 Standard and made only minimal changes. This was possible because when the model was developed, *it was based on managing the processes essential to the efficient operation of the business*—the same basis for the ISO 9000 Standard itself.

One company followed the *implementing the Standard* route and achieved registration. It then found itself saddled with an inefficient, difficult system. Changing to the Process Management Model resulted in the elimination of redundant documentation, a system that met their needs, and that was understood and used by the employees.

Although organizations in similar businesses often use similar methods in their operations, a close examination reveals that each has unique ways of organizing work. The reasons for the differences include managerial style and orientation, personalities of the people, facilities and equipment, relative location of the parts of the organization, and size of the organization.

ISO 9000 allows for these differences and provides companies with ample flexibility. It is not necessary to have a quality system similar to another company's in order to meet the Standard's requirements.

The Process Management Approach: A Totally Different Premise

The previous approaches began with something *outside* the organization—someone else's system or the Standard itself. The Process Management Approach *starts with the organization's own infrastructure*—its own quality system. It is in accord with the understanding that this infrastructure has developed to meet the organization's unique needs and those of their customers. It should not arbitrarily be changed to meet the requirements of the Standard. Each organization already has a quality system, and that quality system makes the only logical starting point.

An organization's quality system incorporates a series of processes that impact the quality of goods or services the organization provides its customers. These processes comprise an organization's means of satisfying customers. The ISO 9000 Standards deal with how companies manage these processes. The Process Management Approach starts with these existing processes—*i.e.* how you now operate your business.

Certain processes form the backbone of the business, dictating how it interacts with its customers, controls its primary processes, and delivers its products and services. These need to be changed only if you think you can improve them or to satisfy the requirements of the Standard. In most organizations, major changes to these backbone processes are not required. To support them, the organization has various other processes such as purchasing, training, calibration, document control, and handling customer complaints. These usually do need to be improved in order to meet the ISO 9000 requirements. Finally, the ISO 9000 Standards require some processes that the organization may not currently have. These usually include internal auditing, management review, and corrective action.

Registration requires the implementation and use of a documented quality system that satisfies the requirements of the Standard. The Process Management Model provides a strategy and tools to enable this to be achieved. It provides the guidance to:

1. Analyze the current situation in your company.
2. Identify the required documentation.
3. Define the necessary documentation scheme.
4. Identify the need for Work Instructions.
5. Write procedures which meet the ISO 9000 requirements.
6. Structure the Procedure Manual.
7. Develop a Quality Policy.
8. Produce the Quality Manual.
9. Implement and operate the Quality System.

The Process Management Approach is a proven, efficient guide for meeting the Standard's requirements. The Standards say what is required; the Process Management Model provides the optimum method for meeting the requirements.

Chapter 3 ◆ ISO 9000 Standards

ISO 9000 is a group of documents that address the features and characteristics of quality systems. There are two types of standards, each with a distinct function.

The first function, provided by Standards ISO 9001, ISO 9002, and ISO 9003, is to define the system features and characteristics considered essential for external quality assurance purposes in contractual situations. These three are the *assessment standards* and are used to assess an organization's quality system, its use, and its effectiveness. They apply to all types of businesses.

Assessment to the Standard is carried out by registration firms hired by the organization seeking registration. These registration firms are referred to as Registrars and are accredited by national bodies. These Registrars employ ISO 9000 auditors to carry out audits which lead to registration. (See Figure 3.1)

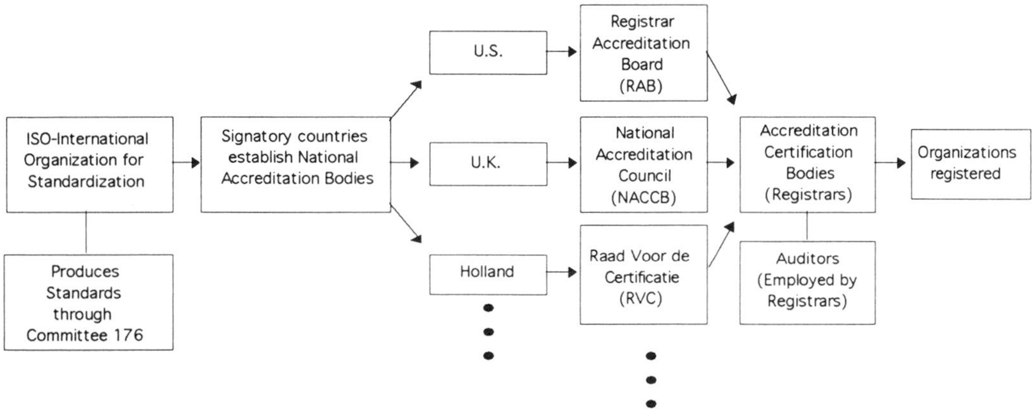

Figure 3.1 ISO 9000 Organizational Structure

The function of the second set of documents is to provide a series of *guidelines* for quality system design. They currently include:

ISO 9000–2: Guidelines for Selection and Use
ISO 9004–1: Guide to Quality Management & Quality System Elements
ISO 9000–3: Guidelines for Application of ISO 9001 to the Development, Supply, and Maintenance of Software
ISO 9004–3: Guideline for Processed Materials
ISO 9004–2: Guidelines for Services

As their titles indicate, these guidelines provide guidance on quality system requirements, control of quality, and satisfying the appropriate assessment standards for the respective type of business. ISO 9000 recognizes that different business/product types are not mutually exclusive and many businesses include more than one of them. For instance, a manufacturer and distributor of photocopying machines would use hardware or product manufacture, service, and software.

This book guides readers as they take an organization through the process of becoming registered to ISO 9001 or 9002. It pragmatically interprets and goes beyond what is included in the ISO guideline documents. The remainder of the book concerns the assessment standards and not the guidelines.

The Standards ISO 9001, ISO 9002, and ISO 9003 do not indicate different *levels* of quality, but relate to the *activities* of the organizations seeking registration.

The following defines the contents of the assessment standards:

- **ISO 9001 Quality Systems:** Model for quality assurance for use when conformance to specified requirements is to be assured by the supplier during design, development, production, installation, and servicing.
- **ISO 9002 Quality Systems:** Model for quality assurance for use when conformance to specified requirements is to be assured by the supplier during production, installation, and servicing.
- **ISO 9003 Quality Systems:** Model for quality assurance for use when conformance to specified requirements is to be assured by the supplier solely at final inspection and test.

To date, the distribution of registrations to each of the Standards in the United States, United Kingdom, Europe, and most other countries has been similar. Approximately 33 percent are registered to ISO 9001, 65 percent to 9002, and two percent to 9003. Standards ISO 9001 and 9002 are the same except for clause 4.4, Design Control. Since ISO 9001 and 9002 represent almost all of the registrations to date and ISO 9001 is the more comprehensive of the two, the book will use the requirements of ISO 9001 throughout. For simplicity of terminology it will be referred to as ISO 9000. Organizations who are working to achieve registration to ISO 9002 can use this book and omit those parts that are not applicable to their business. The next chapter explains how to determine which assessment standard is applicable to your business.

ISO 9003 is not widely used. It only covers organizations who control the output of their processes by final inspection and testing, or who only perform such activities. We believe that the concept of inspecting and testing quality into a product or service after manufacture is contrary to good management practice. In view of our belief, no advice is offered here on ISO 9003.

ISO 9000-2
Guidelines for Application of 9001, 9002, and 9003

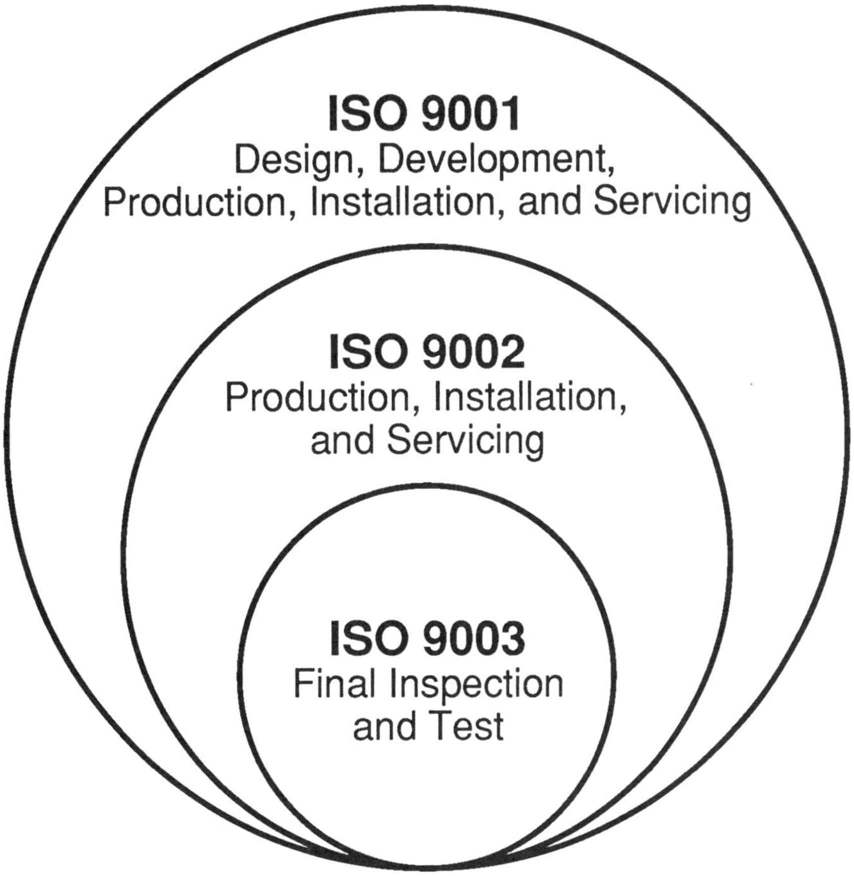

ISO 9004-1	Quality Management and Quality System Elements
9004-2	Guidelines for Services
9004-3	Guidelines for Processed Materials
9000-3	Guidelines for Development, Supply, and Maintenance of Software

Figure 3.2 The ISO 9000 Series of Standards

4	Quality Systems Requirements	9001	9002	9003
4.1	Management Responsibility	X	X	X
4.2	Quality System	X	X	X
4.3	Contract Review	X	X	X
4.4	Design Control	X	N/A	N/A
4.5	Document and Data Control	X	X	X
4.6	Purchasing	X	X	N/A
4.7	Control of Customer-Supplied Product	X	X	X
4.8	Product Identification and Traceability	X	X	X
4.9	Process Control	X	X	N/A
4.10	Inspection and Testing	X	X	X
4.11	Control of Inspection, Measuring and Test Equipment	X	X	X
4.12	Inspection and Test Status	X	X	X
4.13	Control of Nonconforming Product	X	X	X
4.14	Corrective and Preventive Action	X	X	X
4.15	Handling, Storage, Packaging, Preservation and Delivery	X	X	X
4.16	Control of Quality Records	X	X	X
4.17	Internal Quality Audits	X	X	X
4.18	Training	X	X	X
4.19	Servicing	X	X	N/A
4.20	Statistical Techniques	X	X	X

Figure 3.3 ISO 9000 Requirements Clauses

Overview of the ISO 9000 Requirements

The ISO 9001 Standard is relatively brief, consisting primarily of Section 4.0, Quality System Requirements. The requirements are detailed in twenty clauses listed in Figure 3.3 on the facing page. ISO 9001 includes only general requirements and features of the quality system. The appendices of this book provide information about where copies of ISO 9000 Standards can be obtained.

Most companies who have been in business for a while, and are already pleasing customers, find that they already satisfy 70 to 80 percent of the ISO 9000 requirements. They need to change what they are doing or add new procedures for only 20 to 30 percent of the requirements.

Compliance with the Standard is closest in the *backbone* activities of the company: sales, purchasing, production, and delivery. The additional requirements relate to the organizational aspects and include internal auditing, formal calibration programs, management review, formal corrective actions, and document control. An overview of the content of the Standard begins on page 18 and is illustrated in Figure 3.4. For a more detailed analysis of the content of the Standard is given in Appendix A.

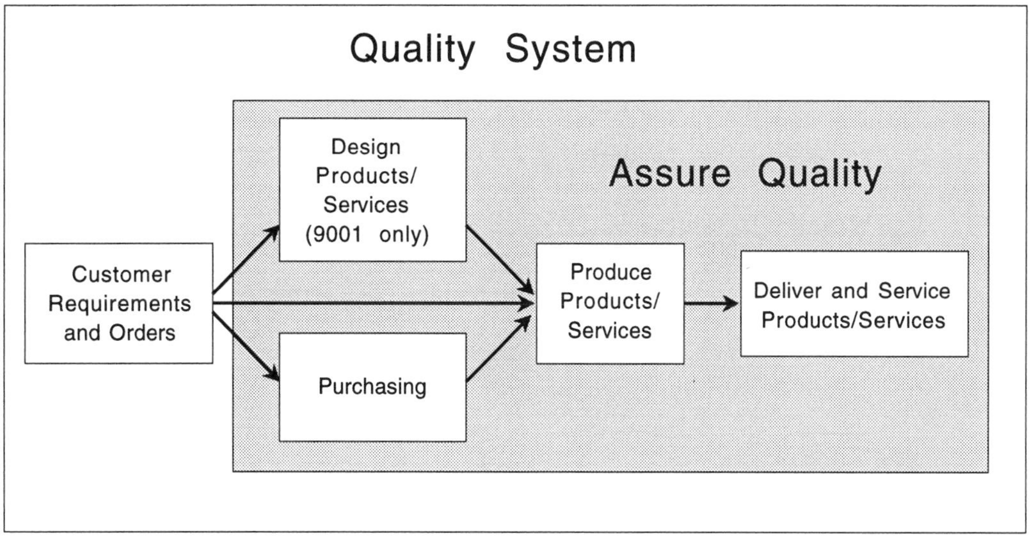

Figure 3.4 ISO 9001—What is Required?

Customer Requirements and Orders

- Clearly define and document orders. Verify verbal orders.
- Ensure the organization has the capability to deliver before accepting an order or contract.
- Communicate contract and/or order changes to all concerned.

Design Products/Services (ISO 9001 only)

- Plan the design activities, identify and assign qualified people.
- Define design and required inputs and manage the design process.
- Verify the design with individuals independent of the design effort.
- Review and approve design changes.
- Validate the final design.

Purchasing

- Clearly state the requirements in purchase orders.
- Select suppliers on the basis of quality requirements and keep records of supplier performance. Evaluate suppliers periodically.
- Verify purchased product before it is used.

Produce Product/Services

- Conduct all work under controlled conditions.
- Provide adequate work instructions, employee training, tools, and equipment.
- Control process and product characteristics.

Deliver and Service Products/Services

- Prevent product damage and deterioration.
- Handle and store products and components to maintain identity and prevent damage and deterioration.
- Control service processes.

Assure Quality

- Verify product conforms with requirements.
- Identify product throughout process and provide traceability (if required by customer contract).
- Segregate and dispose of nonconforming products and components.
- Calibrate inspection and test equipment.

Quality System

- Document how the company conforms to the requirements of ISO 9000.
- Document and communicate management objectives and policy for quality.
- Give employees clear authority, responsibility, and resources to achieve objectives.
- Conduct periodical management reviews of policy, objectives, and effectiveness of its quality system.
- Review and approve all relevant documents before issue; only the most current or relevant documents should be available.
- Have a method for identifying, collecting, indexing, filing, storing, maintaining, and dispositioning of quality records.
- Audit the quality system comprehensively.
- Analyze, correct, and prevent problems that cause nonconformances.

This concludes a quick overview of the Standard requirements. At this stage, it is not necessary to study the Standard, but it is advisable to do so prior to the first ISO 9000 auditor's visit. Looking at the Standard at this stage would be like reading the rules of golf before you learn how to swing the club. You don't need to read the rules until you are ready for your first tournament.

The Process Management Model is the coach.
The ISO 9000 Standard is the rule book by which you must play.

Chapter 4 ◆ Choosing the Appropriate Standard

In practice, deciding which Standard (ISO 9001 or 9002) is appropriate hinges on the extent to which the organization has design responsibility for the product or service it provides. The following definition of design serves as a useful guide.

> Design: the process of task recognition and problem solving with the objective of fulfilling needs by the creation of a product or service.

Design, an inherent part of the business cycle, is part of meeting almost every customer need. The question arises: *Is the design carried out by you or your customer, or has it already been completed (by nature, industry standard, etc.)?*

This chapter discusses different situations—some obvious as to the appropriate standard and some more obscure.

In-House Design Responsibility

First, and the most straight-forward situation, is an organization that designs its products. In this case, ISO 9001 is the appropriate standard.

Accepted Design

Examples of products and services, where the design is complete and accepted by both the supplier and purchaser, include basics such as:

- Standard hardware (*e.g.* fasteners with defined specifications)
- Basic electrical components (*e.g.* resistors)
- Basic engineering processes (*e.g.* heat treatment)
- Standard chemicals (*e.g.* oxygen)
- Raw materials (*e.g.* steel)
- Delivery of standard training programs (*e.g.* software training)
- Delivery of educational product (*e.g.* established curriculum)
- Drafting of standard documents (*e.g.* income tax preparation)

Since the design is established and the supplier of these products or services needs only to adhere to the existing design, ISO 9001 is not appropriate. The design is not one of the organization's processes.

Supplying Goods to Your Customers' Specifications

Determining the design responsibility can also be ascertained from the nature of the relationship between the supplier and the customer. If the customer provides full specifications of the product or service, then that supplier fits into the intended use category ISO 9002. An example of a 9002 organization is a sheet metal fabricator that produces parts to customers' drawings or specifications.

Obscure Examples

There are situations not as obvious as the above illustrations. For example, the supplier has expertise and advises the customer on the contents of the purchaser's design specification. Generally, if the supplier can vary the design of the product *without seeking approval from the customer,* ISO 9001 would be applicable for that supplier. If the customer has to approve any change in the design, ISO 9002 would be appropriate.

Another obscure situation is when the supplier has a series of pre-defined modules to offer to the customer and advises on the selection of those modules that most meet the specific needs of the customer. This is generally considered to be a configuration of the modules rather than a true design and ISO 9002 is the appropriate standard.

Phased Registration

The decision as to which standard is appropriate is clear from a purist point of view. In the early years, there was a tendency to see the achievement of ISO 9002 as a stepping stone towards ISO 9001. Registrars usually do not accept this now. An organization designing products or services is expected to seek registration to ISO 9001, even if it makes registration more difficult. Quality, after all, requires everyone to get involved.

Multiple Sites

Other questions arise with multi-site organizations when product design may be remote from production. In these cases, it is acceptable for each production unit to obtain registration to ISO 9002 and for the design section to register to ISO 9001. It is also possible to register the design and production sites under an ISO 9001 registration, but most organizations register the units individually.

If you are still uncertain about which is the most appropriate standard for your company, refer to Procedure Guide 2 on Design Control in Chapter 9. If you feel the procedure guide could be used to control your design process, then ISO 9001 is appropriate.

Chapter 5 ◆ Planning the Registration Effort

Preparing for registration to ISO 9000 involves developing, improving, formalizing, documenting, and implementing an organization's Quality System. While design and documentation of the Quality System makes up the bulk of the work, *documentation by itself, does not make a Quality System.* The Quality System rests with the *individuals* in the company; the documentation describes the *structure* by which they operate. It must support their work, not inhibit it.

Management Involvement

A Quality System is really a management system. The first and biggest key to ISO 9000 implementation is the total involvement of executive management—perhaps easier said than done. Managers demonstrate their involvement through active participation in the project and maintaining consistency in their priorities and policies. They must make clear through their actions that they are involved—not just committed to seeing others do the work necessary to achieve ISO 9000 registration. Executive management must understand—

- Quality
- Objectives of the Standard
- General contents of the Standard
- The program for registration
- The assessment process

During the project, there are bound to be conflicting pressures and priorities. If it appears that quality and ISO 9000 registration are not a key commitment, the company will not achieve its objective. Chief Executives and their immediate subordinates must establish a common understanding and language. There are many ways to achieve this—hiring a consultant, attending training courses, studying and discussing the contents of this book. Whatever means is chosen, the executives must know the commitment they are making.

One of the dangers inherent in the process of registration to ISO 9000 is that everyone starts to think of an ISO 9000 system as being superimposed on the operating system of the company. This clearly should not be the case. Management should take care to prevent this notion from arising.

Too much publicity early on tends to generate resistance. Allowing the process to start on a fairly low key tends to keep the project in perspective. There are many myths and misconceptions regarding ISO 9000 and these are addressed in Chapter 38.

Management Representative for Quality

ISO 9000 requires executive management to appoint one of their number to be the *Management Representative for Quality.* In this book, that person is called the Management Representative. He or she must have the authority to resolve all matters relating to the quality of products and services.

In small organizations the chief executive may fill this role. In larger organizations another member of the executive management may do it. This assignment need not be a full-time job. The position to which this responsibility is assigned tends to vary, according to the size of the organization. In mid-sized companies with no quality manager, the executive in charge of operations is usually chosen, but financial controllers and sales executives are also common appointees.

The role of Management Representative often seems a natural job for the Quality Manager. It's important to keep in mind that while the Management Representative must be a member of executive management, this does not imply that the Quality Manager must be promoted. If the Quality Manager is not part of executive management, the person to whom he or she reports may be the Management Representative. During the ISO 9000 registration process, the Management Representative is the project champion. The Management Representative is not responsible for writing the detailed documents and carrying out the associated training. The details may be delegated, but the Management Representative is responsible for the project.

Implementation Team

A project of this magnitude requires a trained Implementation Team. The team should be broadly based and include employees who understand their part of the business and know how to document it. There should also be one or more people trained in the analysis and documentation process defined in the Process Management Model.

The Implementation Team must also be able to work with management and employees to capture existing processes and document them to be compliant with ISO 9000 and in line with the Process Management Model. The work can be divided among team members, but frequent meetings are required to establish consistency, monitor progress, collaborate, and define how different parts of the quality system will coordinate with each other. Some or all of this work may be delegated to an external consultant, as discussed on the following pages.

Training

It is always important to keep employees informed and knowledgeable about this or any such project undertaken by the organization. For consistency, it is preferable that all ISO 9000 training follows the same approach to achieve registration. We have seen employees of a company waste time in fruitless debate because they all learned different approaches at various seminars and could not reconcile the differences. If you use the Process Management Model, everyone in the company should be following it.

Training needs to begin with executive management and progress to all levels. As you move the training down through the organization, the numbers to be trained are larger, but the depth of training required is less. Employees mainly need to be aware of the company quality policy: how ISO 9000 defines quality, its contents and aims, and their roles in the registration process. It is usually best to do this in small groups where any operating changes can be explained, the audit process described, the final assessment outlined, and all questions answered.

Fortunately, following the Process Management Model does not result in large changes to existing practices, so there is little need to train employees in new processes. The changes resulting from the model are to make improvements. As such, they justify themselves.

Training the Internal Auditing Team is essential. It is discussed at length in Chapter 12. Training materials which follow the Process Management Approach are available and the details are in the "Where to go for Help" section at the back of the book.

A final training session for all employees, just prior to the assessment, will have a positive impact on the result. It is not possible, under ISO 9000, to hide a deficient system, but it is easy to make an adequate system look unacceptable. This final training session should brief the employees on knowing their part and what the documentation says about their work processes.

Training is an essential part of achieving registration, and assessors will expect to see evidence that it has been carried out. The training records should show the details of any training done as part of the registration project. ISO 9000 auditors frequently check this detail during the audit.

Implementation Plan

One of the most important early decisions is the extent to which the company will use outside resources for training and consultation. This decision should be based on the organization's resources and the available assistance. These pages will provide most of the assistance needed to achieve ISO 9000 registration. If the organization has sufficient resources, there is no reason why, using the information in this book, it could not become registered without further help. A consultant who is not experienced in ISO 9000 registration, or who approaches the task from the Standard rather than the organization's own processes, can increase the required complexity and time. The use of consultants is further discussed at the end of this chapter.

If the project is carried out by an employee, or team of employees using this book, they should be able to take an organization or single site of under 50 employees to registration in about eight months with about 45 days of the team's time. For an organization of around 100 employees, the required time would increase to about 60 days, and for around 500 employees, about 75 days. These time scales, based on experience with many organizations, are typical of those that have been achieved. Other members of the organization must devote an equivalent amount of time working with the team members.

The Implementation Team may advance their expertise by attending workshops based on the Process Management Model. This might be supplemented by training as a lead auditor, although lead auditor training on its own would be of limited use and could be confusing. Its objective is to develop the skills necessary to conduct ISO 9000 audits, not to prepare an organization for the audit.

The Tasks to be Undertaken by the Implementation Team

1. **Education:**

   Management needs to understand the requirements of the ISO 9000 Standards and what is required to achieve ISO 9000 registration. It is also helpful to learn the benefits of ISO 9000 registration, so everyone can commit to the implementation effort.

   Once the decision to proceed is made, determine how to proceed, as discussed above, and choose the individual and team who will lead the implementation effort.

2. **Implementation Plan:**

   The effort required for ISO 9000 registration and the amount of time needed depends on where the organization is, with regard to documentation and compliance with the requirements, and the level of internal and external resources put on the effort.

   It can take from 4 to 18 months to achieve registration. Appendix B provides guidelines for planning the activities and the timing for companies requiring 8, 12, or 18 months. Your plan would also have who is responsible for the various activities.

   Which time frame is suitable for your organization will depend on the factors discussed above.

3. **Design and Document Your Quality System:**

   The activities are presented in Section II of the book. This step requires the most effort—documenting the quality system, including a quality manual, procedures, procedure manual, and any required work instructions.

   During the documentation phase, it is desirable to select and hire a registrar. Registrar selection is discussed in Chapter 31.

4. **Implement and Use Your Quality System:**

   Prior to an ISO 9000 audit, your system must be operational. That is, you must use the system as you documented it. This provides the assurance that the system is operable and effective in controlling quality and meeting the organization's quality objectives. You need to train enough people to ensure the continued operation and effectiveness of the system.

   Since ISO 9000 requires internal quality audits, the organization must choose and train an internal audit team at the beginning of this step. We recommend you audit the entire system at least twice, prior to the registrar's audit.

5. **Getting Registered:**

   As discussed in Section V, your registrar will audit and recommend you for registration. Prior to the Registrar audit, you may want to do a readiness check or pre-assessment as discussed in Chapter 32.

By the time the organization achieves its ISO 9000 registration, everyone should be thoroughly committed to it. Maintaining the documentation and adhering to what it says becomes a daily management activity. None of the organizations we have worked with have added staff to meet the requirements of the ISO 9000 Standard. Any new tasks due to ISO 9000 registration have been allocated to existing staff. The overall improvement in performance and efficiency provides any additional time that might be required for the ISO 9000 effort. These tasks and how they relate to the sections of the book are shown in Figure 5.1 on page 28.

Consultants

It is technically feasible for an organization to achieve registration with its own resources, using the information contained in this book. Some organizations, however, may wish to hire an outside consultant to design and document the quality system and to train employees. This decision would be based on the available resources and the required time scale. The authors had one client who was required to achieve registration in two months—to win a military contract. They were able to provide the resources to enable this to happen.

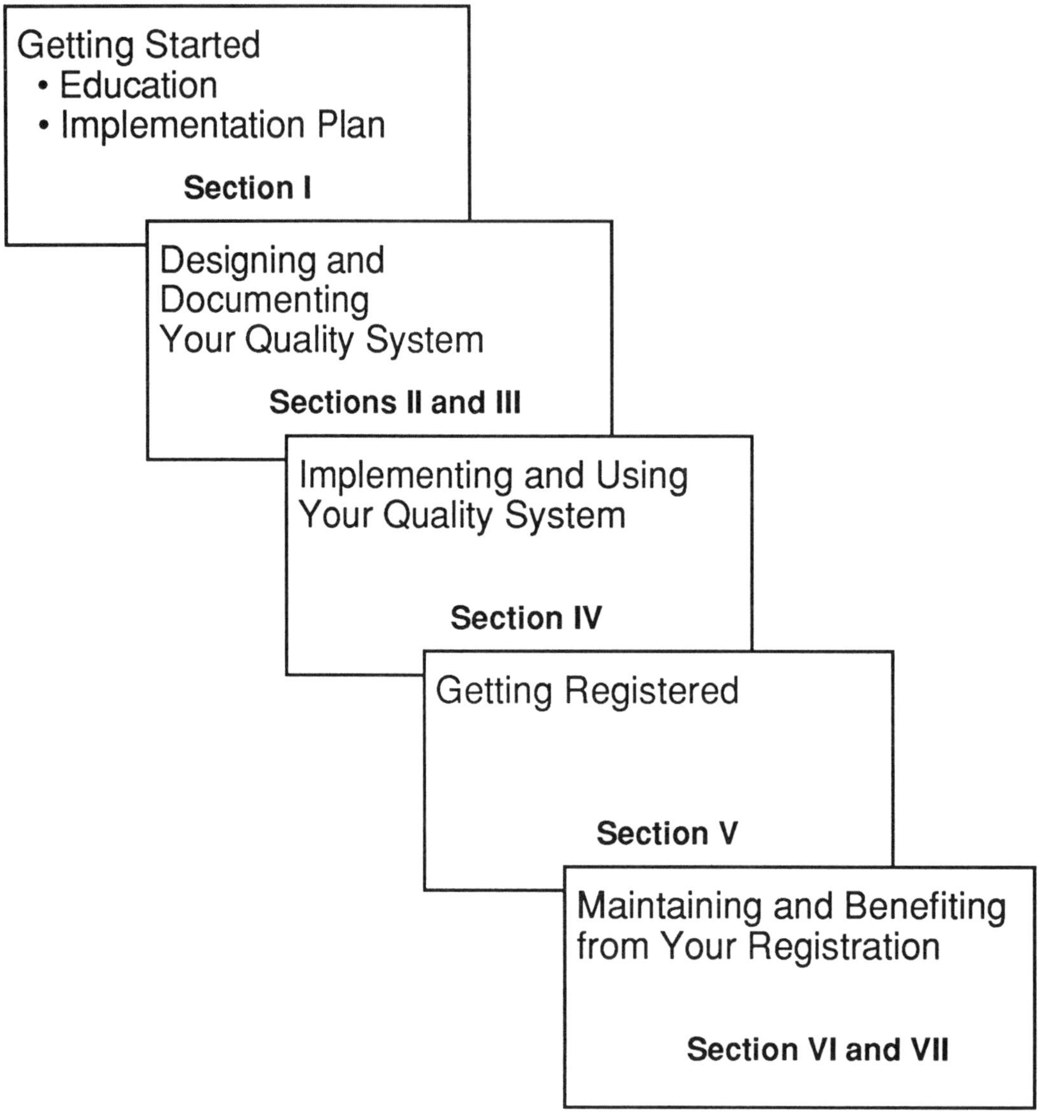

Figure 5.1 Steps to ISO 9000 Registration

The consultant's role and methodology are important. If an organization decides to use a consultant, it is important to establish that the consultant has experience and a successful ISO 9000 track record. The consultant should clarify the approach to be used and say what activities will be undertaken. Beware of consultants who offer only to review the documentation—without taking responsibility for its preparation.

A good indication of the competence, experience, and commitment of a consulting firm is to determine whether the consultancy is itself registered to ISO 9000. This demonstrates whether they practice what they preach. Both Optimum Systems for Quality Ltd. and Process Management International, the quality consulting firms of authors Bryn Owen and Peter Malkovich, are registered to ISO 9001.

The time scales the consultant proposes and the estimated consultant days required give a good indication of the experience of the consultant and the confidence they have in their own work. Using the methods defined in this book, an experienced and well-equipped consultant can take a single site organization of under 50 employees to successful registration in about six to eight months with around 15 total consultant's days, including writing the documentation. A site with 100 employees would take the consultant about 20 days, and a site with 500 would take about 25 days.

Using a consultant to write the procedures has been criticized by those who note that the system must be owned by its users, the line managers and staff who are responsible for it. Usually, however, the consultant can ghostwrite the documents based on information gathered from the staff, who then review and adjust the content until it accurately reflects their requirements. Such an approach brings about the desired staff ownership. It also gives the documents a common style and makes maximum use of the consultant's expertise. The alternate route, having the consultant review and revise procedures prepared by the staff, can result in conflict when the content is changed.

A compromise approach would be to use a consultant to work with and guide the implementation team. This provides the benefits of experienced support and development of in-house skills. The consultant's first job should be to conduct an initial assessment of the organization's quality systems, with recommendations as to the structure and content of the documentation. Then the consultant should monitor the documentation as it is prepared, train the audit team, and do a pre-audit of some parts of the system followed by a review and counseling. This could reduce the consultant's time by about one-half or one-third and still provide a good assurance of success.

SECTION TWO

DESIGN AND DOCUMENTATION IN YOUR QUALITY SYSTEM

Designing and documenting your quality system is the biggest activity in achieving ISO 9000 registration. Many companies have been working on it for years.

This section presents the Process Management Model, which will enable you to efficiently design and document an optimum quality system for your company.

Chapter 9 provides Procedure Guides for all 25 standard elements of ISO 9000.

In Chapter 10 there is a discussion of the requirements for the use of statistical techniques in the control of processes.

In Chapters 6, 7, 8, 11, 12, and 13, all the components of a documented quality system—procedures, work instructions, the Procedure Manual and the Quality Manual—are developed.

CONTENTS

Chapter 6 ◆ ISO 9000 Documentation Requirements

The ISO 9000 Standards do not specify how to document your quality system. Any method of documentation is acceptable. Whatever well established procedures you have should be used as the basis for the ISO 9000-compliant quality system.

The documentation model below has evolved as the best practice, based on what other organizations have done. It is not required, although many auditors expect to see the documentation in this format.

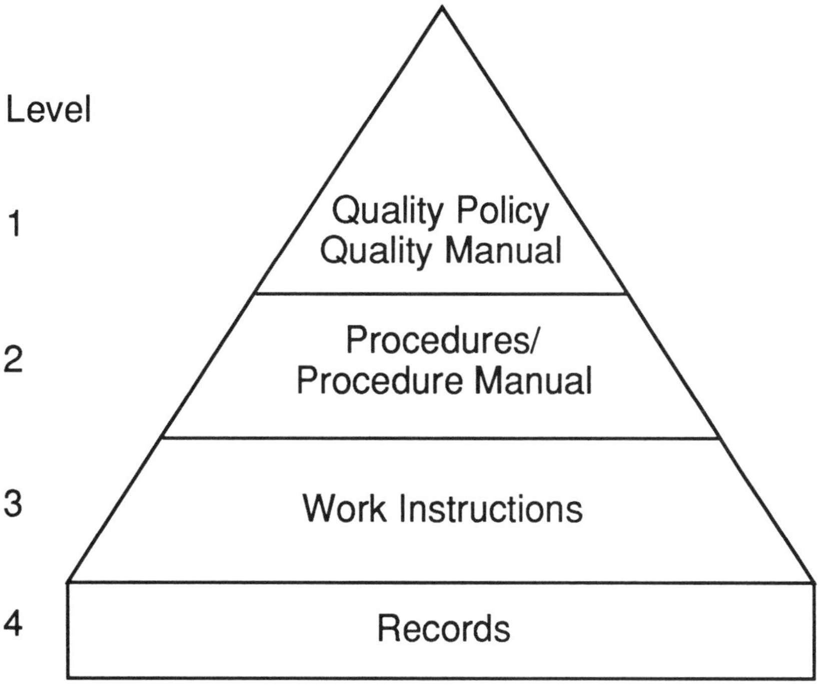

Figure 6.1 ISO 9000 Documentation Hierarchy

ISO 9000 Standards only specify requirements that directly impact the quality of the organization's products or services. Many activities and functions, such as invoicing, recruitment and employee benefits are not requirements. It is acceptable, however, for the organization to document and include these in its system—but they would not be audited by the ISO 9000 auditor.

Documentation Hierarchy

Level	Document	Addresses	Purpose	Responsibility
1	Quality Manual	Why	Policy	Executive Management
2	Procedures	Who, What, Where, When	Strategy	Management
3	Work Instructions	How	Tactics	Departments
4	Records	Effectiveness	Record of Performance	Everyone

Figure 6.2 Documentation Hierarchy

Level 1

The Quality Manual defines the organization's quality policy. It documents how the organization addresses each section of the ISO 9000 Standard. The Quality Manual should refer to the procedures (Level 2) used to implement the quality policy in the text or with a matrix (as in an appendix).

The Quality Manual must be authorized by either the chief executive or the Management Representative. Chapter 12 discusses the quality manual in detail.

In practice the Quality Manual is general and does not change very often. Its content is similar among different organizations. It is often widely circulated, serving as a marketing piece and as evidence of a quality system for customers and potential customers. The Quality Manuals of some organizations include corporate history and other information to make them more complete marketing documents. The ISO 9000 Standard does not require this, but many managers believe it adds a nice touch to the manual.

Level 2

The organization's processes are documented as Procedures. They describe in detail the methods to carry out and control work. Procedures change as the organization's operating practices change. Procedures are usually authorized by management and the Management Representative. Procedures are usually collected in a Procedure Manual. This should not be thought of as an ISO 9000 manual; it is the company's operating manual. Distribution is restricted to those who need the information. Since the manual contains working documents, its binding must facilitate updating; a loose-leaf binder is recommended.

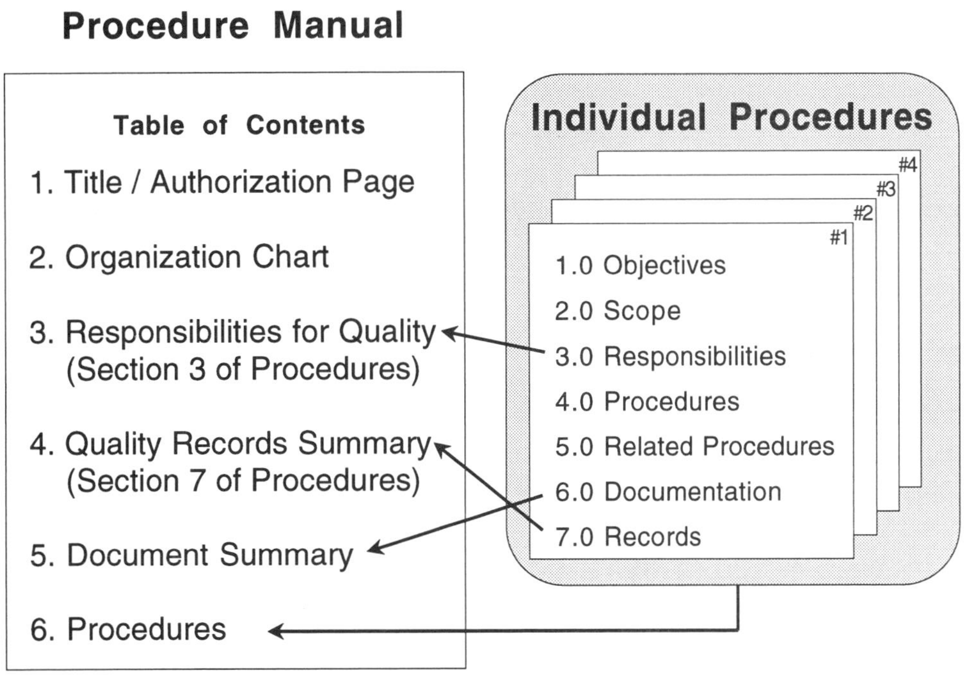
Procedure Manual
Table of Contents
1. Title / Authorization Page
2. Organization Chart
3. Responsibilities for Quality
(Section 3 of Procedures)
4. Quality Records Summary
(Section 7 of Procedures)
5. Document Summary
6. Procedures
Individual Procedures
#4
#3
#2
#1
1.0 Objectives
2.0 Scope
3.0 Responsibilities
4.0 Procedures
5.0 Related Procedures
6.0 Documentation
7.0 Records

Figure 6.3 Procedure Manual

Level 3

In most organizations work instructions are not usually collected in a single manual because they can be so different. They may include work instructions, specifications, engineering drawings, process instructions, pictures, and forms. Work instructions usually are located in—and controlled by—the departments that use them. Work instructions are discussed further in Chapter 11.

Level 4

This level is comprised of records produced in operating the quality system. They are generated throughout the operation and usually are kept where generated.

Summary

The first step to ISO 9000 registration is to design, develop, and document your quality system. The documented quality system will consist of:

- Your Quality Manual
- 15-30 Procedures, best placed in a Procedure Manual
- Work Instructions, the number depending on the need

Most of the effort is in writing the procedures. The Process Management Model enables you to do this. The preparation of the Quality Manual is a simple task and best done after the procedures are written. By that stage, you know how the organization meets all the individual requirements of the Standard. Documenting this in the Quality Manual provides a verification that nothing has been missed. Work instructions necessary for registration already exist in most organizations. The next chapter deals with procedure format and the chapters following it discuss identifying your procedure requirements and writing your procedures.

The above plan has evolved over the years and, in general, is expected by ISO 9000 auditors. There are, however, organizations who become successfully registered who deviate from this plan. We know of companies whose entire quality system is on a computer. Still others maintain documentation consisting primarily of flow charts. The choice is yours as long as you can demonstrate that it works. It is essential, however, that the chosen plan be easily understood by all users of the system, not just the writers. The authors know of one organization who used flow charts that accurately reflected the work of the department. The staff were working according to the flow chart, but when asked to explain it, they could not. It served no real purpose; it was just window dressing.

Chapter 7 ◆ Procedures

A procedure is a description of a process. It serves to tell the user how the process should be carried out. Like every communication, it is written for the reader, not the writer, and certainly not for the ISO 9000 auditors. It should be lucid, understandable, and user-friendly.

The Standard does not say how to structure and write procedures, but a common structure across the organization is beneficial.

Procedures should not be meaningless documents prepared to meet ISO 9000 requirements. Rather, they should describe your quality system and comprise a record and refinement of existing practices. Like every other form of communication, they exist primarily for the receiver, not the sender. Their development should include whoever works in the process.

It may add consistency and save time if staff (or consultants) skilled in procedure writing prepare the procedures, but they must be based on information provided by line management and approved by them.

Procedures define what happens in an organization. Although they may be written before they are implemented, they should still be written in the *present tense.*

Procedures are not a story. They are not a series of orders. They are a record of what is done, by whom. They are best written in the third person, rather than first or second person. Since it is the actions that are important, the use of *passive voice* is most appropriate.

Examples

Not Recommended

- I (You) will arrange for the inspection of the parts when their manufacture has been completed.

Recommended

- The inspection of the parts is arranged by the quality manager when their manufacture is complete.

Not Recommended

- The driver must check his fuel level and tire pressure before setting out on his trip.

Recommended

- The fuel level and tire pressure are checked by the driver before each journey.

Procedures Need to Define the Following:

1. Who

   ...is responsible,
   ...does what activities, and
   ...records what.

2. What

   ...activities are done,
   ...what is recorded, and
   ...where they are applicable.

3. Where

   ...the activities happen,
   ...the records are made, and
   ...the records are filed.

4. When

   ...the activities should occur,
   ...the records are made, and
   ...the records are destroyed.

Procedure Format

It is useful to have a consistent procedure format with numbered sections. There is no prescribed format, but a procedure must have, in addition to content, identifying information such as title, number, and revision level. The next page shows the recommended procedure format.

A procedure covering the opening and sorting of the mail is shown on page 40. This is an example of format and content, used only because it is universally understandable. This process is not usually documented and its inclusion here does not imply that it is necessary to document such a process.

A typical procedure is between two and four pages in length. If it becomes longer, consider whether it has too much detail or if it could be divided into two or more procedures.

Further examples of actual procedures are in Appendix D.

TITLE : NAME OF PROCEDURE — PROCEDURE NUMBER:___
REVISION LEVEL:_____ — SHEET 1 OF_____

1.0 Objective

1.1 A brief description of what the described process should achieve.

2.0 Scope

2.1 Identifies which activities, products, or services this procedure covers and/or excludes. An explanation of any peculiar definitions of items used in the procedures may also be included.

3.0 Responsibilities

3.1 Identifies who is responsible for the various activities defined in the procedure.

4.0 Procedure

4.1 A step-by-step account of what happens, when, where, and by whom.

5.0 Related procedures

5.1 Other procedures in the quality system to which this procedure relates.

6.0 Documentation

6.1 A list of the documents used or referenced in the procedure and a reference to the procedure's Appendices where such documents can be found. It is preferable to have completed, rather than blank, forms in these appendices.

7.0 Records

7.1 Records created during the process described in this procedure, where they are they filed, and how long they are kept.

Figure 7.1 The Seven Parts of a Procedure Guide

TITLE: PROCESSING MAIL — PROCEDURE NO. 7
REVISION LEVEL 3 — SHEET 1 OF 2

1.0 Objective

1.1 To ensure that all mail received by the organization is recorded and processed to the appropriate department.

2.0 Scope

2.1 All mail received by the organization. This specifically includes documents delivered by mail, or other delivery agencies, and faxes received on the central fax machine. Faxes received by other departments are excluded from this procedure.

3.0 Responsibilities

3.1 The Company Secretary has overall responsibility for this procedure.

3.2 The Reception Staff on duty at the reception desk is responsible for processing mail received while on duty.

3.3 The Administrative Assistant is responsible for delivering mail to the various departments in the organization.

4.0 Procedure

4.1 All mail received is given to the member of reception staff on duty. All faxes received on the central machine are treated as items of mail.

4.2 The address on the mail is checked to verify that it is for the organization. If the envelope is marked Private, Confidential, or in other ways that indicate this meaning, the envelope is not opened but is processed in accordance with the procedure. All other envelopes are opened, the contents removed, and date stamped. Loose documents are stapled together. The envelopes are checked to verify that they are empty and then discarded.

4.3 Each item of mail is recorded in the mail log indicating the sender's name, organization, and addressee. The items are sorted for each department. When the addressee is not clear, these items are entered in the log as General and placed with the mail for the Company Secretary.

4.4 When all items have been sorted, they are given to the Administrative Assistant who signs the mail log to confirm receipt.

4.5 When individual items of mail or faxes are received, they are processed by the reception staff member using the above procedure. If the Administrative Assistant is not available, the department for whom the item is intended is informed of its arrival and a representative for the department collects the mail and signs the log.

5.0 Related Procedures

5.1	Processing of Inquiries	Procedure 4
5.2	Processing of Orders	Procedure 5
5.3	Purchasing	Procedure 8
5.4	Control of Deliveries	Procedure 15
5.5	Control of Customer Complaints	Procedure 16

6.0 Documentation

6.1	Date Stamp	Appendix A
6.2	Mail Log	Appendix B

7.1 Records

7.1 The Mail Log is kept in the Reception until full. It is then passed to the Company Secretary and retained for at least another year when it is destroyed.

Chapter 8 ◆ Identifying And Documenting Procedures

The Process Management Model includes 25 Procedure Guides. These guide the user in the analysis of each process that impacts quality. They indicate which parts of the Standard apply to that process. They also indicate what, if anything, should be added or changed to comply with ISO 9000 requirements. This allows an organization to meet those requirements by using its existing practices as a starting point. The resulting procedures formalize the processes, standardize best practices, and improve control.

Figure 8.1 illustrates the relationships between the implementation model, the ISO 9000 Standards, and an organization's procedures.

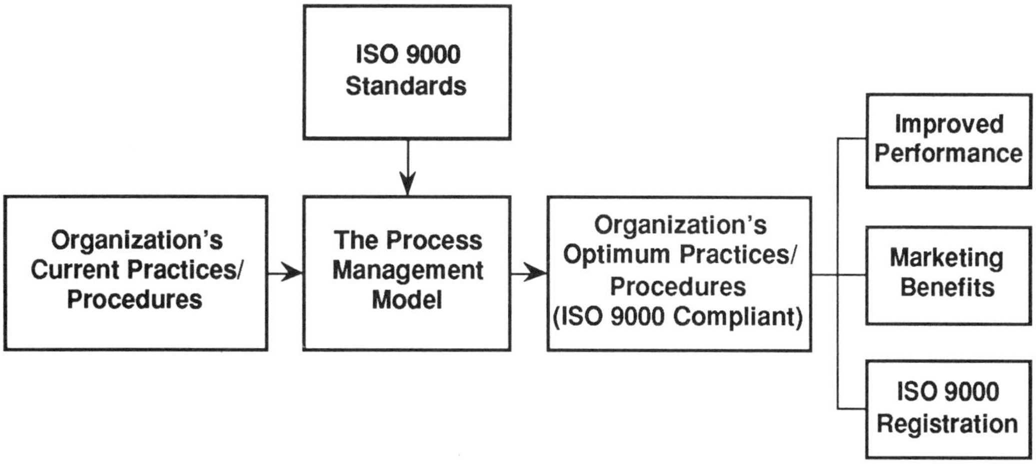

Figure 8.1 Process Management Model and ISO 9000 Standards

In any company, there is a basic operational cycle designed to meet customer needs. It begins with discovering and understanding the customer's requirements and follows through to delivering the service or product to a satisfied customer. To complete the cycle efficiently and effectively, certain organizational factors must be controlled. The factors differ, depending on what the company does, but the systems for control have common features and requirements in all organizations.

The Procedure Guides mirror the operational cycle of the organization. They begin with the definition of the customer's needs and expectations and follow the processes required for the provision of the agreed product or service. The processes may include design, purchasing, receiving, processing, inspection, and testing, storing, packing, distribution, installation, and service. Not all the steps are present in every organization; the modular nature of the Process Management Model allows the user to use only those parts of the model that are relevant to the organization.

The model begins with the company's own processes and by translating these into procedures and work instructions, defines the company's own quality system. The organization must be viewed in terms of its own process, as in Figure 8.2.a, not in terms of its functions and departments, as in Figure 8.2.b.

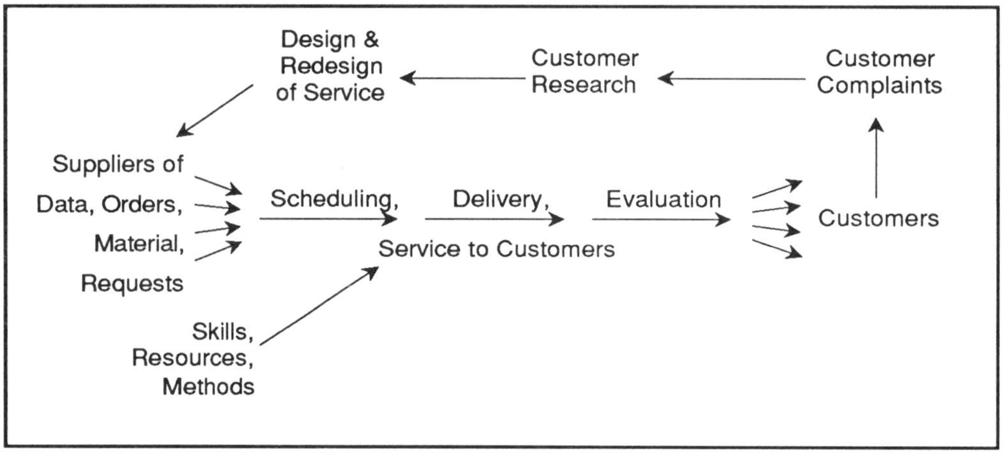

Figure 8.2.a Step 1—Existing System

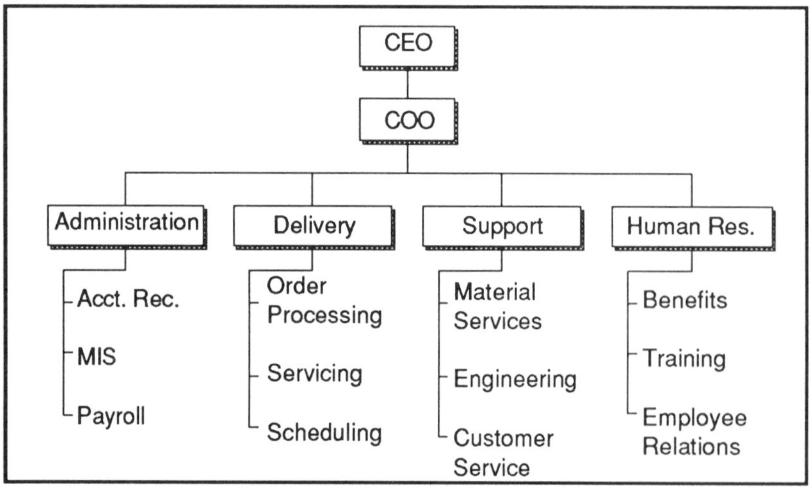

Figure 8.2.b Step 1—Existing System

Organizational and Operational Processes

The Process Management Model includes 25 Procedure Guides which are included in Chapter 9. The Procedure Guides have been divided into *operational* and *organizational* categories. All of the organizational guides are likely to apply in a manufacturing environment. In service environments, certain guides, such as the Calibration Guide, may not be needed.

Determining which operational procedures are part of the quality system is the first step. The model covers all processes that are found in organizations. All of these processes may not be in your company and hence, some of the guides may not apply to you. Just select those you need.

The *Operational* Procedure Guides of the model are:

1. Inquiries/Orders
2. Design Control
3. Supplier Approval
4. Purchasing
5. Receiving and Inventory Control
6. Process Planning
7. Process Control
8. Final Inspection and Testing
9. Packaging and Shipping
10. Control of Reject Material
11. Customer Returns/Complaints
12. Servicing
13. Installation
14. Contract/Project Control
15. Product, Service, and Process Audits

The *Organizational* Procedure Guides of the model are:

16. Control of Quality System Documentation
17. Control of Product/Service Documentation
18. Internal Quality Auditing
19. Management Review
20. Deviations/Waivers/Concessions
21. Training
22. Corrective and Preventive Action
23. Calibration
24. Control of Software Systems
25. Equipment Maintenance

All companies have their own peculiar terminology which may not coincide with that of the model, but which will need to be correlated with the guides. The titles of these sections reflect common names for the activities described, but in some industries other titles are found. For instance, in an automobile dealership, procedures with titles such as Sale of Automobiles, Sale of Parts, and Estimates, are covered by the Inquiries/Orders Procedure Guide. Readers are free to modify terminology to suit their own organizational environment.

Using The Process Management Model

The Process Management Model enables the customized design and implementation of a unique quality system that complies with ISO 9000. As a practical matter, the Procedure Guide's format and presentation are similar to the recommended format for procedures as outlined in Chapter 7.

The format is designed to describe clearly the way work should be documented and performed. Each Procedure Guide has seven parts:

1.0	Objective:	Defines the purpose of the procedure.
2.0	Scope:	Defines processes covered by this procedure guide.
3.0	Responsibilities:	Identifies the key tasks for which responsibilities must be allocated.
4.0	Procedure:	Defines the activities/actions that need to be incorporated into the procedure.
5.0	Related Procedures:	Indicates other sections of the model to which that procedure may interface.
6.0	Documentation:	Indicates the type of documents needed in the procedure.
7.0	Records:	Identifies the necessary records to demonstrate operation of the procedure, including retention time.

Identifying Processes and Procedures

Procedures constitute written documentation of processes. The first step in the documentation process is to survey the company and decide how to divide the business activities into processes. Each procedure should define and detail a process or a series of related processes. Decisions on which procedures to include will vary according to the size and complexity of the company.

Before an organization can use the model, it is necessary to understand—and relate to the model—the organization's current activities.

To Identify Your Procedures and Processes:

- First, list the processes, or chart your business, representing the major activities performed by the organization.
- Then examine the Procedure Guides and decide which sections apply to your organization. Most of the organizational aspects normally apply.

The following illustration is based on the development of the documentation for a consulting/training firm. In Step 1 the basic processes are identified and drawn with their interrelationships (see Figure 8.3.a). In Step 2 (Figure 8.3.b) these basic processes are grouped together into procedures. Figure 8.3.c lists the procedures the firm used to define their quality system.

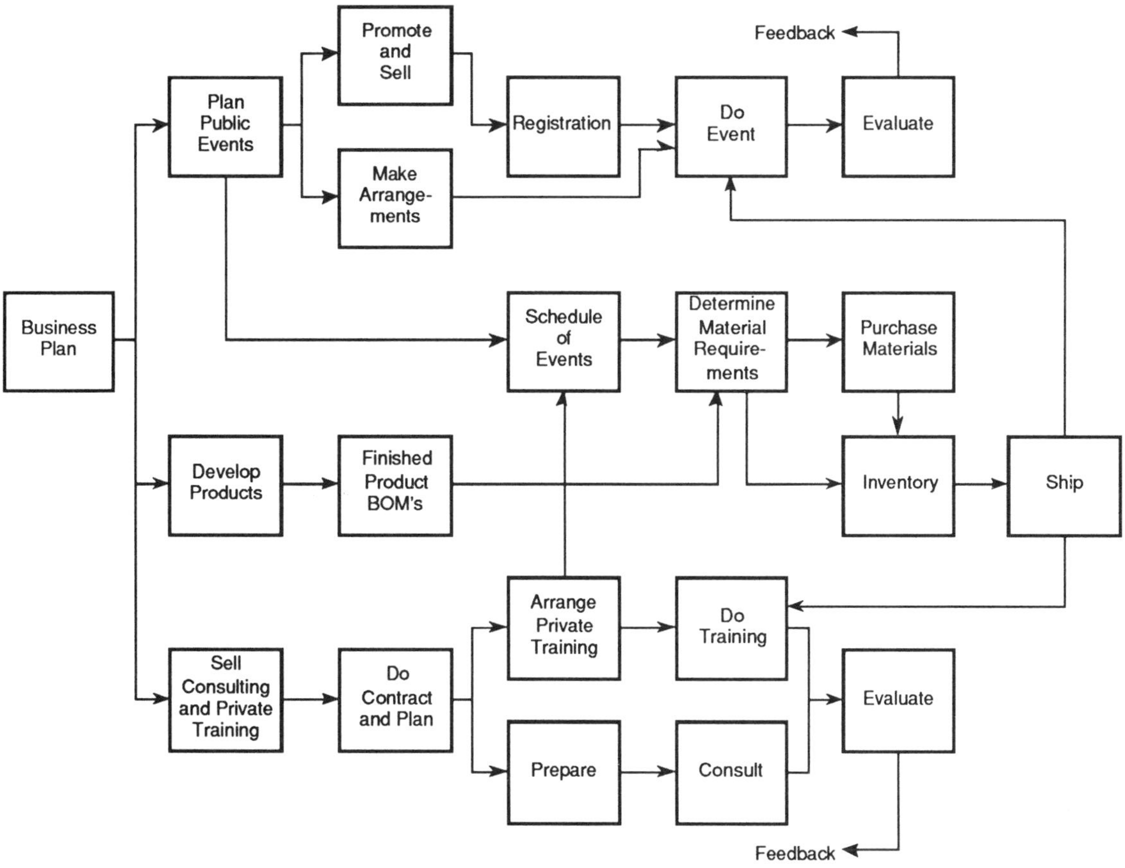

Figure 8.3.a
Step One A — Identification of Basic Processes

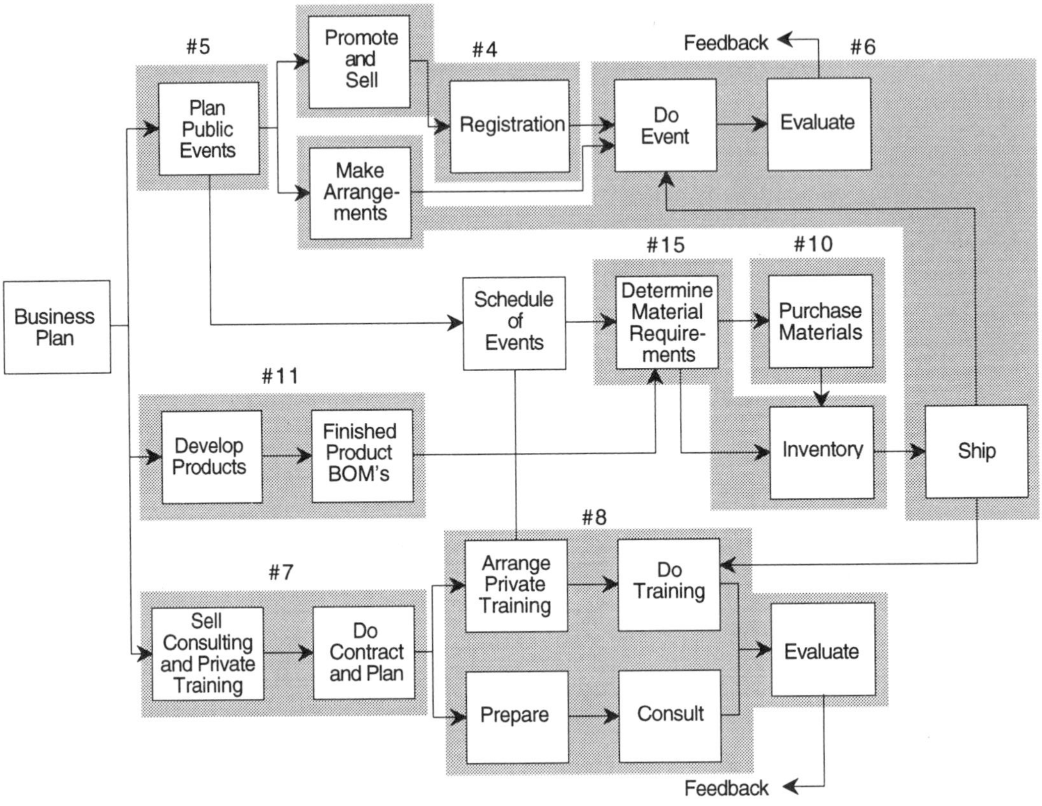

Figure 8.3.b
Step Two — Identification of Operational Procedure Requirements

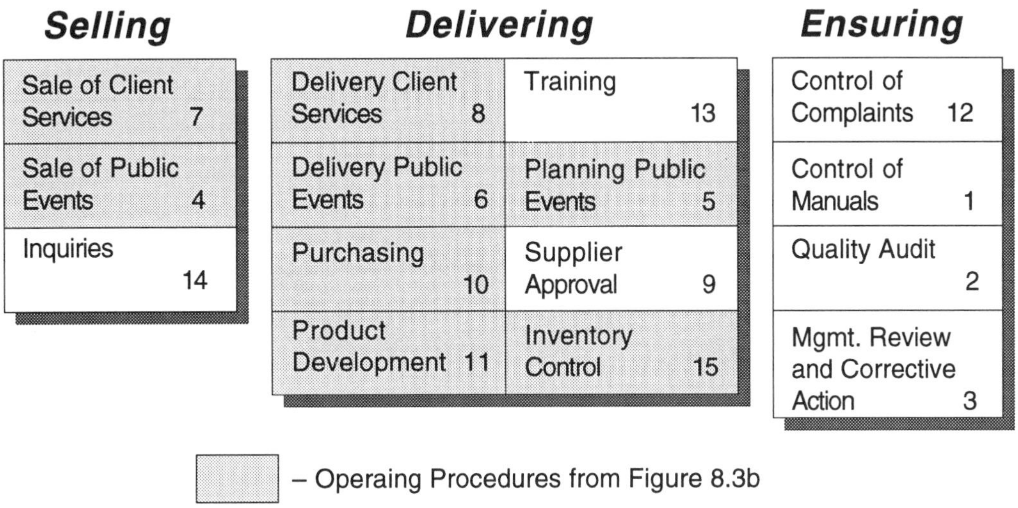

Figure 8.3.c
Step Three — Final Procedure Listing

Note: The Firm ended up with fifteen procedures. Eight of these were identified at Step 2 as operational: Procedure 9, Supplier Approval; 12, Control of Complaints; and 14, Inquiries, are also operational. They were not identified during steps one and two. In reviewing the twenty-five Procedure Guides in the model, it was determined that they are needed to satisfy the requirements of ISO 9001 and these then were added. The remaining four procedures—1, Control of Manuals; 2, Quality Audit; 3, Management Review and Corrective Action; and 13, Training—are organizational and are also necessary to satisfy the requirements of ISO 9001.

Also note that this firm titled their procedures with familiar terminology and did not use titles from the ISO 9000 Standard nor the Process Management Model.

At this time, it may be helpful if you read the relevant industry sectors in Section IV to help determine procedure requirements.

The following examples can also help you identify your procedure needs. These are from organizations that have been ISO 9000 registered. The examples list the procedures used to define their quality system. The titles are the ones used by those organizations. The model has more generic titles for similar procedures.

Organization A—

A two-person design company that provides fire protection system design services to the civil engineering industry.

1. Control of Manuals
2. Internal Auditing
3. Training
4. Corrective Action and Management Review
5. Inquiries and Orders
6. Design Control
7. Drawing Control
8. Document Control
9. Supplier Approval
10. Purchasing and Receiving
11. Control of Customer Complaints
12. Control of Software Back-ups

Organization B—

A 60-employee electroplating organization providing specialty grinding and plating services to manufacturers.

1. Control of Manuals
2. Internal Auditing
3. Management Review and Corrective Action
4. Inquiries
5. Order Processing and Shipping
6. Supplier Approval
7. Purchasing
8. Training
9. Calibration
10. Control of Rejects and Customer Complaints
11. Control of Drawings
12. Control of Plating Solutions
13. Control of Subcontractors
14. Maintenance of Equipment

Organization C—

A small suburban butcher shop employing nine people and supplying meat to the catering trade.

1. Control of Manuals
2. Internal Auditing
3. Management Review and Corrective Action
4. Counter Orders
5. Trade and Frozen Meat Orders
6. Supplier Approval
7. Purchasing and Receiving
8. Hygiene Control
9. Control of Storage of Meats
10. Process Control
11. Control of Complaints
12. Calibration
13. Training

Organization D—

A major automotive dealership employing 150 people in sales, service, parts, and body work for new and used vehicles for individual and commercial customers.

1. Control of Manuals
2. Internal Auditing
3. Management Review and Corrective Action
4. Training
5. Supplier Approval
6. Customer Complaints
7. Calibration
8. Specification Control
9. Retail Sale of New Vehicles
10. Sale of Vehicles to Fleet Customers
11. Stock Control of New Vehicles
12. Sales of Used Vehicles
13. Stock Control of Used Vehicles
14. Pre-delivery Inspection

15. Delivery of Vehicles
16. Sales of Parts
17. Stock Control of Parts
18. Sale of Finance and Insurance
19. Control of Service
20. Control of New Vehicle Stock
21. Control of the Body Shop
22. Control of Nonconforming Products
23. Control of Fleet Sales Contracts
24. Inter-Dealer Trading Procedure
25. Control of Software Back-ups
26. Maintenance of Workshop Equipment

Organization E—

A company employing 2,500 people at three sites designing and producing electrical parts for the automotive industry.

1. Control of Manuals
2. Internal Auditing
3. Management Review
4. Inquiries and Quotations
5. Order Entry
6. Design Control
7. Production of Prototypes
8. Drawing Control
9. Control of Standards
10. Quality Planning
11. Production Planning
12. Supplier Approval
13. Purchasing
14. Receiving
15. Control of Production
16. Final Inspection and Test
17. Packing and Shipping
18. Manufacture and Control of Test Equipment
19. Calibration
20. Product Audit

21. Training
22. Corrective Action
23. Control of Nonconforming Material
24. Modification Control
25. Control of Waivers
26. Process Capability
27. Control of Software Back-up
28. Planned Maintenance

Company F—

A small employment agency providing permanent and temporary workers to local government and industry.

1. Control of Manuals
2. Internal Auditing
3. Management Review and Corrective Action
4. Training
5. Provision of Temporary Employees
6. Provision of Permanent Employees
7. Control of Applicants
8. Control of Specifications
9. Processing of Complaints from Clients

Writing Procedures

Having identified your initial list of the required procedures, you are ready to start the analysis process. The list will probably change as you proceed. It is only a preliminary list and you may combine or subdivide as you proceed. This is a common practice.

The Procedure Writing Process is shown in the flow diagram (Figure 8.4) and described in the steps below.

1. Define the current mode of operation.

Flowchart or describe the current process. Determine if the current mode of operation is acceptable (requiring no change). If not, make the required changes. When documenting work processes, try to change as little as possible. If a process has worked in the past, it should not be changed unless the requirements of the Standard are not being met, or the process is inefficient. If different people use different methods for the same task, a discussion should determine the best practice to adopt. Collect copies of examples of completed forms and other documents. These will become appendices to the procedures.

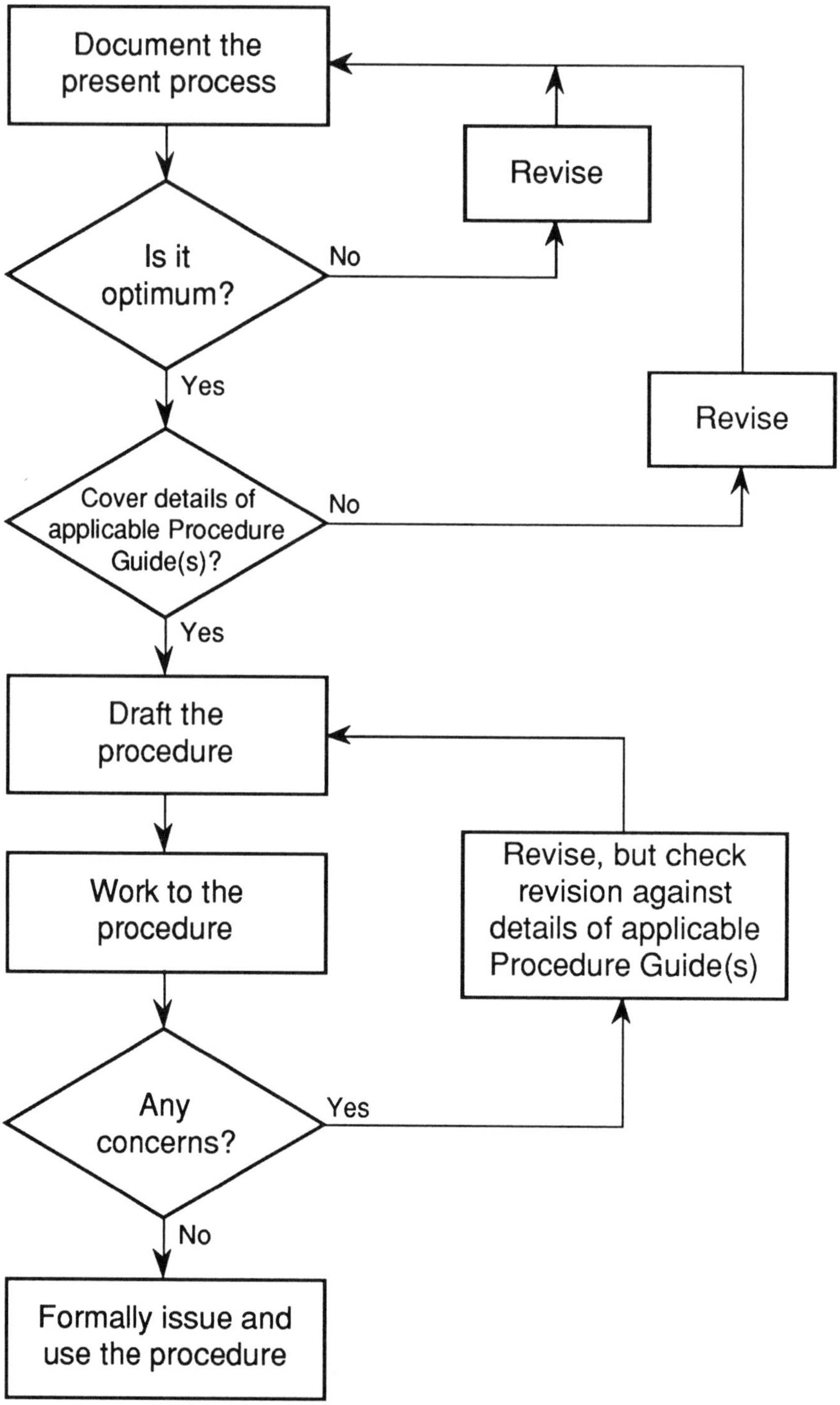

Figure 8.4 Writing Procedure Flowchart

2. Add the ISO 9000 requirements.

   Read the corresponding Procedure Guides from the model and consider the contents of Section 4.0. Examine the current process from Step 1 and use the model to determine any deficiencies in the current processes. If changes are necessary, confer with line managers and refine the current methods.

3. Write the procedures.

   Write the refined method in the format defined in Chapter 7. Take care to record where all documents generated in the process go and are filed, and state who is responsible for the activities defined. Do not include unnecessary operations. If you are not prepared to do something, do not put it in the procedure.

4. Review, refine, and publish the procedure.

   Review the procedure with everyone involved and refine as necessary. Publish it as a draft and implement it. It is recommended that you do not wait until all procedures have been documented before completing these steps. As each procedure is developed, immediately implement any agreed-upon changes, as this reduces the implementation work involved and minimizes the resistance to change. If there are no changes then there is no implementation required.

5. Implement procedures and verify.

   Verify the procedure after it has been in use for about one month and refine as necessary.

6. Issue procedure.

   Formally issue the procedure as Revision 1.

Repeat these steps for each procedure.

This process creates a collection of procedures necessary to define the quality system. These are authorized, issued, and controlled through the Procedure Manual addressed in Chapter 11. The next chapter contains the Procedure Guides for analyzing processes and writing the procedures.

Chapter 9 ◆ The Procedure Guides

Now that you have identified the processes that must be documented to define your quality system, find the corresponding procedure guides in the Process Management Model. Use it in the analysis and writing of the procedure. These guides have been written to ensure that procedures based on them meet the requirements of the ISO 9000 Standards. There is no need to refer to the Standards during the documentation process. The relationship of the Procedure Guides to the Standard is shown in the matrix on page 57.

The Procedure Guides themselves begin on page 59. Each of the 25 sections is presented in a similar way. Each one has introductory comments and the model to be used for drafting procedures. Each ends with commentary, including tips and benefits experienced by various organizations going through the ISO 9000 registration process.

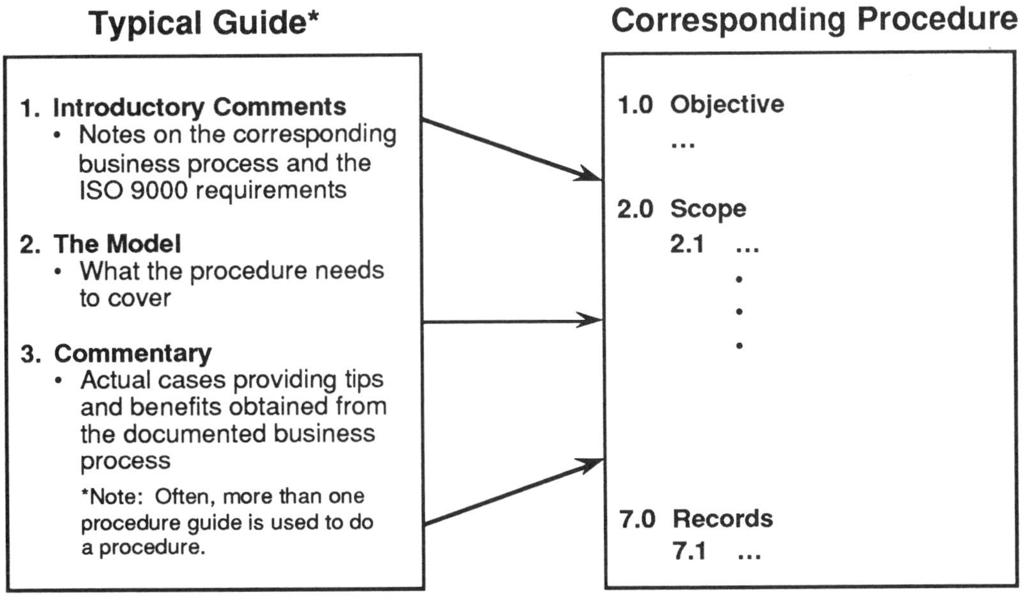

Figure 9.1 Using the Procedure Guides

Control of Documentation

Documents are generated in many processes in the quality system. The short-term control of these documents is generally best achieved by the procedure which describes the process where they are used. There are, however, documents within the quality system which are used for reference in numerous processes and it is useful to have separate procedures to control this documentation.

You can categorize the documentation of most organizations into four types:

- Quality System
- Product/Service Related
- Work Instructions
- Sales Literature

ISO 9000 requires that all documentation supporting quality be identified and controlled. Procedure Guides 16 and 17 deal with controlling documentation.

You can accomplish document control by writing one or two or more procedures based on Guides 16 and 17. The choice is yours and should take account of the number of processes you have and the types of documents that need controlling.

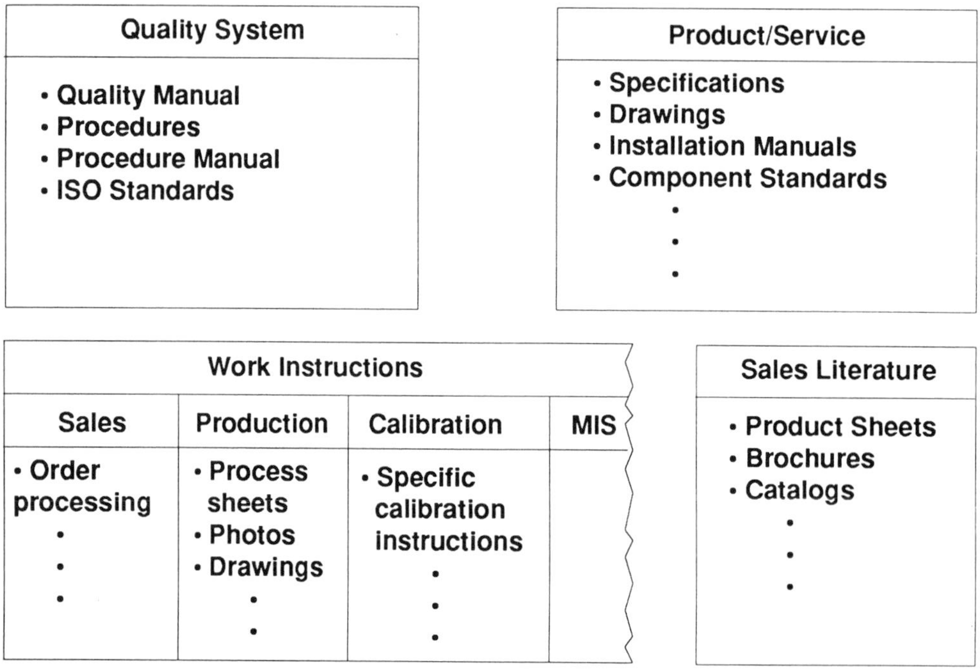
Quality System
• Quality Manual
• Procedures
• Procedure Manual
• ISO Standards
Product/Service
• Specifications
• Drawings
• Installation Manuals
• Component Standards
Work Instructions
Sales
• Order processing
Production
• Process sheets
• Photos
• Drawings
Calibration
• Specific calibration instructions
MIS
Sales Literature
• Product Sheets
• Brochures
• Catalogs

Figure 9.2 Documentation Control: Types of Documentation

Procedure Guide	***Clauses of ISO 9001, Paragraph 4***																			
	1	2	3	4	5	6	7	8	9	10	11	12	13	14	15	16	17	18	19	20
Inquiries and Orders	X	X	X		X		X									X				
Design Control	X	X		X	X											X				
Supplier Approval	X	X				X								X		X				
Purchasing	X	X				X										X				
Receiving/Inventory Control	X	X				X	X	X		X		X	X		X	X				X
Process Planning	X	X							X					X		X				X
Process Control	X	X					X	X	X	X		X	X		X	X				X
Final Inspection and Test	X	X								X		X		X		X				X
Packaging/Shipping	X	X					X	X							X	X				
Control of Reject Material	X	X					X	X				X	X	X		X				
Customer Returns/Complaints	X	X						X		X		X	X	X		X				
Servicing	X	X					X	X		X		X	X		X	X			X	
Installation	X	X					X	X	X	X		X	X		X	X				
Contract/Project Control	X	X	X	X				X	X	X		X	X			X				
Product, Service and Process Audits	X	X								X		X	X	X		X				X
Control of Quality System Documentation	X	X			X											X				
Control of Product/ Service Documentation	X	X			X											X				
Internal Quality Auditing	X	X														X	X			
Management Review	X	X														X				
Deviations/Waivers/ Concessions	X	X											X	X		X				
Training	X	X														X		X		
Corrective and Preventive Action	X	X												X		X				
Calibration	X	X									X					X				
Control of Software Systems	X	X			X											X				
Equipment Maintenance	X	X							X					X		X				X

Figure 9.3 The Relationship of the Procedure Guides to the Standard

Control of Nonconformances

Procedure Guides 10, 11, and 20 deal with identifying and dispositioning of nonconforming material and products. Figure 9.3 distinguishes the three sections of the model. Nonconformances, no matter the source, may need corrective action. Nonconformances are shown as dashed lines.

In all industries, the service provided, as well as any products or material, can fall below requirements. Such shortfalls are considered to be nonconformances and corrective action may be needed to prevent recurrence. Procedure Guides 10, 11, and 12 are also applicable when developing procedures for service shortfalls.

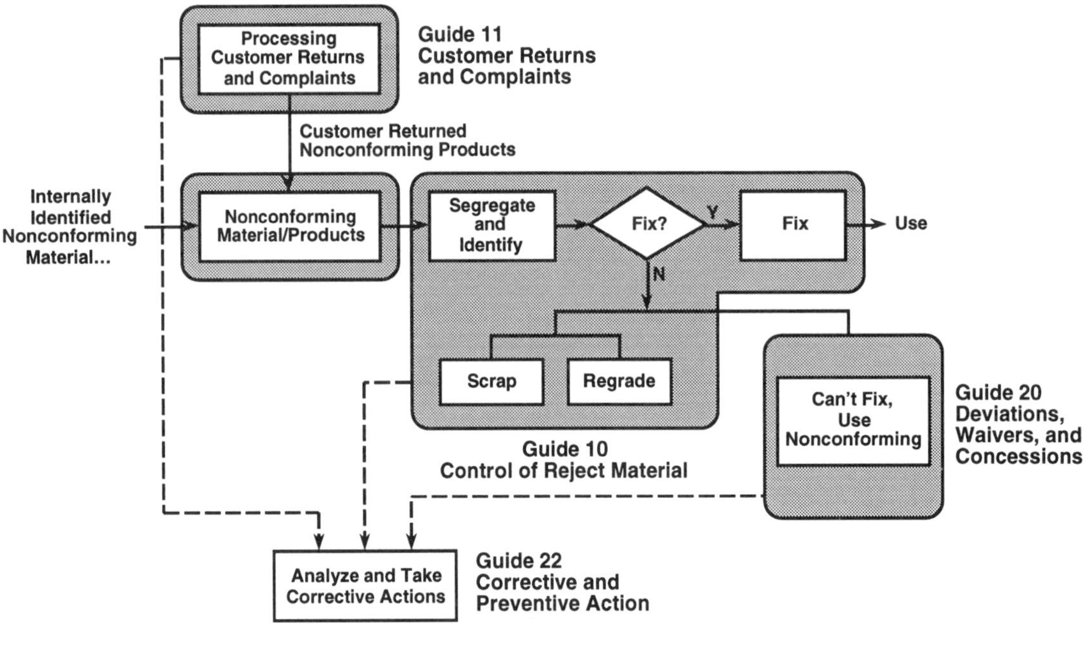

Figure 9.3 Control of Nonconforming Material and Products Relevant Model Guides

Procedure Guide 1: Inquiries/Orders

No organization should contract for anything that cannot be delivered. That sounds very obvious, but how often do you receive excuses from companies who have agreed to deliver certain products or services? It happens all the time. The Standard requires companies to clearly define what they will deliver and when.

The company should also be sure that the customer ordered what the company offered to sell. These contract review provisions seem fundamental, especially from a legal standpoint, but for many organizations, they represent an attempt to bring quality thinking into sales operations.

Contracts are based on what the company says in its advertisements, brochures, and other marketing materials. This information is implied in any contract and must be carefully reviewed to ensure its accuracy.

It makes sense to double-check that the customer asked for the right product and that the company has what the customer wants. It is good practice to read an order back to the customer, especially when it's taken over the telephone. Another good way to confirm an order, especially one having significant technical content, is to have the customer review it on paper.

Sales of technologically sophisticated products, such as cars and personal computers, which are often customized, can require extra checking to ensure that the customer's desires are fulfilled.

The Model

Procedure Guide 1: Inquiries and Orders

1.0 Objective

1.1 To record and control all formal inquiries and orders to ensure that the requirements are precisely defined and that they are within the capability of the organization.

2.0 Scope

2.1 All inquiries and orders received by the organization in the course of its business.

2.2 Four types of contracts with customers are addressed by four different parts of this section. More than one type of contract may be used by an organization for different aspects of its business. It is recommended that there be a different procedure for each type.

2.3 It should be noted that the procedures only cover serious inquiries; casual inquiries can be dealt with informally with no records made.

2.4 Organizations usually have existing procedures for checking the credit rating of potential customers before acceptance of orders. These are not a requirement of the Standard, but where they exist, they should be included in this procedure for completeness.

2.5 Repeat orders for agreed upon and documented products or services do not need to go through the entire procedure. A way to bypass certain steps for repeat orders can be designed into the procedure as applicable.

3.0 Responsibilities

3.1 Responsibilities must be defined in the procedure. There is no need for quality personnel to be involved except where there are special requirements for inspection or testing. Technical capability must be the responsibility of a technical function. Delivery capability may need to be the responsibility of the operations function.

4.0 Procedures

On all contracts where standard terms and conditions apply, these must be available to the customer at the time of ordering. Depending on the type of contract, four situations may be considered. These situations are outlined in sections 4.1, 4.2, 4.3, and 4.4.

4.1 Contracts based on formal inquiries by potential customers with unique solutions.

4.1.1 A record of the receipt of inquiry must be kept, including verbal inquiries, and should be signed by recipient.

4.1.2 Documentation on the development of proposals must be maintained.

4.1.3 All communications with customers or prospective customers must be recorded.

4.1.4 All novel features of proposal need to be assessed as to their feasibility and the conclusion of such assessments must be recorded.

4.1.5 Formal quotation of a proposal, with all technical details, delivery, period of validity of the quote, and conditions of contract should be documented and a copy retained by the organization.

4.1.6 Any changes to the proposal must be recorded in writing and agreed to by the customer.

4.1.7 Upon receipt, an order must be checked against the quotation. Any differences must be resolved with the customer, and all resolutions must be recorded in writing.

4.1.8 Formal acceptance of the order must be documented with reference to proposal, any alterations, and conditions of order.

4.1.9 All post-contract changes to proposal must be agreed to by the customer and recorded.

4.2 Contracts based on defined products or services described in the organization's technical sales literature, but customized or configured for the specific requirement.

4.2.1 Records of the receipt of inquiry must be maintained, verbal inquiries must be documented, and records of their receipt must be maintained. Records must be signed by the recipient.

4.2.2 Any novel features of inquiry must be referred to technical authority for approval.

4.2.3 Formal quotation of the proposal is required, with reference made to standard products and services. All proposals must include delivery dates, period of validity of quotation, and conditions of contract. A copy must be retained by the organization.

4.2.4 Any changes to the proposal are to be recorded in writing and agreed to by the customer.

4.2.5 Orders must be checked upon receipt against the quotation, and any differences must be resolved with the customer and resolutions recorded in writing.

4.2.6 Confirmation of acceptance of an order must be documented and must include reference to proposal, alterations, and conditions of order.

4.2.7 All post-contract changes to the proposal must be agreed upon with the customer and recorded.

4.3 Contracts where the customer buys a defined product or service at a set price without any formal tender or quotation, *e.g.* standard "catalog" of products/service.

4.3.1 If the order is verbal, it must be recorded by the recipient and read back to the customer, then signed by the recipient.

4.3.2 The order must include customer contact name and order number where possible.

4.3.3 Documentation of the order to be sent/given to the customer upon delivery of the goods.

4.3.4 Conditions of the order need to be defined on the customer's order copy.

4.4 Contracts for service when the customer agreed to pay after the work has been done.

4.4.1 A document confirming the work and standard terms and conditions must be available to the customer.

4.4.2 Verbal communications with the customer are to be recorded, the record signed and dated.

4.4.3 A log recording all orders received must be kept.

4.4.4 Any problems encountered must be reported to the customer and instructions on resolution sought. Record of the communications need to be made and signed.

5.0 Related Procedures

5.1 Design Control

5.2 Process Planning

5.3 Servicing

5.4 Contract/Project Control

6.0 Documentation

6.1 Verbal Inquiries/Order Pad

6.2 Quotation Form

6.3 Inquiry Log

6.4 Order Log

6.5 Conditions of Order

7.0 Records

7.1 Records of inquiries, proposals, and orders, together with all amendments to these documents, should be retained for ten years. Where the life of the product or service is considerably less than this, the period may be reduced.

7.2 Quotations which do not convert into orders need not be retained after the expiration of their validity, but in practice, they are retained for a longer period.

Relevant ISO 9001 Clauses:

4.1 Management Responsibility

4.2 Quality System

4.3 Contract Review

4.5 Document and Data Control

4.7 Customer Supplied Product

4.16 Quality Records

Commentary

A company sales representative routinely ignored a company requirement to either get the customer to sign an order sheet or to sign it himself. One day the company refused to deliver an item to a customer because other employees weren't sure it had been ordered. Time was lost while the confusion was cleared up.

A sheet metal fabricator once took a telephone order from a customer who wanted a product with a one-inch hole in it. The sheet metal fabricator dutifully put a round, one-inch hole in the product, only to learn the customer wanted a square, one-inch hole. Transmitting the order by fax would have saved the error.

A bus manufacturer in the United Kingdom once delivered 12 buses to a tour company. The customer complained that they would go only 70 miles per hour. He wanted to take them to Germany where the speed limit was 90 miles per hour. The bus manufacturer's quality manager checked the computer records, which showed the instructions called for the buses' gear boxes to be tested at 70 miles per hour, and that was what had been done. The problem was passed into the hands of the engineering department, which determined that the order indeed specified 70 miles per hour. Eventually it was discovered that when taking the order, the sales manager did not check off a box that would have specified gear boxes able to handle the higher speed. The sales manager had never reconfirmed the order, which cost the company $500,000 in reworking the gear boxes to the required specification.

Many companies accept an order from a customer, deliver the goods or service, and then give the customer an invoice on which the terms of the contract are defined. It is essential for the customer to know the full details of the contract being entered into when the order is placed, if the clauses are to be enforceable. This is particularly relevant in services since once they have been completed, they are not retractable.

Procedure Guide 2: Design Control

Design control is often the most vital link in the chain from idea to product. The design phase is where the idea is developed and put on paper with exact specifications for producing it for the end-user. If the design is flawed, the product will also be flawed. The flaw may show up in customer dissatisfaction, perhaps unstated, and ultimately mean a loss of business. Or it will manifest itself in the form of waste and rework, with inevitable rising costs, or even liabilities.

It is important that the controls included in this procedure are extended to cover all design activities. Special designs and drawings produced for quotations should also be included.

The Model

Procedure Guide 2: Design Control

1.0 Objective

1.1 To record and control the design of products and services, and ensure that the outputs from the design process meet the customer and market requirements and are compatible with the organization's ability to produce the product or deliver the service.

2.0 Scope

2.1 All design activities to develop the organization's products and services. The level of control needs to reflect the complexity and novelty of the design work. Design of less complex products or services within the limits of known technology requires only simple design verification. Design carried out with a high level of innovation needs more design verification. In all cases, the process needs to be documented and the results of verifications recorded.

2.2 Depending on the nature of the product or service, the design process may include the building prototypes or models or pre-production units to validate the design. The control of these activities can usually be better maintained by separate procedures which contain the same features as the design control procedure.

3.0 Responsibilities

3.1 The responsibility for the approval of designs must be clearly defined. This would normally include some type of design review where the technical marketing and production functions are represented. The design review must be approved by someone other than a member of the design team.

4.0 Procedure

4.1 A clear written statement of the design requirements agreed to by all parties should be prepared. The statement needs to identify any standards, regulations, and legislation applicable to the product or service. Target manufacturing cost could also be included.

4.2 The preparation and issue of a plan covering the design project, including the allocation of resources and responsibilities, should be completed.

4.3 A requirement for all documents relating to the design to be retained and filed, usually in a project file, should be included.

4.4 All decisions made during the design, including changes to the design requirements, are to be agreed upon and documented.

4.5 Regular reviews of the status of the design efforts are to be documented. The review period should be defined.

4.6 The approval process for the design output including a record of acceptance criteria (*e.g.* tolerances, operational parameters, and test methods) should be specified.

4.7 Details of all tests and calculations and the results obtained are to be included in the project file. These do not need to be formally written up, as long as the evidence is there that they have been done and the results obtained.

4.8 A final acceptance procedure must be described, with responsibilities clearly defined and the outcomes recorded and logged in the project file. If the design is for a specific customer, the customer's role in this design verification must be established. This completion could be tied to a stage payment; otherwise changes made after this agreement may be construed as extras under the terms of the contract.

4.9 When the design is for a specific customer, changes to the design must be agreed to with the customer and the responsibility for the changes established. This is of particular importance where there is a possibility of the changes resulting in charges under the contract.

4.10 A method of validating the design output must be defined. This could be by building and testing a prototype or model of the product or service, or by the pilot running of a service to confirm its validity.

5.0 Related Procedures

5.1 Inquiries/Orders

5.2 Control of Product/Service Documentation

5.3 Process Planning

5.4 Contract/Project Control

5.5 Purchasing

6.0 Documentation

6.1 All log books, calculations, test results, etc. which are produced during the design process are considered formal documents and must be defined. They do not need to be typed up, just retained in the project file. It has to be possible to identify who carried out the work, so it is recommended that all entries be signed and dated.

7.0 Records

7.1 The project file becomes a record of the design process. Its retention time should be related to the life of the product or service, starting from the last delivery of a product or service based on the design.

Relevant ISO 9001 Clauses:

4.1 Management Responsibility
4.2 Quality System
4.4 Design Control
4.5 Document and Data Control
4.16 Quality Records

Commentary

A company making sophisticated electronic products employed designers who disliked constraints, priding themselves on their creativity in developing new, products. Their designs often changed abruptly due to rapidly expanding electronic technology. Problems arose, however, as the designers continually moved the goal posts for the product designs, even after production had begun. To make matters worse, they did so without keeping records of what they were doing.

The company introduced a system that defined the required output from the designers and then managed the work to meeting the system specifications. This resulted in designs being completed on time with required documentation, and fewer design changes after production started.

Many smaller companies engaged in design frequently depend on one person to organize the design activities. That person is usually under pressure, with little time or emphasis placed on keeping records of the work. Designs are often released without complete documentation, resulting in production problems. The introduction of simple systems to control the design process invariably proves beneficial to the company's operations. It also relieves some of the pressure and increases available time for the individual responsible for design.

When instituting better controls it is important to remember that balance is required in creative work. We seek to create a *structure* to improve the design function, but not to create a *stricture* that may inhibit it. The Standards provide sufficient flexibility to allow either to happen, but the Process Management Model guides an organization to the former rather than the latter.

Procedure Guide 3: Supplier Approval

Suppliers should be carefully selected on the basis of their ability to perform. When a supplier has a track record of reliability, the need to inspect their work is lessened. No amount of inspection can improve quality after a product is delivered. The choice should be based on ability to deliver a part or service that meets or exceeds specifications. Even then, the supplier's performance should be monitored.

Every organization has its own method for selecting and approving suppliers. Often the selection is based on long-standing relationships in which confidence is well established. It is neither necessary nor desirable to discard proven suppliers when a company seeks ISO 9000 registration. Suppliers should be encouraged to seek registration also, but it need not be mandatory.

The Model

Procedure Guide 3: Supplier Approval

1.0 Objective

1.1 To ensure that the suppliers used by the organization are capable of supplying materials and services to meet the organization's requirements.

2.0 Scope

2.1 The procedure need only address the suppliers of materials and services which are directly related to the organization's products and services. This includes providers of material and services, as well as subcontractors used in the production process, for delivering products or services, and for calibrating equipment are to be included.

3.0 Responsibilities

3.1 The responsibility for the approval of suppliers is normally given to purchasing, with involvement of other organizations as appropriate.

4.0 Procedure

4.1 A method of approving new suppliers is required. This may be by one or more of the following methods. The first two options are recommended.

4.1.1 Requesting samples and carrying out trials.

4.1.2 Placing a trial order and closely monitoring it on receipt.

4.1.3 Visiting suppliers and assessing their systems. If this is done, the criteria for the assessment must be defined and evidence provided to show the assessment has met the criteria.

4.1.4 Sending a questionnaire to suppliers and assessing them on this basis. If this is done, the criteria for the assessment must be defined and evidence provided to show the criteria have been met.

4.1.5 Using only suppliers who are registered to a quality standard. This is not a requirement of the ISO 9000 Standard, but valid, albeit restrictive.

4.2 The approval of historic suppliers can be done on the basis of their past performance. If it can be shown that the suppliers have been used for a suitable period, they can be approved on the basis of that alone. There is no need to use any of the methods set out in 4.1 on existing suppliers, but there must be evidence that the past performance has been examined and approved.

4.3 The monitoring of the performance of suppliers should be done formally. It is acceptable to only record instances of nonconformance; it is not necessary to record all conforming deliveries. Nonconformances with respect to delivery or conformance to specification must be recorded and suitable actions taken. Corrective action programs should be agreed upon with the suppliers, documented, and monitored. Failure to conform must result in the supplier becoming nonapproved.

4.4 Nonapproved suppliers can be used, but there must be a system to ensure the quality of what they supply.

4.5 The supply of standard proprietary parts from alternate suppliers should be included to provide flexibility.

4.6 Copies of the supplier approval list must be controlled and upgrades must be made to all copies or the list reissued.

5.0 Related Procedures

5.1 Purchasing

5.2 Corrective Action

5.3 Receiving and Inventory Control

6.0 Documentation

6.1 Supplier approval list: this may be a series of cards, forms, or a computer listing. (An indication of nonconformances and actions taken are part of the record.)

6.2 Documentation on whichever of the above options in 4.1 is used to approve existing suppliers.

7.0 Records

7.1 The records of the past history of the suppliers should be maintained.

7.2 The approvable records of a new supplier must be kept as long as the suppliers are used.

7.3 The records of the actions taken as a result of nonconformance must be kept for at least two years.

Relevant ISO 9001 Clauses:

4.1 Management Responsibility

4.2 Quality System

4.6 Purchasing

4.14 Correction action

4.16 Quality Records

Commentary

A major automotive company once sent letters to its suppliers announcing a deadline for them to become ISO 9000 registered. When the deadline expired, only 60 percent of the suppliers had registered. It was not feasible or desirable to resource all the purchases from the registered suppliers. The company had to retreat from its requirement. This resulted in a loss of credibility and a demand from those suppliers who achieved the target for more favorable treatment.

The Standard does not require a registered organization's suppliers to be registered or to seek registration. The means of approving suppliers is up to the organization itself. It is more important that the organization's suppliers are able to demonstrate that they can take corrective actions when concerns arise.

There are some suppliers who are overlooked when a company is seeking ISO 9000 registration. The applying organization must consider as a supplier any other organization (or person) providing goods or services that have an impact on quality. Some of the suppliers who are routinely overlooked include delivery services, pest control subcontractors in food factories, and testing labs for engineering firms.

Procedure Guide 4: Purchasing

ISO 9000 auditors watch certain things carefully, and purchasing is one of them. The Standard insists that purchasers have clear definitions and agreements with suppliers regarding what is to be provided. Auditors will often challenge them to prove that their purchasing requirements are adequately defined and communicated to suppliers.

The Model

Procedure Guide 4: Purchasing

1.0 Objective

1.1 To ensure that products and services purchased by the organization are clearly described.

2.0 Scope

2.1 The procedure only needs to address the purchase of materials and services which are directly related to the organization's provision of products and services. This should include all purchases of materials used in the product. Subcontractors used in the production process, for delivering products or services, and for calibrating equipment must be included.

3.0 Responsibilities

3.1 The responsibility for the review and approval of purchasing documents should be clearly defined.

4.0 Procedure

4.1 There must be a precise specification of what is being purchased. This may be accomplished by the following:

4.1.1 Having a definitive description on the order.

4.1.2 Referencing one of the organization's drawings or specifications. The revision must be defined, and evidence that the supplier has been sent the document is needed.

4.1.3 Making reference to the supplier's catalog or other published product sheets.

4.1.4 Making reference to a national or international standard.

4.1.5 Where a representative of the company makes a personal examination and selection of the actual items to be ordered, such as at a sale, market, or auction, then it is not necessary to have the same level of documentation. It must be possible to confirm that the items purchased are the items received.

4.2 The purchase document must be reviewed and authorized by a defined delegation of authority.

4.3 Verbal or telephone orders are acceptable, but they must be recorded and the records kept. Ideally they should be sent or faxed to the supplier.

4.4 Conditions of purchase should be specified.

4.5 Any changes to existing orders must be agreed to with the supplier, and this agreement must be documented.

4.6 Orders should normally only be placed with approved suppliers. Exceptions to this can be permitted in defined circumstances, and this should be stated.

4.7 Where the parts being purchased are for inclusion in a contract which states that your supplier's quality system satisfies a specified standard, this must be stated in the order. **Note:** this is not a normal requirement.

4.8 Where the parts being purchased are for inclusion in a contract which states that the purchaser, or his/her representative have the right to verify at source, this must be included in the order. **Note:** this is not a normal requirement.

4.9 When materials are purchased for inclusion in a product or service requiring traceability, the need for traceability and associated certification must be stated in the order.

4.10 If test certificates or certificates of conformance are required, this must be stated. The use of such documentation is not a requirement of the standard, but may be necessary if traceability is required.

5.0 Related Procedures

5.1 Supplier Approval

5.2 Design Control

5.3 Control of Product/Service Documentation

5.4 Receiving and Inventory Control

6.0 Documentation

6.1 Purchase order

7.0 Records

7.1 Copies of the purchase orders should be filed and retained for seven years or longer if applicable, unless the life of the product or service is considerably less than this period.

Relevant ISO 9001 Clauses:

4.1 Management Responsibility
4.2 Quality System
4.6 Purchasing
4.16 Quality Records

Commentary

A company buying electronic components used to order them by telephone, just referring to the catalog numbers. They found that they frequently had the wrong parts delivered. This prompted a change to the use of the fax to transmit the orders. Receiving the orders in writing resulted in a dramatic decrease in the number of errors and in the company's telephone bill. The supplier then had documents filled out in the customer's hand showing what had been ordered.

A seafood processor bought fish and fish products from auction markets through agents. Business was done verbally over the telephone. There was no clear agreement on the meaning of words like "freshness" or "condition." The processor replaced his system with a series of specifications based on military purchasing specifications, including requirements on minimum temperatures. These were circulated to all suppliers with an explanation and a clear understanding that they would be used in all subsequent orders. The specifications defined a scale of freshness and condition to be used in telephone discussions. The scale values agreed to during those sales and negotiations were recorded and the fish were checked against these on delivery. The temperature of the fish was also checked. Anything not up to specifications was rejected.

It is quite common for auditors to find purchase orders with inadequate technical descriptions. Simple descriptions like steel bar, beef steak, zinc plate, plastic pipe, or blue color are inadequate. It is necessary to refer to some standard or specification. This may be an international or national standard, a suppliers specification, or a specification developed by the company and issued to the supplier.

Procedure Guide 5: Receiving and Inventory Control

How many times have you received a shipment that wasn't what you ordered? This happens to individuals and organizations. The Standard requires receipts to be verified to confirm that they are what the buyer ordered. The purchased goods, quantities, and condition must be satisfactory, and meet all customer requirements. When purchased from a proven supplier, acceptance procedures may be based on the customer's confidence in the supplier. The Standard does not require received goods to be inspected. As a practical matter, most organizations would not have the expertise or equipment to conduct such inspections. The Standard simply requires verification; a visual check may be sufficient. This is based on the assumption that the correct item has been shipped.

Once received, items must be identifiable and stored in a way that protects them from damage or deterioration. Items with limited shelf life must be stored so that they are sold or otherwise moved before the expiration date. For items with no defined shelf life, generally the best practice is first-in, first-out.

The Model

Procedure Guide 5: Receiving and Inventory Control

1.0 Objective

1.1 To record and control the receipt of material into the organization's inventory.

2.0 Scope

2.1 All inventory and materials used to produce and deliver the organization's products and services.

3.0 Responsibilities

3.1 The responsibility for checking inventory on arrival should be defined. It does not have to be a quality function, depending on the type of checks done.

4.0 Procedure

4.1 Reference is made to the purchase order on receipt, and a check is made to confirm that the material is as ordered.

4.2 The extent of inspection should be defined. This can be full inspection, inspection of a sample, visual check only, or no check at all. Whatever method is specified, a record must be made that the delivery has been accepted. If test certificates or certificates of conformance are requested on the order, the action to be taken, pending receipt of these, is to be defined, as is the procedure of reviewing, handling, and filing these documents. If statistical techniques are used during receiving inspection then the use of such statistics must be clearly defined within the procedure or by reference to a work instruction.

4.3 The received items must be segregated while pending release. This can be by location, labeling, or both.

4.4 The material in inventory needs to have positive identification by location or labeling.

4.5 The storage location must be appropriate for ensuring preservation of the material.

4.6 Where there are any degradation possibilities, the date of delivery, shelf life, or expiration date should be identifiable. An instruction is needed to routinely check such material and to ensure that the oldest inventory is issued first and that no overdue inventory is issued.

4.7 Where traceability is a requirement of the contract, batch identity must be maintained.

4.8 Material found to be nonconforming must be segregated and the disposition process defined.

5.0 Related Procedures

5.1 Purchasing

5.2 Process control

6.0 Documentation

6.1 Documentation to confirm acceptance and inventory records.

7.0 Records

7.1 Records of acceptance and locations of material are to be kept for at least the life of the material.

Relevant ISO 9001 Clauses:

4.1 Management Responsibility
4.2 Quality System
4.6 Purchasing
4.7 Control of Customer-Supplied Product
4.8 Product Identification and Traceability
4.10 Inspection and Testing
4.12 Inspection and Test Status
4.13 Control of Nonconforming Product
4.15 Handling, Storage, Packaging, Preservation and Delivery
4.16 Quality Records
4.20 Statistical Techniques

Commentary

An automobile parts manufacturer carefully examined items received on its loading docks but did not check whether the goods had been ordered. Prompted by the Standard's requirements, the manufacturer began checking before the trucks were unloaded. During the first month after the procedure was initiated, the manufacturer turned away unordered items valued at $1 million. Many of the company's suppliers apparently knew its receiving personnel did not check whether the goods were ordered, so they sent materials ahead of schedule. After the company accepted and stored the goods, the invoices were processed and paid. This one change resulted in a marked improvement in the manufacturer's cash flow.

Rubber becomes brittle with age. Manufacturers of rubber products should determine shelf life carefully so their products will be satisfactory throughout their life. Use-by dates are particularly crucial for components like brake parts, which must be installed by the proper date so they will remain in a safe condition throughout the intended life. One distributor ignored such dates, believing them to be inappropriate, based on his own experience using outdated items. When the purpose of the dates was pointed out during the ISO 9000 registration process, the distributor began adhering to the expiration dates and disposed of the outdated stock.

While seeking registration to ISO 9000, a car dealer selling imported European cars noticed that one package had a shelf life defined at six months in the language of the manufacturer. A consultant asked the parts manager if he knew when the item came in. A check through a computerized stock control system determined it arrived eighteen months earlier. The parts manager did not understand the foreign language and was unaware of the expiration time. They opened the package and found several warnings pertaining to the hazardous nature of the contents—all printed in the foreign language. The dealer took the problem to the manufacturer, who agreed to supply literature on the parts in the language of the country to which they were sent.

Procedure Guide 6: Process Planning

Process planning is the preparation for producing products or services. The terminology and complexity differs from one industry to another. In a restaurant, process planning could be writing a menu. In an auto factory, it could mean, among other things, analyzing and making make-or-buy decisions for hundreds of parts.

Process planning includes any requirements to produce a quality plan. This should address quality control techniques used in the subsequent processes. Typically, these include how to control materials and parts, the methods and control used during the process, and the method of final inspection and testing. The use of statistical techniques needs to be considered at this stage. If planning includes the use of failure mode analysis or risk analysis, these also should be included in the quality plan.

The Model

Procedure Guide 6: Process Planning

1.0 Objective

1.1 To define the method and processes to be used for producing a product or providing a service to ensure consistent quality of the product or service.

2.0 Scope

2.1 All products and services provided by the organization. This procedure covers setup activities for new product/services, including quality planning and feasibility studies. Procedure Guide 7, Process Control, covers the production, delivery, and installation processes.

2.2 This procedure can be combined with process control in simple processes.

3.0 Responsibilities

3.1 The responsibility for planning the production must be defined.

4.0 Procedure

4.1 The material to be used in the process, and the quantities, should be stated.

4.2 The sequence of operations to be followed must be specified.

4.3 The planned timing of the process is to be defined.

4.4 The mechanism for make/buy decisions should be described.

4.5 The procedure for the preparation of job cards or similar documentation should be defined.

4.6 The identification of jigs, fixtures, numeric control programs, etc. must be included.

4.7 The procedure for handling changes in design should be stated.

4.8 The identification of any new or special inspection and test equipment.

4.9 A definition of the quality control processes to be used, including control points and techniques. The need for statistical techniques to be used to establish process capability needs to be considered. Failure Mode Analysis of the manufacturing process may be included where applicable.

5.0 Related Procedures

5.1 Process Control

5.2 Design Control

5.3 Final Inspection and Test

5.4 Purchasing

5.5 Supplier Approval

6.0 Documentation

6.1 Examples of the process documentation produced

7.0 Records

7.1 The records generated in process planning are usually fed to process control. Alternatively they may be filed as a project file and they need to be retained for a period dependent on the life of the product and the date of its last manufacture.

Relevant ISO 9001 Clauses:

4.1 Management Responsibility

4.2 Quality System

4.9 Process Control

4.14 Corrective and Preventive Action

4.16 Quality Records

4.20 Statistical Techniques

Commentary

The production manager of a small engineering company handled the production planning and purchasing himself. No one else in the organization knew how. As part of ISO 9000 documentation, the production manager gave the procedures and necessary forms to a trainee to prepare. At first, the trainee took longer to do the work, which the production manager revised. Nevertheless, it saved the production manager time, allowing him to focus on more important activities.

Another engineering company received a contract to produce components for the automotive industry. As part of the application of this procedure guide, they developed a Quality Plan that identified how they planned to assure quality at various stages in the production process. This included the definition of requirements of key material to suppliers, process capability to be established prior to hand-over of tooling, the establishment of statistical process controls on key parameters, the functional testing of the sub-assemblies prior to shipment to the customer, and specially designed packaging to ensure safe delivery.

Procedure Guide 7: Process Control

Process control covers the organization's major activities in producing a product and/or delivering a service. Process Control is needed in all businesses—manufacturing, assembly, distribution, recruitment, nursing care, recreation, etc. The controls should include any special elements required to ensure quality, such as hygiene control or control of plating chemicals.

Process control procedures should determine what is to be done and who is responsible for doing it. Work done under process control procedures is generally supported by work instructions, which provide more detail on how a specific job is performed. There is always a relationship between the qualifications of the operator and the level of work instruction needed. If a skilled toolmaker is doing the work, a drawing may be adequate. If the same work is done by a semi-skilled operator, a process instruction sheet describing machine settings might be necessary.

The Model

Procedure Guide 7: Process Control

1.0 Objective

1.1 To control and record the production and/or service processes used by the organization to ensure consistent product and/or service quality.

2.0 Scope

2.1 All processes used by the organization. There may be several procedures referring to different types of processes, *e.g.* assembly, machining, etc. Separate procedures are required when different processes are controlled in different ways. There should be no need to change the existing methods of control, but rather base the procedures on them.

3.0 Responsibilities

3.1 The responsibility for controlling the quality of the work must be defined (not necessarily a quality function). Line management and operator responsibility should be defined.

4.0 Procedure

4.1 A process document, such as a job or route card, should be associated with each order. The process document defines what is to be done, making reference to work instructions as necessary. The level of detail on the document should reflect the level of experience and training of the staff using the document. The document may refer to drawings and other specifications, to provide more detailed work instructions for operators. It should indicate the material and quantities concerned.

4.2 The process document may be used for identification purposes. Where this is not possible, an alternative method of identifying product and status is needed.

4.3 The process document should be used for recording the progress of the work through the process, with a sign-off to indicate the work is completed to specification.

4.4 Completion of the process documentation must be checked before completion of work.

4.5 In-process inspections and tests can be recorded on the documentation. If it is specified in the Quality Plan that statistical techniques are to be used, then these should be included within the procedure. A separate work instruction could define the actual process to be used. If Process Capability Studies are part of the process control, then this would normally require a separate procedure to describe the process used.

4.6 The action to be taken when nonconforming items are found must be defined, usually by reference to the Control of Rejects procedure. Where extensive results are obtained, they can be attached to the documentation.

When Jigs, fixtures or molds, or machine control programs are used in the manufacturing process, the following need to be addressed. This may be done within the main process control procedure or in separate procedures entitled, for example, "Control of Jigs and Fixtures" or "Control of Machine Control Programs."

4.7 Jigs, Fixtures, and Molds:

4.7.1 All such tools must be identifiable and recorded in a log. The identification of parts made by the tools, including revision number, should be recorded in the log.

4.7.2 The accuracy of the parts produced should be checked and the log signed and dated to indicate that the check has taken place. This is normally done by checking the first part produced when a jig, fixture, or mold is set up. If statistical techniques are to be used to confirm the process capability then this should be included.

4.7.3 The tools should be checked for damage before being placed in a suitable identifiable storage location.

4.7.4 The procedure to be followed when the equipment does not produce products or provide a service to specification must be defined.

4.7.5 Procedure for modification of the tools must be defined.

4.8 Machine control programs

4.8.1 All such programs must be recorded in a log with the parts/processes it is used for referenced with revision number.

4.8.2 Programs should be proved by inspecting parts produced and then approved.

4.8.3 Copies of all software should be kept remote to the machine.

4.8.4 When software is altered, the copy must be updated.

4.8.5 Procedure for modification must be defined.

5.0 Related Procedures

5.1 Process Planning

5.2 Receiving and Inventory Control

5.3 Final Inspection and Test

5.4 Packing and Shipping

6.0 Documentation

6.1 A process document may be a printed form or route card, a computer printout, or just a stamp on a drawing where the routing, quantities, and material are indicated. If statistical techniques are used, then the associated charts should be included.

7.0 Records

7.1 The process documentation should be retained as evidence that the processes are completed as planned. It is the means of tracing back who was involved in the manufacturing process. It may be logged or summarized. The retention time should be related to the life of the product or service, but a maximum time of ten years is adequate.

Relevant ISO 9001 Clauses:

4.1 Management Responsibility
4.2 Quality System
4.7 Control of Customer-Supplied Product
4.8 Product Identification and Traceability
4.9 Process Control
4.10 Inspection and Testing
4.12 Inspection and Test Status
4.13 Control of Nonconforming Product
4.15 Handling, Storage, Packing, Preservation, and Delivery
4.16 Quality Records
4.20 Statistical Techniques

Commentary

A plating company relied on the experience of its staff to determine when the plating solutions required strengthening. Asked how such decisions were made, the staff simply said, "We can tell." Establishing a laboratory would require the purchase of expensive equipment and hiring a skilled technician. A supplier offered to do the analysis free, but that would make the company dependent on the supplier to say how much of the supplier's chemical should be used.

To meet the Standard's requirements, the company determined that it had to bring the solutions up to a certain pre-determined strength. After some investigation, it was determined that the quantity of the critical component could be found at a relatively low cost and skill level by checking the specific gravity of the solution.

Once the specific gravity checks started, it rapidly became apparent that the solution concentrations had been too high. During the first month after the change was made, the company saved enough on chemicals alone to pay for the consultant who guided the company in its ISO 9000 application and for the registration process itself.

Another organization had a similar experience with a spray painting operation. The painter did not think he needed to check the viscosity of the paint, instead relying on his own sense of what was correct. The introduction of a simple check of the viscosity determined that the painter was adding too much solvent. Setting the correct viscosity saved $100 per month and reduced the amount of solvent emitted into the atmosphere.

A small engineering subcontractor had no formal production planning procedure. The company ordered materials based on customer drawings. When the material arrived, a foreman gave the material and drawings to an operator who performed some operations and then passed the work to another operator. If a customer inquired about the progress of the job, the foreman had to ask the operators.

Consultants devised a simple system to help the foreman track the work, stamping a form on the back of drawing. The foreman wrote in the names of operators assigned to the work. As each operator completed his part of the job, he passed it to the next operator and told the foreman. The foreman recorded the information on a check list, providing him an instant answer to customer inquiries. It also gave him more control over work flow and priorities. Service to customers improved and the foreman had a record of who worked on each job.

Procedure Guide 8: Final Inspection and Test

Quality cannot be inspected into a product, but some inspection is necessary. The ISO 9000 Standard recognizes this fine line, and the status of inspection as the final act to confirm quality before the product reaches the end-user. Inspection may be a very formal process, with extensive tests to confirm a contract requirement. Or it may be a much simpler, almost implied, process which acknowledges that the requirements have been met. In either case, there must be a record of the final inspection and test, and documentation of any condition or requirement not met.

The Model

Procedure Guide 8: Final Inspection and Test

1.0 Objective

1.1 To record and control the final inspection and test of the product or service to ensure the quality of the part, product, or service released to the customer.

2.0 Scope

2.1 The final inspection and testing of the organization's products and services. This does not have to be a separate procedure; it frequently is covered within the Process Control or Installation Control procedure.

3.0 Responsibilities

3.1 The responsibilities for the final inspection and test activities must be clearly defined, with designated alternates identified. The verification activities do not have to be conducted by staff independent of processing the product or providing the service.

4.0 Procedure

4.1 A check of the control document should be made to confirm that previously defined verifications have been completed. The issue of parts from an inventory is acceptable evidence if parts are verified before storage.

4.2 The features to be inspected and method of inspection should be defined in writing. The method may be in the form of "inspect to drawing," "visual inspection of finish," etc.

4.3 Where there is a formal test, the test method should be defined in writing, indicating the equipment to be used. This is usually a work instruction for each product or group of similar products.

4.4 The results obtained should be documented where these are of a variable nature. If the verification is more in the nature of a check, then a pass/fail indication is adequate.

4.5 There should be a clear indication whether a product or service has passed final inspection. This may entail labeling, documentation, or filing.

4.6 The procedure for dealing with noncompliances should be defined by reference to the Control of Reject Material procedure.

4.7 The responsibility for the final release of the product or service should be defined. This need not be a quality function.

5.0 Related Procedures

5.1 Process Control

5.2 Packing and Shipping

5.3 Control of Reject Material

6.0 Documentation

6.1 Documentation to provide evidence of inspection and test and where applicable the results. This may be in the form of a signature on the manufacturing job card, a stamp or label on the product or, where a major test is carried out, a full set of results.

7.0 Records

7.1 All records of final inspection and test should be kept for seven years, or for the life of the product or service, whichever is the longer.

Relevant ISO 9001 Clauses:

4.1 Management Responsibility
4.2 Quality System
4.10 Inspection and Testing
4.12 Inspection and Test Status
4.16 Quality Records

Commentary

An electronics manufacturer required all units to have a burn-in test before being released. During the ISO 9000 application process, managers found employees implementing the policy erratically, sometimes releasing products with no burn-in. There was a problem with early failures, but the managers, working under the premise that burn-in was being done, failed to explore this avenue as they tried to reduce the problem. Once the employees began recording all tests, the sloppy practices ceased and the instances of early life failure declined.

An electrical company provided another interesting example of how applying the ISO 9000 Standard can reduce costs. The company worked to military standards for many years. It had a relatively large number of inspectors verifying and signing off on items that met the specifications. While preparing for registration, managers discussed the difference between inspector and inspection. Production workers were keen to take responsibility for their own inspection and tests. The inspectors were moved to production, used as product auditors, or trained in corrective action techniques. No change occurred in the quality of the product.

Relating the ISO 9000 Standard's requirements for inspection and test in service environments is more difficult. For instance, in health care situations nurses sign drug or other care administration forms to verify that they provided the drugs or care as ordered. Under the Standard, this verification is an inspection operation. The introduction of simple verifications in all kinds of service environments can increase control and make it easier to know when specifications are met.

Procedure Guide 9: Packaging And Shipping

A customer's satisfaction rests on the condition of the product when received, and that may depend on how it is handled during shipping. Shipping is a vital link in meeting customer expectations. It may include subcontractors whose performance must be monitored.

Packaging must relate to the product, transportation method, and destination. Depending on the nature of the product, efficient planning should include the design of special packaging to suit an individual item. The delivery of spare parts needs to be addressed in this procedure.

The Model

Procedure Guide 9: Packaging and Shipping

1.0 Objective

1.1 To control and record the packing and shipping of the product to the customer to ensure adequate protection and appropriate and controlled shipping methods.

2.0 Scope

2.1 Processes associated with the packing and shipping of products to the customer. In some process industries this may include pumping the product through a pipeline.

3.0 Responsibilities

3.1 The responsibility for these activities must be defined.

4.0 Procedure

4.1 The method of packing to be used must be identified. This will vary with products. Packing could be the last operation in a Process Control or a separate procedure. The choice of packing must ensure adequate protection for the product, taking into account the destination, and method of transport. The basis for making this decision must also be defined.

4.2 The selection of the shipping method to ensure adequate protection to the destination must be defined.

4.3 A document to be signed by the driver or customer to indicate safe receipt of the products must be included.

5.0 Related Procedures

5.1 Process Control

5.2 Final Inspection and Test

5.3 Inquiries and Orders

6.0 Documentation

6.1 Packaging Instruction

6.2 Packing Slip

7.0 Records

7.1 Packing slips must be retained until it is certain that no queries will arise from the delivery of the product. Typically, retention for one month is adequate. However, export orders may require longer retention times.

Relevant ISO 9001 Clauses:

4.1 Management Responsibility
4.2 Quality System
4.7 Control of Customer-Supplied Product
4.8 Product Identification and Traceability
4.15 Handling, Storage, Packaging, Preservation, and Delivery
4.16 Quality Records

Commentary

A meat processor included delivery service. The delivery procedures ensured precise temperatures for the meat during transportation. Cooked and uncooked meat were separated in the delivery van. The procedures also governed how the fresh meat and processed meat products were wrapped and steps to follow if the delivery van's refrigeration unit malfunctioned.

One organization whose managers considered their packing and shipping processes well under control discovered that customers sought credits on approximately 30 percent of the shipments. Further analysis revealed that 80 percent of these claims were associated with damage during shipment. Working with a delivery subcontractor and a packaging consultant, they developed a system of packing that cut the number of credit requests to about four percent.

Procedure Guide 10: Control of Reject Material

A natural aspect of many procedures is the production of waste. Examples are metal or wood removed when turning on a lathe, or excess material left when cutting out a dress. These are natural outcomes of the process. If, however, *during* the operation, there is a lack of control and the product becomes unusable, then it is considered to be reject material.

In considering reject material, we must distinguish between the kind of waste and material that might have been usable, but is rejected due to a fault in processing. ISO 9000 does not address waste as an issue, but it makes clear that companies cannot use rejected material as though it were perfect. Discovery of such material provides opportunity to improve.

Organizations must have procedures to ensure that nonconforming materials are identified and necessary procedures taken to be sure they are not used. With clinical waste or chemical waste, highly controlled procedures must be in place to dispose of the waste.

The Model

Procedure Guide 10: Control of Reject Material

1.0 Objective

1.1 To control and record the actions taken on nonconforming products and material to ensure that they are not used inadvertently or without authorization.

2.0 Scope

2.1 All occurrences of nonconforming products, materials, and components.

3.0 Responsibilities

3.1 The responsibility for the segregation of reject material and products must be defined. This is not normally a quality function.

3.2 The responsibility for the disposition of reject material and products must be defined. This is usually a joint decision among production, quality, and design.

3.3 The responsibility for allowing reject material or products to be used must be defined. This is normally a design function with possible agreement from sales and the customer.

4.0 Procedure

4.1 The method of segregating rejects by their location and/or labeling must be described.

4.2 The process for review of rejects and disposition must be identified. One of the following decisions must be made:

4.2.1 Rework the reject back to specification. Normal inspection/tests must then be applied and the method of rework agreed to and recorded.

4.2.2 Accept the rejects in their present condition under a concession. The concession must be time (or quantity) limited. Details of the period and serial numbers should be identified on the concession in case of subsequent problems in the field. The concession must be correctly approved and corrective action should be identified where applicable. These actions can either be part of the Control of Rejects procedure or may constitute a separate Deviations/Concessions procedure.

4.2.3 Re-grade the reject to a lower level product grade. Labeling must then ensure that this has been done, and care must be taken that employees and the customer do not mistake the lower level product for a higher grade.

4.2.4 Scrap the reject. The method of disposition must be defined. The method of making up for the loss must be identified in order to maintain production.

4.3 The decision taken needs to be recorded and used as input to the corrective action process.

5.0 Related Procedures

5.1 Receiving and Inventory Control

5.2 Process Control

5.3 Final Inspection and Test

5.4 Customer Returns and Complaints

5.5 Deviations/ Waivers/Concessions/

6.0 Documentation

6.1 Reject Notice

6.2 Reject Label

6.3 Concession Request Form

7.0 Records

7.1 All reject data must be analyzed. However, once analyzed, the prime data need not be stored. All concessions must be kept for the life of the product.

Relevant ISO 9001 Clauses:

4.1 Management Responsibility

4.2 Quality System

4.7 Control of Customer-Supplied Product

4.8 Product Identification and Traceability

4.12 Inspection and Test Status

4.13 Control of Nonconforming Material

4.14 Corrective and Preventive Action

4.16 Quality Records

Commentary

Press operators at a company making rubber moldings inspected the products themselves. The operators recorded the number of moldings that did not meet specifications and placed the rejected parts in reject bins. Their standards were high, but the operation was plagued by parts failing final inspection. The company quality manager noticed that the total output at final inspection was higher than the output of good items from the presses. An investigation determined that some products in the reject bins disappeared overnight. An employee who arrived for work early each day was searching the reject bins for items he thought were acceptable. His activities were halted and the numbers of rejects at final inspection dropped to zero. Inspection was replaced by sampling.

Many operations believe they have no rejects. For example, workers at a candy factory tossed broken and cracked candy back into the mixing cauldron. Managers thought since they were reworking the material there was no need to measure it. As part of the ISO 9000 system they gathered information on the extent of the rework and found it to be around 15 percent. While it was true there was no lost material, energy was wasted reprocessing the cracked candy. Fifteen percent of the plant capacity was effectively wasted. The plant operated seven days a week, so, in effect, one day's work each week was wasted. For the first time, the management investigated the causes of the rework, took corrective actions, and slowly, the percentage was reduced.

It is essential that information gained on the nature of reject material goes into the corrective action process. One client regularly received a wheel trim with an important hole missing, but never told the supplier about it. Rather than returning it, they drilled the hole themselves. After a while, the operators more or less accepted the situation. The introduction of a new procedure brought the problem to the attention of the management, who explained the problem to the supplier and eliminated it at the source.

Procedure Guide 11: Customer Returns/Complaints

Customer satisfaction is more than a buzzword for the 1990s. It has become the centerpiece of every successful company's operations. Inevitably, however, there will be problems and complaints. How we deal with these determines how the customer will perceive the company in the future. Dealing with the complaint requires not only a demonstration that the problem has been resolved, but also that a recurrence is very unlikely. Every complaint must be seen as an opportunity to improve.

Sometimes it is difficult to decide when a customer is complaining or when he or she is merely commenting on a service or product. The procedure should allow for recognizing and removing comments that express concerns but not complaints.

The Model

Procedure Guide 11: Customer Returns/Complaints

1.0 Objective

1.1 To ensure that timely and appropriate remedial and corrective actions are taken in response to customer complaints and returns.

2.0 Scope

2.1 Activities associated with complaints and returns from customers.

3.0 Responsibilities

3.1 Responsibility for liaison with the customer on all returns and complaints must be defined.

3.2 Responsibility for the analysis and initiation of corrective and preventive actions associated with complaints and returns must be described.

4.0 Procedure

4.1 A record of all complaints and returns, indicating remedial action taken, must be kept.

4.2 Analysis of all complaints and returns for trends must be completed, and corrective and preventive actions identified. Serious safety related occurrence may require special attention.

4.3 All returns must be separated to ensure that they are recorded and not used for production. Returned products should be disposed of using the control of reject material procedure.

5.0 Related Procedures

5.1 Management Review

5.2 Corrective Action

5.3 Control of Reject Material

6.0 Documentation

6.1 A complaints and returns log, labeling for returned products, and reports recording the actions taken with respect to complaints and returns should be kept.

7.0 Records

7.1 There is no need to keep the above documentation for an extended period once the details have been analyzed for corrective actions.

Relevant ISO 9001 Clauses:

4.1 Management Responsibility
4.2 Quality System
4.8 Product Identification and Traceability
4.10 Inspection and Testing
4.12 Inspection and Test Status
4.16 Quality Records

Commentary

A food processor landed a contract to supply a product in specified portions to the kitchens in a hospital group. One of the kitchens complained about the portion sizes, prompting a visit from the processing company's CEO. The CEO discussed the problem in detail with the kitchen manager and uncovered a difference in how the requirements were interpreted by the kitchen, the buyer and the supplier. The CEO and the kitchen manager shared their thoughts about procedures and requirements, settling on a corrective action. The CEO's visit enhanced the relationship with the kitchen manager by using it as an opportunity to explain and improve the service.

Complaints should always be carefully analyzed. This was illustrated by an incident at a nursing home. A resident complained that a staff member had removed some clothing from her room. The nursing home, as part of its quality system, maintained lists of each resident's clothing. The allegedly missing items were not on the resident's list. A careful discussion with the resident's family revealed that the items of clothing were a figment of the resident's imagination.

As part of its application for registration to ISO 9000, a food caterer serving factory canteens sought to determine exactly what constituted a valid complaint. The catering staff reported some lively conversations with regular customers including comments such as, "Is that all the fries I get today?" The comments were not real complaints. Discussions led to defining a complaint to be relative to an unacceptable feature of the food: dirt on the salad, fly in the soup, etc.

Good records and labeling can help identify the responsibility for returned goods. A supplier of automotive parts stamped the items with the customer's part number, as required in its contract, and added its own final inspector's stamp. When a customer returned items, the supplier determined they had been made by a competitor. Taking preventive action not only showed the supplier had not made the error, but gave them information on a competitor's performance.

Procedure Guide 12: Servicing

ISO 9000 recognizes that service after the sale is a vitally important aspect of quality. When a company services a product after it is in the customer's hands, it must maintain the same level of control as it would if the product were still within the organization.

The Model

Procedure Guide 12: Servicing

1.0 Objective

1.1 To record and control all servicing of the products carried out by the organization to ensure consistent quality.

2.0 Scope

2.1 All service of company products after sale to the customer.
Note: When the company's prime activity is service, this may be covered under process control.

3.0 Responsibilities

3.1 The responsibility for service must be defined. The responsibility for confirming that the service has been carried out satisfactorily must be described. This is not normally a quality responsibility.

4.0 Procedure

4.1 The types of service contracts available should be identified.

4.2 The method of responding to breakdown calls should be outlined.

4.3 The method of scheduling routine service associated with service contracts must be described.

4.4 The documentation used during service should be identified, making reference to service manuals as necessary.

4.5 The method of obtaining and recording the spare parts required should be defined. If local purchases are allowed, the authority for this needs to be defined, as well as any limitations on selection of suppliers.

4.6 The procedure for performing the service and doing the final inspection and test must be described.

4.7 Any customer sign-off procedure should be defined, as well as an exception routine for when the customer cannot be located.

4.8 The method of identifying the cause(s) and feedback for analysis in Corrective Action Procedure must be identified.

4.9 If the product or part is under warranty, the method for claiming the cost should be described.

4.10 The process that service personnel follow to obtain assistance should be described.

5.0 Related Procedures

5.1 Inquiries/Orders

5.2 Control of Product/Service Documentation

6.0 Documentation

6.1 Service Record

6.2 Servicing Inspection and Test Sheets

6.3 Product Manuals

7.0 Records

7.1 A record of the service carried out and the final verification documentation should be retained for the life of the product. Details of the parts fitted, including serial numbers where appropriate, should be recorded.

Relevant ISO 9001 Clauses:

4.1 Management Responsibility
4.2 Quality System
4.6 Purchasing
4.7 Control of Customer-Supplied Product
4.8 Product Identification and Traceability
4.10 Inspection and Testing
4.12 Inspection and Test Status
4.13 Control of Nonconforming Product
4.14 Corrective and Preventive Action
4.16 Quality Records
4.19 Servicing

Commentary

Customers with sophisticated equipment do not always understand the complexity of needed repairs. Many times the technicians cannot determine in advance what needs to be done, and they may not be able to repair the product in the field. Customers often do not understand this.

Sometimes a technician repairs a symptom of the problem, but does not get to the root cause. An example is a client who specialized in rewinding electrical motors. When a customer brought in a burned-out motor, the windings were replaced, and the motor tested. The customer refitted the motor to the machinery. Neither the client or customer sought to determine the cause of the fault, merely assuming it to be the motor. In fact, the problem lay with a seized gearbox driven by the motor. Refitting the motor to the seized shaft resulted only in another burnout, with the customer assuming once again that the problem lay with motor and the rewinding job.

The rewinding company sought to prevent a recurrence by introducing a data sheet spelling out precautions the customers should take when refitting a motor to a shaft. These included checks on the electrical supply and on the free movement of the shaft. The customer's complaint was answered and further problems prevented.

Procedure Guide 13: Installation

Installation may involve spending a short time at the customer's site setting up a machine, or spending weeks or months installing large machinery. No matter the time required or the complexity, installation falls within the installing company's quality system when it is part of a contract. The ISO 9000 Standard requires controls on the installation process and records of how the work progresses. In the construction industry some of the controls and records will be exercised by the client, the architect, or their agent. The documents produced by these people should be integrated into the contractor's files.

The Model

Procedure Guide 13: Installation

1.0 Objective

1.1 To record and control the installation of the organization's products to ensure that the methods used during installation are defined and appropriate.

2.0 Scope

2.1 All installation of products at the customer's site.

3.0 Responsibilities

3.1 The responsibility for installation must be defined. The responsibility for confirming that installation has been done satisfactorily must be defined.

4.0 Procedure

4.1 The details of the methods used for receiving materials on site and their safe storage must be described. The responsibility for this needs to be defined.

4.2 Details of the product to be installed must be provided. The level of detail can be related to the experience and training of the installers. Reference to drawings, manuals, and other specifications is usually preferred over written instructions.

4.3 The procedure for identifying additional work and for obtaining the client's and company's approval should be defined.

4.4 The procedure for requesting site services and accounting for any delays resulting from the failure of others, must be identified.

4.5 The procedure for final inspection, test, and hand-over must be defined.

4.6 A method of identifying which parts of the installation have been inspected/tested and found to be to specification must be described.

4.7 A method for dealing with outstanding issues both before and after installation of the product must be identified.

5.0 Related Procedures

5.1 Contract/Project Control

5.2 Packing and Shipping

5.3 Design Control
5.4 Process Planning
5.5 Final Inspection and Test

6.0 Documentation

6.1 Time sheets, site instructions, and test and inspection results must be retained.

7.0 Records

7.1 All documents generated during the installation are to be reviewed on completion. Final inspection and test results must be filed and retained for the life of the product.

Relevant ISO 9001 Clauses:

4.1 Management Responsibility
4.2 Quality System
4.7 Control of Customer-Supplied Product
4.8 Product Identification and Traceability
4.9 Process Control
4.10 Final Inspection and Testing
4.12 Inspection and Test Status
4.13 Control of Nonconforming Product
4.15 Handling, Storage, Packing, Preservation, and Delivery
4.16 Quality Records

Commentary

A contractor built factories using a team of skilled fitters and electricians who considered it part of their job to correct any problems they found, viewing them as mistakes by the designers. The contractor had no way to control or record these impromptu repair operations, as the workmen did not report their activities.

Procedures introduced to control the installation process resulted in records of the repair activities being compiled. It also required approval if the repairs altered the design. The new procedures allowed the equipment designers and manufacturers to know what was wrong and to improve the designs in subsequent orders.

A major oil company asked its installation subcontractors to become ISO 9000 registered. One electrical contractor improved its installation control procedure en route to registration, keeping precise records on project status and details on when the work went beyond the provisions of the contract. The documentation was so much better than the client's that the client began to rely on the subcontractor's project status data and awarded them more contracts.

The process revealed the costs and implications of alterations performed on work by the oil company's engineering staff, and questioned whether the costs were acceptable. Gradually, however, the client company gained confidence in the subcontractor's quality system, accepted the costs, and sought to control them through better initial designs.

Procedure Guide 14: Contract/Project Control

This part of the model is particularly relevant for the work of lawyers or other professionals who deal with clients. It requires records with sufficient detail to ensure that, in the absence of a specific lawyer or consultant, other members of the firm can readily determine the status of the work and what needs to be done. This provision gives customers almost instant access to any information they need.

The Model

Procedure Guide 14: Contract/Project Control

1.0 Objective

1.1 To control and record the activities related to management of contracts/projects in line with client needs and expectations and the contract requirements.

2.0 Scope

2.1 This procedure applies in situations where organizations provide professional services. It can also apply to the control of large manufacturing or construction projects.

3.0 Responsibilities

3.1 The responsibility for the control of the project must be clearly defined.

3.2 The responsibility for verification activities during the project must be defined.

4.0 Procedure

4.1 A project file must be maintained. Where the project is of a design/build nature, this will be the same project file as in design control.

4.2 An agreed-upon timing and resource plan must be developed.

4.3 The method of identifying, agreeing to, and documenting changes in the contract should be described.

4.4 The procedure for final sign-off of the project must be identified.

4.5 The relative responsibilities for the provision of services must be defined.

4.6 Delays due to the client must be recorded.

4.7 The method of recording the progress on the project and establishing when milestones have been achieved must be described.

5.0 Related Procedures

5.1 Inquiries and Orders

5.2 Design Control

5.3 Process Planning

5.4 Purchasing

6.0 Documentation

6.1 Project plans and documents to control the progress of the project, changes to the specifications, and acceptance of stages of the work must be documented.

7.0 Records

7.1 The Contract file should be retained for a period based on the life of the product.

Relevant ISO 9001 Clauses:

4.1 Management Responsibility
4.2 Quality System
4.3 Contract Review
4.4 Design Control
4.8 Product Identification and Traceability
4.9 Process Control
4.10 Inspection and Testing
4.12 Inspection and Test Status
4.13 Control of Nonconforming Product
4.16 Quality Records

Commentary

The controls introduced by an electrical contractor enabled employees to more readily tell when more work was done than the original contract specified. Quality system documentation helped them to demonstrate the extent of these extras to the client, who then agreed to pay for them. That saving paid for the costs of registration before the registrar's audit.

A consulting firm once allowed its consultants to operate with little or no formal control or reporting. Consultants operated independently with the clients, notifying the central office only with invoicing information. Other records were purely personal, and management knew little or nothing of the status of the projects.

As part of working on ISO 9000 registration, the company realized their mode of operation would fail the Standard's requirements. Although committed to quality and the ISO 9000 philosophy of accountability and documentation, the consultants were reluctant to provide information that would allow greater managerial control over their work.

About the same time, the consulting firm landed a major contract with a large client. The client company wanted the consultants to report on their progress at each of its facilities. The consultants agreed to send the client a report indicating the status of the work and whatever activities resulted from each site visit. The consulting firm's managers designed a simple form for the reports, and the consultants agreed to provide the information.

The consultants then retained copies of the reports in a project file for each site. The reports were used for review meetings and provided the managers with a simple record of the consultants' activities. It also protected the company if a consultant was unable to continue on the project.

Procedure Guide 15: Product, Service, and Process Audits

Product or process audits are a valuable tool for confirming that quality is being maintained. The Standard does not require these audits, but we recommend them as highly useful tools in determining the effectiveness of the quality system. As always, the audits should be handled by staff not involved in the work being audited. Absolute results are often less important than trends. We recommend using statistical tools to analyze the results.

The Model

Procedure Guide 15: Product, Service, and Process Audits

1.0 Objective

1.1 To control and record the audits of the products, services, or processes.

2.0 Scope

2.1 This procedure applies where the organization carries out formal audits of its processes or the products. It is not a requirement of the Standard, but it is an effective method of determining the extent to which procedures are being followed and the condition of products at the point of delivery.

2.1.1 Process audits can be used to confirm machine settings, temperatures, etc. when the process controls the quality of the product or service. They provide feedback for planned maintenance activities.

2.1.2 Product audits examine product in the "ready for shipment" condition. Audits seek trends—not direct participation in the control loop.

3.0 Responsibilities

3.1 Scheduling and conduct of audits should be under the direct control of the Management Representative.

3.2 Auditors should be independent of the audited product, service, or process.

4.0 Procedure

4.1 A process must be set up for preparing and agreeing to an audit program.

4.2 A definition of who carries out the audits must be provided.

4.3 A definition of the actions to be taken as a result of the audit must be developed.

4.4 An analysis of audit results must be conducted, to establish trends to be fed into the corrective action process.

5.0 Related Procedures

5.1 Control of Maintenance

5.2 Process Planning

5.3 Management Review

6.0 Documentation

6.1 Audit program

6.2 Audit results sheet

7.0 Records

7.1 The results of the audits are analyzed and fed to the corrective action procedure. Records of the results should be retained for two years.

Relevant ISO 9001 Clauses:

- 4.1 Management Responsibility
- 4.2 Quality System
- 4.10 Inspection and Testing
- 4.12 Inspection and Test Status
- 4.13 Control of Nonconforming Product
- 4.14 Correction and Preventive Action
- 4.16 Quality Records
- 4.20 Statistical Techniques

Commentary

Organizations can use audits to analyze and evaluate any product or service. They can also use them to confirm whether special features of a process operate as planned. A textile company experiencing problems with housekeeping introduced audits. A sheet listing various features of tidiness in the plant was used to perform audits and members of the management went around areas outside of their direct control and assessed the housekeeping against the standard. The results were then reported to the management meeting and corrective actions taken as appropriate.

A food processing company conducted hygiene audits to confirm that cleaning crews sterilized areas that needed it. This included taking swabs of critical equipment and areas and sending them away for analysis. The results were used to determine the efficiency of the cleaning methods.

A recreation center introduced maintenance audits to determine the effectiveness of the maintenance subcontractor. Various aspects of the contract were randomly audited and the results used to determine efficiency.

Procedure Guide 16: Control of Quality System Documentation

Correct and up-to-date documentation is essential since the quality system describes how you want the business to operate. Every page of every procedure, work instruction, and manual must be up to date, and the documents must be readily accessible to those who do the work. Each document needs to have a revision level if it has been changed. But the first issue does not need to be indicated. This allows the correct parts of the documents to be used as changes occur.

ISO 9000 documents requiring strict control include the Quality Manual, Procedure Manual, and Work Instructions. The title of this procedure may be Control of Manuals or Control of Quality Systems Documentation, depending on the terminology used in the organization. Other documents in the quality system, such as drawings and specifications, require similar control in line with Procedure Guide 17, the Control of Product/Service Documentation.

The Model

Procedure Guide 16: Control of Quality System Documentation

1.0 Objective

1.1 To record and control the issue and modification of all manuals, procedures, and work instructions used by the organization as part of the ISO 9000 quality system.

2.0 Scope

2.1 All manuals, procedures, and work instructions used in the quality system. This will always include the quality manual, procedures manual, procedures, and work instructions.

2.2 Work instructions and other product/service documentation may be controlled by this procedure or by a separate procedure.

3.0 Responsibilities

3.1 The management representative is usually directly responsible for the control of the quality and procedure manuals. Other manuals may be controlled by the head of the department concerned in accordance with the same procedure.

3.2 Each manual holder is responsible for the maintenance of his or her own manual.

4.0 Procedure

4.1 A list of all documents under the scope of this procedure must be maintained and it must include the document's identification, revision level, and holder names or location of each document. Where individual pages are issued, these must be controlled.

4.2 Each procedure, work instruction, and other controlled document must have its revision level clearly shown (preferably on each page of the document).

4.3 An authorizing statement is required on the manuals and revisions.

4.4 The master copy of earlier revision pages must be retained.

4.5 Document and Data Control

4.6 The system of updating controlled documents must have a feedback loop. This can either be accomplished by one person updating the documents and recording this, or by each holder updating and returning an acknowledgment to the controlling person.

4.7 A statement that ownership of the manuals is retained by the organization is useful in maintaining control.

4.8 A record of changes must be maintained.

5.0 Related Procedures

5.1 All procedures in the documented quality system.

6.0 Documentation

6.1 Controlled document Lists

6.2 Acknowledgment Control Slip (if used)

6.3 Revision Record

7.0 Records

7.1 Lists and obsolete procedures are filed for at least three years, or longer if applicable. Control slips, if used, are kept for at least one year, or as advised for legal reasons.

Relevant ISO 9001 Clauses:

4.1 Management Responsibilities
4.2 Quality System
4.5 Document Control
4.16 Quality Records

Commentary

It is common for an auditor to ask to see documentation, and roughly ten percent of the time, someone produces an old, out-of-date copy from the bottom of a desk. This is the very practice the Standard seeks to halt.

In one audit a manager abruptly produced an old Purchasing Manual written five years earlier. No one else knew of its existence, and it was well out-of-date. The manager, who had been involved in an earlier project, showed it to the ISO 9000 auditors, creating a major problem. Fortunately the auditors allowed it to be withdrawn. They cleared the noncompliance and registration followed.

Often ISO 9000 auditors will ask to see the chief executive's copy of a Procedure Manual to determine if it is up to date. Once in a textile company, the executive asked his secretary to bring in his copy which, it turned out, she had not updated, a severe embarrassment to her and her boss. The auditor had to decide whether that constituted a major or minor noncompliance with the Standard.

Procedure Guide 17: Control of Product/Service Documentation

Organizations must control product/service documentation such as drawings and specifications using authorizations and revision levels. This is to ensure that everyone knows when a change is made to a document they may need.

Adequate document control requires some sort of register or log of the location of the documents. Changes to the master copy necessitate new copies for the holders of controlled copies. The old copy should be marked OBSOLETE, destroyed, or returned to a central control point.

There is no need to keep a record of the location of uncontrolled copies of a document, but these should be clearly labeled as uncontrolled. This alerts whoever uses the document to check whether it is current.

The Model

Procedure Guide 17: Control of Product/Service Documentation

1.0 Objective

1.1 To record and control the authorization, issue, and maintenance of all product/service documentation in the quality system with the aim of using only approved and relevant, usually current, documentation throughout the organization.

2.0 Scope

2.1 All specifications and drawings which define the products, services, parts, and processes used by the organization in its quality system. This normally includes: drawings, material specifications, product specifications, process specifications, service standards, inspection instructions, and sales literature that contractually defines the product or service. These may be covered by one general procedure or several covering different document types.

2.2 All national and international standards, copies of legislation, and codes of practice used by the organization in the course of its business need to covered by this procedure. There needs to be a system to ensure that the current copy of such documents is always used.

3.0 Responsibilities

3.1 The responsibility for the control and authorization of all documents covered by this procedure must be defined. It is not necessary for all documents to be controlled by the same person. Control at the departmental level is suitable.

4.0 Procedure

4.1 The identity of who is responsible for the production and authorization of documents must be recorded. Where revisions are made, these must be authorized. Master copies of obsolete documents shall be retained.

4.2 Location and responsibility for maintaining the master documents must be defined.

4.3 All documents must have an identification number and issue or revision number.

4.4 There must be a record of all controlled documents and their distribution.

4.5 There must be a process for withdrawing obsolete documents and replacing them with new documents when changes take place. The process must ensure that all functions, including suppliers and customers, are aware of changes, and that the timing of changes is important. Changes can give rise to a variety of actions, for example, product recall, change all products on site, change as inventory runs out, etc. There must be evidence that the change has been implemented.

4.6 Uncontrolled copies must be clearly identified and any limitation as to their use noted on the document. It is acceptable to issue a specification endorsed "For production order number"—and then not update it. This is suggested for specifications sent to suppliers where control cannot easily be demonstrated and a new copy is sent to the supplier with each order.

4.7 The need to update copies of service and operator manuals delivered with products needs to be considered. Updating can be limited to the copies held by external service staff and agents. Customers have the manual applicable to their machine, and it should not be updated. If the obsolete manuals are still valid for products in the field then they should not be withdrawn, but marked accordingly.

4.8 The date of the implementation of any changes, and the serial number of the products where applicable, must be recorded.

4.9 Where applicable, it is usual to have a separate procedure controlling sales literature. The technical content of all such literature and advertisements should be approved by a technical authority. As much of the distributed literature is outside of the control of the organization, it needs to have a comment such as "may be changed without notice" to alert users to confirm they may not have a current issue.

5.0 Related Procedures

5.1 Design Control

5.2 Control of Deviations/Waivers/Concessions

5.3 Purchasing

5.4 Process Planning

5.5 Servicing

5.6 Inquiries and Orders

6.0 Documentation

6.1 Examples of the Documents Controlled

6.2 List of Documents

7.0 Records

7.1 The lists and obsolete documents should be maintained by the responsible person for a period that relates to the life of the product or service.

Relevant ISO 9001 Clauses:

4.1 Management Responsibility

4.2 Quality System

4.5 Document and Data Control

4.16 Quality Records

Commentary

Brochures displayed in a car dealership offered a particular feature—lumbar support—that had been added after some of the vehicles in stock had been delivered from the factory. The brochure prompted a customer to buy the car to help with back problems. When the unhappy customer complained that the car had no lumbar support, the dealership had to pay for the installation of another seat with lumbar support. The ISO 9000 Standard's requirements for documents, which include advertisements and brochures, attempts to prevent such misunderstandings and misinformation. The dealership, which later became ISO 9000 registered, learned that the Standard prevents it from using inaccurate brochures and risking unhappy customers who could be misled.

Engineering companies often find the ISO 9000 requirements provide the discipline for thorough and complete documentation. A company that acquired another engineering organization inherited drawings that contained many alterations not reflected on the master drawings. It took the company six months to determine the drawings' correct details. While they were working on the problem, they were unable to seek out new suppliers because they did not know what to buy.

The ISO 9000 document control requirements also help prevent problems from a rather common practice by employees who use and then store an old specification or drawing, unaware that the design may have changed.

A major automotive company frequently rejected parts at receiving inspection and sent them back to the supplier. The supplier checked the parts, found nothing wrong and in frustration, sent them back—only to be rejected again. After the parts had traveled several hundred miles back and forth, the supplier learned that the buyer had failed to inform him of a change in the specifications. ISO 9000 makes clear that the supplier chain should be included in the control of drawings and specifications.

Another problem encountered by a client, an architect, related to assigning numbers to drawings The existing numbering system left employees confused as to when a number should be assigned. They did not know when the drawing should be logged and finally two drawings ended up with the same number. One drawing was intended for internal use only, and the other gave details of carpentry. A subcontractor telephoned for a copy of the drawing, quoting the drawing number, and received the wrong drawing. The architect sent the correct drawing after discovering the mistake, but the system required a change to prevent the episode from recurring.

Procedure Guide 18: Internal Quality Auditing

Internal quality auditing is one of the most important requirements of the ISO 9000 Standard. It commits the organization to systematic and repetitive examinations of its quality system. Internal audits review the system, but do not evaluate personnel. They must not become witch hunts. A cross-section of the organization, including top management, should be on the audit team and conduct internal audits. Internal auditors must view this as a high-level activity and be trained for a consistent approach. Chapter 30 discusses in detail internal auditing, internal audit planning, and preparing internal auditors.

The audits often reveal differences between what people thought was happening and what actually was happening. Internal audits are an opportunity for management to demonstrate how a documented quality system becomes a living entity, affecting all those who serve in it and receive services from it.

The Model

Procedure Guide 18: Internal Quality Auditing

1.0 Objective

1.1 To ensure that internal auditing is planned, recorded, and controlled in accordance with the Standard and achieves verification of the implementation, monitoring, and improvement of the organization's quality system.

2.0 Scope

2.1 All formal internal audits of the quality system.

3.0 Responsibilities

3.1 The Management Representative usually has control of the planning, organization, and control of the audits.

3.2 The audits must be carried out by an audit team drawn from management and staff including the senior management of the organization. Each member of the team is responsible for his or her own audits.

4.0 Procedure

4.1 An audit program must cover at least a six-month period. Initially, each procedure must be audited within the six-month period. If problems are found, more audits may be necessary. Conversely, if no problems are found then the time between audits can be extended to a maximum of one year.

4.2 The auditor(s) must be independent of the procedure being audited.

4.3 The organization must be able to demonstrate that internal auditors have been formally trained.

4.4 Audits must be conducted with the knowledge of line management.

4.5 Audits must check nonconformances and corrective actions taken since previous audits.

4.6 The details of the audit, including references to documents checked, must be recorded on the audit report.

4.7 All system nonconformances must be recorded and concurred with the staff being audited.

4.8 Corrective actions with planned completion dates must be agreed to with line management, and line management must sign the audit report.

4.9 Corrective actions must be signed off when completed.

4.10 Audits should be analyzed and a summary report given at the management review meeting.

5.0 Related Procedures

5.1 All procedures in the documented quality system.

6.0 Documentation

6.1 Internal Audit Program

6.2 Internal Auditing Report

7.0 Records

7.1 Audit reports and program are to be filed and kept for at least three years.

Relevant ISO 9001 Clauses:

4.1 Management Responsibility
4.2 Quality System
4.14 Corrective and Preventive Action
4.16 Quality Records
4.17 Internal Auditing

Commentary

A manufacturing company had not completed its audits as scheduled. ISO 9000 auditors considered this a major noncompliance and did not recommend registration. The company quickly understood the importance of completing the audits on time.

The managing director of an automobile parts supplier had worked his way up from the shop floor. He welcomed the quality system audits, which gave him an opportunity to go back and look at the activities of various departments he had worked in—areas where he normally might not go. While the managing director looked forward to the assignment, it could cause problems in the organization. Internal auditors and managers must respect the role of the line managers who run departments. They must ensure that the quality systems audit does not become an excuse to criticize the managerial style of peers and subordinates.

A catering company passed its ISO 9000 audit and became registered but did not continue its internal audits. Just before the auditors were to arrive for a surveillance audit, the managers panicked and started doing audits. To their surprise, they found they had changed many processes without changing their documentation. They had to quickly rewrite their procedures before the auditors arrived. If they had followed their audit schedule, they would have been ready for the ISO 9000 audit.

Procedure Guide 19: Management Review

The ISO 9000 Standard requires executive management to review the quality system at appropriate intervals to ensure "its continuing suitability and effectiveness." The management review is intended to ensure that the organization is achieving its quality policy and the requirements of the ISO 9000 Standards.

Management review meetings should be held at least every six months, but monthly, bimonthly or quarterly is preferable.

The Model

Procedure Guide 19: Management Review

1.0 Objective

1.1 To confirm the continuing suitability and effectiveness of the quality system.

2.0 Scope

2.1 A total review of the quality system.

3.0 Responsibilities

3.1 The review should be under the chairmanship of the chief executive.

3.2 All executive management should be present and all functions represented.

4.0 Procedure

4.1 The frequency of the review meeting should be indicated. Minimally, this is usually every three months.

4.2 The participants at the meeting must be specified. This is usually the executive management and includes the Quality Manager.

4.3 The meeting should have an agenda and consider the items on it. A sample agenda is given in the appendix to this procedure.

4.4 The responsibility for recording the minutes of the meeting is assigned, usually to the Management Representative.

4.5 Where actions are decided at the meeting, these must be followed up at subsequent meetings.

4.6 The training plans of the organization must be reviewed. **Note:** In small organizations the management review meeting may be combined with another meeting.

5.0 Related Procedures

5.1 Corrective Action

5.2 Internal Quality Auditing

5.3 Customer Returns and Complaints

5.4 Control of Reject Material

5.5 Training

6.0 Documentation

6.1 No formal documentation is required, although a typical meeting agenda may be included as an appendix. (See appendix.)

7.0 Records

7.1 Minutes of the meeting are filed and retained for at least three years.

APPENDIX: Management Review Meeting Agenda:

1. Minutes of the Last Meeting
2. Outstanding Action Items
3. Quality Policy and Objectives
4. Customer Complaints
5. Supplier Concerns
6. Corrective Actions
7. Internal Audits Review
8. Registrar Communication
9. Organizational Issues
10. Changes in Regulations/Standards
11. Review of Training
12. Other Business

Relevant ISO 9000 Clauses:

4.1 Management Responsibility
4.2 Quality System
4.16 Quality Records

Commentary

Small, family-owned companies are subject to the managerial style of the chief executive officer. One such chairman almost never met with his managers and kept information to himself, rarely involving others in policy or strategy. Once the decision was made to seek ISO 9000 registration, however, he initiated meetings to comply with the requirements of the Standard. Slowly the meetings evolved into a more open examination of the company's activities. The chairman's previous style faded, replaced by a more open style. At last word, the chairman was studying the question of managerial succession, with an eye to retirement.

The ISO 9000 Standard does not require that management review be conducted in a meeting held only for that purpose. The management review can fit into the company's current scheme of managerial meetings and activities as long as the management review agenda is covered. One company added the Standard's managerial review into its monthly steering team meeting, making it part of that team's duties.

Procedure Guide 20: Control of Deviations, Waivers, Concessions

Waivers, deviations, and concessions are all terms used in various industries for the same thing. They refer to the practice of authorizing products, materials, or services outside of the specifications. Concession is the word used in ISO 9000, so we will use it here.

In a perfect world, there would be no need for concessions. In reality, however, there are times when management, and sometimes a customer, may accept goods or services that do not meet specifications. Recognizing this, ISO 9000 makes provisions for these concessions.

It is necessary that a concession be approved by the same function that approved the original design. So if the engineering department approved the design, the engineering department must approve the concession. This ensures that the person authorizing a temporary change understands the reason for the original specification.

Occasionally a concession results in a product or service which is satisfactory in the short term, but not in the long term. In these cases, controls should be used to ensure that the appropriate actions are taken.

The Model

Procedure Guide 20: Control of Deviations, Waivers, Concessions

1.0 Objective

1.1 To ensure that the use of material, parts, products, or services which do not meet specifications is controlled by written permission from the design authority and/or customer.

2.0 Scope

2.1 All instances of the use of material and parts which do not meet specification. In service industries there are occasions when the client is prepared to accept a level of service which does not comply with the original agreement. Such circumstances are covered by this procedure.

2.2 If material, parts, products, or services that deviate from specification are never used, a procedure based on this guide is not needed.

3.0 Responsibilities

3.1 The responsibility for authorizing concessions must be defined. This is normally for the original design. A reference to the customer may be necessary, and if so, this should be defined.

3.2 The responsibility for any additional work or precaution resulting from the use of nonconforming goods or services must be defined.

4.0 Procedure

4.1 The method for requesting a concession must be described. This is usually as a result of the identification of nonconforming material or products which may be usable or a service level which may be acceptable.

4.2 The method of gaining approval of the concession must be covered and recorded in writing. This may include contact with the customer when the final product is affected.

4.3 The action to be taken if the concession is rejected must be defined.

4.4 The action to be taken if the concession is granted must be specified. This can include notifying customers, changing documentation, repricing, rework, reinspection, or retesting. The limitation of the concession by time or product/serial numbers must be specified.

4.5 The corrective action to be taken to prevent recurrence should be indicated, and a procedure for checking that corrective action has been taken is required.

4.6 The recording and numbering of the concession in a log.

5.0 Related Procedures

5.1 Control of Specifications

5.2 Corrective Action

5.3 Design Control

5.4 Control of Reject Material

5.5 Control of Customer Returns and Complaints

6.0 Documentation

6.1 Concession Request Form

6.2 Concession Log

7.0 Records

7.1 All concessions must be retained for a period that relates to the life of the product or service.

Relevant ISO 9000 Clauses:

4.1 Management Responsibility

4.2 Quality System

4.13 Control of Nonconforming Product

4.14 Corrective and Preventive Action

4.16 Quality Records

Commentary

The use of concessions is widespread in the automotive industry. It was common practice in one automobile plant for inspectors to decide whether to use out-of-specification parts. The inspectors' decisions were based on whether they considered the parts fit for the intended purpose. The production manager only asked the Engineering and Design Department for a concession when the inspectors said the parts were not suitable. When ISO 9000 controls were introduced, responsibility for allowing use of items out of specification was given solely to Engineering and Design. That department found itself being asked to concede so many parts that they realized that the tight tolerances used in the design were not needed. They re-examined tolerances and changed many, resulting in production cost savings without sacrificing quality.

The operator of a franchised food restaurant had trouble obtaining a regular supply of fresh spinach. The chef applied to the franchiser for permission to change the content of the salad. The restaurant's quality system provided for testing the proposed alternatives, and the tests established that the changes would be acceptable. The requirement for fresh spinach was conceded.

Procedure Guide 21: Training

Training is a necessity. More and more organizations have begun to realize that the knowledge and skills of employees are a most important asset. ISO 9000's requirements for training are fundamental, requiring that records be kept of each employee's training, education and experience. The Standard requires that people may only be given tasks for which they have been trained. This improves the organization's ability to optimize utilization of employees and also advances the employees' interests.

The Model

Procedure Guide 21: Training

1.0 Objective

1.1 To demonstrate that all personnel whose work affects quality have the necessary training for such work.

2.0 Scope

2.1 All employees whose work affects quality.

2.2 There is a trade-off between the level of training and the level of work instruction. If there is a high level of training, then work instructions and specifications can be less detailed.

3.0 Responsibilities

3.1 The responsibility for organizing training and keeping records must be defined. This does not need to be one individual, and delegation to the level of department head is acceptable.

4.0 Procedure

4.1 A brief description of all jobs covered in the scope is required indicating that the training, experience, and education necessary to carry out the job satisfactorily is required.

4.2 A record must be maintained for each employee indicating the training received, experience, and qualifications. The record needs to be signed by the responsible person and indicate a level of competence or the jobs for which a person qualifies.

4.3 Work by employees-in-training is allowed if a process for controlling the work is included. Monitoring by a supervisor is an acceptable practice and should include a competence sign-off at the end.

4.4 The current training records or plans are to be reviewed at least annually and whenever there is a significant change in the organization's operations. Relating the training needs to the organization's plans link training into the business plan of the company.

5.0 Related Procedures

5.1 All Procedures

6.0 Documentation

6.1 Job Specifications

6.2 Employee Training Records

7.0 Records

7.1 Training records must be retained for a period relevant to the life of the product or service. If a defect shows up during the life of the product or service, it may be necessary to demonstrate that the employee concerned was adequately trained for the duties undertaken.

Relevant ISO 9001 Clauses:

4.1 Management Responsibility
4.2 Quality System
4.16 Quality Records
4.18 Training

Commentary

The manager of a fish processing company personally trained his employees how to filet different types of fish—cod, trout, or salmon. He showed them how to cut the fish, then watched them until he felt they were capable of doing it correctly on their own. After applying for ISO 9000 registration, the manager began using photographs to illustrate the correct method, how the finished product should appear, and what was unacceptable. The photographs—work instructions in the new scheme—were kept where the employees could easily see them. This standardized the training and acceptance criteria, making the company less dependent on the knowledge and skills of one man. Employee records reflected this training.

As part of its effort to meet the Standards' requirements, an electronics company kept training records for each employee. Previously unknown skills were discovered. For instance, one employee spoke Spanish; the company had been paying for Spanish translations. After all the employees' training had been documented, the company made better use of the employees' talents.

A car dealership computerized training records of service area employees and gave the service manager easy access to the information. This allowed the service manager to quickly cross-check which mechanics were capable of handling the jobs as they came in.

Procedure Guide 22: Corrective and Preventive Action

Work processes break down at times, producing undesirable outputs. The Standard requires organizations to analyze such situations and take corrective actions to fix the problem and prevent recurrence.

- *Corrective action* occurs when the organization alters a process to make sure the problem does not recur.
- *Preventive action* occurs when the managers and employees anticipate the problem and stop it before it happens.
- *Remedies* are the steps to fix a problem with a product or service after it happens.

This procedure guide addresses the process of collecting and using data of inadequate performance and problems from the entire business. A strong corrective action procedure will result in ongoing continual improvement.

The Model

Procedure Guide 22: Corrective and Preventive Action

1.0 Objective

1.1 To record and control corrective actions taken by the organization to prevent the recurrence of defects and problems.

2.0 Scope

2.1 Corrective and preventive actions arising from problems and occurrences of nonconformance, including internal rejects, receiving rejects, customer complaints, and returns. Major individual occurrences, or trends in minor nonconformances, must be formally addressed in this procedure.

3.0 Responsibilities

3.1 The Management Representative is responsible for ensuring that corrective and preventive actions are taken and monitoring their progress and efficacy.

3.2 Individual line managers and staff are responsible for taking and controlling corrective and preventive actions in their areas of responsibility.

4.0 Procedure

4.1 Analysis of all nonconformances must be completed, and the most significant instances must be determined.

4.2 Agreement should be gained on corrective and preventive actions to be taken. This may be a straightforward single action or an investigation to find the root cause of the problem.

4.3 Monitoring the progress of the corrective and preventive actions is required, as well as an eventual sign-off on their effectiveness.

4.4 The corrective and preventive action processes may be controlled in regularly scheduled meetings. Minutes of such meetings should be recorded, including actions, responsibilities, and evidence of the actions taken. This could be part of the management review meeting. In small companies, the corrective action process may be operated by the Management Representative. Whatever the format, records must be maintained to demonstrate effectiveness.

4.5 The application of preventive techniques at the planning stage, where appropriate, are included in the Process Planning Procedure Guide. The progress and effectiveness of these activities should be analyzed and reviewed in this procedure.

5.0 Related Procedures

5.1 Management Review
5.2 Control of Reject Material
5.3 Control of Customer Complaints and Returns
5.4 Process Planning
5.5 Control of Concessions

6.0 Documentation

6.1 Minutes of the Meetings or Log of Problems and Actions
6.2 Corrective and preventive action form

7.0 Records

7.1 The minutes or log must be kept for a period that relates to the life of the products and services.

Relevant ISO 9001 Clauses:

4.1 Management Responsibility
4.2 Quality System
4.14 Corrective Action
4.16 Quality Records

Commentary

The manager of a car dealership said he didn't need Corrective Action Procedures to tell him what was going on in his company. Nevertheless, the dealership introduced a process to record concerns expressed by external and internal customers. These were fed to a meeting chaired by the manager, who later declared that he had learned more about the dealership's internal working than he had expected. This enabled him to begin improving company systems.

An example of one improvement came from the practice of routinely putting used cars on the lot without service—until they were sold. A problem arose when a salesman sold a car needing major work to a customer who wanted it immediately. Simultaneously, there was another issue over how the service shop allocated mechanics' time. Most customers were bringing cars in for service an hour or so after the shop opened, wanting to pick them up an hour before it closed. This left dead time for the mechanics at both ends of the day. The dealership decided to service unsold new cars during this idle time. The result was more efficient use of the mechanics' time, and faster and more ecomical deliver of sold cars.

Corrective Actions do not always have to be big issues. A consulting firm received complaints from two clients who received letters addressed to each other. The letters had been put in the wrong envelopes. The remedial action was easy—the letters were resent with an apology. The corrective action—the use of window envelopes. This eliminated the possibility of letters being misdirected and the need to type the addresses on the envelopes—a win-win solution for everyone.

Procedure Guide 23: Calibration

Accurate measurement is an essential component of any quality system. The Standard requires that any equipment used for measurement, however sophisticated or simple, must be regularly examined for accuracy and dependability. The model defines a procedure for ensuring that all measurements affecting quality are performed with a calibrated tool or instrument. After all, what good is measurement if the accuracy of the measuring device is unknown?

Measurement takes place in virtually every kind of operation. Manufacturers measure components to determine dimensions and other characteristics. In service industries, measurement may be more difficult. Some instruments need a high degree of precision; for others, such as measuring tapes, calibration may mean a simple visual check of the equipment to ensure its integrity.

Calibration is an area in which it's difficult to predict auditors' interpretation of the Standard. They have been known to suggest that the wall clock in a bakery be calibrated if the cooks use it to time the cooking. *But it is only necessary to calibrate measuring equipment that affects the quality of the product or service.* Whether it's a simple measuring cup or voltage measuring device, it need only be calibrated if it fulfills some vital role in the system. The Standard clearly states that the level of calibration being sought should relate to the accuracy that is being measured. If you measure baking time with a wall clock, split-second accuracy isn't necessary. If you use the clock to alert you to examine the goods and base your decision on physical appearance, the clock would only need a periodical check. If you are making computer chips or photographic lenses, however, it is essential to have highly precise calipers and other measuring equipment.

We sometimes encounter auditors from precision engineering environments who impose their experience on other types of businesses. It's a good idea to call the auditor before the visit and ask what they expect in measurements and calibrations. Their reply should depend on the type of business you are in and what measuring equipment you currently use.

The Model

Procedure Guide 23: Calibration

1.0 Objective

1.1 To ensure that all measuring equipment used to control the quality of the product or service is of known and acceptable accuracy and precision.

2.0 Scope

2.1 All measuring equipment used to check the product, service, or its constituent parts.

3.0 Responsibilities

3.1 The responsibility must be defined. It can rest with the quality department or line management.

4.0 Procedure

The following should be included in the procedure. There needs to be a careful examination of what equipment is included in the procedure.

4.1 A record of all measuring equipment used to check product or service quality is needed, and the equipment must be identified.

4.2 Measuring equipment used for controls which do not confirm product or service quality may be marked "For indication only, not calibrated."

4.3 The accuracy and precision of measuring equipment must be defined on the record, and must be related to the tolerance of the measurements being made. A guideline is that the precision of measuring equipment should be a factor of one tenth or less of the tolerance band.

4.4 The frequency of calibration must be defined. This is dependent on the use of the equipment. Items in everyday use should be calibrated in line with manufacturer's recommendations or every six months. If no faults are found, this time span may be increased.

4.5 For those reference items held by the organization which are only used for calibration, a frequency of three to five years should be satisfactory. For those reference items linked to the National Bureau of Standards, this link must be demonstrable by documentary evidence.

4.6 Calibrations can be carried out in-house, but there must be a calibration instruction, and the readings obtained must be recorded. The environmental conditions must be suitable for the measurements being taken. Pass/fail, without data, is not acceptable.

4.7 Adjustable devices must be sealed to prevent unauthorized adjustments.

4.8 When equipment is found to be out of calibration, the measurements taken must be reviewed to determine significance of inaccuracy. If significant inaccuracies are discovered, the items inspected/tested with the equipment are suspect and may need to be recalled.

4.9 Measuring equipment owned by employees must be included in the calibration system.

4.10 Color coding systems are not required but are a useful way of indicating the equipment due to be calibrated. If it is decided to use a color coding system, then this should be described in the procedure.

5.0 Related Procedures

5.1 Process Control

5.2 Final Inspection and Test

5.3 Control of Reject Material

5.4 Servicing

5.5 Installation

5.6 Product, Service, and Process Audits

6.0 Documentation

6.1 Logs or record cards or computer files for each piece of equipment

7.0 Records

7.1 Records demonstrating the accuracy of measurements are needed for the life of the product or service, to demonstrate that the products or service are to specification. Keeping records for long periods can be useful in determining the degradation of equipment.

Relevant ISO 9001 Clauses:

- 4.1 Management Responsibility
- 4.2 Quality System
- 4.11 Inspection, Measuring, and Test Equipment
- 4.16 Quality Records

Commentary

A good example of precise calibration is a company that manufactures equipment for the electrophoresis and molecular biology research. The quality system named the director of engineering responsible for determining which equipment must be calibrated and how often.

The company numbered each item of test equipment and recorded the number on a *Calibration Record Card* which defined the frequency of calibration and whether it was done internally or by a contractor. The record card provided a space for each calibration to be dated and signed by the manager. A work sheet was used to record the measurements. The director of engineering maintained a master calibration schedule. Equipment requiring calibration carried a label showing dates of the last and the next calibration. The company avoided inaccurate measurements by using the results of the calibration to adjust the time when the equipment must be recalibrated.

One of the simplest examples of calibration is that of a company that contracted to clean kitchens for restaurants, hospitals, and other commercial facilities. Their employees, who were not highly educated or skilled, did most of their work during the early morning hours when the kitchens were not in use. The work involved the use of industrial grade cleaning solutions to loosen congealed or baked-on fat from ovens and ducts, and cleaning dirt from floors. It was their job to see that every nook and cranny of the kitchen met a health inspector's requirements. The cleaning workers had no work instructions or measuring equipment and mixed their solutions differently each time.

As the company sought registration to ISO 9000, supervisors told the workers to use an exact level of cleaning solution each time. Using the manufacturer's recommendations for the cleaning solution and their own experiences, the managers determined optimum solution concentrations. The company purchased several pint-sized measuring containers and issued them to the workers with specific instructions on the ratio of solution to water. The amount of cleaning solution was reduced to a third of what it was before they sought ISO 9000 registration. Once a week a supervisor checked the measuring cups, replacing any that had been damaged.

The cleaning company owner later said ISO 9000 registration didn't cost him anything, since he recouped all of his costs in the savings on cleaning solution. This simple routine also met the calibration requirements. The owner said his customers were more satisfied with the cleaning jobs they were getting. He bought certificates to place in a customer's kitchen saying the facility was cleaned by an ISO 9000-registered contractor. These certificates were seen by visitors to the kitchens and led to new business.

Procedure Guide 24: Control of Software Systems

Computers form an integral part of most quality systems. They may control the sales/order intake, the purchase ledger, stock control, production control, and computer-aided design, as well as word processing and spread sheet applications. All such software systems should be controlled to ensure the integrity of the data and information.

The three main areas for computer system control are:

- backup that allows for recovery of data in the event of a failure,
- security to control access, and
- data input integrity.

The Model

Procedure Guide 24: Control of Software Systems

1.0 Objective

1.1 To ensure the accuracy and reliability of information produced by software systems that are part of the quality system.

2.0 Scope

2.1 All software systems used in the quality system. These typically include sales order entry, purchasing, inventory control, MRP, production control, and CAD systems.

3.0 Responsibilities

3.1 Responsibilities must be defined in the procedure. There is no need for this to be a responsibility of the quality personnel.

4.0 Procedures

Depending on the type of software system the procedure should define—

4.1 Backup

4.1.1 Where and how master copies of software is stored and who is accountable. For standard software packages someone needs to be accountable for the master disks. Multiple copies in different locations are not necessary when it is possible to obtain additional copies from the supplier. For proprietary or customized software, at least two copies should be kept in separate locations.

4.1.2 When and how backup copies of data files are made and stored and who is responsible for storing them. Copies should not be stored in the same location. A log or other record should be available to demonstrate when copies have been made. All copies should be clearly identified.

4.2 System Control

4.2.1 Where software is controlled by password or otherwise, a log of access codes, by individual or department, is required.

4.3 Data Integrity

4.3.1 Suppliers' software manuals are adequate work instructions for the operation and setup of the system. In-house software systems need to be documented to a similar level.

5.0 Related Procedures

5.1 All procedures which use software systems.

6.0 Documentation

6.1 Backup log

6.2 Password log

7.0 Records

7.1 The logs of the backups should be retained for at least twelve months to allow system integrity to be demonstrated at an audit.

7.2 Password logs are live documents and need to be retained while valid.

Relevant ISO 9001 Clauses:

4.1 Management Responsibility

4.2 Quality System

4.5 Document and Data Control

4.16 Quality Records

Commentary

An organization experienced a break in the power supply during a vital computer operation, resulting in a hard disc crash and subsequent loss of all the data. Fortunately, two weeks earlier, as part of their preparation for ISO 9000, the company had started regular back-up procedures. Copies of the software and all the data files from the night before were available and recovery only took two hours. If the back-up procedures had not been introduced, the downtime alone would have been several days, not to mention the costs.

A company using a material control system for years had a long-established system of backing up their computer-aided design system and data. They never thought to implement the same disciplines for their material control systems. Fortunately, as part of their drive for ISO 9000 registration, they realized their error and brought the system under the same control.

Procedure Guide 25: Control of Equipment Maintenance

For an organization to make products or provide services, it is usually dependent on some form of machinery or equipment. In a production environment these may be machine tools and material handling equipment. In a service environment they may be delivery vehicles, telecommunications equipment, and computers. If the organization relies on these machines to provide quality, it must maintain them as part of the quality system.

An organization needs to minimize the risk of breakdowns and ensure employees know what to do when breakdowns occur. Depending on the environment, this may mean a comprehensive preventive maintenance system and a periodic shutdown for maintenance.

The Model

Procedure Guide 25: Control of Equipment Maintenance

1.0 Objective

1.1 To provide suitable maintenance of equipment for continuing process capability.

2.0 Scope

2.1 The maintenance of equipment that has a direct effect on the ability of the organization to produce its products, process its material, and provide its service.

3.0 Responsibilities

3.1 Responsibilities must be defined in the procedure. There is no need for the quality personnel to be involved.

4.0 Procedures

Depending on the type of equipment the procedure should define —

4.1 The method by which breakdowns are recorded, reported to appropriate functions, and the system for controlling and recording the repair needs to be documented. As downtime has a direct effect on quality the system should allow for the calculation of downtime. This can then be monitored using statistical techniques and used as the basis for justifying planned maintenance. If maintenance is subcontracted then the subcontractors need to be on the approved list of suppliers.

4.2 When planned maintenance is appropriate, the rationale for defining the maintenance, and the system for conducting and recording the actual maintenance, needs to be defined. If maintenance requires a shutdown, any special precautions or product verification after restart should be defined as necessary.

4.3 If the organization relies on the process capability for the control of the products or service, the determination of process capability should be part of this procedure.

5.0 Related Procedures

5.1 Process Control

5.2 Servicing
5.3 Installation

6.0 Documentation
6.1 Breakdown Report
6.2 Breakdown Log
6.3 Planned Maintenance Schedule

7.0 Records
7.1 The records of the breakdowns and the associated maintenance should be analyzed and retained for a period relevant to the life of the equipment.
7.2 The planned maintenance schedules and records of the maintenance should be kept for the life of the equipment.

Relevant ISO 9001 Clauses:

4.1 Management Responsibility
4.2 Quality System
4.9 Process Control
4.14 Corrective and Preventive Action
4.16 Quality Records
4.20 Statistical ctechniques

Commentary

A manufacturing company had problems with breakdowns on a piece of production equipment resulting in a 30 percent loss of production capacity. In addition, the machine also frequently malfunctioned, causing high scrap rates. The machine and the processes performed on it were monitored over time and causes of the breakdowns analyzed. The company introduced a regular maintenance procedure. As a result, downtime was reduced to less than one percent, and the scrap rate also fell—to less than two percent.

A catering company had a fire in the exhaust duct over the cooking stoves, caused by a spark igniting a heavy layer of oil and grease that had built up on the duct. The kitchen was closed for some time, with a considerable loss of business. A planned maintenance program that included deep-cleaning all ducts and other equipment was instituted in all their outlets. The result—no more fires.

Chapter 10 ◆ ISO 9000 and Statistical Techniques

There are numerous excellent books on using statistics in business. This is not the place to explain statistical techniques, but to discuss how they relate to ISO 9000.

The quality of a product or service, is determined during conception, design, development, production, delivery and even use. Statistical techniques can help us to study and improve each of these steps.

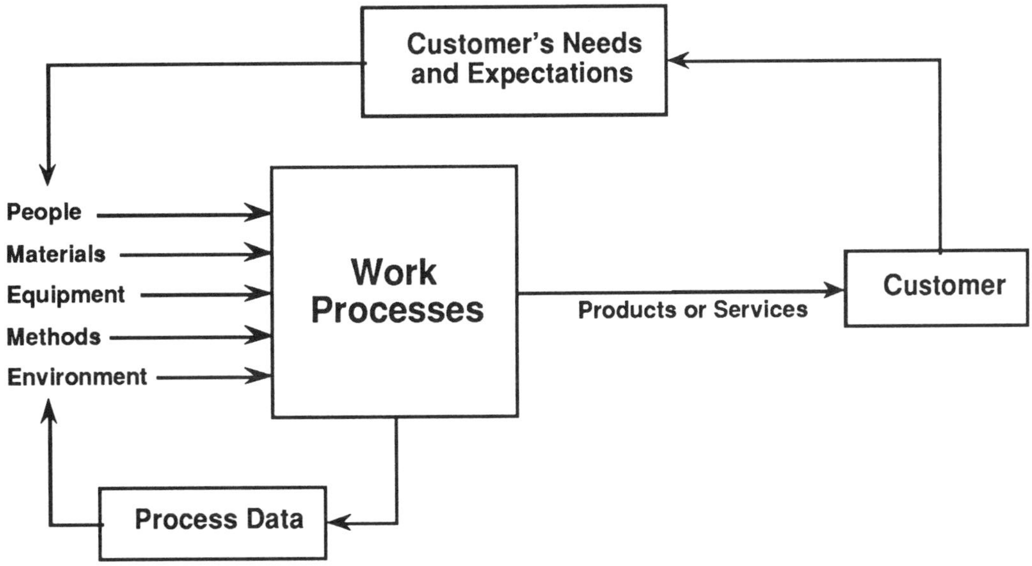

Figure 10.1 Simple Control Loop

All processes have inputs and outputs. The inputs include materials, methods, people, equipment, and environment. The inputs have an effect on the outputs, and to control the process, the inputs must be studied and understood.

Formerly, quality was thought of in terms of conformance to specifications. This naturally resulted in efforts to control the quality of the output by sorting good products from bad ones. This proved to be highly inefficient.

Today, however, quality is more often defined in terms of "on target with *minimum variation*." This places an emphasis upon using the inputs to control the process. This approach requires an understanding of the relationship between the inputs and the outputs. This understanding can best be achieved by the use of statistical process control.

Statistical process control (SPC) was developed as a means of listening to the *voice of the process*. Is the process operating as consistently as possible, or not? If not, what upsets occur?

When a process is operating as consistently as possible, it is said to display a *reasonable degree of statistical control*. Only when this state has been achieved can the process be said to possess a certain *capability*. This capability defines what the process will produce as long as the system is not fundamentally changed. In short, the capability of a stable process is the *voice of the process*.

In contrast, specifications can be thought of as the *voice of the customer*. Obviously, the objective is to get these two voices into alignment—by improving the process. SPC is used to determine whether the two voices are aligned.

The problem comes with processes which do not operate as consistently as possible. Such processes do not possess a well-defined capability. What they have produced in the past is not a prediction of what will happen in the future, and this lack of predictability is a quality problem waiting to happen.

Thus, SPC is primarily concerned with the predictability of any process. If it is unpredictable, SPC provides a way of working to make it predictable. If it is already predictable, SPC identifies what the process can be counted on to produce in the future.

Achieving quality depends on establishing a method of ensuring that the voice of the process is properly aligned with the voice of the customer. SPC is the most thoroughly proven method of achieving this objective.

Using SPC represents a large improvement over final inspection of products, since it allows the organization to prevent nonconformance, rather than inspecting out nonconformances after the fact. It allows companies to reduce the variation in the output from the processes, reducing the risk of producing unsatisfactory products or services and raising productivity.

Although there has always been a clause in ISO 9000 on statistical techniques, to date, ISO 9000 auditors have not generally demanded that organizations use statistics to measure their processes. That may change as the Standard itself changes between the 1987 and 1994 versions.

The 1987 version of ISO 9000 says in clause 4.20:

> Where appropriate, the supplier shall establish procedures for identifying adequate statistical techniques required for verifying the acceptability of process capability and product characteristics.

In the 1994 Standard this is changed in 4.20 to:

> 4.20.1 Identification of Need
>
> The supplier shall identify the need for statistical techniques required for establishing, controlling, and verifying process capability and product characteristics.
>
> 4.20.2 Procedures:
>
> The supplier shall establish and maintain documented procedures to implement and control the application of the statistical techniques identified in 4.20.1.

Based on the 1987 version, ISO 9000 says an organization should demonstrate and document that it has considered using statistical techniques for verification—*as appropriate*. Those who already use statistical tools describe their use in the procedure which facilitates registration. Many companies choose to exercise the option of simply stating that they do not consider the use of statistical techniques appropriate for their operations. Thus, they hide behind the words "where appropriate." ISO 9000 auditors rarely challenge this, even in industries where the use of statistics has a proven track record.

It remains to be seen whether the change in wording will mean auditors will change their practices. The 1994 Standard removes the words "where appropriate." It states that the organization "shall identify the need for statistical techniques." This appears to be more definitive, but depends on how you define the word *need*. If the organization can achieve quality without statistical tools, even though their use would improve control and efficiency, is it true that there is no need?

Auditors are always mindful that it is not their job to tell management how to run the organization. So is it their responsibility to declare that such a need exists? The 1994 wording could still lead to an organization declaring it has no need for statistical techniques for verification purposes. The auditor might disagree, but would have to refute the statement by showing that quality was suffering and could be improved through the use of statistical tools.

Putting auditors in that position might require them to be trained extensively to be able to recognize when statistical tools are necessary. Most auditors, after all, are not statisticians.

Process capability is also mentioned in the 1994 Standards' clause on process control. It states that:

> Controlled conditions shall include...suitable maintenance of equipment to ensure continuing process capability.

As noted above, process capability has a precise meaning to a practitioner of SPC. Such an expert might interpret the clause as meaning that it is necessary to use this method of measurement on almost all processes.

Using statistical tools has preventive aspects as well, and these are also addressed in ISO 9000. The 1987 version states that:

> The supplier shall establish, document, and maintain procedures for initiating preventive actions to deal with problems to a level corresponding to the risks encountered;

The 1994 Standard expands this to a whole clause on the issue. This too could prompt an SPC expert to argue that statistical tools are the only route to prevent nonconformance. However, other methods might be equally effective, in some circumstances. For instance, preventing a boiler from overheating can be achieved by fitting a thermostat that switches off the boiler when a pre-set temperature is reached.

There are other statistical techniques, problem solving methods, and management tools a company might use, along with SPC, to collect information on the quality of products, services, and processes. These would appear to be an inevitable result of implementing a sound quality system. They will also help to determine appropriate preventive and corrective actions.

At this stage, despite the benefits these tools might bring, they are not considered requirements of the ISO 9000 Standard. This does not in any way deprecate the value of the techniques but may imply something about the difficulty of requiring them. Having established a sound quality system as part of their registration, however, many organizations may want to continue working toward Total Quality and introduce these techniques.

The Process Management approach identifies the need for statistical techniques in Procedure Guide 6, Process Planning. The implementation of the identified quality control process is covered in Procedure Guide 7, Process Control.

Chapter 11 ◆ The Procedure Manual

By now, you have prepared and implemented individual procedures—level two of the ISO 9000 Documentation Hierarchy shown in Figure 11.1.

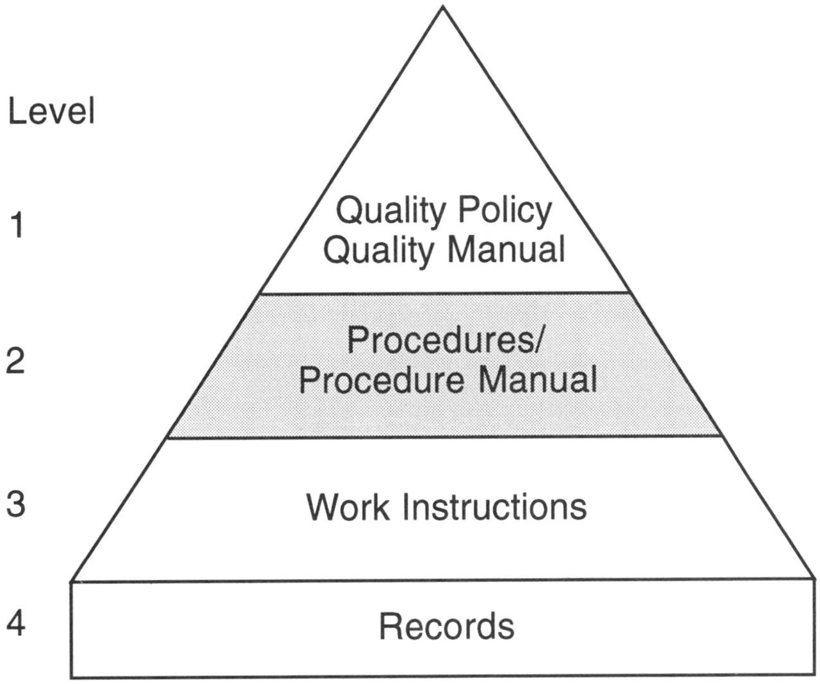

Figure 11.1 ISO 9000 Documentation Hierarchy

These, collectively along with the work instructions, describe your quality system and satisfy the ISO 9000 Standard requirements. Achieving ISO 9000 registration requires that you use your system as documented. The way to ensure ongoing use of the system is to package and distribute the procedures to individuals and areas of the company who need them. They should be placed in a book called the *Company Procedure Manual*. The use of titles such as the "ISO 9000 Manual" should be avoided as these tend to create the impression that the contents relate to the Standard, rather than its true role of helping to control the operations of the company.

Procedures, once written, are not chipped in stone. As the company changes there will be changes in the processes it uses, the organizational structure of the company, and the responsibilities of its staff. As these changes occur, they need to be reflected in the Procedure Manual. To allow for changes to be efficiently incorporated, it is advisable that the manual be placed in a loose leaf binder.

The Procedure Manual should include the following titles (discussed below):

Title/Authorization Page
Table of Contents
Organization Chart
Responsibilities for Quality
Quality Records
Document Summary
Each Procedure, with its appendices

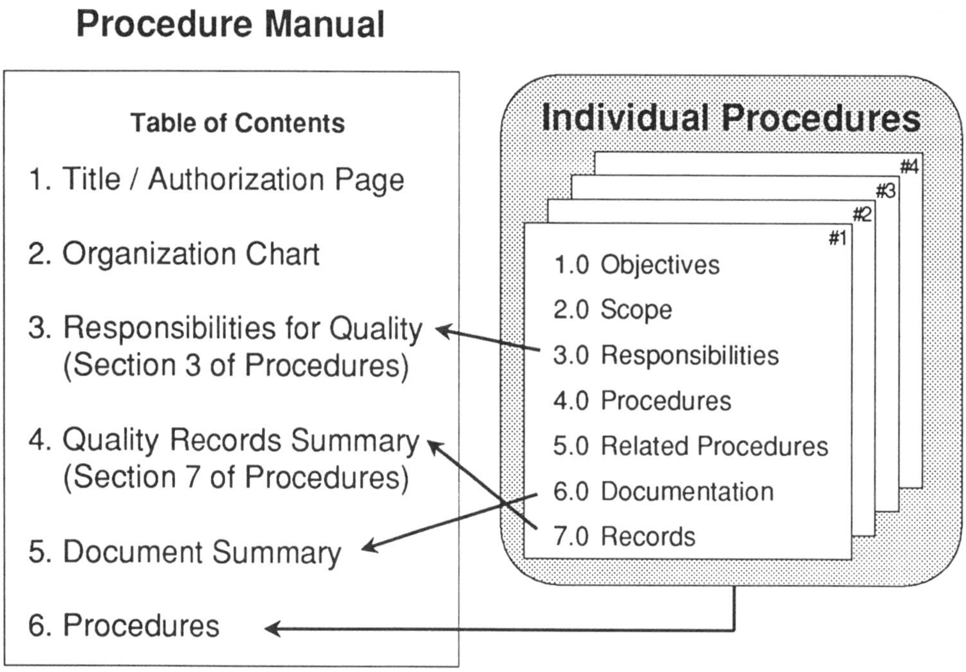

Figure 11.2 Procedure Manual

The **Title/Authorization Page** of the Procedure Manual should include a statement on the content of the manual and indicate its ownership and authorize its use. This page is followed by a **Table of Contents** that lists the procedures included in the manual and the issue, or revision levels, of each one. There are many ways to authorize procedures, but the two most common are at the individual procedure level or the Procedure Manual level. In the former, each procedure has an authorizing signature. In the latter, the Table of Contents page shows the current revision level of each procedure and authorizes all of them. The bottom of the page contains a statement saying, "The above procedures are authorized for issue at the revision levels indicated and must be adhered to by all employees at all times."

With either approach, the revision levels of all the procedures and the manual itself are shown on the Table of Contents. This allows the user to easily check that the manual is a current issue and to confirm that updates have been incorporated within the manual.

The next section is an **Organization Chart** that defines the relationships between members of the organization. It includes the positions referenced in the procedures and identifies the duties of the Management Representative. It is better to show titles for the various positions in the company rather than the names of the individual incumbents. Writing the procedures using titles allows for greater flexibility. Employees may then change jobs without requiring an update of the manual. If the structure changes, however, the organizational chart must be updated.

Some people believe the Organization Chart should also be in the Quality Manual, *including some ISO 9000 auditors who insist on it.* They are in a minority, but readers should be aware that *their* auditor may expect this. The organization should put the chart in the Procedure Manual, since that document refers to the job titles shown on the chart. All holders and users of the procedures may not have a quality manual and hence would not have access to the information. Another reason for having the organization chart in the Procedure Manual is that organizations change and the Procedure Manual is designed to change.

Another useful addition to the Procedure Manual is a summary of **Responsibilities for Quality.** Section 3 of each procedure lists responsibilities for the activities and actions defined in the procedures. They are summarized by title or position so that everyone can easily see their responsibilities within the quality system. This listing should include identifying the person to whom each reports, brief descriptions of the overall responsibilities, and a statement regarding substitution in the case of absences. (See the sample in Appendix D-3.)

Similarly, the records defined in Section 7 of each procedure can be copied and summarized into a **Quality Records Summary** section, allowing the same easy reference to the records being maintained within the quality system. The introduction to this section should define the policy of the company with respect to the storage of records, where they should be archived, and the name of a person who is responsible for them. Once this section is prepared, it is an ideal opportunity to examine the retention times of all the various records being held. Retention times are not specified in the ISO 9000 Standard, and it is left to each organization to decide what meets its requirements. A sample of a Quality Records Summary is in Appendix D-4.

While the documents used in each procedure are listed in the procedures with examples in the appendices, it is useful to have a **Document Summary** section. This is a listing of the documents from Section 6 of each of the procedures, and provides an easy reference guide. The introduction to this section should indicate that the documents are at Issue Level 1, except where indicated to the contrary. When documents are revised, this is indicated by adding Rev. 2 or a date to the document. This approach removes the need to add issue levels to existing forms and is in harmony with the Process Management Approach of not introducing a change except where absolutely necessary. An example is shown in Appendix D-5.

The remainder of the **Procedure Manual** consists of the procedures themselves. These are in order by identifying number.

Typically, a Procedure Manual will be a 75 to 150-page manual. The pages should not be numbered from beginning to end, but each procedure/section should be numbered within itself. Since the procedures are in numeric order, they are easily located. Numbering throughout the manual complicates matters when an individual procedure changes in length.

Once the Procedure Manual is completed, it should be duplicated and distributed. Some companies adopt a policy of only issuing manuals which contain a full set of procedures, while others issue abridged manuals with contents selected on a "need to know" basis. For example, a buyer may only be issued those procedures that directly affect the purchasing function. There are advantages to this approach in large companies as it reduces the number of copies required. On the other hand, it increases the complexity of control. Other companies issue one or two procedures for display on bulletin boards in appropriate locations. This is beneficial for production and storage areas where the instructions need to be available for all to read. However, posted procedures also need to be controlled.

The advisability of issuing uncontrolled copies of procedures is often questioned. Within the company, it is recommended that all copies be controlled—to avoid the danger of individuals having out-of-date procedures. When someone needs a procedure, they need a current one, *i.e.* a controlled copy. A case can be made for issuing uncontrolled procedures to internal auditors who might mark them up for use during internal audits. In this case, they should be collected at the end of the audit and destroyed. Again, this approach removes the need to add issue levels to existing forms and aviods introducing changes unless they are absolutely necessary. A sample of a Documentary Summary is shown in Appendix D-5.

These summary sections are not difficult to prepare if the procedures are on a word processor. It is just a cut, copy, and paste exercise.

Chapter 12 ◆ Work Instructions

The third level of documentation is called Work Instructions. These documents, which may be highly diverse, tell people who work in the system, the details of what to do, and how to do it. There are three types of work instructions: documents, instructions, and reference standards. These are not mutually exclusive; some items could be placed in more than one of the three categories, but the division is useful.

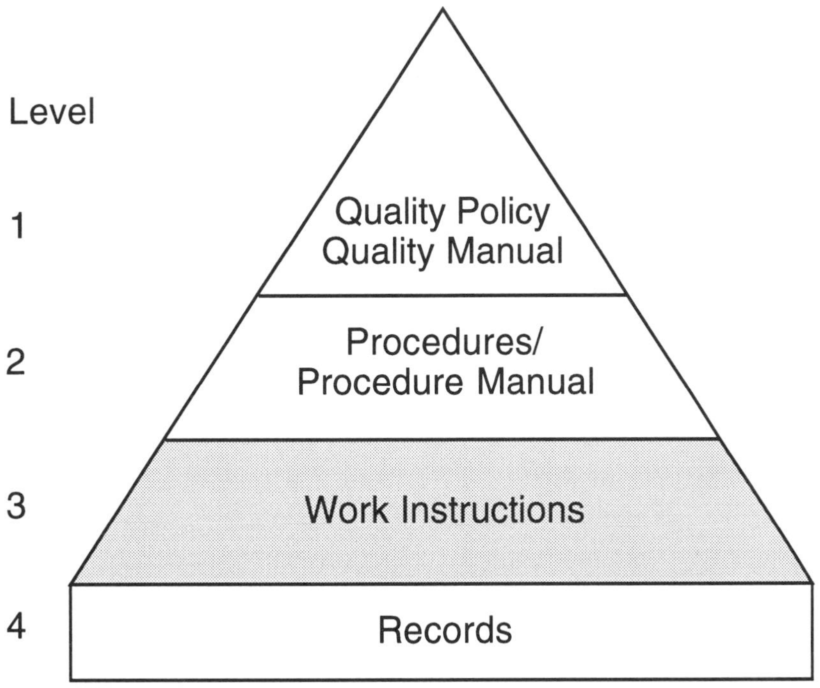

Figure 12.1 ISO 9000 Documentation Hierarchy

Documents are identified in the procedures describing the quality system. They typically include forms and records. Examples are Sales Orders, Work Orders, Inventory Requisitions, Job Cards, and Invoices. Each of these serves as an instruction to carry out some level of work. They might indicate the number and type of item to be supplied, or describe in general terms the service required. If the documents are revised, it is necessary to indicate the new revision level on the form.

Instructions define what is required from a process and often include a description of how the work should be done. The level of detail in the instruction should relate to the qualifications, skills, experience, and training of those who will use them. Examples of Instructions are Engineering Drawings, Recipes, Formulae, Process Sheets, Photographs of Products, and Cleaning Instructions.

Reference standards also cover a wide range of documents and include drafting codes of practice, computer operating manuals, maintenance manuals, ISO 9000 Standards, laws, other government regulations, and other standards. These documents may be produced outside the company, but must be controlled within the company.

Regardless of the category of the work instructions, they should be controlled by a document control procedure, as defined in Procedure Guide 17 or 18 of the Process Management Model. Control involves approval, issue, and distribution ensuring that only the pertinent revisions are available to employees.

Need For Work Instructions

Questions of where, if, and when work instructions are necessary, tend to touch off considerable discussion in organizations seeking ISO 9000 registration. The Standard clearly requires documentation of the quality system, but the level of documentation hinges on the needs of the organization. The acid test is whether the absence of such instructions would adversely affect quality.

As you will by now know, the Process Management Approach seeks to change as little as possible to define the Optimum Quality System for the organization. If the organization has been operating successfully without work instructions, and it can demonstrate that quality has not suffered, then it should not be necessary to produce additional work instructions. If there are problems with staff not knowing what to do, then the introduction of a work instruction will help control the process—the objective of the ISO 9000 registration process.

As the above indicates, the ISO 9000 Standard is not definitive, so you must decide where and when work instructions are needed. An auditor cannot say, "You need a work instruction here"—or anywhere. Auditors can only respond to "objective evidence" that there is lack of control or a problem. Hence, if an operation or process is producing nonconforming product, or causing concerns about quality, this would be objective evidence that the "process is not carried out under controlled conditions." The solution to the problem could be a work instruction, or it could be training, a new machine, or whatever. The solution will most likely be some combination of these. Again, you decide, hopefully after exercising your corrective action procedure, what is the best way to alleviate the problem and prevent its recurrence. If the solution involves working with an employee, it is usually some combination of work instruction and employee enhancement (training, experience, and education). This is illustrated in Figure 12.2.

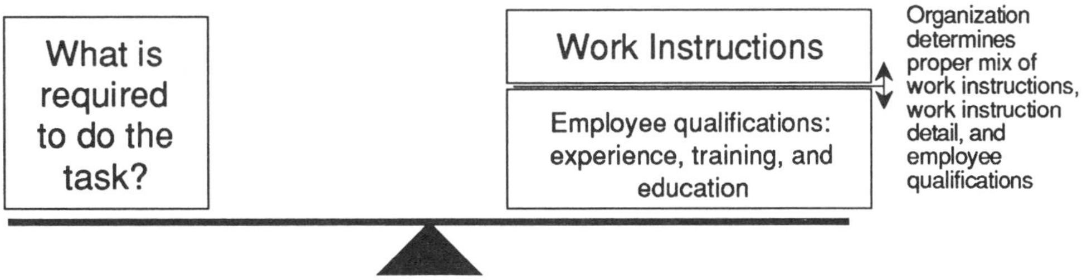

Figure 12.2 Qualification Work Instruction Trade-Off

Hence, you need to look at your operations and processes and decide where changes are necessary, and if work instructions are part of the solution. Figure 12.3 on page 135 illustrates the decision process.

Work Instructions not only are diverse in type, but also in content and need. To illustrate this we consider three restaurants, each with different employee qualifications and customer expectations.

Types of Work Instructions

A fast food restaurant offers fixed dishes prepared by staff trained only to prepare those meals. They are not fully trained chefs. The employer only expects them to know how to prepare what is on the menu. The franchise owner or manager must maintain the product standards and must follow guidelines or instructions provided by the franchiser pertaining to food purchases.

The fast food restaurant requires detailed work instructions on quantities, cooking times, temperatures, and purchasing specifications. These documents may be in the form of Instruction Manuals, Cooking Instructions, and/or Photographs of the required dishes and must be available to the staff.

The second type of restaurant is *the catering company* that operates factory canteens in various locations. A trained cook manages the canteen and devises and delivers menus that meet the requirements of the workers in the factory. The catering company does not attempt to standardize the products offered in all canteens, leaving it to each cook to buy the necessary food.

Work instructions for the factory canteen are less detailed than those of the fast food restaurant. They might consist of a menu for the week and a standard recipe book. The caterer need not write an original recipe book, but may buy any suitable cookbook, chosen by the cook, who must be trained and qualified. Detailed food purchasing specifications are unnecessary since the cooks vary the recipes according to variations in supplies and local customer likes or dislikes.

The third example is a *haute cuisine restaurant* offering food prepared by cordon bleu chefs whose skill, experience, and use of fresh and exotic ingredients delight the customers. The meals may lack the consistency of a fast food restaurant, but variety adds to the customers' pleasure.

The menu, written by the chefs themselves, might be the only work instruction for the preparation of meals. They would select the raw materials from the suppliers, based on their own assessment of availability, and then design the meals.

Obviously, the number and level of work instructions vary at each type of restaurant. Menus, training material, purchasing specifications, product descriptions, and recipe books all serve as work instructions.

In addition to these instructions for food preparation, the restaurant would probably use other documents which would be similar in many respects. The waiters would have a simple order pad to record the customers' precise requirements. The ingredients would be ordered with a purchase order form from approved suppliers, and the customers would be given a bill indicating the amount to be paid.

In each restaurant type, there is equipment with operating and maintenance manuals which employees use for reference; also examples of work instructions. Similarly there are handbooks on the dish washing machine, health regulations, instructions on the use of chemicals, disposal of waste, and other items.

Where work instructions are available from outside sources, there is no need to rewrite the outside documents into a prescribed company format, but they still must be controlled. A system to ensure that the documents are the latest issue is required, if that is important to the quality of the service or goods. In the case of a standard recipe book, this may not be important. Just because a new edition comes out does not mean the company has to use it. In the case of a standard, legislation, or product instructions, however, it is essential to use the current version.

A classic example of a reference standard that is often overlooked by organizations is the ISO 9000 Standard itself. There is no requirement for an organization seeking registration to have a copy, but how can they claim to be adhering to it if they do not? If they have a copy, they must ensure that their copy is the latest version. In practice, the registrar informs the organization when the Standard changes, though ISO 9000 auditors are reluctant to accept this as a valid method for ensuring up-to-date documentation.

ISO 9000 does not require the documents produced by the company to be in a predefined format. Many of the required instructions already exist. All the organization must do is set up a system for authorizing and controlling them. When there are changes in the issue or revision level, managers should review and reapprove the instructions. Any replaced copies should be destroyed or marked as superseded.

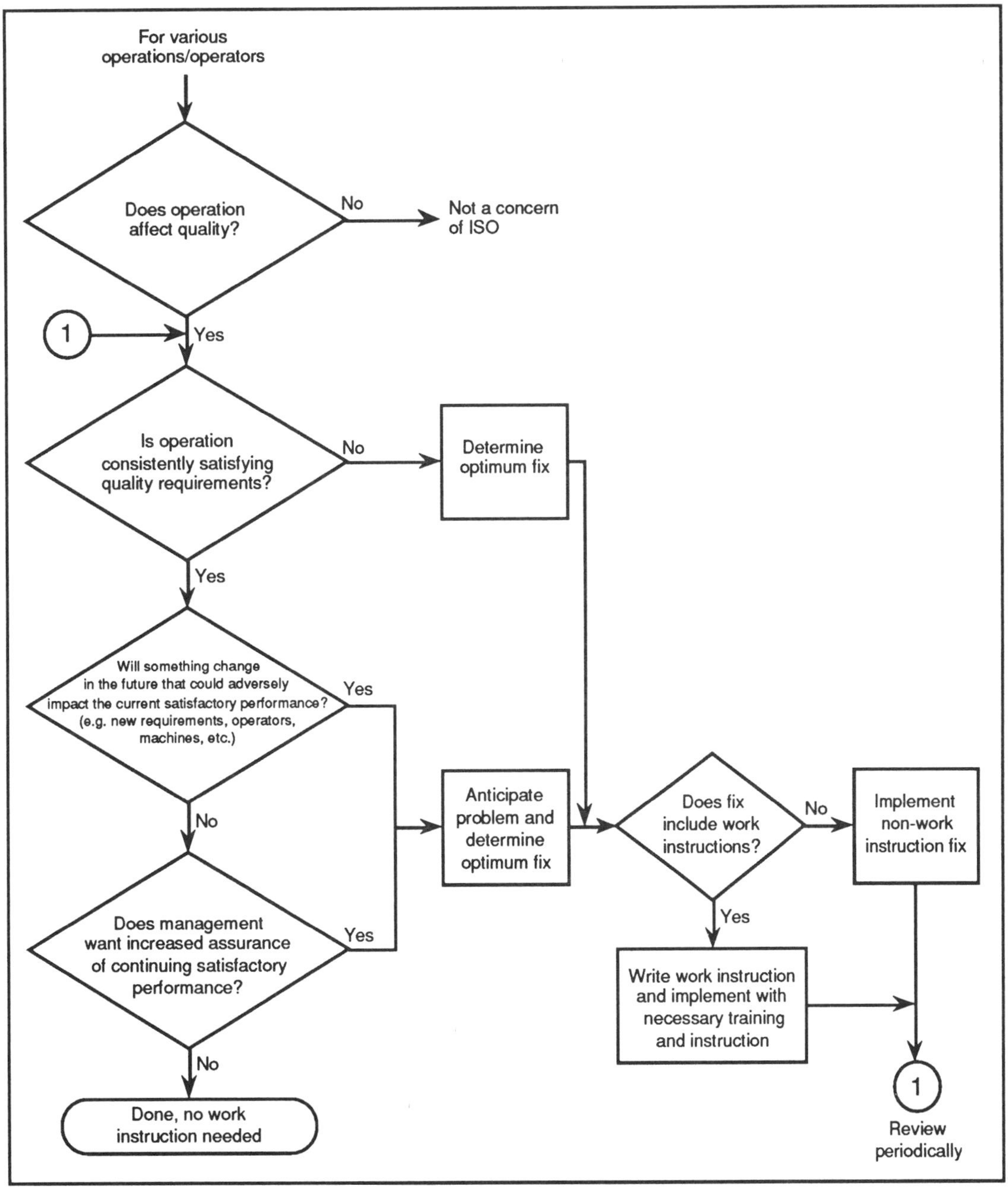

Figure 12.3 Determining Work Instruction Needs

Although the Management Representative for Quality is usually responsible for controlling the Quality Manual, Procedures, and Procedure Manual, that person does not have to be responsible for the control of Work Instructions. Control of Work Instructions is usually best accomplished by the department that generates and/or uses them. For example, laboratory methods used only within a particular laboratory are controlled by that laboratory.

The method of control should always be in line with Procedure Guides 16 and/or 17 of the Process Management Model. Since document control is a common noncompliance in ISO 9000 audits, it should receive extra attention during internal audits.

Examples of different types of Work Instruction are given in Appendix D-6. Early in the project, managers should survey and analyze the existing Work Instructions. Often a table, as shown in Figure 12.4, is useful. For each Work Instruction the method of control should be decided and entered into the table. This information may not be known initially, and should be added as it becomes available.

Work Instructions			Procedure	
Name	Rev	Purpose	Referring	Controlling
Sales Inquiry Form	1	Record Sales	Inquiry Procedure	Control of Sales
Estimating Form	2	Determine Price	Inquiry Procedure	Inquiry Procedure
Price List	0	Current Std	Inquiry Procedure	Control of Specification
Order Entry Systems Manual	1	Details of System	Inquiry Procedure	Control of Manuals

Figure 12.4 Work Instruction Table

Chapter 13 ◆ The Quality Manual

ISO 9000 originally did not explicitly require a Quality Manual as part of the documented quality system. That has now changed. Virtually every registered organization has a Quality Manual and registrars expect to see one. The Quality Manual is part of the Process Management Model discussed in this chapter.

ISO 90013—Guidelines for developing quality manuals, provides guidance on the content and format of quality manuals. The content of this Standard and the Process Management Approach to documentation are compatible.

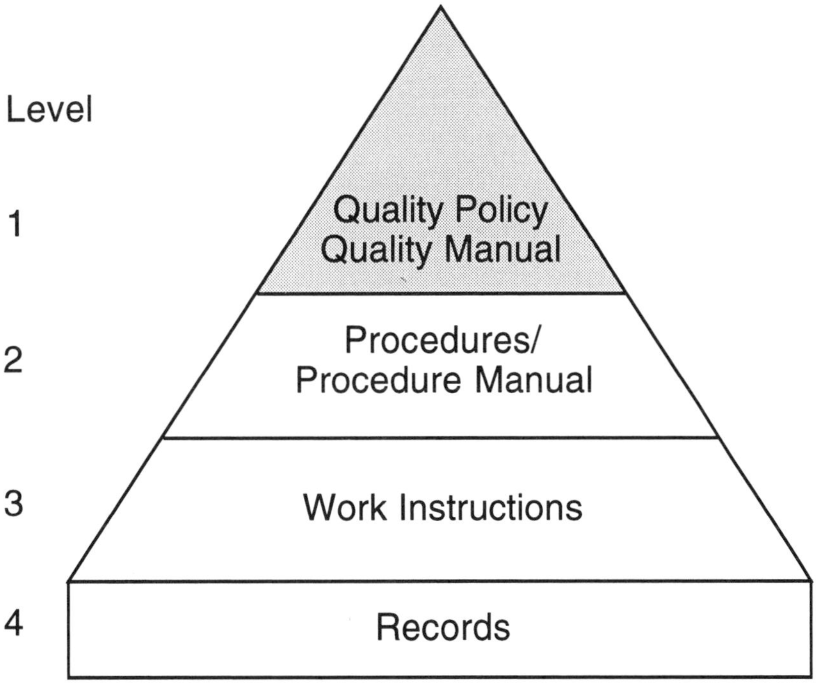

Figure 13.1 ISO 9000 Documentation Hierarchy

As explained in Chapter 6, the top level of documentation for the quality system is the Quality Manual. It is defined in ISO 8402 as:

> A document stating the quality policy and describing the quality system of an organization.

In considering this definition of a Quality Manual we will start with the first of the two requirements, the Quality Policy. With respect to the Quality Policy ISO 9000 requires that:

> ...the management with executive responsibility for quality shall define and document its policy for quality including objectives for quality and commitment to quality. The quality policy shall be relevant to the supplier's organizational goals and the expectations and needs of its customers.

Developing a Quality Policy

The quality policy is a policy for the entire company. Executive management must develop it, believe it, and adhere to it. By having the management team develop the policy, their minds focus on what quality means in their situation. It also illustrates to them what is involved in registration to ISO 9000. This is far more beneficial to the company than adopting a standard policy or asking the Management Representative or Consultant to write the Quality Policy.

Consideration of a few simple questions can help an organization shape and formulate its quality policy.

Quality Intentions

What does the organization intend to do about quality?

Is the organization prepared to allocate the necessary resources?

Direction for Quality

What is the vision and direction of the organization?

Does it intend to get better?

Does it believe in continual improvement?

Objectives for Quality

Is the overall goal for quality clearly defined?

Does the policy define the route to be taken as well as the goal?

Commitment to Quality

Does the policy make the organization's position on quality clear?

Does the organization put quality first?

Customer Expectations and Needs

Does the policy address the expectations of the customers?

Does the policy include the needs of the customers?

Once the Quality Policy is drafted, it must be approved, communicated, and distributed. Minimally, this should include the approval by top management—the signature of the Chief Executive Officer on behalf of the organization—and public display in a prominent location (or locations).

Sample Quality Policies

Below are the quality policies of five companies registered to ISO 9000. Get the management team to read these policies and criticize them. They should be mindful of the points in the preceding section as they go through this exercise. Try to identify the extent to which these policies cover the concepts already noted. Using this process, your management team should be able to develop its own Quality Policy, thereby developing a sense of ownership.

◆

Black Plating and Engineering Company is committed to providing customers with efficient electroplating, plating jig design, and manufacturing that meets their needs with respect to specification, delivery, and price. The company believes itself to be the best in its field, but intends to become better.

Customer satisfaction is a priority within the company. Our customers have a right to expect this. We must maintain a constant dialogue, determining both present and future needs. It is our objective to promote progressive development to ensure improved user choice.

Quality is achieved by working to audited procedures throughout the organization. It is the responsibility of every employee to ensure that these procedures are followed. Accreditation to ISO 9002 and keeping abreast of current standards are the cornerstones of this policy.

It is essential for the company's success and long-term prosperity that we maintain an excellent name for quality. Complete customer satisfaction is our objective.

◆

White Design is committed to responsively producing technically sound designs with a high standard of presentation while providing professional site supervision and project control service for the fire protection industry and related pipe work disciplines.

The Company seeks to achieve this objective by maintaining an effectively managed Quality Assurance System which meets the Standard defined in ISO 9001. This policy assures the Company's customers that the services it provides meet their requirements of performance and delivery as specified in its contracts.

◆

It is the policy of **Brown's Butchers** never to let their customers down. We are committed to ensuring that at the point of delivery to the customer, the product totally meets all of the customer's requirements. This is achieved by the operation of an efficient quality system, subjected to regular independent assessment, and by having sound hygienic conditions and procedures.

◆

Green Services offers an innovative integration of products and services of the highest standard, designed to provide its customers in the catering industry with safe and hygienic working environments. The service, which is tailored to meet the customers' needs, may include:

- a consultancy service that analyzes and designs suitable systems with objective professionalism;
- a training service that assists the development of the hygiene standards of customers' staff; and
- a monitoring service to ensure that the objectives of the system are achieved.

At Green Services, quality is achieved by working to audited procedures throughout the organization. It is the responsibility of every employee to ensure that these procedures are adhered to properly. Accreditation to ISO 9002 is the cornerstone of this policy.

Customer satisfaction is a priority within Green Services. Our customers have a right to expect this. We must maintain a constant dialogue, determining both present and future needs. We pride ourselves on the continual development of a product range that is in harmony with the environment. We believe we are the best and strive for perfection in our field.

◆

The management and staff of **Blue House Nursing Home** are committed to providing the highest standard of care and support to our residents. We seek to provide a professional, holistic service which addresses the social, physical, intellectual, emotional, and spiritual needs of those in our care.

We work in a loving partnership with our residents providing freedom of choice, maintaining dignity and independence, while respecting the rights of the individual and the residents as a group. Fulfillment of the individual's changing potential is a key consideration at all times.

In the home we provide care within a multidisciplinary framework, in close cooperation with families, medical practitioners, paramedics, physiotherapists, clergy, social workers, and others appropriate to the residents' needs. To monitor the health of our residents, we routinely screen for diseases common to later life and work with their own Medical Practitioner to provide appropriate interventional care.

We recognize that the residents of our home have responsibilities in the wider community. We provide confidential counseling and patient advocacy, calling on professionals as necessary.

It is our policy to provide privacy and dignity within a warm and friendly home environment which is constructed, furnished, and maintained to a very high standard. Through a structured system of nursing care, we ensure that our policies are implemented. To demonstrate the efficiency of this implementation, our systems are independently assessed to the Quality Standard, ISO 9002.

We welcome residents from all walks of life, all races, all religions or none, and endeavor to cater to and enable them to maintain their individuality. We believe we provide a service we would be proud for our own families to receive.

◆

Whether the Quality Policy is prominently posted or given to each employee, management must communicate with all employees and help them understand it. Employees should attend a training session in which its content and meaning are examined. The company may also wish to use it on promotional material.

QUALITY MANUAL

Table of Contents

1. Title/Authorization Page
2. Quality Policy
3. Organization
4. Satisfying ISO 900X Requirements – by Section 4.0 Clause
5. ISO 9000 – Procedures Relationship

Figure 13.2 Quality Manual: Table of Contents

Describing the Quality System

The Quality Manual's second function is to describe the quality system. The detail of description in the quality manual needs to correspond with the ISO 9000 hierarchy and documentation format introduced in Chapter 6.

The Quality Manual describes the quality system in accordance with the company's quality policy and objectives and with the applicable ISO 9000 Standard. The Quality Manual's contents should be kept as simple as possible and address all the clauses of the Standard (see Figure 13.2 and the sample in Appendix D-1).

There is no predefined format for a Quality Manual, but it should be clear, accurate, and complete. A good method of organization is based on the clauses of the ISO 9000 Standard, beginning with a statement similar to that of the Procedure Manual. Two sample Quality Manuals are included in Appendix D-1. A sample page is shown in Figure 13.3.

The Quality Manual should include:

Title/Authorization Page
Table of Contents
Definition of Terms (optional)
Quality Policy
Organization
Satisfying the ISO 9000 Requirements
ISO 9000 - Procedures Relationship Matrix

XYZ Inc.

QUALITY MANUAL

This Quality Manual is a description of XYZ's quality policy, organization and responsibilities, quality system, procedures, and controls implemented and maintained to conform with the requirements of ISO 9001.

The requirements of this Quality Manual extend to all employees with responsibility for implementing and maintaining the quality system referenced in this manual. The relationship between this manual, ISO 9001, and the Company Procedure Manual is defined in Appendix I of this Manual.

The contents of this Manual are authorized and approved by the Chief Executive Officer of XYZ Inc. and must be followed by all employees at all times.

This manual is the property of XYZ Inc. and must be returned to XYZ Inc. when requested. This manual must not be copied, in whole or part, without the written consent of XYZ Inc.

Chief Executive Officer
Authorized Date

Issue ___
Manual ___

Figure 13.3 Quality Manual: Title/Authorization Page

If the documented quality system uses terms or concepts unique to the organization or its industry, the Quality Manual may include a section defining these terms. If the manual uses ordinary language found in a standard dictionary, industry publications, and ISO publications, no such section is needed. Any attempt to define standard terms should make sure the definitions are clear and accurate.

The Quality Policy should be the next section of the manual, along with a statement that it has been effectively communicated to everyone in the organization.

A brief description of the organization structure, the responsibilities and authorities of key positions with responsibility for quality is the next section. It is recommended that this section be kept to a minimum and reference the detailed organization chart and responsibilities for quality in the Procedure Manual. This reduces the necessity of modifying the document when minor changes are made in the organization.

The remainder of the Quality Manual describes how the organization meets the requirements of whichever ISO 9000 Standard it seeks to be registered under. It is recommended that this be done by starting with Clause 4.1 of the ISO 9000 Standard and continuing through to 4.20 indicating how the organization meets the requirements of each clause. The manual should say which clauses of the Standard have no application in the organization. This is all that needs to be said under such a clause. For instance, a law firm would have no equipment to calibrate and would write "Not Applicable" for Clause 4.11.

This part of the Quality Manual is best written after completion of the Procedures and Procedure Manual. Until all the procedures have been documented, it might not be clear how the organization meets the requirements of a particular clause of the Standard. Also reading the Standard and writing how the clause is satisfied provides a valuable cross check that all elements have been covered in the procedures.

The Quality Manual is completed with a cross reference between the clauses of the Standard, the Quality Manual, and the Procedure Manual. This may be in the form of either a matrix or a series of statements. Both alternatives are illustrated in Appendix D-1.

Unlike the Procedure Manual, the Quality Manual should rarely change. Any change in it would necessitate reissuing the entire document, so the pages can be sequentially numbered.

The Quality Manual can make a good marketing piece. When used as such, it can also include information about the company and its activities. It should include the company name, address, and telephone number. If the same Quality Manual applies to more than one location or plant, the manual should say so.

SECTION THREE

ISO 9000 IN 15 DIFFERENT BUSINESS SECTORS

ISO 9000's origins can be traced to quality standards developed by NATO for the purchase of military hardware, and the basic principles developed in the NATO military standards. The language in the ISO 9000 standard refers more to goods than services, although there is a note saying:

> *For the purposes of this Standard, the term "product" is also used to denote service, as appropriate.*

The note appears almost as an afterthought, signaling that probably no one foresaw the wide range of service industries to which ISO 9000 eventually would apply. Philosophically there is no reason the Standard should not apply to services; the problem arises with the terminology.

Despite the note about services, ISO 9000's general content is more understandable when related to manufacturing. Concepts such as control, calibration, inspection, concessions, test and inspection fit naturally in the manufacture of hardware products and a host of other industries. Problems arise, however, when we begin to interpret the terminology and apply the concepts in the service industries.

To address those problems this section examines how the Standard is applied in a variety of industries and organizations. The list of industries is not exhaustive, but indicates the range of organizations achieving registration and using the Standard to improve their operations. Each chapter shows how organizations in a particular sector interpret the Standard. They also illustrate the thinking behind the Standard. Comment is made on interpretations of specific elements of ISO 9000 which may be troublesome or noteworthy. A lack of comment on a particular element in a given industry indicates that it operates there in a straightforward way, with no need of further comment.

At the start of each section there is a guide as to which Procedure Guides of the Process Management Model are likely to apply to that industry. This is only a guide, since there is considerable variation within the generic industries. If a Procedure Guide is not indicated, it is unlikely to apply.

Contents

Chapter 14 ◆ Design and Manufacture of Discrete Products

(Applicable Procedure Guides 1–25)

ISO 9000 was developed around the requirements of designing and producing discrete products, such as a fastener, an automobile, or a piece of electrical equipment. It still applies with relative ease to such industries. Products may be mechanical, electrical or electronic, simple or complex. They may be the manufacture of single items, small batches, or mass production lines. It is, however, possible to identify the product at all stages of manufacture.

Complex machines often incorporate software, but when software is only part of the overall design, its specification, development, testing, and acceptance become part of the overall product design. Companies that only produce software for specific customers or the marketplace should refer to Chapter 28.

Appropriate Standard

The choice of standard in the manufacture of discrete products revolves around the responsibility for the design of the product. If design is included in the scope of registration then it is appropriate to use ISO 9001. The complexity of design has nothing to do with the choice. A company *making* complex machines to the customer's designs should use ISO 9002; a company *designing* simple toys should use ISO 9001.

Customer Contracts

The methods of marketing and selling of discrete products are nearly as diverse as the products themselves. The activities are well covered in the Procedure Guide on Inquiries/Orders. The only complexity arises in ensuring that the responsibilities for design are known.

The design function includes the responsibility for defining acceptance criteria. In some sectors of this industry, these are not well defined. Many subcontractors are not given clear requirements on the level of finish to be achieved and the associated tolerances in these levels. They are left to do the best they can and hope this meets the customers requirements. This is particularly true in industries such as printing, where there can be a subjective element in deciding what is acceptable. A clear definition benefits both the customer and supplier.

Design Control

Design can vary in complexity from the development of new aircraft to the design of a pair of scissors. In every case it is necessary to define the requirements of the design output and ensure that the process achieves them. The level of control in this process is determined by the risks involved, but the customers' requirements need to be considered at all stages.

Design control is required both for unique designs for specific customers and for the development of items for the company's range of products. In both of these instances the customer should be represented in the design review, although in the latter case, where there is no specific customer, this representation is usually the sales or marketing department.

It is important to include in the design process a definition of acceptance criteria. These may be simple tolerances or the detailed test specification on the performance of the products. Prototypes or models built to validate the design should be tested against the acceptance criteria.

Process Control

Most manufacturing companies have systems using route cards, or traveling documents, that accompany the products or parts through the processes. Usually there is a drawing, specification diagram, or instructions providing the details of what needs to be done. The operator acknowledges completion of an operation and verification of this as work progresses. These records provide the basic documentation necessary to meet the Standard's requirements pertaining to process control, product identification and traceability, inspection and testing, and inspection and test status. Keeping copies of this paperwork meets the requirements of Quality Records in manufacturing.

The control can be more complex in a mass production environment where it is often not possible to have documents traveling with the products. Records are needed to identify the product at all stages. These can be achieved by indicating the products currently on a transfer line.

Chapter 15 ◆ Textiles

(Applicable Procedure Guides: 1–13, 15–25)

The textile industry is very diverse, with manufacturing and service activities ranging from yarn production to high fashion design. Companies frequently subcontract much of the work to bleachers, dyers, or merchants who buy, process, and sell fabrics without ever setting eyes on them.

Appropriate Standard

The industry's wide array of activities can confuse companies that are choosing the appropriate ISO 9000 Standard to use. The answer usually revolves around how much design the company does. Do its customers define its products? Does it manufacture standard products to customer specifications? If the answer to these questions is yes, the company should register under ISO 9002. If the company *designs products to meet customer requirements,* or as part of its own product line, ISO 9001 is appropriate.

Customer Contracts

Historically, textile industry contracts or agreements have been somewhat casual, and often detailed specifications similar to those of other manufacturing businesses do not exist. This is a problem when a textile company seeks ISO 9000 registration. Textile companies sometimes have to develop new ways to describe and define their activities and services so that the customer can understand and agree to them. It is common in this industry for merchants to buy cloth that they never see and arrange to have it processed by a number of different subcontractors with no clear specifications for what is required at each stage. This creates complications for contract control.

Matching an organization's products with the customer's exact requirements may require considerable research for the company to meet ISO 9000 registration criteria. The organization must be able to reference its own specifications to national, international, or trade standards, and show that the products conform to those standards. Colors can be particularly hard to define. Buyer and seller should use samples to reach agreement on colors, and then preserve the samples for future reference.

Many textile companies adhere to long-established industry practices regarding the length of cloth on a roll and responsibility and acceptance of minor defects, joins, or snags. The industry also has standards for shrinkage during processing. Contracts should spell out these practices and standards.

When considering textile products, specifications need to be agreed on for the detailed requirements. These would typically include a definition of the threads to be used, the number of stitches per inch or centimeter on a seam, and the number of stitches retaining a button. Such specifications can be best done on a generic basis with, for instance, a specification for all shirts, and this specification can be referenced for a specific shirt.

Design Control

Any design work must be controlled under a design control procedure that will address the requirements of the ISO 9000 Standard. If there are technical features in the design, the procedure must consider any current standards and codes of practice. If the finished design has to pass particular tests, such as fire retardation testing, then the company should produce and test prototypes, with the results recorded.

In fashion, it is important to consider aesthetic features—with a means of confirming that the design specifications have been met. Storing samples and patterns from the initial design must include a means of inhibiting deterioration, particularly of color.

Purchasing

Textile companies often order items without the precise specifications required by ISO 9000 clauses on contract review and purchasing. Often a buyer may not have a specification, but may know that a particular product does just what is needed. Producers, however, usually have specifications, and the buyers may ask for them. Specifications should spell out acceptance and rejection criteria and perhaps even the means of verifying compliance.

Buyers often are subjective in their assessments of textile products, particularly those made of natural fibers. Buyer and seller need to clarify and formalize their subjective criteria, which can be complicated when they buy products through intermediaries or commodity markets. Assessing quality on this basis requires skill and experience on the part of the merchants or third parties. Once buyers develop confidence in them, however, those parties become approved suppliers.

Customer-Supplied Product

Customer-supplied product is often a major issue in textiles. Contract finishers working simultaneously with several customers' materials (in wet processes) require a foolproof system of identification. Labeling is impractical, but finishers may meet the ISO 9000 requirements by recording the material being processed by each machine or by use of indelible inks and ultraviolet-detectable marks.

Process Control

Work instructions, geared to the skill and training levels of the operators, will provide the process control mandated by ISO 9000. These instructions may simply be optimal settings on various machines. If the process includes chemicals, operators must establish and record temperatures, concentrations, and times. The definitions of many parameters and settings should be in a language that allows skilled operators to use them as a starting point, but allows some degree of freedom for the operators to adjust them in order to properly control the process.

Some textile processes, such as dying, are almost *mysterious arts,* with the dye master as the *guru* who senses when the dye mixture is just right. ISO 9000 requires companies to document formulas, which when required, a dye master can usually do. Controls are needed to monitor the concentrations and to meet the established levels. This demystifies the process and leads to less variation.

Like other products, textiles can have critical safety features, such as flame-retarding materials, which may require testing. Companies should not release the materials until they complete tests. As always, appropriate records should be kept.

Chapter 16 ◆ Building and Construction

(Applicable Procedure Guides: 1–25)

The building and construction industry has many features in common with the engineering industry. Controls used by an organization constructing buildings, plants, and such facilities are similar to those in engineering.

Appropriate Standard

In building and construction, architects and engineers handle the design, while the builder does the actual construction. A construction company with no architectural or engineering services should seek registration to ISO 9002. An architectural or engineering firm would seek registration to ISO 9001.

If a developer or builder takes responsibility for the design and construction of a building and subcontracts the design, then the builder should register to ISO 9001. The construction firm, however, would have to establish control of the design activity even though the process is subcontracted.

Customer Contracts

Contracts in the building industry vary from small jobs, such as replacing a door, to the construction of skyscrapers. Managers must control all contracts although the level of control may differ considerably.

Builders usually find it beneficial to have two procedures for business development: a simpler procedure for informal inquiries and a more extensive one for making bids on major projects. The construction company's employees can cover the informal inquiries by recording what the customer requires and the price quoted. Bidding on a large project necessitates creating a file that will grow until the company loses the bid or completes the project.

To confirm that their company has the capability to do the project, managers and project supervisors should visit the site and study all the requirements. For instance, assumptions on the ability to gain easy vehicle access could seriously affect the cost, and even the feasibility, of a contract.

Document Control

The organization should control all documents associated with the contract. The architect usually issues the drawings, and the construction managers receive enough copies to supply all involved personnel. A master copy stays in the office. From time to time, modified drawings will arrive. Builders should identify the modifications and give copies to all concerned, including subcontractors.

Purchasing

Purchasing tends to be an informal activity with small companies in the building industry, but it is essential to establish control. Written orders, mailed or transmitted by facsimile machine, are best. This is a particularly good idea when using subcontractors because it provides documented evidence of what service or product the customer wants.

Construction contractors need to approve their suppliers. Most purchases, such as windows and prefabricated joists, will come from distributors or a subcontractor for manufactured components. This makes the approval of subcontractors more important than purchasing standard building supplies. Managers should assess and monitor subcontractors continually. An initial evaluation through a trial order on a small, non-critical but closely supervised contract, is a good idea. The contractor should record the results and, if everything is satisfactory, follow the project with others until he or she feels confident with the subcontractor's performance.

Product identification in the building industry is generally provided either by visual identification, that is, sand, gravel, nails, etc., or by labels on items such as paint or cement. ISO 9000 considers these methods adequate, and the contractor's procedures should include them. If clients require traceability on a specific item or material, that should be treated as a special requirement and controlled separately.

Process Control

Skilled operators, carrying out and inspecting their own tasks, provide process control in construction. Supervisors, and sometimes a customer representative, inspect and may test the work as it progresses. ISO 9000 requires records of these inspections. The records may be simple indications on drawings or signing of work cards by the operators after they complete the work.

Work instructions are generally not required by skilled operators. It is not appropriate to prepare additional work instructions since drawings and the like meet the requirements. For critical work, however, like that in a special process such as mixing concrete, careful monitoring, and accurate records may be required. For instance, if the concrete requires tests, these should conform to a test work instruction done by a qualified employee or subcontractor.

Calibration

Most of the measuring equipment on a construction project is either self-calibrating (such as spirit level which is checked by turning it back on itself) or used in relatively low accuracy situations (such as a measuring tape). Low accuracy equipment should be checked visually for damage, but it is generally not necessary to calibrate it. Records of the checks, however, should be maintained.

Equipment used for special tests, such as the moisture content of wood or the strength of concrete, needs to be calibrated to national standards.

Final Inspection

Building industry practices usually involve the customer's inspection on completion, along with identifying punch or snag lists. Many of these are subjective interpretations of the requirement, but the inspect-and-fix ethos is endemic in the industry. The punch list becomes a record of inspection. There is, unfortunately, a perception that snags are inevitable. Management should analyze the information, not only act to fix the snags, but also reduce the likelihood that the same snag will occur on the next job. Seeking out corrective actions, after all, provides everyone with avenues for progress. It is better to work with the customer's representative as the work progresses than to try to inspect quality into the job at the end.

Chapter 17 ◆ Food Processors and Producers

(Applicable Procedure Guides: 1–13, 15–25)

Strict safety standards and comprehensive control are essential in the food industry. Food is handled by growers, middlemen, and processors and is often shipped hundreds or thousands of miles before being consumed. Food producers and processors find that ISO 9000 is a good way to show they have systems to prevent contamination or food poisoning.

Appropriate Standard

Most food companies have no design activities and would, therefore, register to ISO 9002. A company that develops food products, however, should register to ISO 9001.

Customer Contracts

Companies in the food industry must deliver what they say they can provide. Claims made in contracts, specifications, and advertising should be demonstrable. Special conditions of packing and delivery, such as temperature and life span of the product, should have written definitions. If the customer specifies or designs the product and packages it with its own name (often the case with retail chains), the agreement should define any deviations from the supplier's standard product.

Design Control

Companies that develop new products need to apply Procedure Guide Number 2. This requires them to clearly define the product to be designed, and specify the ingredients, the processing methods, and the final packaging materials. They need to include product tests and pilot marketing to validate the design. If the initial products are made under laboratory conditions, then the full production process must be validated.

Document Control

Document control should cover all specifications associated with the quality system, including packaging and artwork, which may include claims on the content or performance of the product. Also, the companies involved in the transaction should maintain copies of any state, federal, or local laws pertaining to the products. They must stay up to date on changes, of course.

Purchasing

Purchasing procedures should cover all supplies and services used in processing food. For instance, if water is a major part of the product (as in beer or soft drinks) the supply source becomes a control point. The use of external hygiene and pesticide services should be included in the supplier approval procedure.

The food industry routinely uses numbers to identify batches of products so they can be traced from the plant to the customer. They should also record batch numbers at delivery locations in order to facilitate product recall.

Traceability

In the food industry, possible contamination and the resulting need for product recall is ever present. It is essential to be able to isolate and locate a contaminated batch, with minimum cost. This is achieved by labeling each batch with a number and keeping records when the batch is produced. It may also be advisable to maintain records of the distributors or customers who take various batches.

The batch identity may be based on a coded number, or a date indicating the date of manufacture, the date by which the item should be sold, or the date by which it should be used. Each alternative has advantages and disadvantages. Each company makes its own decision, possibly in consultation with the distributors.

It is also advisable to retain samples from each batch so it can be tested in the event of a suspected problem. This can enable the suspect batch to be defined more clearly. The tighter the definition the less impact on customers and the company.

Some organizations bond the finished products while accelerated life tests are conducted on samples from the product, only releasing the batch when it has been cleared by tests. This is a solution that may be considered extreme if the risk and consequences of contamination is low.

It is generally considered necessary to have a procedure in place which defines the actions to be taken if contamination is suspected. It is easier for executive management to decide on the guidelines that will be followed before there is urgency or external pressures. If the contingency arises the procedure is automatically followed, even in the absence of the executive management.

Process Control

Process control in the food industry means that every aspect of food processing, including the environment, must be clean and maintained at a consistent temperature. Companies must set up, and adhere to, suitable facilities for storage, packing, handling, transportation, and the personal hygiene of employees.

The health of employees who come into contact with the product is critical. The organization needs to have clear procedures for controlling any contagious diseases and a procedure for the actions to be taken if staff members become infected. Plant design needs to ensure, and make clear, that there is minimal chance of contamination as workers cook or otherwise process the food. Documented procedures should also detail a safe, sanitary means of disposing of waste products.

A food company's quality system must provide for the avoidance of cross-contamination. One technique used to do this is a Hazard Analysis of Critical Control Points in which the whole process is carefully analyzed for potential danger of contamination. Then the operators must act to remove or reduce these hazards.

Hygiene levels should be determined by taking swabs and other analyses of food preparation surfaces and equipment. Due to delays in growing cultures, tests of this nature become part of internal service audits, as defined in Procedure Guide 18, to confirm the existence of the highest possible levels of hygiene.

Inspection and Tests

Inspections and tests in the food industry often rely on human senses of sight, smell, taste, and touch. Tests should be controlled through training and retraining (if necessary) the staff doing the tests. Photographs, descriptions, and reference to standard items can be used.

Calibration

Food companies should maintain a regular schedule for calibrating scales, volume meters, and thermometers used for cooking or storage.

Packaged food includes minimum or average weights, which companies must verify and statistically demonstrate. These weights also should comply with industry standards or legal codes.

Stock Control

Supervisors should exert tight control over stock rotation, maximum storage times, temperatures, and cleanliness in storing raw material and finished products. Temperature and time also are critical in transportation. Food company procedures must include contingency plans for breakdowns of refrigeration systems or vehicles. They also must segregate and dispose of any nonconforming product after thorough consideration of hygiene or other safety factors.

Training

Anyone who comes into contact with food must have documented hygiene training.

Chapter 18 ◆ Chemical and Process Industries

(Applicable Procedure Guides: 1–11, 15–25)

Processing chemicals is a major industry across the globe. Thousands of organizations develop, process, buy, sell, and distribute massive quantities of petroleum-based products, pharmaceuticals, gases, and other products every day.

Appropriate Standard

Chemical companies must first decide whether their activities are covered by ISO 9002 or ISO 9001. Many chemical companies research and develop new products, but these activities often occur in remote research centers far from operating plants. The processing plants should each seek registration to ISO 9002, while facilities with research and development laboratories should pursue ISO 9001. There are also organizations producing chemicals defined by nature, or with established formulas, thus not requiring design. In such cases ISO 9002 is appropriate.

Remote operations are a common feature in the chemical industry. Many clauses of ISO 9000 which pertain to processing may not be pertinent to every plant of a given organization. For example, sales and purchasing functions for several plants may be centralized. In this case, a good strategy is to seek separate registration for each plant and for the central services. Registrars will accept this approach provided the separation is real and the organization plans to address all the parts of the operation.

Customer Contracts

Chemical products have sales literature, and these documents must be correct. Organizations should define the acceptance criteria for chemical products and details pertaining to safety and usage. They should also describe methods for packaging and delivery, including how to measure chemicals flowing through pipelines. These documents form the basis for formal contracts with customers.

Arrangements can become complicated, with companies processing their customers' products for them or swapping products. In such cases it becomes difficult to differentiate between the customer and the supplier. The respective positions must be defined and controlled to meet the ISO 9000 requirements.

Contracts may provide for a formal schedule of usage or informal requests for deliveries. Both means are acceptable and are covered by the Process Management Model.

Contracts involving traceability should consider whether a high degree of traceability is justified.

Design Control

If a company develops products, it must control product and process research and development. This could include developing prototype plants to manufacture new products, since products in the chemical and process industries are often closely tied to these plants.

Purchasing

Purchasing should cover all suppliers and subcontractors, who must be assessed and approved. If the plant uses process water, it may need to agree with the supplier, probably the local municipal water authority, on the purity standard for water and a method to monitor it. If the company has its own source of water, such as a well, then there is no supplier, but a method of controlling the purity would still be necessary.

Customer-Supplied Product

Products processed for customers through subcontracts may be difficult to track through a pipeline or other delivery method. Procedures must state what happens and how it is controlled. The specific yield and quality of the products should be fully documented and reported to the customer.

Similar disciplines should be followed when processing material for several customers. The processing company must demonstrate to its customer that it has processed—and returned—the materials put into its care.

Process Control

Producers and customers alike often cannot see the product being processed, making product identification difficult. Companies should address this by labeling the tanks and pipes. Labeling on different batches processed through a plant can be updated as the batches change.

Many companies make several different products within the same plant, sometimes running one batch into another. During the changeover process, there is typically some waste which should be recorded and controlled.

Traceability may be a contractual requirement, further complicating the identification process. Total traceability requires that holding tanks be drained and cleaned before introducing the next batch.

Two levels of work instruction are advisable. The first level covers the data sheets and settings required to produce the various products. The second level covers startup and shutdown procedures, preventive maintenance, and instrumentation and control procedures.

The chemical industry uses many special processes, creating a need to record the results of inspections, tests, and settings used during a process. These usually go into the plant's log books—or automatically show up on chart recorders.

The organization or plant should have up-to-date records of its operators' skills and training.

Once a bulk-processed chemical enters distribution channels, it may be difficult to isolate, making prior inspection and testing critical. For instance, when material comes in from a supplier, or from another process, and goes into a tank or silo with other similar material, its identity is lost. In the event one of the materials is contaminated, recovering the untainted material would be difficult, expensive, and perhaps even impossible. That makes it vital to ensure that the two materials conform before mixing occurs. This may require the use of holding tanks or silos where material can be temporarily stored while operators perform inspections or tests. When dealing with suppliers, it is a good practice to make the supplier hold the material until it has been cleared.

This principle applies at all stages of processing. At final inspection and test, the procedures should ensure that no material leaves the plant until the requirements are fully met. This is not always easy to do, since some tests take time or may require special procedures or specialist staff who may not be immediately available. Chemical and process organizations frequently operate continually on a 24-hour cycle, and delays are expensive.

Calibration

Chemical and process industries generally need considerable instrumentation and associated calibration to ensure quality. There are a number of things to consider relative to what needs to be calibrated, and where:

1. The nature and degree of use of the instrument;
2. The accuracy of the measurement; and
3. The stability of the measuring device.

Here is a basic guideline. If an instrument gives readings related to a specification, calibration should establish an accuracy level of approximately 10 percent of the tolerance of the value being measured. For example, measuring temperature to the nearest ten degrees would suggest a temperature measuring device accurate to one degree. If the reading can be replaced by a description, such as hot or cold, and the setting is then dictated by the performance of the plant's climate controls, no calibration is required.

Nonconforming Product

Operators must identify and segregate nonconforming material immediately upon detection. Often chemical and process industries have no opportunity to rework nonconforming material, but it may be possible to blend a small amount with good material. Managers and supervisors must take care to authorize, record, and control any such blending activities. If the resulting blend meets specifications, there is no need to inform the customer. Any blend outside specifications requires a concession, however, and the customer's agreement.

Stock Control

Handling chemicals may be hazardous. Safe, secure handling practices must be documented and established. These need to take into account legislation and professional codes of practice. They should also define how to prevent contamination. These procedures also extend to the work of subcontractors.

Storage should suit the products and materials being stored, (including shelf life). This is particularly important when products are stored in contract warehouses not controlled by the company. Operators should ensure that the temperatures and other storage conditions are correct for the stored materials.

Packaging should protect the product and whoever handles it. The presence of hazardous chemicals should be clearly signaled in languages used in the locations where the products are to be sold. The batch or lot numbers should be marked on the packages.

Managers must ensure that their delivery agents can meet customer requirements and handle the products safely. This may necessitate specialized delivery vehicles which then must be cleaned to prevent contamination. Managers or supervisors should ensure that any customer requests for special couplings or fittings on the delivery vehicles are met.

Pipelines require procedures for maintenance and statements naming who is responsible for the pipeline.

Statistical Techniques

Statistical Process Control is widely used in the process and chemical industries. Indeed, this is the optimum method for controlling the processes. Operators should measure not only product characteristics, but also the key processing parameters. The effective use of statistical process control not only allows a process to be controlled, but it also results in the continual improvement of both process and product.

Chapter 19 ◆ Transportation

(Applicable Procedure Guides: 1, 3–11, 15–25)

Total quality involves meeting needs and expectations, from the designer's original idea to the consumer's use of the product. That includes transporting the product to the point of sale or use. Transportation companies are included in the quality chain and many have sought registration to ISO 9000.

Customer Contracts

Since most organizations require transportation services, industry practice is to have a formal written contract for a defined period of time. Subsequent individual orders for specific deliveries are based on the contract.

Contracts must fully define the extent of the service and any limitations on the hauler's liability in the event of mishaps. Insurance covers damage to the goods, but a customer's losses due to late delivery are handled through contract and negotiation. Other concerns, such as waiting time for goods not ready for shipment or loading, or problems at the delivery point, also require definition.

Procedures should be set up in advance, with customer approval, to handle emergencies with hazardous chemicals or items requiring special temperatures or other environmental conditions. Both parties should know what to do when problems arise. The agreement should state whether the transportation company takes responsibility for such situations. It should define potential compensation issues.

Document Control

ISO 9000 provisions for document control pertain to the company's quality system documents and other laws or regulations. Transportation companies should publish a handbook for drivers, defining their responsibilities.

Drivers should have names, addresses and directions to the delivery points of all regular customers. Route planning (incorporating road repair and other possible delays), should be part of the drivers' information. Giving the delivery drivers clear maps and directions for pick-up and delivery sites can improve the efficiency of the service. It also provides a visible indication of how a good system should work.

If any of these documentation efforts are formal documents, the organization should create a system of periodically updating and replacing them.

Purchasing

Subcontractors who are used to augment the transportation company's own drivers and vehicles must be included in the supplier assessment system. The subcontracted drivers are subject to the same controls as the company's regular drivers, including updated records of their training. Subcontracted services may also include vehicle maintenance and hauling services, training, cleaning, and cargo handling.

Contracts or other purchase documentation should provide the details of what is required in clear, unambiguous language. In practice, an order or contract may define the general conditions of the agreement and this is supplemented when the order for specific service is made.

Customer-Supplied Product

Since transportation companies transport customers' goods, the Control of Customer-Supplied Product clause is important to successful ISO 9000 registration. Trucking companies are clearly responsible for maintaining and delivering goods in the same condition they receive them. For perishable products, they must understand and agree with their customers on the requirements and demonstrate that they have been met. Transporting bulk commodities may involve some shrinkage. The hauler must demonstrate that predetermined shrinkage levels are not exceeded. Transportation companies must also account for returnable pallets and other returnable packing material.

There should also be a mechanism for informing the customer and taking corrective action when someone finds defects or damage to the customer's goods.

The ISO 9000 Standard requires a transportation company to maintain identification and traceability of the customer's goods. The company must keep records of which vehicles and drivers were used to move a particular shipment.

Process Control

Process control covers the preparation, pickup, transport, storage, and delivery of goods. It should include emergency procedures, handling hazardous substances, temperature control, maintenance procedures, and special cleaning of vehicles used to carry goods that might be contaminated.

Inspecting and testing vehicles is part of any transportation business, and as such, automatically falls into its quality system. The same goes for periodical checks during delivery to make sure a shipment has incurred no damage. Any time loads approach the maximum axle weight or overall allowable weight of the vehicle, the whole truck should be weighed before leaving and again at highway weight stations. If weather conditions can result in an increase in the weight of the load being carried, the ramifications must be taken into account. If the load is over the maximum allowable weight, action must be taken and recorded immediately. Such records would be crucial in defending the company if it were later accused of carrying an unsafe load.

Calibration

Truck scales, pressure gauges, temperature equipment, speedometers, tachometers, and other speed-recording equipment also require calibration. Speedometers are calibrated to assist drivers in traveling at a safe, legal speed. Prosecutions resulting from inadequate calibration may affect the organization's ability to maintain a good team of drivers.

Maintenance

Any faults found on vehicles should be recorded properly, according to the maintenance procedure guide. Responsibility for finding the faults may belong to drivers or to management, depending on the type of problem. But everyone concerned must be informed. Both drivers and managers should have guidelines for determining when a malfunction will affect the safety of the vehicle. They should have a mechanism that quarantines the vehicle until the problem is solved.

Stock Control

Material handling procedures should detail all aspects of safe loading, unloading, and securing of the shipment. This can be provided by including in the Driver Handbook a series of work instructions covering the type of goods normally carried by the company. They should include any products requiring special handling. The instructions should mention laws and regulations pertaining to certain types of loads. The handbook must, of course, conform with the regulations.

The instructions also should include the customer's requirements on storage, segregation of products, orientation, how items can be stacked, or other conditions. Packages should be marked accordingly, either by the customer or the shipper.

Work instructions should cover the handling of shipments with high value or which are otherwise subject to theft. The instructions should advise the driver on parking and related procedures if the driver must leave the vehicle unattended. They must mention any security devices or procedures. The instructions themselves should be secured.

Training

Employee records should include all driver training and licensing information. Companies handling hazardous material must be particularly careful to train drivers in handling the material. They must keep records proving the training occurred.

Chapter 20 ◆ Distributors, Wholesalers, Stockists, Retailers

(Applicable Procedure Guides: 1, 3–5, 7–12, 15–23, 25)

Wholesalers, stockists, retailers, and distributors are all descriptions of companies whose role is to keep goods in stock until they deliver them to a retailer, customer, or dealer. They rarely change the product, and their scope sometimes includes delivery. These are referred to as *distributors* in this chapter.

Appropriate Standard

Under this definition, the distributor performs no process on the product, other than to possibly repack it or subdivide it into smaller lots. A steel distributor might cut steel for a customer, or a sand distributor might buy it in bulk and sell it in bags. These are minor processes which make no significant change in the product. Distributors apply for registration to ISO 9002.

Traceability

There are two types of distributors covered by ISO 9000 requirements—those who supply products with traceability, and those who do not. This does not suggest a hierarchy among distributors. The distinction is made because some customers require products that are traceable to the manufacturer. A good example would be the steel market. Customers often purchase special grades of steel requiring certificates noting the content and properties of the steel. For the certificates to be meaningful, the steel distributor must have a system to identify which steel goes with which certificate. The ability to accurately identify a batch of steel is batch traceability. It requires positive identification of each batch, not just the type of steel.

Other examples of traceability on discrete products involve the recording of the serial numbers of the products.

Whether the distributor must maintain traceability depends on the nature of the products being stocked or the customers being supplied. The ISO 9000 certificate and registration mark, however, specify whether the distributor provides traceability. This provides guidance for potential customers who require traceability.

Customer Contracts

There are no special requirements for contract review. Orders may be received verbally, recorded, and confirmed with the customer. Before accepting the order, the distributor must confirm that the product can be supplied. This implies a stock control system with information available to the person taking the order, although the Standard does not explicitly require it.

Some distributors have retail-like facilities that allow the customer to select an item from stock and present it for payment. Under these circumstances, stock information is not required since the customer can see, or can determine by inquiry, that an item is out of stock.

Where bulk items are sold by the bag, with possible inference on the weight of the product, then the true position must be clearly defined. For instance, sand may be sold by hundredweight, or 50 kilo bags, but unless these are weighed, it should be made clear that the contract is for so many bags—not so many hundredweight or kilograms.

Document Control

Document control extends to catalogs, data sheets, price lists, and other sources of information relating to the distributor's products. In many cases these documents are produced by manufacturers, and the distributor merely has to ensure that the catalog relates to the models currently in stock. Any time such literature is used, there must be a way to verify the accuracy of the data and authorize and control issue levels and modifications.

Assured Sources

Since distributors supply goods under an assured system, they are required to distinguish between items provided by companies registered to ISO 9000 and non-registered companies. Customers must be informed, when they order an item, if it comes from a non-approved source. Distributors may achieve this by a standard note on all documentation given to the customer.

The exception to this occurs when a customer requests a specific brand name. In these circumstances it is assumed that the customer has selected the supplier, regardless of whether the source is registered.

The distributor should provide, at the time of purchase, the full technical details of the items being ordered, including the packaging, delivery time, and any certification, test results, or other documentation required. If the customer requires traceability, this too should be stated at purchase.

The distributors must have a method for identification of all items in their inventory. They must also be able to trace back to the supplier all items in their inventory. They can usually do this by using the suppliers' own markings or labeling. In most cases, there is no need to introduce an additional procedure.

Process Control

Distributors have no significant manufacturing processes, but should have documented work instructions covering any dividing, combining, and repackaging activities that occur.

A policy for verifying goods on receipt should be carefully defined. In practice, when items come from approved suppliers, the only checks needed should confirm that there are no visible signs of damage and that the quantities are correct. Such a policy will meet ISO 9000 requirements, if it is in the documented quality system. Generic inspection plans for different types of products are generally appropriate.

Procedures should address situations in which the distributor arranges for goods to go directly from the supplier to the customer—without passing through the distributor's warehouse. There needs to be some confirmation, possibly by the customer or by occasional audits, that the items have been delivered in acceptable condition and are what the customer ordered.

Calibration

A distributor's calibration system only needs to include inspection and the test equipment used to assess the items being supplied. If goods are sold by weight, volume, or length, the accuracy of the equipment must be demonstrated. If the measurements are only for large tolerances, that is, the length of electrical cable, then a visual check of the tape measure or scale would be adequate. There must be records of such checks.

Control of Nonconforming Items

Items found to be out of specification must be identified, or segregated and disposed of. Disposal may include scrapping, reclassification, selling them as substandard (in an approved manner), or returning them to the supplier. Records must show what the disposition was. Since a distributor, by definition, has no manufacturing capability, distributors do not rework damaged goods, although they may subcontract for such work.

Stock Control

Storage and packaging should preserve product quality and prevent damage or deterioration. This may include temperature and/or humidity control. Items with a limited shelf life must be controlled to ensure the rotation of stock and prevent out-of-date stock being sold.

Chapter 21 ◆ Professional Services

(Applicable Procedure Guides: 1–4, 6–8, 11, 16–22, 24)

This chapter covers professional service providers, such as accountants, lawyers, and engineers. Although consultants are used as examples, many of the comments apply to these other businesses.

Appropriate Standard

There are two key factors in deciding whether a consulting firm should seek registration to ISO 9001 or ISO 9002.

First, consider whether the company is responsible for the finished design it produces. If the consultants use their skills and experience to advise a client on the design of a system or product, but the client is free to reject the advice and alter the design, the consultant is not the design authority. This would be covered under process control and ISO 9002 would be appropriate. If the consultant takes full responsibility for the design (including for example, stress calculations) and the client requires the consultant to evaluate any change in the design, then the consultant is responsible for the design. Design control is necessary and registration to ISO 9001 would be appropriate.

Second, consider whether the consulting organization uses a defined methodology in its work. If the consulting firm designs a methodology, proves it, and controls any modifications to it, control of the methodology or design is required. So ISO 9001 would be appropriate. The definition of methodology should include established training processes used by the consulting firm. Any new or modified methodologies and training programs that are customized or developed for clients must be controlled under the design control procedure.

Customer Contracts

Contract review presents a critical stage in a client relationship. Consultants must clearly define the work they are expected to do. This can be stated in terms of tasks to be done or results to be achieved. It is essential to define all terms and conditions relating to the contract. Consultants should check written orders upon receipt to ensure that none of the terms have changed.

Consultants making a proposal for a project should first confirm that they have the capability to complete the project. This should happen before accepting the order. In cases when the work is straightforward, the person handling the sale may confirm the company's ability to perform. In the event of unique elements or a large contract, however, a senior member of the firm should review it.

Purchasing

Purchased items may have little or no impact on the service being offered, in which case purchasing procedures will not be needed.

Supplier approval needs to be addressed in cases when the consulting firm subcontracts work to other professionals or service organizations. In such cases an assessment of the subcontractors is critical to the quality of the service. The assessment must be formally documented and based on the work actually to be done. The extent to which the subcontractors must follow the organization's own control systems should be carefully considered. A method of control should be established.

Customer-Supplied Product

ISO 9000's Customer-Supplied Product clause pertains to any temporary accommodation provided to the consultant while working for the client. The amount of time the consultant uses an office or other accommodation must align with the length of the project.

The parties should address the security of any information provided by the client to the consultant. The consultant should treat any such information as confidential and control the files carefully.

Product identification also applies to consultants, who must be able to identify the status of a project at any stage. A project file in which the status is kept current is a good means of doing this. Relevant correspondence, minutes of meetings, and any reports relating to the project should go in the file so that the status is apparent to others (usually a colleague not working on the project but aware of operating procedures) at any time. This method of recording and control meets any requirements for tracing who worked on the project at various times.

Process Control

The level of work instructions necessary to meet the requirements of process control is minimal. Consultants are, by their nature, experts in their respective fields. Project control means defining areas of responsibility, project planning, and review of progress. The procedure needs to state that the assigned personnel will work in accordance with the terms agreed to by the client, and that management will review the progress of the project.

An independent assessment of the service provided is useful in establishing customer satisfaction. This is usually done by reviewing the status of the project with the client at critical milestones, near the midpoint, and at the conclusion. This provides a means for identifying any need for corrective action.

Due to their professional competence, consultants may carry out their own inspection or test activities and record the results. As with other types of operations, any evidence that objectives have not been achieved should prompt necessary action to achieve them. Inspections and test status is useful to allow an examiner to know the status of the work.

Calibration

It is unlikely that management consultants will use inspection, measuring, and test equipment in their work, and therefore unlikely that they will have to address this part of the Standard. Engineering firms and consultants, however, use measuring devices which may have to be calibrated.

Corrective Action

ISO 9000's clause on control of nonconforming product applies to consultants and their work. We interpret this to mean instances when the service falls short of the requirements. When this occurs, action is necessary to ensure that the client is inconvenienced as little as possible. It may be that the original objectives are no longer achievable, and the consultant should ask the client if another set of objectives will suffice.

Consultants should take corrective action whenever the level of service falls below the requirements. In practice this is not a common occurrence, but when it occurs, the consultant should make clear to the client what he intends to do.

Chapter 22 ◆ Employment Agencies

(Applicable Procedure Guides: 1, 3, 4, 7, 8, 11, 15–22, 24)

Employment agencies and recruiters—or headhunters, as they are often called, provide a service to industry. We find that organizations seeking registration to ISO 9000 frequently use agencies to fill vacancies. In the United Kingdom this has led many such organizations to seek registration for themselves and there is little doubt that this pattern will be repeated in other countries.

Appropriate Standard

To determine whether an agency should seek registration to ISO 9001 or ISO 9002, it is necessary to ask if the service includes any design. This might be the case if the agency designs advertising campaigns for a client, but normally, employment agencies are covered by ISO 9002.

Customer Contracts

A signed contract is the initial key event in the service. At the outset the agency must record and confirm the client's requirements and make sure the client knows what the service includes. This may be accomplished by standardizing and defining the different levels of service available. In the case of different levels, the contract must clearly state what service the client agreed to accept.

The terms and conditions of the contract should be fully documented, including the amounts and timing of payments, and special situations—such as when the vacancy is not filled by the agency, or the recruited person leaves after a short period. Any continuing relationships between the client and the recruiting company must also be defined.

If the company quotes service fees, it must ensure that the orders subsequently received are consistent with the original quotation. The agency should discuss and resolve any differences with the client. This is particularly important if the client sends an order on its own standard form, with terms and conditions printed on the back. These terms-and-conditions statements are usually formulated with the supply of goods in mind, so they may not adequately relate to the agency's services and terms.

Agencies having long-term relationships with clients do not need to define the work in each contract. They may have instead, a blanket contract, which should be reviewed with the client on a regular basis.

On some occasions, an agency may need to check out a client or prospective employee. There are instances of people taking advantage of employment agencies for nefarious purposes. The agency's reputation can suffer enormous damage from this, and more importantly, the safety of the candidate or temporary employee could be compromised.

Any specific design functions done by the agency for the client, such as advertising campaigns, follow the normal disciplines of design control.

The agency should have document control procedures for its documented quality system. This should include all pertinent legislation and any applicable professional codes of practice. If the organization uses any type of data base, either software or hardware, it must be controlled.

Purchasing

The primary purchased service may be advertising. Purchasing procedures should provide control and approval of these services.

When subcontractors are used to perform some of its services, perhaps those in distant cities, the subcontractor must be assessed and approved. Their subsequent performance should be monitored.

Verifying information provided by candidates is a vital function. The client relies on the agency's advice in making a selection, and the agency's reputation rests on providing accurate information. Documents presented by the candidate and information from references are suitable sources. In cases of high level positions, or those involving security or other sensitive work, the agency may have to investigate the candidate—including interviews of family and friends. The client contract should clearly define the procedure in such cases.

Customer-Supplied Product

Customer-supplied product, a key area of any professional service, relates to information provided by the client. It requires precautions to ensure security and absolute confidentiality.

The actual control of the recruitment process, the associated product identification, traceability, inspection, and test requirements are fundamentally the same as those applying to professional services (Chapter 21).

Calibration

Agencies who use tests in a selection process may come under ISO 9000's requirements for control of inspection, measuring, and test equipment. They must have a documented method of qualifying such tests and instructions on how to conduct the tests. The agency must also define qualifications of staff who conduct tests and make assessments associated with the tests. Anytime the tests are psychologically based, interpreting the results will probably require qualified psychologists.

Data Control

A recruiting agency's records are clearly an important asset, especially those of candidates who were unsuccessful but hold promise for future opportunities. The records should be carefully stored and cross referenced, since they may facilitate placing a candidate later.

Retaining records on successful candidates is also a standard practice. Confirming that the candidate has settled into the new position can be a good idea, but must be handled in a diplomatic manner which does not disturb either the candidate or client. No agency's quality policy is well served by recruiting candidates who have just been placed.

Statistical Techniques

Various types of statistical data on the placement of candidates, dropout rates, time taken to fill vacancies, and many other aspects of the work of the agency will be valuable to the recruiting company. The statistical techniques should be included as part of the quality system. Any statistical techniques used in assessing candidates should also be described.

Chapter 23 ◆ Commercial and Industrial Training

(Applicable Procedure Guides: 1–4, 6–8, 11, 15–24)

Rapidly changing technology and the need to improve service to customers have made training imperative for organizations seeking to get ahead—or even keep up. Managers who once saw training as a necessary burden now see it as a competitive edge. Consumers also see continuing education as a requirement of modern life, as witnessed by the proliferation of self-help books and well-attended seminars on many topics. Companies selling major products, such as industrial machinery or computer software, often accompany the sale with an offer of training.

Commercial and industrial training organizations form a major industry, providing services to a wide range of organizations and individuals with very different, though related, requirements. Successful training often begets the need for more training and assistance in determining the training needs of the organization or the individual.

Appropriate Standard

Which ISO 9000 Standard is appropriate to a training organization depends on the extent to which that organization designs its own courses. If standard, predefined courses with little variation are offered, ISO 9002 should cover the activities. If the courses receive periodic redesign and updating to meet changing demands, or tailoring to meet specific customer requirements, registration to ISO 9001 would be more appropriate.

Customer Contracts

The Standard's contract review clauses require companies to define their training product and service, either as an outline of the course content, or in the form of an expected outcome. If the training leads to qualifying the organization or person, for some activity or level of expertise, the parties should define the goal and the course entry requirements.

The contract should state what the course offers, what it costs, hours of attendance, and number of participants allowed. The training providers should also inform the company what meals, refreshments, and/or accommodations come with the course so the attendees will have all the details.

Accepting a contract for customized training requires a review to ensure that the training organization has the capability to develop and deliver a suitable course within the required time frame. For public courses, planners should monitor the number of available spaces in order to preclude the possibility of overbooking.

Design Control

If the organization designs its own training courses, the procedure should cover planning activities, definition of the design stages, design review, provision for a pilot program, allocation of necessary resources, and evaluation materials used to validate the course and its use. The design output must contain all documents needed to teach the course and the tests used to evaluate its effectiveness.

Document Control

Companies must control course materials. This means they must indicate the issue or revision level, updates, other modifications, and formally distribute them, with instructions to return or destroy old versions. The documentation required for course presenters will depend on their experience and the nature of the course.

Any external regulations or guidelines relating to course material or training methods, either upcoming or already in use, must also be controlled. This includes manuals on equipment, software, the documented quality system, governmental regulations, and flyers or brochures advertising the training provided.

Purchasing

Purchasing is not usually a major issue for training organizations. Their suppliers are usually printers, subcontractors, and hotels or meeting centers which provide training facilities. Organizations should carefully assess any subcontractors who deliver training, both before and during their work.

Companies must also examine nearby sites used for courses, but this can be handled by examining documentation pertaining to those facilities. Managers should review the facility's services after use, with corrective action if the requirements were not met.

If freelance or self-employed staff are used, they must be treated as suppliers and subject to a supplier approval.

Customer-Supplied Product

Customer-supplied product may be pertinent if a client provides materials or facilities for the training. This is most likely when training is conducted on the client's premises. Equipment checks, before and after training, are essential, with a prompt report to the client if any of the equipment fails to work properly.

Trainers often find themselves obtaining confidential information belonging to a client. ISO 9000 considers such information to be customer-supplied, requiring total confidentiality. This can be an issue when it comes to disclosing student performance and results of assessments and attendance. Before any information changes hands, trainers should establish an understanding regarding confidentiality.

Process Control

Trainers providing extensive courses should maintain records so they can readily report what training occurred. A training log will usually suffice. Trainees often produce work intended to be returned to their managers or used to assess the training. Training companies should have a means of identifying the work so the details will be obvious to the trainee and their manager.

The training delivery also requires planning and control. The trainers should teach on a level of instruction commensurate with their level of expertise. The company's documentation should define the training aids which are to be used.

Companies should control participant assessment in accordance with ISO 9000 procedures. An assessment may come before acceptance to the course, during the course, and/or at completion. Assessments may be informative with feedback provided as necessary. Assessment results should be recorded.

The assessments may be accompanied by certificates of attendance and performance. Written assessments may need to be qualified to ensure their validity.

Calibration

Companies should calibrate any inspection or test equipment used for training to ensure it is sufficiently accurate to handle the course demands. They also need to verify the software and courseware that they develop. There is no need to verify commercial software packages.

Corrective Action

When participants fall short of assessment requirements, managers should consider additional training. If many of the participants fail, companies should consider redesigning the content or delivery of the training.

Records

Keeping records of training is important for a training company. Participants often lose certificates or other records of what they learned, and they expect the trainer to have such records. Often this need is identified when they are applying for promotion, or a new job, or otherwise need documentary evidence of the training. Thirty or forty years is a reasonable retention time, since careers span that time frame. Computer storage is ideal, but retrievability could be an issue with software changing so rapidly. It is always a good idea to retain paper copies as well.

Training

Maintaining a high degree of expertise among the trainers is also crucial. The trainers must not only know their material, they must be able to present it well. Contracted staff, used for absent regular staff or for overflow work, must have the same qualifications as regular staff. Contracted trainers also must go through an induction program to acquaint them with safety issues, company policies and knowledge of the training company's quality system. The contract trainers must maintain the same kind of record keeping, teaching standards, and assessments as the permanent staff.

Statistical Techniques

Many training organizations use statistical techniques to monitor the overall performance of course and student performance. The techniques used must be appropriate for the data obtained, and they need to be built into the documented quality system.

Chapter 24 ◆ Automobile Sales and Service

(Applicable Procedure Guides: 1, 3–12, 15–25)

Auto dealerships typically consist of several closely related, but independently-operated, business units. The units include new vehicle sales, used vehicle sales and purchase, financial services, rentals, parts sales, mechanical services, and sometimes a body shop. To the consumer, the differences in these units seem negligible, but their operations are quite separate from each other. The distinctions between them become more visible when we consider the contract review requirements of ISO 9000.

Customer Contracts

Dealers usually sell new cars to individuals or organizations at fixed prices (with some negotiation) and perhaps with discounts. The manufacturer usually sets the terms and conditions. The customer and the sales agent come to terms once the dealer establishes that he can get the car the customer wants. The dealer also must ensure that the car is the model described in the literature given to the customer. The sales contract should clearly define any extras ordered by the customer.

The deal becomes more complex if the customer asks for a loan. The dealership, acting as an agent for the finance agency, has to check the customer's credit record and may provide advice on the best method of payment. The terms must be clear to the customer. The dealer's procedures must incorporate all instructions from the finance agency.

The deal takes yet another turn when the customer wants to trade in a vehicle. The dealer must assess the value of the used vehicle, quote the buyer a trade-in price, and provide an agreement in writing. There should be controlled price guidelines, based on age and condition of used vehicles. The dealer should define how long the quoted price will stand. If the transaction is set for completion later, the agreement should spell out anticipated mileage and deterioration. It is also essential to record the condition of the car and for the customer to indicate agreement about the condition. Some customers find it tempting to switch items, such as tires, after the assessment, and the agreement should preclude this possibility. The dealer should have a policy for re-assessing the vehicle when it is turned in.

Parts Department

The parts department is almost a separate business. Sales of parts to the dealership's service department or body shop is almost the same as to an outside customer. Customers—internal or external—seeking parts often require advice. The dealer has a system to identify the required parts, which are usually sold at fixed prices, but may be discounted. Personnel should identify after-market parts when the customer places the order, and offer to obtain parts from the original manufacturer if the customer prefers. The parts department also must say when urgently needed parts may be expected to arrive—if they are not immediately available.

Most auto dealers, particularly the large ones, receive orders for parts by telephone, with delivery by the supplier or pickup by the dealer. Control of such transactions should be included in the procedures.

Servicing and Repair

Customers rely heavily on the dealer, or the manufacturer, to define what services come with warranties or other contracts for service. There must be procedures to cover what happens when additions to the standard service become necessary. If additional costs arise, the service department contacts the customer for consent before doing the work.

Reliance on the dealer is even higher when body repairs are done. The contract may become more complicated by the need to have the approval of the insurance company who pays for it. In effect, the dealer has two related customers, the owner of the car and the insurance company. Insurance companies often have defined procedures for approving work on a car, and these need to be referenced from the procedures. Any time there are alternative methods of repair, for instance repairing a panel or replacing it, the customer must be made aware of the alternatives and agree to the chosen method.

Document Control

Document control is a major issue with dealerships, particularly if they provide service and body work. The shops require service information on current as well as older vehicles. This means keeping up a continually growing set of service manuals, since few of them ever become totally obsolete. Today's dealerships, usually equipped with computers and microfiche files, have ready access to large amounts of information.

These files, other paper documents, and sales literature on new vehicles must also be controlled. This causes some problems, since manufacturers regularly change the options they offer, and dealers may be hard pressed to keep up-to-date literature. When a customer reads a piece of literature listing certain features, the vehicle is expected to have those features.

Purchasing

Unlike other features of ISO 9000, purchasing is less challenging for auto dealers. The vast majority of their purchases, apart from used cars, are from the manufacturers whose franchise they hold. These manufacturers are approved suppliers. They define in detail the method of ordering new vehicles and parts. Typically, some form of computer system is used, and orders are by unambiguous part numbers. The related manuals can be referenced in the procedures.

Auto dealerships also buy specialist services such as tire fitting, calibration, crankshaft regrinders, delivery services, windshield installers, and supplies such as hoses and light bulbs. They may become approved suppliers based on their past performance and continual monitoring. Other suppliers to auto dealers include sellers of used vehicles as mentioned above.

Purchasing used vehicles, whether for cash or trade-in value, falls under the purchasing requirements of the Standard. Obviously, individuals within the general public cannot be approved suppliers. Therefore, ISO 9000 requires the dealer to make sure the vehicle is owned by the seller, carries no outstanding debts, and has accurate odometer readings. To achieve this the dealer may use pre-approved agencies to perform checks on the vehicle.

Used car sales differ from new car sales, since the condition of the vehicle is assessed by the customer. Some dealers provide independent reports on the vehicle's condition, and may have it serviced prior to display for sale. Used car warranties, when they exist, must be clearly defined. Registration to ISO 9000 really benefits the dealer here, since these requirements raise the dealership's credibility.

Customer-Supplied Product

Service and body shop activities which center on the customer's vehicle falls under the Standard's clauses on customer-supplied product. Staff should inspect the vehicle when it comes in, preserve its condition during service and storage, and verify its condition with the customer on completion. Dealers are not responsible for the overall condition of the vehicle, but they are responsible for maintaining its condition while it is in their care.

There is always a danger in repair shops that a part removed from one vehicle during service could inadvertently be fitted to another, similar vehicle. Dealer service departments must have a system to prevent this. Small items should be placed in labeled containers; larger items marked with the vehicle number.

Stock Control

Identification of parts is not a major challenge. Most automotive parts are clearly marked with numbers. This makes the dealer's job easier, and the system should make use of those numbers.

Dealers must be able to trace parts covered by warranties. Employees should make a record of serial numbers on such parts when they are installed.

For safety, dealers should define the methods for handling and storing chemicals. The storage facilities should prevent damage, particularly with glass and body panels. The Standard requires careful monitoring of parts with limited, well-defined shelf life, such as rubber seals, rubber brake components, solvents, and paint.

Recording numbers on new and used vehicles is a system requirement. Dealers will also find it useful to keep records of key numbers, radio codes, and any security codes relating to vehicles. Dealers should keep the numbers in a secure place and divulge them only to people whose identity has been verified.

Process Control

An auto dealer must look at process control aspects of the business. The Standard's requirement for work instructions is provided by the manufacturer's workshop manuals. When these are not available at the dealership, there should be a defined method of obtaining critical data on equipment settings or instructions. The sources may be other dealers or the manufacturer. Either way, the dealer must have documents saying how the information is to be obtained.

Special processes should include painting and welding in the body shop. Welding must strictly adhere to industry-wide recommendations on the number of spot welds. The integrity of the spot welds should be tested on similar materials. A simple destructive test would qualify the spot-welding equipment.

Inspection and testing are key activities in the automotive industry, even on new cars fresh from the assembly plant. The dealer is expected—and paid—to carry out a pre-delivery inspection and test of the vehicle. Dealers must keep records of this and any associated remedial work. Manufacturers also usually track customer and dealer complaints or feedback so they can begin corrective actions deeper in the system.

Dealers usually limit the inspection of parts received from the manufacturer to checks for damage. Then they separate the damaged parts and return or destroy them with the manufacturer's permission. The procedures must conform with the manufacturers' requirements and instructions. Mechanics, electricians, or other shop personnel should handle inspections during service and repairs. Most shops have an independent final inspection and road test carried out by the foreman before completion. The Standard does not require this, but accepts operator control instead, with records of results and a sign off.

Calibration

The inspection and test equipment required to be within the calibration system includes a wide variety of instruments. These include multimeters, tire pressure gauges, torque tools, tire thread depth gauges, temperature gauges on paint ovens, emission measuring devices, brake testers, and the jig used to align damaged bodies. Feeler gauges may be calibrated within the dealership, using a calibrated micrometer.

Delivery

Dealers should carefully control vehicle delivery, with particular attention to driving new vehicles at the reduced maximum speeds usually required for them. Dealerships should also instruct new vehicle drivers on these requirements.

Training

Most manufacturers have extensive training programs for dealers' employees. These cover all aspects of sales, parts management, finance systems, as well as mechanical, electrical, and body shop skills. These courses are usually certified, and dealers should keep records of the training. Staff should be assigned to jobs for which they hold the necessary manufacturers' training certificate.

Chapter 25 ◆ Hotels and Catering

(Applicable Procedure Guides: 1, 3–8, 10, 11, 15–25)

Hotels and catering services basically serve two types of customers: groups and individuals. We distinguish between them by referring to individuals as *customers* and groups as *clients*. Clients may be corporate travel agents making block bookings on behalf of customers, companies booking facilities for training courses, or companies arranging for caterers to provide food service for employees.

Appropriate Standard

Members of this industry should seek registration to ISO 9002.

Customer Contracts

As in other instances, the Standard maintains in its contract considerations that organizations may not offer something they know they cannot deliver, and that means no deliberate overbooking.

Other contract considerations include segregating contracts into formal agreements and casual, perhaps verbal, agreements. The formal contracts cover major activities, such as conventions and meetings, while casual contracts would be for occasional drinks and food. The circumstances vary, but in all cases, it is essential to clearly define the requirements.

Major formal contracts must be recorded and confirmed with the client, with conditions pertaining to cancellations carefully defined. This protects both the organization and the client. There is no need to record casual contracts, such as for drinks, but since such services are usually part of the service offering, they are part of the documented quality system.

Document Control

Document control addresses all the external reference standards which managers may need to interpret. These may include local or state or federal laws and regulations pertaining to food, hygiene, safety, and security.

Purchasing

Material purchases are divided into proprietary goods and produce, ordered by description from distributors/stockists. Produce includes natural foods such as fish, meat, and vegetables, which are highly variable. Specifying produce is difficult. Hotel and catering company buyers often procure produce by visiting markets and selecting the goods personally, or by using approved suppliers who understand their requirements. In the latter case, the purchaser should define the requirements through detailed descriptions.

We recommend working with the supplier to draw up produce specifications, which the supplier can use for reference when receiving an order. The specifications should refer to appearance, freshness, and the method of storage and delivery, paying particular attention to temperature control and any preparation done by the supplier.

A trained employee should check the items when they arrive. This verification must include measuring and recording any defined temperatures and assessing the condition of the produce. If produce freshness is unacceptable, or if it has other signs of poor condition, the caterer should reject it. A clear procedure for doing this eliminates the need for segregation and disposal of unusable produce.

Purchasing special services is also important. These typically include delivery services, hygiene services, laundry supplies, pest control, and temporary help agencies. Those who supply these services must be approved and the details of the service fully defined. In the case of a temporary help agency, the company should make sure that temporary or part-time staff have the necessary training and qualifications for the work. This should include the same safety and hygiene requirements as for full-time staff. Other job skills could be at a lower level if good instruction and supervision are available.

Customer-Supplied Product

In the catering industry, the client often supplies the kitchen facilities and equipment used by the caterer. This is considered Customer-Supplied Product and is subject to special care and control by the caterer. Maintaining the equipment is usually the responsibility of the client, but there should be a system for reporting the need for maintenance and then ensuring that it is done.

Customers routinely bring personal belongings into hotels and restaurants. The hotel or restaurant must have a system to ensure the safe storage of such items when requested to do so. Hotels often also receive personal items such as mail, messages, or deliveries, which require careful handling.

Process Control

Product identification should consider the knowledge of the people handling the goods. There is no need to label items such as vegetables which can be clearly identified by their appearance, and no other method of identification is necessary. Packed goods can be identified by a supplier's label. The use of labels or additional marking need only be considered when no other method is available.

The age of fresh and cooked foods is critical. The date of processing should be recorded on a label attached to the goods or their containers. When such foods are consumed within a short time, the hotel or caterer may restrict the labeling to unused items which are being stored. Cooked and uncooked foods should be segregated in storage.

When food problems arise, it is essential to isolate the foods concerned. To do this, it may be necessary to have a method of tracing food and drink from arrival at the facility through to the customer. The labels on packaged goods can be used to identify the source and age, but in the case of fresh produce, a disciplined system for storage may be needed. If the caterer only uses one or two suppliers, this lessens the problem, but if they use many, it may be necessary to introduce some type of batch control.

The hotel or caterer must document and control the delivery of services to the client or customer. These services typically include cooking, serving food and drinks, housekeeping, and associated services. The work needs to be written out in a procedure and/or work instructions and specifications appropriate for the skill and training level of the staff.

When chefs prepare or create meals, there is no need for detailed work instructions or even recipes. Chefs have the experience, training, and skills to produce food to the customers' requirements. In the case of fast food restaurants, where semi-skilled employees prepare identical dishes, there is a requirement for precise instructions defining the ingredients, the method of preparation, and the times and temperatures of cooking. The same instructions and qualifications of staff applies to all areas of the operation. Work instructions are needed to ensure quality and consistency in areas such as cleaning and presentation of rooms, setting tables, and serving drinks. Hotels and caterers also need to define drink recipes so customers receive a consistent product, and managers can plan for product usage.

We interpret ISO 9000's clause on process control to consider hygiene control as a special process. Records of cleaning activities must be kept. Detailed work instructions are required indicating the frequency and methods used and definitions of process characteristics such as temperatures and concentrations.

Inspection and Test

The operators themselves normally inspect the work as it progresses. This is particularly true for chefs and other skilled workers. The ISO 9000 Standards, however, require them to keep records of these inspections, whether the record is a detailed checklist or only a signature confirming that the requirements were met. This type of control also applies to setting tables, cleaning rooms, and preparing and serving meals.

There are few areas of food preparation where tests, or accurate measurements are required. The main ones are the temperature of food and bacterial levels found on equipment after cleaning. Temperatures must be routinely checked and recorded. When a problem such as above-minimum temperatures for cold storage of food occurs, the equipment must be adjusted or fixed. There should be a record of the action taken. The main reason for measuring bacterial levels is to demonstrate the integrity of the cleaning process. Internal service audits are recommended to achieve this.

Calibration

Caterers and hotels should carefully consider the need to calibrate measuring equipment. Since the temperature of a food storage locker is critical, the temperature measuring device must be calibrated. When dishes or beverages require specific quantities, such as an eight-ounce steak, the instruments that make these measurements need to be calibrated. If Work Instructions or recipes define the actual quantities and the cooking temperatures, the instruments that make these measurements need to be calibrated. If, on the other hand, these details are not defined, and the chef uses his skills and experience to gauge the ingredients and the cooking temperature, these measuring instruments are only needed as indicators, not to produce absolute readings. These can be marked—

FOR INDICATION ONLY - NOT CALIBRATED.

Stock Control

Food storage should take account of shelf life limitations. There must be a system of dating such items to demonstrate control. Temperature is critical with many foodstuffs in both storage and delivery. It is also essential to pack food in a way that maintains cleanliness and prevents cross-contamination. Operators must also establish well-defined, segregated storage areas for cooked and uncooked fish and meat.

A nonconforming product in the hotel and catering industry often means contaminated food, which must be disposed of in a way that takes account of any potential hygiene problems arising from the disposal.

Chapter 26 ◆ Recreation Facilities

(Applicable Procedure Guides: 1, 3, 4, 6–8, 11, 16–25)

When we pay for recreation, we expect to have a relaxing and enjoyable experience. Leisure time separates us from the rat race and the relaxation we derive is important. We hope—no, we demand that those offering such services provide satisfaction. That demand compels organizations offering recreation to strive for higher quality. Many of them are doing so by seeking registration to ISO 9000.

Leisure industries comprise a major economic growth area, prompting both investment and high expectations by all concerned. Many facilities are packed with people, all of whom expect quality service. Many recreational activities have safety related concerns, requiring dependable control systems so customers can be confident of a safe environment. If a leisure complex has catering facilities, these activities are covered by Chapter 25.

Customer Contracts

As with hotels, a leisure center has two types of customer: the casual visitor who comes with friends or family, and sports clubs who make regular bookings. The second group may also include professional instructors who lease the facilities for training or coaching purposes. All customers have basically the same requirements, but group contracts are handled differently.

Contract Review procedures require that facilities and instructors be qualified for the activities in which they engage. This is critical if the organization provides potentially hazardous equipment or experiences. Safety and liability are also considerations. For example, operators should determine who provides lifeguards for swimming pools, what certification the lifeguards must have, and may require an insurance certificate from the user before accepting a booking.

Often a hotel, or sports facility, will subcontract with a specialized leisure management company to provide certain services, including swimming pool or golf course management. In this case the hotel becomes the customer of the subcontractor, a relationship that should be covered with a formal contract defining the responsibilities of both parties. The management must also assess and monitor any subcontractors used to instruct or coach customers.

Managers must define for employees (and possibly customers) a facilities booking system for the different users. This should include the terms and conditions relating to bookings, particularly with respect to cancellations.

Customer-Supplied Product

ISO 9000 provisions for customer-supplied product require that procedures and facilities exist for securing equipment and clothing brought into the leisure center by its guests.

Process Control

Recreation facility operators must have procedures to identify their activities and services at all times. They should identify which staff members are responsible for each activity and establish minimum staffing level for areas in which safety is a factor. A facility plan should include the names of staff allocated to each area.

Process control requires managers to address the cleaning and preparation of the facilities prior to use. They may need to issue work instructions to define the cleaning methods for various areas and the procedure for setting up equipment. Managers must define the duties of staff who supervise hazardous activities. These may include the location of staff observing pool areas, emergency procedures, and the control of potentially dangerous facilities to prevent unauthorized use.

The control of any water treatment and filtration activity associated with pools is a special process, requiring complete records of readings and actions required when the process goes outside tolerance levels.

After the facility has been set up for a specific use, *i.e.* a lecture or awards ceremony, operators should inspect the facilities and test the equipment as appropriate. Trained staff or supervisors may do the tests and create a record, such as a check list, to demonstrate the results of the inspection. If the inspection or test indicates a problem, the Standard requires remedial or corrective action, and a record of any such action.

Calibration

Calibrating measuring equipment should include the instruments used to control temperatures, assess swimming pool water, and measure physical features (such as strength or training equipment). Other measuring equipment is used mostly for indicators and need not be calibrated. You must, however, regularly check to see that it is in working order.

Sports events often require accurate timing and measuring equipment, which in turn requires that equipment to be calibrated. If the sports events are non-competitive, or merely casual games, the equipment is for information only and calibration is not needed.

Training

Staff must be carefully trained for supervision of hazardous activities. Records are required, supported by qualification certificates as appropriate, for all such staff, whether permanent or temporary employees. The records should include first aid and emergency training.

Chapter 27 ◆ Nursing and Residential Homes

(Applicable Procedure Guides : 1, 3–8, 11, 15–25)

The ill and aged are the customers of nursing and residential homes, where many of them come knowing it may be a last refuge. The standards for serving these customers have to be high. Most of the ISO 9000 provisions for hotels and catering apply to this industry as well, but there are additional factors of medical care and greater concern for customer welfare. Many of the points made in this chapter also apply to hospitals and medical clinics.

Appropriate Standard

Registration to ISO 9002 is appropriate, since the provision of nursing and residential care has no significant design elements. As with businesses that provide food and housing, the organization providing these services must be fully aware of the provisions of any laws and regulations pertaining to its activities.

Customer Contracts

To meet ISO 9000's requirements for contract review, the provider must conduct a full assessment of the prospective resident's needs prior to offering him or her a place. Usually this means testing the person's capabilities and classifying his or her needs. Discussions with health care professionals are a must. All this makes it possible to confirm whether the provider can meet the customer's needs and identify when space is available.

Once agreed to, the arrangement requires a detailed contract spelling out all aspects of the service and the rights and responsibilities of the resident. If the prospective resident cannot understand the implications of the contract, a relative or legal adviser should review the contract and guide the person.

Medications, other treatments, religion, birthday and anniversaries, dietary requirements, and all other personal information should go into the files upon admission.

Purchasing

If the nursing home uses agencies to supply substitute staff, such as doctors and nurses, then such agencies need to be approved and controlled under the supplier approval system. The same is true of self-employed staff. But these staff members could also be treated and trained as employees.

Customer-Supplied Product

Nursing home personnel should make a list of personal possessions, with the inventory updated periodically. ISO 9000 requires this through its Customer-Supplied Products clause, although auditors generally recognize that it may be inappropriate, if not impossible, to record gifts and many other items the resident owns. Major items such as furniture, however, should be listed.

Training

Since nursery and resident home services include specialized nursing care, clearly written qualifications and selection procedures for employees must be defined. The qualifications apply to temporary as well as full time employees who provide nursing care. Records must reflect staff changes and additional training.

Process Control

A system is required to control and document the control of drugs and other medications by the nursing staff. An inventory system that includes shelf life and storage temperature is also required.

ISO 9000's product identification and traceability provisions require the home provider to identify which staff person is responsible for nursing care on each shift.

The Process Control provisions require providers to maintain plans for care and medication for each resident and provides for verifying these activities. This should include recording communications with physicians, other health care providers, relatives, or lawyers who represent the resident. Procedures to follow during admission, discharge, and death of residents must be documented.

Identification

A system for identifying the residents is needed as in emergency conditions it might not be possible to rely on the residents identifying themselves. In practice the staff generally rely on personal recognition and this is satisfactory if there is a system in place to ensure that there are always staff on duty who know all residents. The issue becomes critical when substitute staff are used and the administration of drugs, or the serving of special diets, are involved.

The system may be based on photographs of the residents, but these need to be kept up to date as there can be marked changes in appearance as time goes by. It is only in extreme cases that wrist labels would be appropriate as the dignity of the residents must be respected.

Chapter 28 ◆ Software

(Applicable Procedure Guides : 1–25)

The ISO Committee 176, the committee responsible for the ISO 9000 series, considers software design, development, and maintenance to be a very specialized process. So special, in fact, that it made software the subject of a separate guideline document, ISO 9000-3: Guidelines for the application of ISO 9001 to the development, supply, and maintenance of software: 1991. The purpose of this guideline is to help interpret the requirements of ISO 9001 for software development companies.

The guideline addresses contractual situations in which a supplier develops unique software for a customer. This requires close cooperation between the supplier and customer and a clear understanding of who is responsible for what. The ISO 9000-3 guidelines are used in this chapter to provide guidance on the concepts covered, but the Standard itself is a necessary source of information for organizations seeking registration as software designers.

Appropriate Standard

This chapter, and ISO 9000-3, are only for organizations in the software industry. In manufacturing industry today, there are many products which have certain control activities undertaken by software in process controllers, such as machine tool programs and cycles on photocopying machines. This software carries out simple control activities and analyses. It forms an integral and important part of the product, but is incidental to it. The actual control activities and analysis may be unique to that product, and may have been developed specifically for that product by a software engineering section within a design department. The customer for the software is the department that specifies what the product requires. The software engineers develop the software. If the entire organization seeks registration, the software activity would constitute a minor activity, albeit complex and important. Such organizations would register to ISO 9001, with the software section and activities treated as part of the design function.

If the product manufacturer has no software programmers, however, it will probably choose to contract with a software developer to write the software. The customer has no direct control over the software as it develops, but requires assurance that adequate controls are present. In this situation the Standard ISO 9000-3 applies to the software developer.

ISO 9000-3 further specifies requirements to those defined in ISO 9001. The following comments, therefore, are unique to registration of software designers and should not be used for other products.

Customer Representative

Due to the need for close cooperation between the purchaser and supplier, the guideline requires that the purchaser assign a representative to interact with the supplier. The representative is responsible for providing timely information and other support for the software development effort. The representative should also assist through joint reviews of specifications, verification activities, and acceptance test results. The guidelines require the purchaser to define interfaces and hardware requirements and to approve responsibilities. It emphasizes the need for mutual cooperation between the purchaser and supplier. This includes establishing the purchaser's requirements, methods of changing those requirements, definitions of terms, and background to the requirements and methods for recording and reviewing discussion results on both sides.

Customer Contracts

The contract review requirements expand considerably with the requirement for a common terminology. Contracts should cover all contingencies, identify risks, and define the proper handling of proprietary information. Contracts must identify specific quality requirements, including acceptance criteria, changes, problem solving after acceptance, applicable standards, and facilities to be provided by the purchaser.

Project Planning

Planning the project is a major ISO 9000-3 requirement. It should include a project definition, a resources plan encompassing associated responsibilities, development phases and milestones, and a schedule. Managers or staff should update the development plan as the project progresses.

The quality system must encompass the need for quality throughout the life cycle of the software product. A quality plan for each new software development should identify and define a method of control to use at key points in the project.

Phases of the project—the management, development methods and tools, progress control, input, output and the verification of each phase—are important parts of the plan.

The organization must define its requirement for quality planning as part of development planning and update the two together. The plan should express the quality objectives and how the organization intends to measure them. It should also specify input and output criteria, types of tests, responsibilities for reviews and tests, configuration management and change control, defect control, and corrective action.

Design Review

Software companies' plans for design and implementation must include reviews, which in turn lead to testing and validation of the software. Tests should occur early in the project, with the results analyzed and recorded. The software must be validated again, this time as a final product, in situations that resemble the application environment as closely as possible. Only then can it be delivered to the customer.

The scope of the plans should include a formal delivery, with demonstrations and tests, and a procedure for handling any problems or concerns that arise during delivery.

Document Control

The quality system documents must define these steps—replicating, delivering, and installing the software—along with the requirements for maintenance and support procedures. The documentation must define protocols, the technical languages and terminology used in the documentation, and indicate what documents to draft as the project progresses.

As the above indicates, the contents of ISO 9000-3 go beyond ISO 9001 in scope and depth. ISO 9000-3 is more prescriptive because it addresses a particular industry. The Standards have the same objective: to assure quality to the purchaser. ISO 9000-3 recognizes the vital role of the purchaser in designing and/or specifying the product and the need for close cooperation between the supplier and purchaser during all phases of the project. ISO 9000-3 is so comprehensive it leaves little doubt that you will have a system for achieving quality. It makes an ideal international standard for companies developing major software packages.

SECTION FOUR

IMPLEMENTING AND OPERATING YOUR QUALITY SYSTEM

Any organization wishing to achieve ISO 9000 registration must do three things:

1. Design and document a quality system that satisfies the requirements of the selected ISO 9000 Standard.
2. Implement and use that quality system as documented.
3. Generate evidence that the quality system works and is effective.

Section II dealt with designing and documenting a quality system. If you use the Process Management Model to document your quality system, it will satisfy the ISO 9000 requirements.

This section deals with the second and third issues. Chapter 29 discusses what is involved in implementing and using your quality system. Chapter 30 covers internal auditing.

CONTENTS

Chapter 29 ◆ Implementing Your Quality System

Assuming you have done everything this book has recommended so far, you now have a documented quality system—that is, Procedures and Work Instructions that describe how you operate your business. Many of them probably existed before you began this effort. Others will have been implemented as they evolved.

You no doubt still have a few things to do to complete the documentation phase, such as completing the Procedure Manual as discussed in Chapter 11 and the Quality Manual covered in Chapter 13. However, it's time to start implementing and using your quality system. This chapter covers implementation, operational suggestions, and issues that will ensure successful and complete implementation.

At this point you want to advise all employees that the quality system is fully defined and that it is essential for everyone to work according to its parameters. Keep in mind that you may want to make changes as you go through this implementation phase.

Using the Quality System

Using the system means operating the system as it is documented.

Management—and the entire work force—must be trained and have the pertinent documents at their disposal. This means the documented system needs to be officially issued to everyone requiring documentation. To achieve the most successful and meaningful registration, the whole work force should be committed to quality, and know of the ISO 9000 Standard's objectives and assessment process.

Using the quality system in accordance with the Process Management Model guidelines means you are doing internal audits, conducting management reviews, generating records, controlling documentation, and following up all the actions identified within the system.

Internal audits are covered in the next chapter. The Management Review Procedure Guide in Chapter 9 suggests that management meet regularly to review the operation and effectiveness of the quality system.

As the implementation unfolds, executives need to review what is happening. It is easy to make these a formal management review, as described in the Procedure Guide. This brings that procedure into force almost effortlessly. As the organization starts to identify concerns with quality, the Corrective Action procedure begins to address these concerns, and becomes operative on its own.

Each procedure identifies records generated, along with those who will maintain the records, and for how long. If the records do not already exist, file space needs to be set up so records can be easily maintained and retrieved. ISO 9000 auditors will review records for evidence that your quality system is working and effective.

Your operating results, internal audits, and customer feedback all provide data that require some action. The corrective action requirement means that data will be analyzed to determine the root causes, and corrections will be made not only to fix the problem, but also to prevent recurrence. The ISO 9000 Standard requires you to identify the need for action, complete the action, and then verify that the action was effective.

Certain parts of the quality system involve customers and suppliers who should be informed of any changes that may affect them. This will improve the company's image—especially if follow-through improvement is evident.

Most procedures can be installed and started immediately, but some require the generation of records. The two that generally require the most work to implement are the Training Procedure and the Calibration Procedure.

Unless the Company already has comprehensive training records, these need to be collected for all employees. This can usually be achieved by circulating a form to all staff, asking them to provide information on their education, qualification, training, and if needed, experience. In some circumstances this task may need to be assigned to a supervisor who will interview the personnel involved.

Calibration, when necessary, can be one of the most costly and time consuming aspects of meeting the Standard. It is worthwhile for managers to survey each piece of measuring equipment and establish its purpose and required degree of accuracy. Management should decide whether the item must be calibrated or if it can be considered as a work aid. If calibration is needed, it must be decided whether it can be handled in-house or by a subcontractor.

The Control of Quality Systems Documentation procedure is not necessary when the procedures are issued in draft form. The first issue level, however, will require formal control. This is a critical element and a source of most nonconformances in a registrar's audit.

Chapter 30 ◆ Internal Auditing

Introduction

ISO 9000 requires internal auditing of the documented quality system to assure that the quality system is operating as planned and that the system is effective. Once started, internal audits become the primary mechanism for monitoring and continually improving the system and the business. ISO 9000 requires internal audits to examine the quality system described in the ISO 9000 procedures and supporting work instructions. Internal audits are best done by employees selected from all levels and functions of the organization, including the executive management. All auditors need to be formally trained in internal auditing techniques. Audits are usually carried out by a single auditor who is independent of the function being audited. To gain confidence in the process, early audits may be performed by two auditors.

ISO 9000 defines the purpose of internal auditing as "verifying whether quality activities comply with the planned arrangements and determining the effectiveness of the quality system."

The procedures prepared, using the guides in Chapter 9, define the processes and activities of the organization's quality system. If the model is followed, the quality system meets the ISO 9000 requirements. These procedures define the organization's *planned arrangements* for achieving its aims.

The Standard, however, is concerned with what actually happens. To ensure that the documented quality system is implemented and used, ISO 9000 requires the organization to audit its quality system and identify areas where the quality system is not followed. In addition, internal audits assess the situation when the system is not effective in controlling the processes. In simple terms, to be effective means:

Procedures & Work Instructions:	Say what you do
Implementation:	Do what you say
Internal Audits:	Show me you do what you say

Each audit requires a written audit report, which is reviewed with the Management Representative and line management. The report identifies nonconformances and areas for corrective action to bring the actual practices in line with the quality system, as well as potential improvements to the system. The corrective actions are the responsibility of the line management. The Management Representative is responsible for ensuring that corrective actions are effective.

The audit cycle represents the traditional total quality approach of Plan–Do–Study–Act:

Plan	•	The procedures are the Plan
Do	•	The implementation is the Do
Study	•	The audit is the Study
Act	•	The corrective actions make up the Act

The commencement of the audits marks the point at which the company's management becomes involved in the progression towards registration. Experience shows that internal auditing can be of enormous benefit. This is especially the case when management participates and views the internal audit process as a way to improve the business. When the chief executive and the management are part of the audit team, the importance management places on quality and registration becomes clear to the rest of the organization. Most executives see the auditing process as a key feature of ISO 9000 registration, which they view as an opportunity to help the organization improve its overall quality.

ISO 9000 auditors use the internal audit results to understand if and where the organization is acting to correct and improve their operations. They expect the audits to show that management and employees are concerned about the system. The results also provide evidence that the concerns are being addressed and that such actions are effective.

The failure of organizations to implement an effective audit program is one of the more common reasons for not achieving registration. An organization that does not take auditing seriously is not taking quality seriously, and registration is clearly inappropriate.

The remainder of this chapter discusses the essential ingredients for an effective internal audit program.

Audit Team

An effective audit program requires a trained audit team. The Standard requires that internal auditors be independent of the audited function. A designer cannot audit the company's design procedures, but is acceptable as an auditor for sales procedures; a purchasing manager can audit design, but not material control. Consequently, the audit team should come from all functions of the company. Managers who have few other activities in the registration process (such as finance), can be members of the audit team, thereby increasing their involvement.

This independence can be hard, or even impossible, to achieve in small organizations. As long as the organization demonstrates that it has done all it can to ensure independence, the ISO 9000 auditors should accept their efforts.

Having a cross-functional team also allows the load to be shared. A typical audit with preparation time and follow-up work takes about half a day. Some of the simpler procedures take less time, while more complicated procedures may take longer. Large companies may have about thirty procedures, some of which are repeated over several areas. Employing one or two full-time people to audit all the procedures might seem an attractive alternative, but full-time auditors usually develop a certain tunnel vision regarding the company's operations and may lack the status of a management-based audit team. A team of twelve to fifteen auditors, with each of them doing only three or four audits, can handle the job. This is a better option and is not too much to ask from a committed management team.

Having a large cross-functional audit team also produces other useful spin-offs. All functions have personnel who are trained and understand the auditing process. This enables them to monitor their own functions and to keep these operating according to the quality system. They gain an understanding of what happens during an audit, the importance of documented procedures, and they become part of the team guiding the company to registration.

Internal audit team members can assist during the actual ISO 9000 registration audit and may identify possible concerns before they become apparent to the ISO 9000 auditor.

Audit Plan

The Standard does not define any frequency for audits, but once every six months is recommended. When the audits reveal causes for concern, the frequency should be increased. For example, if an audit uncovers five instances of nonconformance, it should be followed by another audit within a couple of months. Conversely, when several audits reveal no problems in a process, the audit time interval may increase to twelve months. It is necessary, at least, to audit each part of the quality system annually.

During the implementation phase it is desirable to carry out two complete internal audits prior to the ISO 9000 audit. These can smooth any leftover wrinkles in the system. Managers should make sure the final round of audits prior to the ISO 9000 audit produces a fairly clean set of audit reports. This is necessary for confidence, or if many concerns are identified, rescheduling the Registrar's visit.

The ISO 9000 audit should be scheduled a minimum of three months after completing the procedures in order to allow time for using, enhancing, and auditing the system. For larger organizations, this could mean as many as fifty to sixty audits. But with a team of fifteen, that is still only four audits per member.

The Management Representative normally prepares and distributes the actual audit plan to all members of the audit team and function heads. It is comprised of a simple time-based program by week, with weeks across the top (X-axis) and the procedures/areas to be audited up the side (Y-axis). The auditor's name or position is indicated in the body of the matrix. This is shown in Figure 30.1, which represents an unfinished fragment of a planned program.

PROCEDURE		WEEK NUMBER									
NO	**Title**	1	2	3	4	5	6	7	8	9	10
1	Control of QS Document	GH									
2	Internal Audit							AF			
3	Management Review								HT		
4	Training						RG				
5	Order Entry									HT	
6	Design Control			TH							
7	Drawing Control				AF						
8	Production A	RG									
8	Production B				AF						
8	Production C	PM									
9	Purchasing									TC	
10	Supplier Approval									TC	

Figure 30.1 Extract from an Audit Program

This extract from an audit program shows the plan for carrying out the various audits. Initials show who is doing each audit. Auditors schedule the audit with the line manager to occur within the time indicated in the program. For example, the plan shows the audit of "Drawing Control" scheduled in Week 4.

The auditor and the line manager agree on a suitable time and day within that week. Line management should be present, or represented, during the audit. This is particularly important, since auditing is intended to be an open program to improve the system, not a covert operation to catch people doing something wrong. Auditors should consider their job to be helping the audited function or area benefit from a sound, working quality system.

The program in Figure 30.1, illustrates how one procedure, Number 8: Production, is applicable in three areas designated as A, B, and C. The program indicates that each area is to be audited separately. This situation arises when separate areas use the same procedures, and it could apply to sales offices, warehouses, or design teams.

The plan also shows that in some cases, more than a single procedure may be evaluated during one audit. In this case, Purchasing and Supplier Approval are audited together since they both pertain to purchasing.

In addition to auditing the activities specified in the procedure, the scope of the audit should include all referenced work instructions that support the procedure.

When making audit assignments, the Management Representative must take care that every auditor is independent of the area or department he or she is auditing. A good method is to assign auditors whose departments have interfaces or similarities and have them audit each other. That way the auditor has a more detailed knowledge of the procedure.

Checklists

The audits are performed—step by step—against the processes documented as the organization's quality system. The audits' function is to confirm that all procedures and work instructions are being used and, when they are not followed, determine what corrective action is necessary.

The procedures provide the technical details of what should happen. It is not necessary to reproduce them as a check list before carrying out the audit. For instance, let's say the procedure states: "The order is recorded in the Order Log by the Sales Clerk." That gives the auditor the necessary information on what should be happening. All the auditor needs to do is check that it *is* happening. To have a checklist that says: "Is the order recorded in the log?" is not necessary or required. The auditor can confirm directly from the procedure textt hat the procedure is being followed .

Generic checklists which cover any procedure are, however, a useful tool. They can cover more general points which might be missed when checking over the actual text of the procedure. Some checklist questions might be:

1. Does the person being audited have access to the procedure and applicable work instructions?
2. Is this procedure at the correct revision level?
3. Is the organization structure correct with respect to the responsibilities in the procedure?
4. Does the scope cover all of the present activities?
5. Are the documents kept, as indicated in the Documentation section, and are the examples in the Appendices correct?

6. Are the records kept as stated in the record section?
7. Are records filed in the sequence described?
8. Are records secure and easily retrievable?
9. Are the retention times followed?
10. Have previously specified corrective actions been taken and are they effective?
11. Is there any immediate necessity to modify the system to improve its effectiveness, reduce the cost, accommodate new requirements, or resolve any inconsistencies?

In addition to a check list alerting the auditor to what needs to be checked, a set of guidelines on the conduct of the audit is also helpful.

1. Before starting an audit, the auditor should study and understand the procedure and area to be audited.
2. It is necessary to probe for objective evidence of nonconformance. Mere suspicion is not enough.
3. Ask the personnel using the system to explain what they do, and compare it with the written procedure.
4. Do not ask leading questions. Let the employee explain things the way they want.
5. Check records and work in progress to see if the procedure has been followed in detail.
6. Record findings in detail and get the personnel involved to confirm your findings. You do not want to argue facts at the end of the audit.

Audit Reports

A function of internal quality audits is to learn where the organization's quality system needs to be improved. For this to be effective, the audit findings must be reported, corrective actions taken, and evidence provided that the corrections were effective. This perpetual quest for improvement is an important feature of the ISO 9000 standard which is often overlooked. It is also a vital step on the road to total quality, which is discussed more in Chapter 39.

It is best to record the results of an audit on a standard report form. No provision of ISO 9000 requires this, so an organization could simply write audit reports on a plain sheet of paper. A form, however, helps the auditor, prompts follow-up action, simplifies record-keeping and control, and enables the ISO 9000 auditor to easily determine what has happened.

Since ISO 9000 does not require the form, it provides no guidelines on a format. The example below has evolved from working with many organizations and many registrars. It is an example, however, not a definitive standard.

Most organizations design their own form, but they should keep in mind certain features required by the ISO 9000 Standard. These are listed below with the reasons for their presence. The reader may design any form that suits their operation—within these guidelines—or adopt the sample in Figure 30.2.

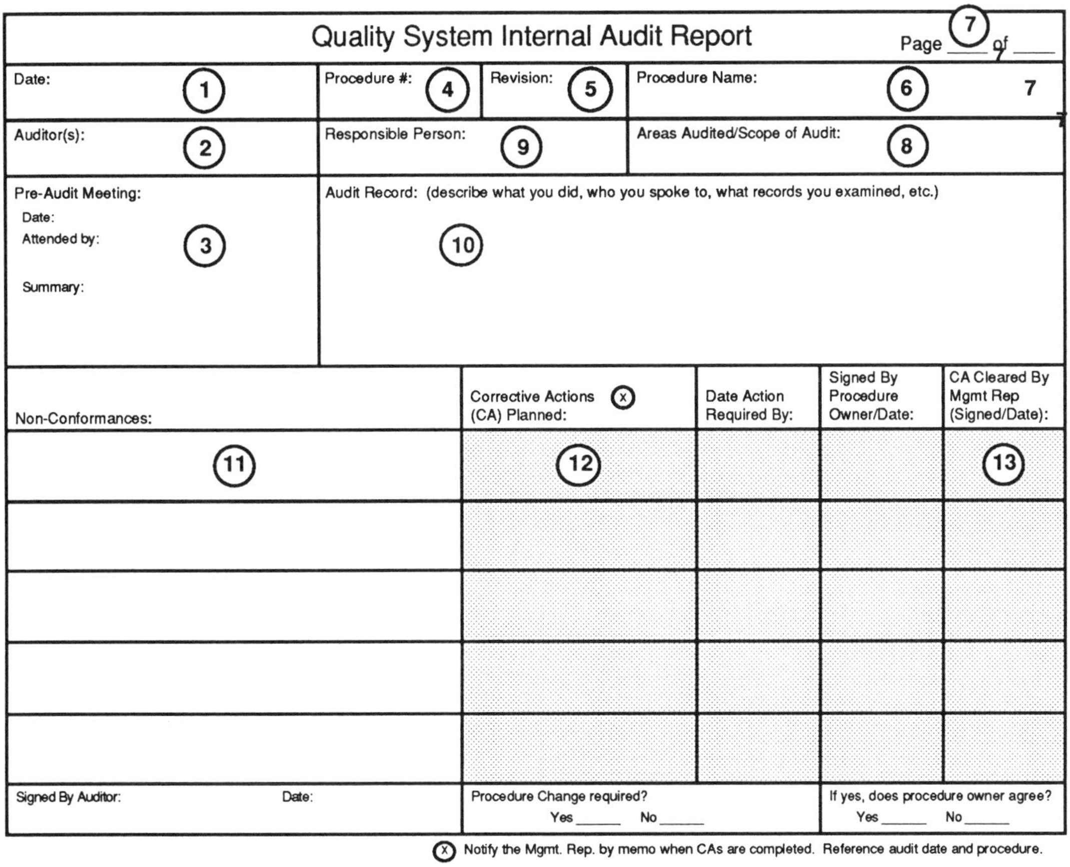
Quality System Internal Audit Report — Page (7) of ___

Date: (1) | Procedure #: (4) | Revision: (5) | Procedure Name: (6) 7

Auditor(s): (2) | Responsible Person: (9) | Areas Audited/Scope of Audit: (8)

Pre-Audit Meeting: Date: Attended by: (3) Summary:

Audit Record: (describe what you did, who you spoke to, what records you examined, etc.) (10)

Non-Conformances: (11) | Corrective Actions (CA) Planned: (x) (12) | Date Action Required By: | Signed By Procedure Owner/Date: | CA Cleared By Mgmt Rep (Signed/Date): (13)

Signed By Auditor: Date: | Procedure Change required? Yes_____ No_____ | If yes, does procedure owner agree? Yes_____ No_____

(x) Notify the Mgmt. Rep. by memo when CAs are completed. Reference audit date and procedure.

Figure 30.2 Quality System Internal Audit Report

1. Date:
   The date of the audit is essential for reference purposes and to demonstrate that the audit plan is being followed.
2. Auditors:
   The name(s) of the auditor(s), is required for reference, for subsequent resolution of any questions on the report, to establish the independence of the audit, to confirm the audit plan is being followed, and to enable a check on whether the auditor was trained. The auditor's signature verifies that the audit was carried out by the named individual.

3. Pre-audit briefing and audit plan:
   A record of the briefing by the Management Representative prior to the audit.
4. Procedure(s) number:
   For reference purposes, the audit reports are generally filed first by procedure number and then by date order.
5. Revision level:
   It is vital, when reviewing corrective action, to know what the procedure said at the time of the audit.
6. Procedure name:
   This is needed for complete description and easy reference.
7. Page number:
   To allow the audit report to be more than one page, there should be an indication of the total number of sheets in the report (*i.e.* Page 2 of 3).
8. Area:
   This is only relevant where a procedure is used at more than one location or department. A sales procedure may be operated in the head office and at a branch office and the location of the audit needs to be known.
9. Responsible person:
   This states the name of the line manager who was present during the audit, or who agreed to the audit time.
10. Audit details:
    A record of what was asked, confirmed, and with whom, demonstrates that the audit was carried out. Strictly speaking, the Standard only states that there shall be a record of the audit results, so it could be argued that this is not essential. But there are advantages in recording this information. Documenting the number of records checked puts into perspective any that are found to be incorrect. That is, if the audit shows that one in fifty orders were found unsigned, this tells a more complete story than merely saying one order was not signed. It also makes it easier to demonstrate that the audit was carried out. It demonstrates to management the fact that the procedure is being followed and is working. It records the activities examined on the audit, providing guidance on the activities to be chosen in the next audit.
11. Nonconformance:
    This is a record of failure to comply with documented procedures or Work Instructions. To cite a nonconformance, auditors must obtain objective evidence and provide the details of that evidence. Sometimes an auditor may decide to make an observation on the way an activity is handled even though the work is not, in the strictest sense, a nonconformance. This is permissible, but must be marked as an observation—not a nonconformance. It may be, for

example, that the procedure is being performed correctly but records are not securely stored. This should still prompt corrective action.

12. Corrective Action:
    For each nonconformance listed a corrective action must be determined. The responsibility for carrying out the corrective action must be assigned and recorded. It must include a completion date. The audit form should include a space for this information.
13. Clearance:
    For each corrective action identified, there must be a provision for recording the actual date the action is completed. The Management Representative has to acknowledge when the action specified was implemented. Subsequent audits should be used to confirm the effectiveness of the implementation.

Corrective Action

It is essential to have a clear understanding of what constitutes *corrective* action and what constitutes *remedial* action. If the audit revealed that an employee's training record was incomplete, then completing the record would be only remedial action. If all such records were checked and completed as required, that would be an improvement, but real corrective action needs to prevent the nonconformance from happening again. In this case, it might be necessary to train those responsible for the records. Evidence is needed that this training (or retraining) has occurred. Only after the Management Representative sees evidence of completed training can the corrective action be cleared. Sometimes organizations attach a copy of the evidence to the audit report, such as the timetable of a training program.

Line management is responsible for corrective actions. Management decides what actions to take and sees to it that they are taken. The actions may be delegated to other members of the organization, or require assistance from other departments. If so, this should be recorded on the form. The date for completion of the corrective action should be feasible and should be monitored to ensure that it is achieved.

The Management Representative must be satisfied that all corrective actions are complete before closing out the audit. Some organizations choose to have the audit team review the audits and associated corrective actions at a monthly Corrective Action meeting. The decision to sign the audit is then confirmed by the meeting. This approach increases involvement of the audit team and ensures that all the auditors know how the Quality System is performing.

Audit Process

The diagram in Figure 30.3 details a typical audit process. Auditors should be briefed by the Management Representative prior to the audit. The briefing is to prepare the auditors and ensure the audit is complete and effective by bringing up issues, areas to cover, and numbers of records to examine. At this briefing the results of previous audits should be brought to the auditor's attention. The audit will verify that corrective actions have been implemented and are effective.

Psychological Considerations

The internal auditing process revolves around human interaction. The auditor endeavors to determine the extent and effectiveness of the documented quality system. Any human interaction can be stressful, but this one—which involves executive management and often results in changes—is particularly stressful. It must be controlled and managed by the auditor if the organization is to enjoy the maximum benefit of ISO 9000 registration with minimum disruption.

A member of management serving as the internal auditor can seem especially threatening. This perceived threat can be minimized if the executive managers are careful to ignore their organizational authority and focus on their temporary role. *During the audit, even the chief executive is only an auditor.* Those being audited can be put at ease if the auditor role and management role are kept separate. The auditor must let the line managers choose and execute any corrective actions.

An audit examines how the system functions. It must not be a witch hunt. The people being audited must be reassured that the auditor does not seek to place blame. Every nonconformance should be seen as an opportunity for improvement. Auditors should not attempt to deliberately catch people's mistakes. They should assume that nonconformances will be found and dealt with appropriately, but they should avoid antagonizing the people being audited.

An audit is not an interrogation. In fact, a good auditor is a good listener. When you listen, you learn what is going on in the process. The auditor should spend about 20 percent of the time asking questions and 80 percent listening.

Auditors should introduce themselves and explain clearly the objective of the audit. A line manager or supervisor should be present, or at least be aware that an audit is taking place. But the auditor should make it clear *who* is to answer the questions. The employees in charge of a process must demonstrate that they know what they are supposed to do and that they can demonstrate it. If there are problems in understanding the requirements, the auditor may ask the manager or a supervisor to help, but the auditor must control the audit.

Executive managers whose offices or departments are being audited must take care to maintain a sympathetic attitude toward the auditor and cooperate totally—especially when caught in a nonconformance. This provides an opportunity for senior personnel to demonstrate their commitment to quality and to provide a constructive model for others. If managers—and other senior employees—fail to demonstrate a strong professional attitude toward the audit, the negative impact on the other members of the organization can be profound.

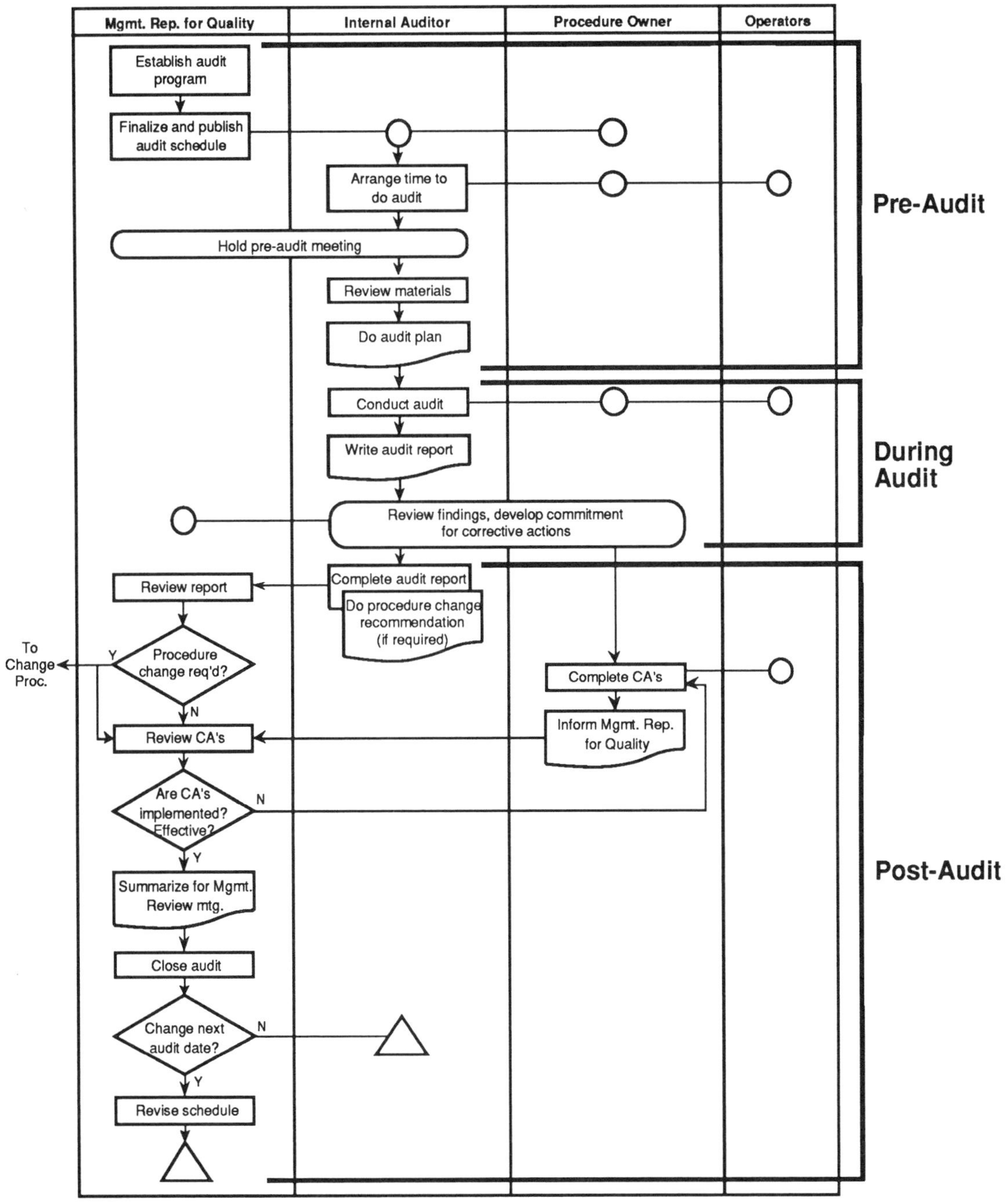

Figure 30.3 Internal Audit Process

Training

The Standard requires that the company "assign trained personnel for verification activities including internal quality audits." From this, it is inferred that internal quality auditors require some formal training.

The Standard does not define any level of training. ISO 9000 auditors generally require documentary evidence that training has been done by someone with proven competence in the subject. In the past this has been rather subjective, but at the end of 1992, the Institute of Quality Assurance in the United Kingdom issued guidelines for training internal quality auditors. These guidelines suggest accredited courses of at least fourteen hours duration to be conducted by a qualified internal auditor and include an assessment of each student.

Whether such courses become accepted practice or a requirement of the Standard remains to be seen. Conversations with the heads of assessment bodies tend to indicate that this will not happen. Training is essential for a successful internal audit program. This needs to include some knowledge of the content of the Standard and the process of registration, but this will normally have been provided early in the project. The formal training on internal auditing can be left until the quality system is documented and the audit program is ready to start.

Irrespective of any external requirements—explicit or implicit—for training internal auditors, it is advisable to train all the internal auditors in the same way to ensure that they will conduct the audits in a similar manner and at the same level.

Some companies send one person to an outside course and then have that person train the auditing team. It's an attractive option from the standpoint of cost. It may prove shortsighted, however, when viewed against the importance of the internal auditing process in ensuring an effective quality system and with the potential for continual improvement. It is also unwise to limit the size of the team based on the cost of the training. The most cost-effective way is to hire a consultant to conduct a course for the company. But you must confirm that the consultant has a fully documented course which adequately covers the subject.

The question may arise as to whether an internal auditor needs to be trained at the same level as a registrar's auditor. The answer is no. The role of an ISO 9000 auditor is completely different from that of an internal auditor. A registrar's auditor is trained to go into an organization and assess their quality system against the requirements defined in ISO 9000. The result may have a profound effect on the organization. The preparation for such a role has to be detailed and control must be tight. Internal auditors, on the other hand, examine their own organization to determine whether the documented quality system is adequately implemented—a considerably different role. An ISO 9000 auditor needs to have an intimate knowledge of the Standard and has to deal with interpersonal relationships that are far more stressful than those encountered by an internal auditor. An internal auditor requires no more than a passing knowledge of the Standard and deals only with internal relationships.

The ISO 9000 Standard requires internal audits. More importantly, however, internal audits are a way to continually improve the quality system and, hence, the business.

SECTION FIVE

GETTING REGISTERED

Everything done so far—designing and documenting the quality system, implementing and using it, internal audits, management reviews and so on—are essential steps to achieving ISO 9000 registration. This section covers the remaining activities. Although finding a registrar is included in this section, you may need to make the choice soon after you begin the registration effort. In some areas, lead times for engaging a registrar are long, and securing an appointment in your desired time frame may require early action. But whenever you make the choice, Chapter 31 discusses what is involved.

The remainder of this section deals with the ISO 9000 audit, preparing for the audit, the audit itself, and following up on the findings of the audit.

CONTENTS

Chapter 31 ◆ Selecting a Registrar

Choosing a Registrar is a major decision that an organization makes en route to ISO 9000 registration. The relationship with the Registrar is not a one-shot situation, but could continue indefinitely. The hope is for a partnership that proves to be long and harmonious. There are a number of criteria used to select a Registrar:

- Accreditation
- Expertise
- Experience
- Mode of Operation
- Cost
- Availability

These are discussed in this chapter and a worksheet used to compare Registrars is included. You can add your own criteria and give weight to those most important to you.

Accreditation

The first issue to be addressed is accreditation credentials. Are the credentials issued by a recognized national body that is relevant to your organization and your customers? Some customers only recognize Registrars accredited by certain national bodies. While this is contrary to the spirit of ISO 9000, an organization must be pragmatic.

All Registrars are subject to controls by their accreditation bodies. This process gives credence to the Registrar and ensures recognition of the registration. There are a large number of accredited Registrars working in North America and Europe.

Some Registrars hold accreditation from more than one national body. A company is free to choose one or more registration plans under which it wishes to be registered. Be aware that the accreditation process is long and exacting and a statement indicating that an organization is applying for accreditation means very little.

Scope of Expertise

The second issue is whether the Registrar's accredited scope includes the organization's activities. When initially applying for accreditation, Registrars have to define and demonstrate the scope of their expertise. Some Registrars specialize in specific industries and others have a wider selection of expertise.

Before Registrars can add to their areas of expertise, each has to conduct an audit in that particular business and in the presence of a representative of the accrediting body. In this way the scope of expertise can be increased as time goes on. It may be advantageous to select a Registrar who has already established expertise in your organization's business. Such a Registrar is more likely to understand your processes and be more able to objectively evaluate the relevance of the controls necessary to meet the requirements of the Standard.

Some Registrars operate outside of their accredited scope. They do not always make this clear when offering to carry out a registration. *Check this out carefully and beware*. If your business is not within the accredited scope of the Registrar's expertise, your company can only display the Registrar's mark and not that of the accrediting body.

As important as expertise and experience in your industry is the Registrar's experience in dealing with companies your size. It can be difficult for auditors used to assessing large companies to come to terms with small ones—and vice versa.

Mode of Operation

Having selected Registrars with the right expertise and experience, the organization should next examine the differences in the mode of operation of the various Registrars. All accredited Registrars must operate in accordance with ISO Standard 10011, Guidelines for Auditing Quality Systems. This Standard has three parts:

- Auditing
- Qualification Criteria for Quality Systems Auditors
- Management of Audit Program

Between them, this three-part standard ensures that all accredited Registrars throughout the world operate to the same standard. Like companies registered to ISO 9000, Registrars do not have to operate in the same way, but their operating systems and practices have to satisfy the same standard.

In all cases a Registrar's ISO 9000 auditors make a recommendation during the initial audit. The Registrar then acts on this recommendation.

There are, however, differences in the way Registrars operate. The first difference arises with the pre-audit. Some Registrars will visit to estimate the job, but will not usually bring a qualified auditor. In this case, little or no definitive information can be gained about the impending audit.

Other Registrars visit in order to plan the initial audit, review the quality system documentation, and identify deficiencies. Uncertainties about specific areas in the Standard can be discussed then. This enables the organization to implement the interpretation before the audit and improves confidence that the documented system complies with the ISO 9000 requirements.

The third approach, most common in North America, is for the organization to submit its documentation for a desk review. If you choose a Registrar who is some distance away, a desk review will save some expense. This can provide definiive feed back, but it is easier to establish a relationship when you join the auditor in a face-to-face situation. It also enables the auditor to judge whether the documented system relates to your operations.

There are differences in the evaluation of the findings during the audit and these fall into two major practices.

In the first, the organization's quality system is evaluated against each element, or clause, of the Standard. The auditor decides if the requirements have been met or if the element does not apply to the organization. If the company meets all the applicable sections of the Standard, the auditor makes a recommendation on registration as a pass or fail.

In the second practice, the system is evaluated against each applicable element and given a score on each element. To be recommended for registration, the organization has to achieve an average score of 75 or more out of 100 points, with no score below 65. The auditors still give a pass/fail at the end, but also provide scores. If decision is for a deferral, then the auditor indicates which elements the company needs to address to bring the score to the required level. The organization may publish the score. Potential customers may ask suppliers for their ISO 9000 Audit score. The problem with this practice is that an ISO 9000 audit is only relevant to that point in time. Corrective actions and improvements are ongoing in all registered organizations. The score is only of historic interest.

Either option allows an organization falling just below the requirements—providing the fundamental quality system is intact—to correct the problems within a certain time, usually a maximum of three months, and still achieve registration. Then the auditor re-assesses those elements and, assuming the corrections are effective, recommends registration. Depending on the type of corrective actions needed, this may require another visit or it may be achieved by providing documentary evidence. For instance, any required procedure changes could be demonstrated by sending copies for review. If product identification was the issue, however, a visit would be necessary.

After an organization achieves ISO 9000 registration, the Registrar conducts surveillance visits; a requirement for maintaining the registration. There are usually two to four such visits a year, depending on the findings during the assessment.

Surveillance visits are not as long or as detailed as the initial audit. The auditor usually covers Internal Auditing, Management Review, and Corrective Action each time, and examines the other elements over a three to four year cycle. Any noncompliance found during a surveillance visit must be corrected, although it will not be rechecked until the next surveillance visit (as long as it does not represent a major breakdown in an element of the Standard). A major breakdown requires extra visits to review the corrective action. If these are not effective, registration may be withdrawn. This process is covered in more detail in Chapter 35.

Registrars differ greatly on their post-registration policies. Some Registrars maintain registration simply through surveillance audits. Some perform full re-audits every three or four years, which is generally more expensive. Registrars who require complete re-audits argue that partial audits of the system are insufficient. for continued registration

Cost

Another criteria for selecting a Registrar, and often the most important, is cost. Registrars usually charge a daily fee plus fixed fees for preliminary and post-registration activities. Their travel costs may be additional. Needless to say, costs rise when a Registrar has to re-audit.

Registrars charge different daily fees and spend different amounts of time doing audits. In the United States, the Registrar's travel expenses can be substantial, so the location of the auditors should be considered. This is a consideration with respect to the initial assessment and the surveillance audits. If possible, have the Registrar agree not to use an auditor from a remote location, expecting you to pick up the expenses.

Organizations should expect the relationship with the Registrar to be long-term and take this into consideration when comparing costs. We recommend doing cost comparisons on the basis of a five-year period.

Availability

Availability for the assessment audit could become an over-riding consideration. If demand for Registrar time exceeds supply, companies may not be able to achieve registration within the desired time frame. We suggest that the search for a Registrar start early in the registration process. You should at least call a number of Registrars to determine availability and complete the selection process accordingly.

These are the major factors in choosing a Registrar, but others may come into play as well. The following form has more criteria and may prove useful in selecting a Registrar.

REGISTRAR CHOICES

	Registrar		
	A	B	C
Name:			
City			
Contact			
Phone #			

I. ACCREDITATION:

- Is the Registrar acceptable to my customers?
- Who are their accrediting bodies?
- Is the accrediting body acceptable to my customers?
- Is Registrar's mark recognized in pertinent countries?
- Any memos of understanding?
- Other

II. EXPERIENCE / MODE OF OPERATION:

- Do they have relevant experience?
- Do they provide a list of their registered companies?
- Does their accredited scope cover my operations?
- Stability of the business
  - Part of bigger organization?
  - Time in business?
  - Other
- Do they provide references?
- How do they work?
- Will they sign confidentiality agreement?
- Do they use own staff or contractors?
- Do they use only lead auditors?
- Do they require pre-assessment?
- Do they require a pre-audit visit?
- Pass/fail criteria?
  - Which plan of assessment do they use?
  - What is the time to correct deficiencies?

III. SURVEILLANCES:

- What's covered each time?
- What is the frequency of surveillances?
- Do they give advance notice of surveillance?
- Will they use the same auditors each time?
- Do they use a Lead Auditor each time?
- Other

	Registrar		
	A	B	C
IV. RE-ASSESSMENT:			
• Registration period (years)?			
• Do they do full audits for re-assessment?			
• Do they rely solely on surveillance?			
• Other			
V. AVAILABILITY:			
• Desired time frame is:			
• Are they available in required time frame?			
• When is a commitment required?			
VI. COST FACTORS:			
• Billing rate per day?			
• Do they charge for travel time?			
• Do they charge for travel expenses?			
• Initial Audit:			
• Application fee:			
• Documentation review			
• Pre-visit			
• Pre-assessment			
• Audit			
• Report/Registration			
• Subsequent Visits:			
• Surveillance Audits			
• Re-assessment audit			
• Other			
VII. TERMS AND CONDITIONS			
• Prepayment required (for what and when)?			
• Do they invoice as service is delivered?			
• Other			

Chapter 32 ◆ Pre-Assessment

Many registrars offer a pre-assessment in which the same auditors who will do the final audit perform a dry run, complete with a report of nonconformances. The assumption is that identified nonconformances can be fixed, making it easier to pass the final audit. But that doesn't always happen. Many companies still fail the final audit because the pre-assessment is only a sample of the quality system. Different parts of the system may be examined at the final audit, or a change in interpretation by the Registrar may cause failure in a final audit.

The pre-assessment differs from the final audit because it doesn't count and some pre-assessments are not thorough. Even if the organization passes the pre-assessment, a final audit must be done, and both must be paid for.

If a company follows the Process Management Model, they will have a quality system that complies with ISO 9000 requirements. If they implement and use that system, they will achieve registeration with or without a pre-assessment.

Many organizations choose pre-assessment because of registrar recommendation. And some companies have said they are glad they had a pre-assessment, because they had the pre-assessment early in the process, before they were adequately prepared—and they didn't have resources such as this book.

The organization can choose to go right for the full ISO 9000 audit. If only a few nonconformances are found, the ISO 9000 auditors will recommend a provisional pass and then later confirm that the corrective actions were effective. This saves both time and money. The organization only faces a full re-audit if a large number of nonconformances are found, and even this ends up, from a cost viewpoint, about the same as preassessment and audit.

A *pre-assessment is clearly a no-win for the organization.* Even if the pre-assessment uncovers nothing, undiscovered nonconformances may still be found. If the pre-assessment finds nonconformances, they must correct them and still face a full audit. If the pre-assessment finds total noncomformance, they still have not won. Going directly for an audit gives a win in all but the last scenario. If the preparation has been right, that scenario is most unlikely.

Table 32.1 shows that a well prepared company can save $5,000 to $8,000 by not doing a pre-assessment. If they are not ready, the no pre-assessment option would add only $1,000 to $3,500.

This is illustrated by a client who insisted on having a pre-assessment. Afterward, they were told that if it had been the real audit they would have passed. They had to wait another six weeks and go through the whole process again, with a risk of failure—definitely a no–win situation.

Readiness	No Pre-Assessment Audit		
	First	Re-Audit	Total
OK	Pass Registered* $9K	X	$9K
Not OK	Not Registered, Re-Audit Required $9K	Pass Registered* $9K	$18K

Pre-Assessment	With Pre-Assessment Audit		
	First	Re-Audit	Total
$5.5-8K	Pass Registered* $9K	X	$14.5-17K
$5.5-8K	Pass Registered* $9K	X	$14.5-17K

* Assumes outright pass or conditional pass not requiring additional expense.
Note: K = $1,000

Assumptions:

Audit (Re-Audit)
- 2 Auditors; 2 days @ $1500/day
- Cost – $9K (includes daily fee, travel, and admin)

Pre-Assessment:
- 3-4 days @ $1500/day
- Cost – $5.5-8K (includes daily fee and travel)

Figure 32.1 Pre-Assessment: Hypothetical Case

ISO 9000 auditors only examine systems and documentation. They are not consultants, and are usually careful *not* to suggest how nonconformances can be removed. There are many ways to remove a nonconformance, but the optimum solution will come from someone who is both familiar with the ISO 9000 requirements and with the system in question. A good consultant can help and is an excellent alternative to a pre-assessment by the registrar. A consultant who understands quality systems can help managers identify and remove nonconformances and inefficiencies and develop optimum solutions for the organization.

If you decide to do a pre-assessment, you have different alternatives:

- Your Registrar
- An Independent ISO 9000 Consultant
- Internal Employees
- A Knowledgeable Employee from a Parent Firm or Customer

The cost, thoroughness and confidence of the pre-assessment will vary with these alternatives.

If you decide to have a pre-assessment, the timing needs to be considered. Generally your audit is scheduled months in advance and the pre-assessment should be scheduled six to eight weeks before the audit to allow time for corrective actions.

Chapter 33 ◆ Preparing for the ISO 9000 Audit

Using the Process Management Model, an organization should not need to prepare a great deal for the ISO 9000 audit. It is not possible to paper over cracks in the system at the last minute. The functioning of the whole system is being assessed, and the records kept by the company will demonstrate to the ISO 9000 auditors the extent to which the system has been efficiently implemented.

The date of the ISO 9000 audit needs to be carefully selected so that the company is presented in its best light. If part of the production operation is on vacation, or the sales force are at a major exhibition, it is a poor time to plan the ISO 9000 audit. It is inevitable in large organizations that some of the staff will be off site. This still needs to be minimized and care must be taken to ensure that all key players in the quality system are present, or other staff are fully briefed as stand-ins.

The ISO 9000 audit is a time for testing and proving. It is an important event and can be stressful for the employees who have been intimately involved in the preparation. The ISO 9000 audit's methodology usually seems familiar, since the organization used a similar approach in its internal audits, but the objective and implications are different.

The objective of an internal audit is to seek out nonconformances and make improvements. The process is a positive route to improvement. In theory the same is true of the ISO 9000 audit. At the end of this audit, however, the organization is informed not only about areas for improvement, but also whether the ISO 9000 auditors recommend the company for registration. This is an important strategic and prestigious difference, and the organization should plan accordingly.

Before the audit, managers should meet with employees to heighten their awareness of quality. While most employees will not encounter the auditor, managers should discuss the audit and the employees' role in it.

- Employees should be told to be honest with the auditor and answer all questions to the best of their knowledge.
- They should not volunteer any extra information.
- Employees should know where documents pertinent to their operations are located and know the basic contents of the company's quality policy.

- Managers must encourage workers to see the audit as a positive event, since registration to ISO 9000 will benefit them through greater job security and the pride of knowing they are part of a quality team.

Managers should order a special cleanup before the final audit so that offices, factories, warehouses, and other facilities look sharp. Many organizations use ISO 9000 registration as the impetus for making decisions about old equipment or files that have been kept too long. Employees should remove any outdated supplies or merchandise from warehouse or other storage facilities. Waste, or even dust, cleared from work areas or machinery will improve appearances significantly. Checking paper work such as route cards, orders, or job tickets to ensure accuracy and correct processing can prevent headaches during the ISO 9000 audit.

The ISO 9000 audit is a challenge, but should be viewed as an opportunity to demonstrate how smoothly the company is running. Inevitably some things will have been missed in the eyes of the ISO 9000 auditor. But if you got this far and followed the Process Management Model, you should be in good shape.

Chapter 34 ◆ During the ISO 9000 Audit

To present the organization in the best light during the ISO 9000 Audit, it is essential that the executive management be:

- Available
- Committed
- Involved

The ISO 9000 auditors observe whether the whole organization seems involved. If there is no way to avoid the absence of a manager or other key individual, other managers should be ready to explain the absence.

ISO 9000 auditors should work according to a schedule that has been reviewed with the management. This will inform managers in the various departments when they can expect visits. The managers should relay the schedule to their departments and make sure the department heads are present during the auditor's visit. *The schedule is only a plan and ISO 9000 auditors may deviate from it as the findings dictate.*

For the ISO 9000 auditors to work effectively, it is necessary to provide them with an office, or at least a desk, where they can discuss their findings. The company is responsible for providing any special safety training or equipment required to enable the ISO 9000 auditors to conduct the audit. Auditors should not want to spend time on long lunches and may prefer to have sandwiches brought in. If they are away from home they often do not wish to socialize with company personnel in the evenings—but the offer can be made.

Every ISO 9000 auditor should be accompanied by a guide who knows the quality system, its documents, and how they relate to the Standard. Internal auditors are ideal for this role. ISO 9000 auditors assess the system against the clauses of the Standard and how the organization's quality system relates to each element. The more help they get relating the documents in the quality system to the ISO 9000 Standard, the better the audit will go. The appendix to the quality manual, discussed in Chapter 13 and illustrated in Appendix D-1, is a useful guide in providing this information.

Assuming the organization used a consultant to prepare for the ISO 9000 audit, should the consultant have a role during the audit? The auditors are evaluating the organization, not the consultant, and expect the organization to provide answers to their questions. If consultants are present, they should be there to advise the organization, only discussing issues with the ISO 9000 auditor when invited to do so. A consultant trying to dominate a conversation will annoy the auditor, and perhaps even lessen the company's chance of being recommended for registration. The consultant's job is to help get the organization ready, and then take a back seat. The absence of a consultant at this stage demonstrates confidence in the client and the strength of the quality system.

As the audit progresses, the guides witness what the ISO 9000 auditor finds. Employees asked questions by the auditor should respond as best they can.

If nonconformances are found, the company may take corrective actions immediately, *even while the audit is under way*. They must be careful, however, that whatever actions they take are appropriate long-term actions, and not mere stop gap measures. For instance, if the auditor finds a nonconformance in the wording of the quality manual, the document can be rephrased on the spot, a useful job for the consultant if present. Clearing the nonconformance does not remove it from the audit findings, but may prevent it from becoming an obstacle to recommendation for registration. Even major nonconformances can be cleared during the audit.

Examples of nonconformances that have been addressed during the audit have included:

1. ISO 9000 auditors found a calibration certificate that did not show the results of a measurement. Employees obtained a new certificate with the required data for the auditors.
2. The final ISO 9000 audit turned up a procedure that failed to include the recording of quotations in a log. The company added the use of the log and reissued the procedure.
3. ISO 9000 auditors found no records for training internal quality auditors, even though the training had taken place. The company had copies of the certificates sent by fax from the training provider, in order to update the files.
4. Auditors found backup copies of computer disks stored near the machine, and no other copies stored in a remote place as indicated in a procedure. Employees copied the disks and stored the second copy in a safe.
5. The ISO 9000 audit discovered an appendix missing from a procedure. The company made copies of the appendix and issued them to all manual holders.

As the examples demonstrate, the nonconformances can be minor and even trivial. Managers and employees who worked hard to prepare for the audit often find this exasperating and may be tempted to argue the points with the auditor. *Avoid this*. The constructive thing to do is let go of the frustration and get on with clearing the nonconformances. Arguing the point could antagonize the ISO 9000 auditors, whose findings may be quite sincere and in line with their training.

This is not to say that you cannot debate a point with the auditor, but conventional wisdom says that you can only do this a few times before appearing to be uncooperative or obstinate. The ISO 9000 auditor may rightfully conclude that the manager who argues every point with an auditor may be inclined to do the same with a customer. You can only debate a few points, so be sure they are important.

It is, nevertheless, important to be on your toes during the audit. For instance, the ISO 9000 auditor may identify a nonconformance that is fundamental to the organization's quality system. The guides, and possibly the consultant, consider the requirements outside the scope of the Standard. There is nothing wrong—or argumentative—about asking the auditor to show where the Standard defines the requirement in question. If the procedure guides in Chapter 9 have been followed, this should not happen, but occasionally auditors interpret the Standard incorrectly. Examples of this are discussed in Chapter 38, Myths and Misunderstandings.

Nonconformances inevitably occur during an ISO 9000 audit. Nonconformances of a trivial nature will not prevent a recommendation for registration. The Authors know of organizations that had more than 30 nonconformances and still achieved registration. Once the nonconformances are cleared, the organization should notify the auditor and seek to reach agreement on the clearance quickly.

Audits end with a closing meeting during which the audit team goes over the audit results, explains the appeals procedure, and informs the organization of their recommendation. The recommendation can be:

- for registration.
- for registration subject to nonconformances being cleared.
- for registration after demonstrating clearance of nonconformances.
- for a complete re-audit.

Sometimes the outstanding nonconformances are too vague for the organization's managers or employees to understand. The ISO 9000 auditors should be asked to clarify what they mean and it is permissible to ask if a certain corrective action would clear the nonconformance. It is not permitted for the auditors to tell the company what to do to clear the nonconformance, but ideas can be bounced off the auditors for confirmation. Ask the auditors whether another visit to confirm the corrective actions is warranted or if documentation will suffice.

Whatever the ISO 9000 auditor recommends must be ratified by the Registrar's governing body. Ratification is usually a rubber stamp procedure, but until the organization receives its ISO 9000 registration certificate number, it should refrain from publicizing the registration except to say that it has been recommended. However, the employees (who worked for the registration and are keenly interested in the audit results) should immediately be informed. The immediate result will be high morale, followed by long-term pride in their work.

Clearing Nonconformances

ISO 9000 auditors leave an audit report which details the nonconformances. The findings should be clear, and the organization should immediately begin implementation of the optimum method for clearing the nonconformances. There are deadlines for informing the Registrar what the company will do and when it will be done. Registrars vary in their requirements for these deadlines, but three weeks to three months is the usual range.

These deadlines must be met and failure to do so may prejudice an ISO 9000 auditor's favorable recommendation. However, care should be taken to ensure that the optimum long-term solution is adopted, not a short-term expedient to clear the nonconformance. Corrective actions should be recorded and sent to the Registrar. If there is any doubt or delay, managers should make informal contacts with the Registrar to ascertain whether the proposed actions meet the ISO 9000 requirements.

The corrective actions should be accomplished by assigning them to specific managers or staff. Any needed resources, such as funds, clerical help, computer time, etc. should be determined at the same time. Executive managers should monitor the corrective action progress and report to a weekly meeting or review, which should be chaired—at least occasionally—by the chief executive.

Once the corrective actions have been completed, an internal audit should be performed. The internal audit should be submitted to the weekly meeting to determine whether further action is necessary.

The Registrar must be informed once managers agree that corrective actions are complete. Depending on what was involved, the registrar may choose to visit the site again or clear the nonconformances based on the documentation submitted to them. The outcome should be a recommendation for registration, and ultimately, registration itself.

SECTION SIX
AFTER REGISTRATION

A recommendation for registration to ISO 9000 is a significant milestone for any organization. It is recognition that they are in the first division for quality—not just a national division but an international one. The whole company contributed to this. This contribution should be recognized.

While arranging for the presentation of the certificate and the associated publicity, it should not be forgotten that ISO 9000 registration is not a one-time deal. It is the start of a long-term commitment to quality. While it is great to tell everyone of your success, it is humiliating to have to tell them that you lost it—and that does happen on occasions.

Your registrar will be auditing you on a regular basis—surveillance audits—discussed in Chapter 35. Two chapters of this section deal with taking advantage of ISO 9000 registration. The last chapter discusses the implications of ISO 9000 registration to your suppliers.

CONTENTS

Chapter 35 ◆ Surveillance Audits

Once registered, a business receives regular surveillance visits by ISO 9000 auditors. This assures customers (and potential customers) that the supplier continues to comply with the ISO 9000 Standard. Surveillance is an important part of the ISO 9000 Registration process, and everyone in the organization should view the auditor's visits as opportunities to demonstrate their continual improvement.

Registrars usually schedule surveillance audits well in advance. Normally, surprise visits only occur when the ISO 9000 auditor suspects that an organization is trying to hide something. For a time, surprise visits were routine for some Registrars. But the practice proved unworkable because the people they needed to see were often not present.

The preparation for the surveillance visit should be similar to the initial audit (as discussed in Chapter 33). Managers should tell everyone when it will occur and make themselves available. Managers and employees should check for and eliminate any obvious deficiencies. By this time, however, operating the system should be second nature with little or no need for last-minute actions.

The ISO 9000 auditor—who may not be the same one (or ones) who performed the initial audit—only covers part of the quality system in a surveillance visit. They normally start with a review of outstanding nonconformances from the previous visit. The review then proceeds to the documented system. The ISO 9000 auditor examines any changes made since the original assessment. The record of internal quality audits and management review meetings are also examined. Then they look at the ISO 9000 elements scheduled for review during the visit. Each surveillance audit will follow roughly the same pattern, but with different elements of the system under scrutiny during different visits.

The auditor and the company should treat nonconformances the same during a surveillance audit as they did during the initial audit. A new auditor may sometimes try to *move the goal posts,* but managers must tactfully resist this. If the original assessment approved a major feature of the documented quality system then it should not suddenly become unacceptable. An organization cannot be expected to make fundamental changes to meet the whims of individual auditors.

If the ISO 9000 auditor finds that the organization has not been following the approved system, management must decide on corrective actions. If these are isolated examples (and do not indicate that the system has collapsed) the ISO 9000 auditor would normally record these and request action by the next visit. If the findings indicate a major breakdown of the system—with the system out of compliance with a major element of ISO 9000—immediate action would be required. A visit will be scheduled to confirm that it is effective. If the action taken is subsequently found to be ineffective, or if the organization does not propose to take the required action, the assessor can recommend the withdrawal of the registration.

The first surveillance is critical. During preparation for the initial ISO 9000 audit, a company often makes modifications to its operating practices which it believes are necessary to pass the audit. If these are not viable in their own right, but are only being adopted to meet the Standard, the commitment to them will be low and they may not have been sustained. Everyone may have made an extra effort for the initial assessment, but once registration had been achieved, various individuals or departments may relax too much. The first surveillance will reveal any lack of sustained commitment.

On the average, ISO 9000 auditors return for surveillance visits about every six months (or four to six visits during a three-year registration period). If the selected Registrar has a policy of periodic full re-assessment, there should be no need for extra preparation. If the system has been running for several years, meets the company's requirements, and has no major nonconformances, there should be little concern.

Registrars do not generally publicize it, but ISO regulations allow companies to change Registrars without requiring a complete re-audit. If the company has no outstanding nonconformances, it is acceptable for another Registrar to assume the surveillance activities.

This practice has occurred in the U.K. when a company is not satisfied with the service provided or with the costs. This could occur, for example, when a new Registrar opens a new office closer to the company and a switch could save expenses. The company is the customer and has the choice of who should conduct its ISO 9000 audits. Of course there may be some extra costs because it would be necessary to dispose of any paperwork with the old Registrar's mark and reprint with the new mark.

Through this process of continual surveillance, the Registrar assures that the organizations it has registered continue to meet the requirements of ISO 9000.

Chapter 36 ◆ Advantages of Registration

People often ask how registration to ISO 9000—and the effort that leads to it—benefits an organization. As mentioned earlier, some companies have improved efficiency enough to pay for the expense of registration. Others have reported a market advantage that brought new business. But not all benefits are as quantifiable as these.

Unfortunately many companies do not approach ISO 9000 registration as it is taught in this book. Instead, they develop and impose inappropriate systems and documentation, only to find the whole process a burden. When the Process Management Approach is adopted, the results are real and the outcome is different.

Market Advantage

The growth in ISO 9000 registrations is undoubtedly customer-driven. Many large firms and government agencies are indicating that they intend to make registration a requirement for their suppliers. While this may be your motivation in seeking registration, the ISO 9000 Standard brings other opportunities. It clearly tells your customers, and potential customers, that you have placed a high priority on quality and have achieved international recognition as a company that has a quality system in place.

Announcing your registration can be an opportunity to get free exposure in the media. This alone is a good reason to inform your customers and market of your achievement. Your ISO 9000 registration can and will set you apart in your market. You should use it to its full advantage.

Other Recognition

The C-E mark in the European Economic Community may be the most prominent seal of approval. Many countries require it in order to demonstrate that a product so stamped meets certain pre-defined standards. There are two ways an organization may receive permission to use these marks. The first is for the company to send product samples to accredited test labs to be checked against the specific requirements of that product standard. In the second route, the company self-certifies its products through a theoretical assessment during the design process. The organization uses calculation and other means to confirm that the design meets the product standard. The company keeps documentary evidence of these confirmations in a product file. For this second route to be credible, the organization must control its design and production process. Registration to ISO 9000 provides the evidence of control and establishes the credibility.

Safety

No government or international agency currently requires organizations to become registered to ISO 9000, but doing so can be an asset when safety issues arise. Since ISO 9000 registration requires adherence to all legal and industry regulations, it shows a commitment to product and service safety and documents its compliance with all applicable laws or guidelines. The improved control of safety factors reduces the likelihood and severity of litigation.

Some insurance companies are taking ISO 9000 registration into account when determining premiums for safety-related insurance. If a defective product causes an injury, a set of ISO 9000 records will demonstrate that the organization sent the product out of its plant in the planned condition.

In some countries, failure to adhere to safety standards can result in criminal prosecution. The management of accused companies are able to use the argument in their defense that they operated with due diligence. The presence of an internationally recognized quality registration could only help to establish such a defense.

Public Image

Many companies in the U.K. report their ISO 9000 registration to their stockholders to demonstrate their commitment to quality. The managing directors of those companies believe registration enhances the value of their stock.

One company even used its ISO 9000 registration as a weapon in fighting off a hostile takeover bid. Their ISO 9000 registration plans served as a demonstration to stockholders that theirs was a more efficient management than the predator.

Performance Improvement

All surveys indicate that the process of achieving and maintaining ISO 9000 registration will improve operating performance. Some improvements occur just because the registered firms use their ISO 9000-registered systems. Others result from management taking advantage of those systems and using them for ongoing continual improvement.

First, let's look at why operating improvement occurs from an ISO 9000-based quality system. Figure 36.1 shows the built-in mechanism for continual improvement. Internal audits, management reviews, and corrective action are all requirements of the Standard. These require (and provide) data on deficiencies and results and ensure attention and discipline to correct and prevent recurrence. If your organization seriously performs internal audits, management review, and corrective action, you will continually improve.

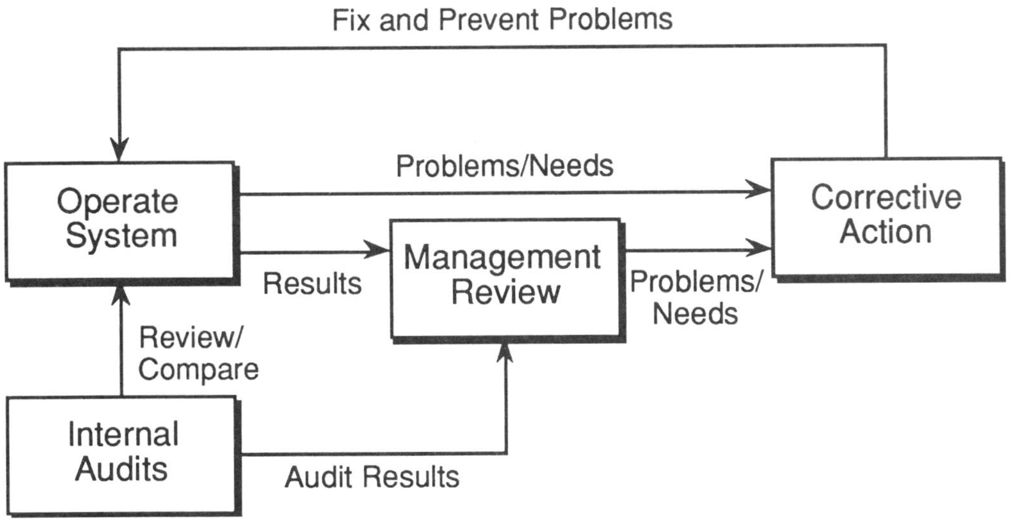

Figure 36.1 ISO System Improvement Loop

The word audit doesn't usually sound very appealing, because it conjures up an image of regulators and piles of paper. An ISO 9000 audit is different. It provides an opportunity to improve. A team of trained, independent experts visit the operation and evaluates it against an internationally accepted standard, deliberately set higher than the operating norms for the vast majority of non-registered companies. The company learns which areas in the organization may not be performing as well as they should. The auditors, both internal and external, look for nonconformances which lead to corrective action, and thus, improvement.

The audits may be likened to a medical examination. You hope there is nothing wrong to be found, but it's a good idea to have check-ups on a regular basis. The examination doesn't improve your health. But if something serious is found, it is an opportunity to take any necessary actions.

The discipline of regular systems audits, internal and by the ISO 9000 registrar, force management to keep quality at the top of the agenda. The audits probe and uncover areas for improvement, as well as provide evidence that quality is high in some areas. ISO 9000 registration is important because it signifies commitment to quality and demonstrates real actions arising from that commitment. Managers put themselves on the line when they open their operations to outside review, with published results. For many, this is a new idea. But when they adjust, it becomes a source of pride. Their customers and competitors can see that they have a clearly-written quality policy and a steadfast commitment to it,

Many chief executives have learned surprising things about their business when engaged in the new activities associated with ISO 9000 registration. During the management review, one chief executive found a processes with waste and rework rates of about 30 percent. The figure dropped to less than two percent after the necessary attention and resources were invested. ISO 9000 forces people to deal with issues which they soon realize should have addressed before. There are many more examples.

Quantifiable Benefits

Some research in the U.K., the country with the largest number of ISO 9000 registrations, provides evidence of operating performance gain. One survey of 2,300 small companies, conducted in 1991 by the University of Salford, U.K., found companies could attribute savings of at least five percent of sales to their ISO 9000 registration efforts. Other sources make larger claims.

Another survey studied liquidation of U.K. companies. During 1991 and 1992, about seven percent of all corporations in the U.K. went into liquidation. The similar figure for companies registered to ISO 9000 was 0.2 percent.

Redundant Audits

Many companies spend considerable time and money on large numbers of quality audits of their suppliers and subcontractors. Large supplier companies may receive many such visits, forcing up the overhead cost of their goods and services. Registration to ISO 9000 reduces the need for such visits.

Management Change

In addition to measurable benefits, our clients have identified numerous benefits that are less easily quantifiable. Managers, including both line managers and executives, become more aware of other departments' operations. Once they understand how other departments work and begin to participate in internal audits, the managers tend to meld as a team. They see the organization as a system, and themselves not as isolated components, but as process managers of that system.

Some managers undergo a different metamorphosis. Challenged and renewed by a chance to serve on the internal audit team, they cease to cut corners or otherwise bypass the best practices and methods. Spending time on internal audits and dealing with problems builds their understanding and commitment to the quality system as a whole—and makes it more difficult to compromise.

Employee Change

An enthusiastic involvement in ISO 9000-related activities demonstrates the managers' commitment to quality and continual improvement. When other employees see managers, particularly executives, putting time into audits, they begin to take quality more seriously as well.

ISO 9000 demonstrates to all employees—designers, planners, sales people, managers, production line workers—what their roles in quality are. If the company did not already have a Total Quality policy, it begins to develop one. In the majority of companies, employee attitudes change when they see their company develop and use a sound quality system.

Employees also begin to respect management more and take more pride in their own work as the change in attitudes cascades through the company. They often seek to become involved in corrective actions. Research shows an improvement throughout the work force, correlated with the extent of corrective actions. Opportunities to improve are often greeted with relish.

The availability of documented procedures, which can be used as training materials, makes it easier to prepare new employees. Once the organization defines its method of working in a given procedure, control becomes easier, as does delegating work to subordinates. The same is true when key individuals go on vacation or cannot work because of illness.

Many organizations have a traditional view that quality is only the role of the inspection and production departments. These departments are responsible for making the products correctly and it is their job to identify and remove any defective products. This ensures that only perfect products are delivered to the customers. ISO 9000 spreads the responsibility across the whole organization, indicating to sales, design, planning, purchasing, and personnel that they all play a role in meeting the customers' requirements. This company-wide appreciation is inherent in the Standard. Companies lacking a company-wide approach to quality must develop it to meet the ISO 9000 requirements. Figure 36.2 illustrates the change in attitude that may be experienced when a company is committed to the ISO 9000 requirements—and quality.

Standardization

When documenting its quality system, the company examines all of its working practices and evaluates the best ways to meet its objectives. Unauthorized subsystems within a department are often revealed. Sometimes these have been designed to make the work easier—sometimes in defiance of orders from higher management. These subsystems may work better or worse than what was authorized. Either way, an analysis will prove worthwhile. Once the results are in, the organization can formally integrate the best practices. The benefits of the improvements go out to the whole company, providing uniformity of use and easier conditions for staff transferring between departments. This is illustrated in Figure 36.3.

Purchasing

Purchasing activities are markedly improved as a direct result of introducing systems to meet the ISO 9000 requirements. This happens for two reasons:

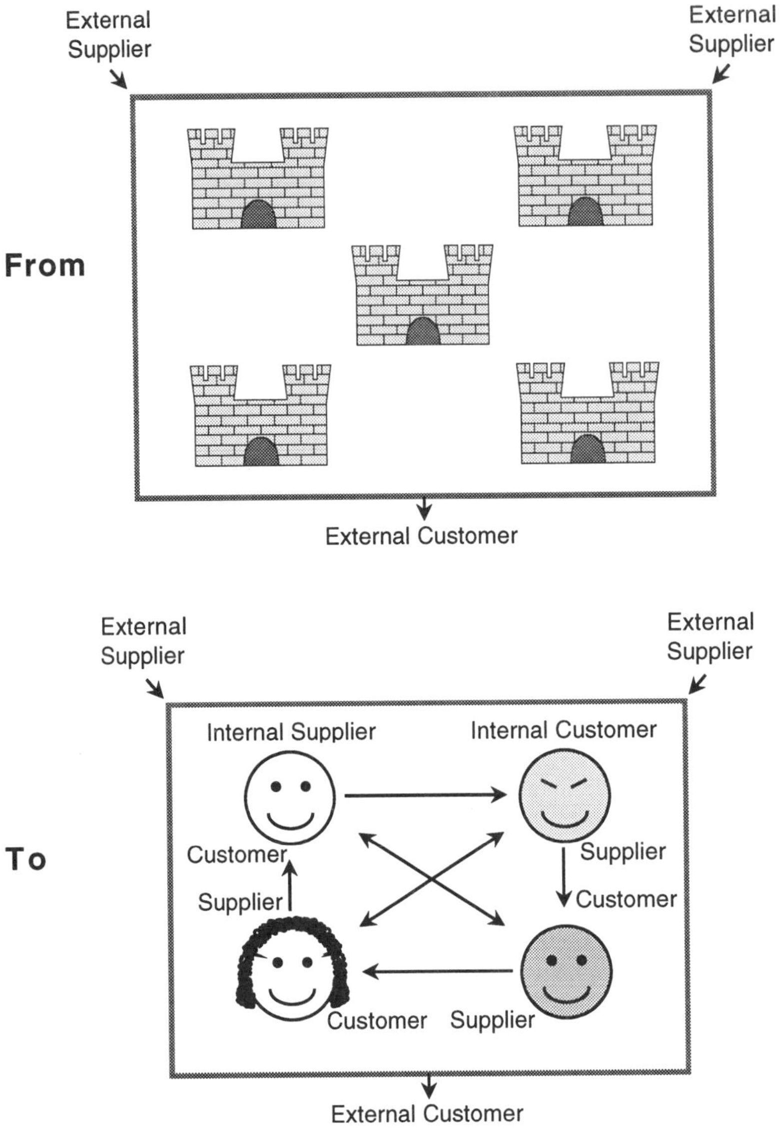

Figure 36.2 Organizational Change Inherent in ISO 9000 Registration

1. The ISO 9000 Standard requires clear definitions of ordered material. In some organizations, developing and reaching agreement with suppliers on purchasing specifications is a major task, but one with big dividends. Only if a supplier is aware of the customer's precise requirements can satisfaction be provided. When the supplier helps develop the specifications, satisfaction is more likely.

2. Formal approval of suppliers leads to more lasting relationships. Changing suppliers, just to save money, becomes more difficult to defend. The result is long-term relationships with suppliers who demonstrate their ability to meet requirements.

A reduction in the number of rejects follows. Initially the opposite may be true, as new standards and specifications are used with purchased material. As the new requirements become understood, however, the number goes back down.

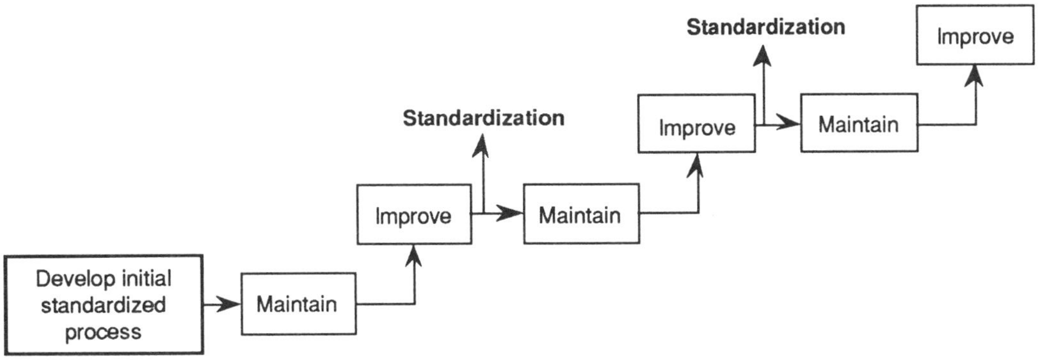

Figure 36.3 Standardization – Improvement Cycle

Summary

Few, if any, companies keep figures to show whether the cost of quality declines as a result of introducing quality systems. Many executives, however, say there is a clear increase in corrective actions, which change the processes that cause nonconformities. ISO 9000 quality systems force management to address nonconformances and to treat them as opportunities to improve. As that happens, the overall cost of quality falls. No company using the Process Management Approach has added personnel to operate the systems introduced. The need for documentation increases, but the overall result is greater efficiency—which more than makes up the difference.

Registration to ISO 9000 produces operating and marketing benefits. The benefits are only limited by management's desires and use of its quality system.

Chapter 37 ◆ ISO 9000 and Your Suppliers

ISO 9000 contains no requirement for the registered company to request its suppliers to become registered. As companies discover the benefits of improved quality control and the reduced cost resulting from registration, many see the advantages of asking their suppliers to consider ISO 9000. The suppliers would achieve similar benefits and the supplier-customer chain would be strengthened.

The selection of new suppliers is a critical task. If a poor supplier is inadvertently selected it can jeopardize a company's performance and be costly to fix. A supplier with a committed management, who routinely audits its quality system and treats problems as opportunities to improve, would naturally be a more attractive supplier than a competitor without those attributes.

The practice of assessing suppliers is both costly and time consuming. It is difficult to manage and can lack objectivity. A company desperate to find a new supplier might be obliged to temporarily approve a supplier it considers inadequate. And customer assessments do not necessarily result in good working relationships with suppliers, especially with the ever present threat of non-approval. Contracts based on such practices will probably not build good customer-supplier relationships.

It is more rewarding to find suppliers who are registered to ISO 9000 and work with them to develop products and services that meet your requirements. Using their quality system to improve your operations develops win–win situations.

ISO 9000 was born out of the need to address this customer-supplier assessment problem. It is inconsistent for registered companies to conduct their own supplier assessments.

Suppliers also benefit from customers using ISO 9000 registration as a criterion for selecting suppliers. Any supplier who provides products to more than one customer is subject to working and being audited under more than one standard. The suppliers to the automobile industry in the United States faced this confusing and costly situation and asked the industry to adopt a single quality system standard. They did so—it is ISO 9000.

Of course, the availability of registered suppliers in your business and location needs to be considered. If there are none available, such a policy will obviously fail. As the number of registered companies grows, however, it will become more viable.

Resale of Goods and Services

If an ISO 9000-registered company sells products or services it purchases from non-registered sources, it must reveal this information. This occurs frequently with distributors. As explained in Chapter 20, a registered distributor must ensure that the customer knows whether the goods came from a registered system. This requires a clear statement to that effect on any quotations, order acknowledgments, delivery notes, and invoices.

This requirement also stands for registered companies that sell goods made by others, alongside those they manufacture themselves. If the company publicizes its registration, as most do, it must ensure that customers know which items come from non-registered quality systems.

This might seem a little strange. It would be stranger still, however, if a small manufacturer achieved registration and then expanded its product line by purchasing finished goods and selling them as if they were made in the registered system.

The situation is not always so clear cut, of course. A public relations company might arrange the design and production of brochures through a freelance graphic designer and a printer. The printer might subcontract the color proofing to a specialized color separation shop. If the public relations agency registers to ISO 9000, indicating its scope is public relations, no problem arises. If it claims to provide design and printing services, however, it operates outside the scope of its registration, unless its suppliers are also ISO 9000 registered.

Unfortunately, a company is not required to define the scope of its registration when it includes the registration mark on its stationery and literature. A customer can check with the Registrar, but more often will assume the mark covers all the activities of the company.

Prior to the ISO 9000 audit, the auditor will take care to clearly define the scope of the registration and to audit all of the company's activities within that scope. They also ask if the company has any activities outside of the scope. If so, they must ensure that the excluded activities do not appear to others to be within the registered scope. An ISO 9000 auditor will monitor this on surveillance audits. This situation most often arises when one site within a group achieves registration. The extent of the registered system must be made clear to customers and potential customers.

To avoid the necessity of these exceptions, your suppliers should be encouraged to seek registration. Then you may freely publicize that all products and services are provided by registered systems.

SECTION SEVEN

AND FINALLY...

If you are following this book from cover to cover, by now you will be registered and enjoying the benefits of a well-tuned quality system and delighted customers. The section addresses some of the ill-founded criticisms of the Standard and how your registration *can* lead you into Total Quality. It looks at the future development of the ISO 9000 Standard and its use.

CONTENTS

Chapter 38 ◆ Myths and Misunderstandings

Introduction

ISO 9000 is the first global quality system standard. Many industries and nations pursue quality beyond the scope of the ISO 9000 Standard. The Japanese show that relentless pursuit of improvement—*kaizen*—can be a way of life. Throughout the world, however, there are millions of organizations with no quality program and no understanding of what comprises a quality system. The ISO 9000 Standard is achievable and rewarding when it is understood and implemented.

Unfortunately, there are some myths and misconceptions about the ISO 9000 Standard that persist despite its overwhelming record of success. Some of these are inspired by the nature and requirements of the Standard itself; others seem to have simply sprung from the ground like weeds.

Bureaucracy

One of the most persistent myths states that ISO 9000 is an attempt to bureaucratize quality, setting up regulations and a new host of functionaries to maintain them. This argument focuses on the documentation required by ISO 9000 and audits performed both by internal and external auditors. Documentation is an element of the ISO 9000 Standard. It requires that *you say what you intend to do* and then *do what you said.* To do that, your plan must be written down.

The Process Management Model produces documentation that is optimized to ensure efficient control of processes. Whether the documentation, or the activities of the auditors, result in a bureaucratic approach to quality will depend on the attitude of the company's managers. If they create documents for the sake of creating documents, that's bureaucracy. If they view the creation of documents as the embodiment of an efficient system, it will serve a vital purpose in the control of the company. The documents, as they are presented here, serve to communicate, not to confuse.

The role of auditors is positive. Their activities help to tune the system, finding opportunities for improvement, not creating useless requirements. ISO 9000 does nothing to instill waste; it drives it out. The ISO 9000 auditors are a unique type of supplier, selected and hired by the organization for their expertise—and ultimate recommendation—for registration to ISO 9000.

Consistency, Not Quality

Another major myth holds that the ISO 9000 Standard is not about quality at all, but merely about consistency. It has been suggested that if a company makes a poor product or provides inferior service, and consistently does just that, it can still achieve registration. This is not true. The ISO 9000 Standard requires a company to have a quality policy that addresses the needs and expectations of its customers. They have to define the product or service they offer, meet all applicable legal requirements, and respond to any complaints they receive. In other words, the standard requires registered companies to strive for customer satisfaction and to use any shortfall as an opportunity to improve. By committing to these concepts, the organization locks itself into a continual improvement cycle.

Inspector-Oriented

Some say the Standard requires an army of inspectors and testers to check on the output of others. The word inspector does not appear in the Standard, but the words *inspection* and *test* and *verify* (and their derivatives) appear many times. The Standard emphasizes that someone must confirm that processes and products meet requirements. It doesn't say the company must have an inspector. The verification may come from the same people who are responsible for the processes. We know of no organization that has followed the Process Management approach to registration and increased the number of its inspectors to meet the Standard. Many, in fact, reduced the number.

Quality Manager

A few quality professionals maintain that the quality manager should be a member of executive management. The Standard identifies the role of Management Representative, but not of the quality manager. Companies may name the quality manager as the Management Representative, but ISO 9000 does not require it. The quality effort may be represented at the executive level by someone who oversees the quality manager. Organizations may use various officers, *i.e.* the Chief Financial Officer, the Vice President of Operations, or the Vice President of Marketing as the Management Representative.

Registered Suppliers

Yet another myth alleges that once registered to ISO 9000, companies may only purchase products and services from other ISO 9000 registered organizations. The Standard says only that a registered company must determine that its suppliers and subcontractors can meet its requirements. The supplier does not have to be registered in order to do that. The registered company may introduce the requirement of ISO 9000 registration, but alternative options, such as an analysis of previous performance or screening on receipt, are also acceptable. The acid test is effectiveness, based on how well the product or service satisfies the customer.

Supplier Visits

The purchasing requirements written into contracts are sometimes also misunderstood. Some companies think they must reserve the right to visit a supplier to confirm the quality of the goods. The Standard does state this, but with the reservation "where specified in the contract..." Correctly interpreted, the clause limits verification at the source to situations where this requirement is defined in the contract with the customer. This is a throwback to the old military standards and has little relevance in normal commercial activities.

Traceability

Issues also arise over traceability; that is, the ability to positively identify a specific item or material batch throughout the entire manufacturing cycle, from raw material to finished product. Traceability demonstrates that the manufacturer used the specified material and provides information for product recalls. These requirements mainly apply to industries with high safety risks such as food and drug manufacture, aerospace, oil and chemical production, and the nuclear industries. ISO 9000 makes clear that the customer must specify that product traceability is wanted. But any manufacturer may use it to meet legal or other requirements.

Excessive Inspection

The clause on receiving inspection and testing allows a company to define what procedures it will use to verify incoming products. Often companies interpret this to mean they must inspect incoming goods. Actually, it allows a company to define how it intends to verify incoming goods. The company may decide not to inspect items purchased from approved suppliers. If such a policy is not effective, the company takes corrective action, which may involve inspecting certain predefined items, or showing what the Standard calls "documented evidence of quality conformance."

Documented evidence could be in the form of Certificates of Conformance from the supplier. But ISO 9000 does not require certificates of conformance. In our experience, a certificate of conformance from a poor supplier proves little, and one from a good supplier is a waste of paper. Test or inspection results are a better means of accomplishing the same thing.

Some mistakenly believe the ISO 9000 Standard's requirements on final inspection and test mandates that everything has to be inspected and tested. It does not. The organization itself has to define what to inspect and test in quality plans or procedures. Then it has to do what it says it will do.

Secure Stockrooms

The Standard says a company must have an effective system to prevent the inadvertent or unauthorized use of nonconforming products. That doesn't mean, as some believe, that goods have to be locked up. A label may be sufficient. On the other hand, if the organizational culture indicates to managers that a lock is necessary, then a secure place with a good lock is in order. The company chooses a policy and demonstrates its effectiveness. An ISO 9000 auditor can question the policy if he finds the system to be ineffective.

Security issues should be considered in the context of the organizational environment and the production methods being used. Few companies would consider locking up machines or demanding a receipt for every nut and bolt.

Summary

All of these myths, misunderstandings, and misinterpretations tend to confuse managers and employees seeking to learn about ISO 9000. When properly interpreted and understood, the ISO 9000 requirements are simply based on sound management and common sense.

Chapter 39 ◆ ISO 9000 and Total Quality

The pursuit of quality in industry and business is a crucial issue today, equated with success or failure or even survival. Some organizations pursue quality according to the ideas of W. Edwards Deming, Joseph M. Juran, Philip Crosby, or through a mixture of their ideas. Others seek quality through registration to ISO 9000.

These theories and practices are referred to by many as Total Quality. How do they differ? How are they alike? Do they complement each other? If so, how? These are some of the typical questions that arise about the two. There is no attempt here to explain Total Quality in detail. Our aim is to help readers understand some of the basic precepts of Total Quality and how ISO 9000 relates to them.

For the purpose of this discussion, every organization fits into one of two categories—those already involved in Total Quality and those not.

If you already pursue Total Quality, you might ask:

Do we need ISO 9000?

How will ISO 9000 fit with my Total Quality philosophies and methods?

If you have not addressed Total Quality, you might ask:

Do we need Total Quality, ISO 9000, or both?

Where should we start?
- With ISO 9000?
- With Total Quality?
- With both?

Before we consider these issues, however, let's look at the background and develop some basic definitions for some of these terms. For instance, what is quality? What is Total Quality?

Quality

Achieving quality requires a clear definition of quality. Outside of the confines of business and industry, the measure of quality is subjective. To move away from this subjectivity, business and industry ties quality to the customer through a specification or standard. In some quarters, quality becomes the consistent meeting of specifications or standards. Quality Professionals often define quality as meeting specifications with the lowest rate of variation possible.

The failure to meet specifications, or producing products or services which are unsuitable for use, certainly indicates the lack of quality. This is not the same as saying that meeting specifications, or producing suitable products or services do constitute quality. The customer may demand products and services better than the standard. Ultimately, quality is defined by the customer.

If quality is equated with goodness, and specifications are associated with rules or laws, then it must be good to adhere to the laws. Mere adherence to those laws, however, does not indicate goodness. There is, in the meaning of these terms, a neutral position where goodness is neither demonstrated nor negated. Goodness, or quality, begins a level above this neutral position.

Quality has to relate to the needs and expectations of the customer. This is an eternal truth. Plato said it more than 2,000 years ago. The same principle is embodied in ISO 9000 today. Customers seek products and services that meet their needs and expectations—at a price they agree to pay.

Total Quality

There is no commonly accepted definition of Total Quality. Companies define it differently and seek it differently. But there are some important basic elements that most companies consider part of their Total Quality effort. These are:

1. Satisfying and exceeding the needs of customers—internal as well as external.
2. Involving, utilizing, and empowering all employees.
3. Striving to continually improve.
4. Basing decisions on facts and using analytical tools to solve prob lems and improve processes.

Your definition may include other philosophies and concepts. But this basic list provides a conceptual foundation on which to discuss the similarities and differences between ISO 9000 and Total Quality.

It is easy to argue that ISO 9000 and Total Quality are compatible and complementary. However, Total Quality goes further than ISO 9000, and there is some speculation that the 1996 ISO 9000 update will bring more features of Total Quality into the Standard.

ISO 9000 and Total Quality share the same underlying aim of achieving customer satisfaction. ISO 9000 does not address internal customers directly, but the defining of the quality system clarifies internal interfaces and enables improvements in communication and teamwork to happen.

The search for Total Quality is strongly customer-focused. ISO 9000 registered companies have quality policies that address the needs and expectations of their customers. The registration of their quality system demonstrates the implementation of this policy.

The ISO 9000 Standards, as discussed throughout the book, are not prescriptive. That is, they do not say how to meet the Standard or how to run your business. Hence the standards do not specifically discuss empowering employees, but if a system is well defined, it facilitates empowerment. You must include employees in the development and documentation of your quality system. Employees are required to be adequately trained for their jobs. After all, the quality system is their system too. They use it and are in the best position to help improve it.

While assisting companies to achieve ISO 9000 registration, the Authors have observed a pleasing byproduct. Organizations frequently become less compartmentalized, more focused on the common goal, and particularly focused on the policy for quality.

ISO 9000 acts to encourage continual improvement. In fact, four specific requirements—internal auditing, management review, statistical techniques, and corrective and preventive action—provide the necessary mechanism and discipline. Companies with effective corrective action processes use analytical tools for analysis and fact-based decisions.

ISO 9000's requirements for document control, sometimes viewed as "just more paperwork," are, in fact, a discipline that proves helpful to employees. People learn how to use the system and see its value. *Seat-of-the-pants* management becomes less necessary—and less acceptable.

There has been considerable discussion of the need for standards. The need for, and the benefits of international standards are obvious and incontrovertible. However, some people think standards are an end point fixed in concrete, and they believe working to a standard excludes continual improvement. The fact is, all companies, those who seek Total Quality and those who do not, have standards and must work to standards. Standards must not be viewed as a limit to continual improvement, innovation, and creativity. Standards provide guides and structure that should encourage the search for better products and services.

Total Quality is a never-ending effort. You can always get better. ISO 9000 should be thought of in the same way. No organization can survive unless it is continually changing and improving to meet the evolving needs of its customers.

ISO 9000 registration benefits the organization by giving recognition to its quality system; that it satisfies the requirements of an international standard. It is not an end point, but a recognizable milestone. Everyone can take pride in the achievement, but it's not time to lean back, put your feet on your desk, and light up a big cigar. You must still continue to improve—all your competitors are doing so.

If your customers need and expect your organization to become registered to ISO 9000, you have little choice. *The Process Management Model is a Total Quality approach to getting registered.* It is also the least painful or disruptive approach and brings the most benefits to your system.

ISO 9000 and Total Quality are complementary. Both are needed. Depending on where your organization is today, the next section discusses how to proceed.

Total Quality Companies

Total Quality and ISO 9000 are entirely compatible, as already shown by the many companies using both. For instance, many industrialized countries have awards which include definitions of quality and recognize organizations with advanced Total Quality programs (such as the Deming Prize in Japan, Malcolm Balridge National Quality Award in the United States, and the European Quality Award in Europe). Many winners of these awards have become registered to ISO 9000. Examples are Zytec Corporation, IBM, and Xerox. These organizations say that ISO 9000 has helped them standardize, formalize, and improve their processes. They also cite marketing and other operational benefits.

Non-Total Quality Companies

If you are new to quality, ISO 9000 is an excellent place to start. Many companies address quality for the first time when they embark on a program leading to ISO 9000 registration. It is often the first executive management discussion aimed at developing a quality policy: management holding review meetings to discuss the achievement of quality. Then they begin the internal quality auditing program. All of these are a normal part of the process of preparation for registration. They bring quality issues to management's attention.

The documentation of the quality system often results in improvements in operating methods. Management sees these as benefits of the quality program. They begin to accept the fact that quality improvements result in operating improvements.

Many managers have seen benefits from the ISO 9000 program and want it to continue. They believe that ISO 9000 registration has improved their companies, and Total Quality is the next logical step. The use of the Process Management Model starts a company off on the right foot, and leads naturally into Total Quality.

Overall, there is no conflict between Total Quality and ISO 9000 registration. In many respects there is harmony and support. Indeed, ISO 9000 registration is a fine way to begin a Total Quality effort.

Chapter 40 ◆ ISO 9000 in the Future

Before it becomes accepted in a market or country, a new product, service, or profession must achieve a critical mass. For ISO 9000, as a successful new standard for quality, this was reached in the U.K. in the metal-working industries around 1990, in other manufacturing industries in 1992, and in many service sectors in 1993. Total U.K. registrations are now around 25,000, but with hundreds of assessments taking place each month, it is an impossible task to obtain an accurate up-to-date figure.

The rest of the world, however, has been slower to adopt the Standard, with about 40,000 organizations registered across the globe. Exponential growth began in 1993 in the United States, Europe, Canada, Japan, and other nations. As the numbers grow, acceptance of the Standard grows.

Total Company Registration

As more businesses accept ISO 9000 and see its value to their operations, its application to the whole company has emerged. This development is known as Total Company Registration.

Within companies, primary processes are used to directly meet customers' requirements, which are supported by secondary processes. In a manufacturing business, the primary processes are activities such as design, production, purchasing, and delivery. Secondary processes are activities such as security, catering, finance, and personnel. ISO 9000 registration mainly applies to primary processes since these directly impact customers' needs and expectations.

In large companies, the scope of registration to ISO 9000 does not involve employees in the secondary processes, leaving them feeling somewhat left out. To them, it may appear that their work is less important.

Many companies, seeing the benefits from improved control of their primary processes, have decided to do the same for their secondary processes. They have chosen to treat these processes as external suppliers to the primary processes. The secondary processes then have had to meet the needs and expectations of the primary processes—their customers.

Managers of these secondary processes have defined their own quality policies, developed their own quality systems, and obtained ISO 9000 registration.

This new practice, registering both primary and secondary processes, is Total Company Registration. It enables all employees in a company to feel part of the quality system and the quality team.

Changes in the Standard

Its remarkable flexibility and universality give ISO 9000 an appeal beyond what anyone expected when it first emerged as BS 5750. There is every indication that ISO 9000 will be established on the world scene by the time its next major revision occurs in 1996.

The widespread acceptance itself becomes a problem since the larger numbers and widely diverse industries and cultures make changing the Standard a more complex process. Also, the impact of the changes will be much broader and deeper.

Revision, however, is always necessary to reflect changes in the environment. The current language of ISO 9000 is clearly more applicable to manufacturing than to service industries. Meanwhile, the ISO 9000 Standard's controllers, ISO Committee 176, are publishing guidelines for four generic product types: hardware, software, processed materials, and service. The guidelines should make the current version of the ISO 9000 Standard easier to understand and apply.

The debate now is over how much to change the Standard in 1996. Some say that for ISO 9000 to be universally accepted as a quality standard, it should take more of a Total Quality Management approach. Needless to say, that would mean a complete makeover, with an effort to pin down what must be involved in the concept of total quality. Many of the companies currently registered have less than 20 employees. How will they adopt a total quality approach?

The first drafts of the revised Standard, due for release in 1996, are already in circulation. Some of the proposed changes would place greater emphasis on training and educating employees, recognizing their roles as carriers of the organization. Marketing and the need for continual improvement also appear to be marked for more prominence.

The proposed changes are still under debate—a process that will probably be both long and contentious. A detailed examination of its content is not worthwhile now, but the Standard will almost certainly continue along the lines in this book. This edition is designed to take companies to successful registration to the 1994 issue of ISO 9000.

This revision process is looking forward to providing an international standard that will anticipate the critical features of standardization of quality systems by the year 2000. Called "Vision 2000," the revised Standard is intended as a vision for quality in the next century. The changes are not so radical that the current Standard will cease to exist. Meeting the ISO 9000 Standard today will start organizations on their journey toward this vision.

Indeed, ISO 9000 is well established as the international standard for quality. Like democracy, it isn't perfect, but it's the best we have. Its flexibility and global appeal allow it to fit each environment, across both corporate and ethnic cultures. The process for registration is well-known and respected internationally. Its central themes of customer focus and recognition that quality systems must be understood in order to be efficient have a simple yet powerful message. Registration, with its accompanying audits and surveillance visits, provide a way to measure the quality system's efficiency and improve it.

An organization that embraces these notions of customer focus and quality systems will improve and enjoy good relationships with employees, customers, suppliers, and society in general. Intangible benefits of pride and satisfaction will pervade its own culture, setting the stage for never-ending process improvement, individual development, and ultimately, high quality products and services enjoyed by delighted customers.

APPENDICES

INTRODUCTION

The appendices are intended to help you design and develop your quality system and to effectively achieve registration to ISO 9000. They include the following:

Appendix A: Chapter 3 and the Procedure Guides of Chapter 9 interpret ISO 9001 requirements so you can comply in the optimal way for your business. Appendix A provides further insight on the meaning and interpretation of the ISO 9001 requirements.

Appendix B: This appendix supplements the discussion on planning your registration effort (covered in Chapter 5). It shows the major milestones for achieving registration, in either 8, 12, or 18 months.

Appendix C: Flowcharts are useful tools to understand, document, communicate, and improve processes. They are used to document existing and new processes. This appendix provides basic information on flowcharting.

Appendix D: This appendix contains sample documentation from organizations who have achieved ISO 9000 registration. The appendices will guide you in designing and developing your unique quality system. But remember, *they are someone else's end point, and should not be your starting point.*

Appendix E: This appendix provides sources for the ISO 9000 Standard, Consulting and Training assistance, and other ISO 9000 related services.

Appendix F: The glossary is designed to provide consistent definitions of the terms used in this book.

CONTENTS

Appendix A

A Detailed Review — ISO 9001:

Quality Systems: Model for Quality Assurance in Design, Development, Production, Installation, and Servicing

This Appendix is a section-by-section review of the ISO 9001 Standard and its requirements. While Chapter 3 provides an overview of the Standard's requirements, and the Procedure Guides in Chapter 9 translate those requirements into quality system activities and tasks, the explanations and interpretations found here are presented in an easy-to-use format. This Appendix will be helpful when the reader is not sure about the meaning of a particular clause of the Standard.

0.0 Introduction

The purpose of ISO 9001 and the two associated Standards, ISO 9002 and ISO 9003, are to provide buyers of goods and services with a level of confidence that their suppliers meet certain external quality requirements. The ISO 9000 Standards detail the provisions of a quality system that can ensure that the buyers' requirements are agreed to and met.

It is intended that the ISO 9000 Standards be universally accepted in their present form. The Standards are generic and intended for application to the quality system of any organization. ISO Standards do not address the specifics of products and services.

A quality system that is developed to meet ISO 9000 requirements must reflect the needs of the organization, the products and services it provides, and the processes it uses. Some organizations use the ISO 9000 Standards as a basic system and introduce additional requirements for their own specific needs.

Such specifics, referred to as "technical standards," define the characteristics and requirements of products and services to be delivered to the customer. ISO Standards are to be complementary with technical standards.

1.0 Scope

ISO 9001 applies to organizations that design products and services. These organizations must demonstrate certain capabilities in design, development, production, and installation and service. ISO 9002 and ISO 9003 define a more limited scope. The distinction between ISO 9001 and ISO 9002 is the design capability.

2.0 Normative References

This paragraph links the ISO 9001 Standard to other ISO Standards. It encourages users of ISO 9000 to apply the most recent Standard and to incorporate other ISO Standards in developing their quality systems.

3.0 Definitions

ISO 8402 is referenced as the source for definitions when using the ISO 9000 Standards.

"Product," as used throughout the ISO 9000 Standards, is "the output of a process." Such output is called "hardware" (physical items), "software" (information usually associated with computer systems), "processed materials" (materials from continual processes), and "services" (usually delivered by a person). Often the output of an organization is a combination of these items.

4.0 Quality Systems Requirements

This section defines the features and characteristics of a quality system. Organizations are assessed against this section of the Standard. The following is intended to aid in interpreting an organization's requirements. Some key terms used in the Standard are:

Supplier	=	the organization applying ISO 9001
Customer	=	its customer
Subcontractor	=	its supplier
Operator	=	anyone in the organization
Product	=	output broadly defined to include both goods and services
Shall	=	a requirement of the Standard that must be met
Notes	=	explanations which are not necessarily requirements

4.1 Management Responsibility

The management and control of quality within an organization must be the responsibility of its executive management.

First, executive management must define a quality policy. This policy should address the activities of the organization and the needs and expectations of its customers. It must be communicated to and understood by employees at all levels of the organization. This policy must be the basis of a quality system, which will assure that the policy is implemented and maintained.

Second, executive management must define and document the responsibilities for implementing the quality policy and delegate the necessary authority. Management must provide the resources required for the implementation of the quality policy and ensure that assigned employees are adequately trained.

A Management Representative for Quality must be identified and take specific responsibility for the establishment, implementation and maintenance of the quality system. This executive, at minimum, should provide management oversight of the system and may delegate associated tasks.

The Management Representative for Quality is required to keep executive management informed of the operation and effectiveness of the quality system.

Third, management must review the progress of the organization against its defined objectives. The reviews must be formal, and records must be kept. The frequency of these reviews ensures that management controls and is aware of the performance of the quality system. Most organizations schedule Management Reviews every one to three months.

4.2 Quality System

This section establishes the need for a documented quality system. The system needs to include a quality manual and procedures. The quality manual relates the system to the ISO 9000 Standard. The quality manual does this by referencing the corresponding parts of the documented quality system to the ISO 9001 requirements. Procedures document the organization's processes.

Detailed work instructions for the performance of such procedures may be needed. The need and level of detail depend on the qualifications and experience of the personnel performing the tasks. Work instructions need to relate to the procedures.

A separate quality plan is not needed provided that the documented quality system defines how quality requirements are met. New projects, either initiated from within or because of a customer contract, require a quality plan if existing systems do not sufficiently define how quality is to be achieved. The quality plan requirement is a recognition that the quality system must change to ensure control as the organization develops. Such quality plans need to be integrated into the quality system.

4.3 Contract Review

Every order and contract with a customer must clearly define the goods and services to be provided. Prior to accepting a contract or order, the organization must verify its capability and capacity to complete the transaction. A contract exists when an offer by one party is unconditionally accepted by the other party. It need not be a written legal document. For example, an order from a catalog constitutes a contract.

Hence, it follows that ISO 9000 requirements should be applied to all offers made by the company. The details of the offer need to be clearly articulated, and the organization must have the wherewithal and capability to provide what is being offered. Where this is not possible, then the terms and limitations of the offer need to be defined and included in the offer. For example, a seminar or concert provider offers seats, but only subject to availability.

The acceptance of an offer is normally in the form of an order. Orders may be written or verbal depending on the nature of the business. Verbal orders need to be recorded. The details of an order should be reviewed to confirm that they are understood, are in accordance with the offer, and can be fulfilled.

The processing of contracts and orders and possible changes to those contracts and orders need to be defined. It is especially important that all those who need to know are made aware of the contract and order changes.

4.4 Design Control

In the design of a product or service, control procedures must ensure that all activities are performed and that records of work and results are generated and maintained throughout the design process.

Design needs to commence with a plan which defines milestones, responsibilities and time scales, assigns qualified personnel, and provides necessary resources to the work. Design Plans need to be reviewed and updated as the project progresses.

The relationships between the design function and other groups and functions, both inside and outside of the organization, must be defined. A process must be established for efficient communication and interaction with other groups and functions.

The design process starts with inputs which normally are product requirements or product briefs. Statutory and regulatory requirements relevant to the product must be included in the requirements.

The output of the design process is normally in the form of specifications and drawings which define the product or service. Critical features of the design must be identified and "acceptance criteria" established. The design is then evaluated to determine if these requirements are met. All output documents need to be reviewed and approved prior to the release of the product or service.

The design should be reviewed at defined stages by interested parties such as sales, purchasing, production, quality personnel, and by the customer, if appropriate. Design verification can be achieved by calculations, comparisons with proven designs, tests, or demonstrations.

Once the design meets requirements, it should be validated. Validation can be by prototype, model, initial batch of production, or pilot delivery of a new service. During the validation, further tests are carried out.

Changes to the design need to be documented and approved before being implemented.

4.5 Document and Data Control

All documents relating to the quality system must be controlled, and procedures defining this control must be established. Document control means that changes to the documents are only made by a proper authority, and that only current/pertinent issues are available. Controlled documents include quality system documents—quality and procedure manuals, work instructions—and product specifications and drawings, sales and product literature, and externally-produced documents such as standards and customer and supplier specifications.

The content of the organization-produced documents must be reviewed and approved by authorized personnel. This can be any member of the organization and can be the same person who prepared the document. The position needs to be defined in the document control procedure.

Changes to documents must be reviewed and approved by the function that initially approved them.

Changes made to documents must be indicated on the document by a change in revision or issue level. A method for removing or marking all obsolete documents needs to be defined and a distribution list maintained.

Where data is on computer systems, there must be a procedure to ensure its security and safe storage. This requires a procedure for controlling the production and storage of data backup and the control of access to data through methods such as passwords.

4.6 Purchasing

Purchased products and services must meet the requirements for which they are intended. This is accomplished with three controls—the use of qualified suppliers, precise descriptions of what is purchased, and verification of those purchases.

The Standard refers to the evaluation of subcontractors whose products and services impact the quality of the products or service provided by the organization. Subcontractor or supplier evaluation can be done by a variety of methods depending on how critical the purchased product or service is to the quality of the products and services of the organization. The evaluation may be based on a supplier's past performance or performance on trial orders. The supplier's quality system can also be evaluated either by third party assessment, such as ISO 9000, or by second party assessment. Whatever method is used, it must be defined and documented in a procedure.

For control purposes, purchase orders can specify that the products or services being purchased shall be supplied within a registered quality system such as ISO 9000. This is not a requirement of the Standard. If this is used, the order must fully define the title, number, and issue of the standard, *e.g.* ISO 9001:1994 Quality Systems.

Purchasing documents need to clearly define the product or service being purchased either by detailed descriptions or by reference to catalog numbers, specifications or other technical data.

Before orders or other purchasing documents are released, they must be reviewed and approved by designated personnel. Verbal orders must be recorded and maintained, including reference to the subcontractor.

It is the responsibility of the purchaser to verify that purchased products and services are as ordered. Verification can be done visually or by inspecting/testing key product characteristics. ISO 9001 does not specify how an incoming product is verified. The organization determines what is appropriate.

If verification at the supplier's premises is desired by either the organization or its customer, it must be specified in the purchase order. ISO 9000 does not require on-site verifications. This does not remove the organization's responsibility to ensure that the supplier performs.

4.7 Customer-Supplied Product

In some business relationships, the customer supplies material, parts, documents, equipment or tools to its suppliers. ISO 9000 refers to these items that are owned by the customer as customer- or purchaser-supplied material. In some industries it is known as free issue material.

Some examples are parts sent to a subcontract plating firm for plating and special labels for placement on a customer's products. In service industries customers may supply information and documents. Records should be kept of the receipt of such items, and the items should be kept in a safe place. Lost or damaged items need to be reported to the customer.

4.8 Product Identification and Traceability

Product identification is a means of positively identifying either in-process parts or completed items. Where identification is obvious, there is no need to introduce an identification system. For example, apples and potatoes can be identified by appearance, so there is no need to label them. If, however, different varieties of a product are stored together, it may be necessary to introduce a labeling system. Documents, which are usually the products of a service business, can be identified by title, number, date, and revision.

Traceability is a means to identify and locate products that have critical components or were produced from a particular batch of materials. In some industries where concerns of health, safety and environment are an issue, traceability is a requirement. In the pharmaceutical, food and aerospace industries, traceability is common. Traceability can be requested by the customer or required by industry or government regulation.

Organizations may implement traceability for their own purposes. If a product liability claim is filed, for example, traceability can help identify the date of purchase and the supplier of critical components. If a warranty claim arises, traceability can establish the date of production.

4.9 Process Control

Process Control requirements apply to all processes used in the production or supply of products and services. In manufacturing environments these are typically inventory control, purchasing, fabrication and production, assembly and test processes. In service environments all processes that contribute to the delivered service are included. For example, for a personnel agency seeking ISO 9000 registration, the process of selecting candidates comes under the requirements of this section. (In a manufacturing plant, personnel recruitment is outside the scope of the Standard.)

All processes necessary to produce, deliver, install, and service a product should be performed so that quality policy and objectives are achieved. Organizations must employ the necessary resources to ensure this. A means of control should ensure that what is required is actually done, and accompanying records kept.

Instructions such as procedures, specifications, recipes, drawings, etc. are needed "where the absence of such procedures can adversely affect quality." The complexity of the process and the qualifications of the employees doing the work determine whether or not instructions are necessary. A thorough explanation can be found in Chapter 11.

The Standard requires that equipment used in the operation of a process be suitable for the process. The quality of products and services must determine suitability of equipment. Procedures may be required to assess equipment suitability. There need to be procedures to control the maintenance of equipment to ensure continued process capability.

Where external standards, codes of practice, legislation, plans or procedures are applicable, the quality system must determine and ensure that they are adhered to.

The standard of quality required is defined by specifications, tolerances, examples, illustrations, or other similar means. These should illustrate or define both what is acceptable and what is not acceptable. The standards can be specific to certain products or operations or generic to process outputs.

"Special processes" are those where it is not possible to determine from the output whether or not the process has been successfully carried out. In these cases, verifying that the output is to specification can be done by controlling and recording process input parameters, by testing (and thereby destroying) extra products or items, or by using qualified operators who can demonstrate their control of the process by special tests.

An example of a special process is precision welding. Weld penetration can only be confirmed by cutting the weld. A sample weld can be tested with the same parameters as the required weld to "qualify" the process and establish a level of confidence in the process. Other examples are heat treatment of steel, cooking of soufflés, etc.

4.10 Inspection and Testing

Process outputs (products and services) must conform to specified requirements. This can be done by any suitable verification means—even inspection by the process operator. There is no requirement for independent inspections or any kinds of tests. The organization determines what is suitable to ensure quality. This section of the Standard addresses receiving, in-process, and final inspection and testing.

Not all purchased material needs to be inspected. Purchased items must be verified to confirm that they meet requirements. The method of verification is left to the organization, and needs to relate to the nature of the items, their source, and their importance to quality.

When purchased items come from an approved source and are clearly identified, verification can be based on physical observation and the supplier's documentation. In reality, customers accept the majority of items they purchase on this basis. Inspecting or testing purchased items is beyond most buyers' expertise and can be counterproductive.

When purchased items are to be tested or inspected, they should not be released until the results are known. If they are released earlier, there should be a method of identifying them for possible recall.

In-process inspections and tests may be necessary to confirm that components, products, and services are to specification. These can be carried out by the process operators. Records indicating such verification must be kept. Where verification is required, the release of the items should be controlled until the verification results are known.

Prior to delivery to the customer or finished goods inventory, confirmation is required that all specified inspections and tests have been completed and there are no concerns outstanding. The authority for the release must be defined and a record kept of who authorized each release. The organization must define the mechanism for releasing products and services. Records should demonstrate that such policy is implemented and effective.

4.11 Control of Inspection, Measuring, and Test Equipment

When measuring devices and equipment are used to verify product or service quality, the instruments must be accurate and job-appropriate. Measuring equipment should have a known accuracy of at least 10% of the tolerance band of the measurement.

The accuracy of measuring equipment is determined by comparing their measuring performance to the performance of "masters" of known accuracy. This is the start of a chain of checks that needs to be traceable back to national or physical standards. The link to national standards must be demonstrated by documentation.

The Standard requires a formal calibration program that includes all necessary information and instructions for calibrating equipment. Equipment should be labeled so operators know the calibration period. Adjustable calibrated equipment must be sealed to prevent unauthorized adjustments. ISO 9000 auditors are interested in seeing calibration certificates from outside bodies.

Calibration must be done under special environmental conditions when needed for the accuracy of the measurements or to simulate where the measuring equipment is used.

4.12 Inspection and Test Status

When products and components are inspected, the outcome must be clearly indicated. This may be done on the accompanying documents, by where the product is placed, or by marking the product.

This clause also applies to service organizations which require records for verification.

4.13 Control of Nonconforming Product

Items not conforming to their specifications have to be identified and/or segregated to prevent their use. A means of disposing of nonconforming items must be established and documented. There are four possibilities:

1) Items may be reprocessed or reworked to bring them back to specifications. The items would then meet the requirements after reprocessing and could be used.
2) The items may be accepted by a "concession." A concession gives permission to relax the specification for certain items or periods only. The design authority and/or the customer (if appropriate) must approve. The items may be used in the original nonconforming condition or reworked to a more acceptable level—but still not to specification. For example, a cabinet may be dented, but the dent is in the back and not visible. If the customer agrees to accept it anyway, this would be an example of original nonconforming condition. If the dent is on the front and clearly visible, the customer may agree to buy it, but only after the dent is filled and the cabinet repainted. The cabinet still may not be to specification, but it would be acceptable. In either case, documented acceptance by the customer is required.
3) The items may be regraded and used for different applications. This can include blending faulty material with good.
4) The items may be scrapped and disposed of. The method of disposal needs to be defined to prevent re-use of the items.

4.14 Corrective and Preventive Action

The philosophy of ISO 9000 is to produce and provide goods and services that meet certain specifications, and when they don't, to make the necessary changes and improvements. The changes and improvements should not only be remedial to correct the problem (corrective action), but must also prevent the cause of the problem and its recurrence (preventive action).

Executive management must ensure that the corrective and preventive action process analyzes shortfalls in performance, identifies corrective and preventive actions, and ensures that such actions are effective.

4.15 Handling, Storage, Packaging, Preservation, and Delivery

The Standard requires the products, components, and materials to be preserved and protected in handling, storage, packaging, and delivery. These activities must be included in the documented quality system.

For controlled usage, dates must be tracked on items and materials with limited lives. Procedures need to be in place to control items requiring special storage conditions such as temperature, hygiene, and humidity levels.

The contract with the customer must specify the party responsible for delivery, and documentation must show that the products were delivered in accordance with the contract requirements.

4.16 Control of Quality Records

The operation of the quality system produces records which demonstrate the operation and effectiveness of the quality system. They must be readable and stored for a defined period in a manner that allows easy retrieval. The period is not specified in the Standard but should relate to the life of the product. If the product has only a short life, *e.g.* fast food, there is no point in retaining records for years. If the product has a life of several years, records need to be kept for years. In some instances, the contract specifies the length of time for record retention.

Hard copy, microfilm, and electronic media are all acceptable means of keeping records. If electronic media is used, precautions must be taken to ensure retrievability and readability, especially when computer hardware changes.

4.17 Internal Quality Audits

Internal audits of the quality system are required and are used to confirm that the quality system is being operated as defined. These audits must be planned and performed by employee auditors who are independent of the area being audited and who are trained in auditing techniques. The results are reported to the executive management.

The results of the audits must be recorded, and appropriate corrective actions should be agreed to and taken. The responsibility for corrective actions belongs to the line management. The effectiveness of these actions is confirmed by subsequent audits.

Internal audits are not meant to confirm compliance to ISO 9000 requirements. Compliance is built into the quality system when it is designed and documented.

4.18 Training

The qualifications for each position in the organization must to be defined. Employee records should show current qualifications—skills, experience and training of employees. When assigning work, employee qualifications must match the requirements of the job.

4.19 Servicing

Where the contract specifies the servicing of a product, the servicing must be done within the quality system. The discussion in 4.9, Process Control, applies to this section.

4.20 Statistical Techniques

In practice it is left to the organization to decide when and if it is appropriate to use statistical techniques for controlling processes and establishing product acceptance. This requirement is discussed in some detail in Chapter 13. When statistical techniques are required, they are part of the documented quality system and done under "controlled" conditions. Employees using such techniques need to be trained and qualified.

Appendix B

Implementation Plan Guidelines

Three "Typical" Organizations Achieving ISO 9000 Registration in 8, 12, or 18 Months

	Calendar Months to Registration		
	8	12	18
Time Lines for Activities:	Month	Month	Month
1. Education • Study ISO Standards • Determine Requirements • Determine Applicable Standard (9001, 9002, 9003)	1	1	1
2. Assessment • Determine where the Standard relates to you and what needs to be done • Commit to getting registered	1	2	2
3. Implementation Plan • Assign individual responsible for Quality • Identify the implementation team • Develop implementation plan (activities, accountabilities, due dates) • Communicate to employees	1	2	3
4. Document the Quality System • Develop documentation scheme and formats • Write procedures and procedure manual • Write work instructions • Review for consistency, soundness, and compliance with Standard	2–4	2–6	3–10

Time Lines for Activities:	Calendar Months to Registration 8 Month	12 Month	18 Month
5. Complete Documentation • Complete quality manual	4	6	11
6. Registrar • Select and hire Registrar	4	7	12
7. Internal Auditing • Do audit plan • Select internal auditors • Train internal auditors	5	8	13
8. Implement and Operate Quality System • Communicate to employees • Do internal audits • Do management reviews • Make corrections and improvements	5–8	8–12	13–18
9. Pre-assessment (optional) • Independent assessment of readiness prior to third party audit	6	10	16
10. Third Party Audit • Audit by registrar • Certification and registration	8	12	18
11. Surveillance and Improvement • Periodic (approx. every 6 months) audits by registrar • Continue operating and improving the system			

Appendix C: Flowcharting

Purpose: People often try to solve a problem without first having a clear picture of how the process currently works. A flowchart helps to define a process by:

- visualizing sequential steps of a process;
- identifying what the process does; and
- identifying what the process should do.

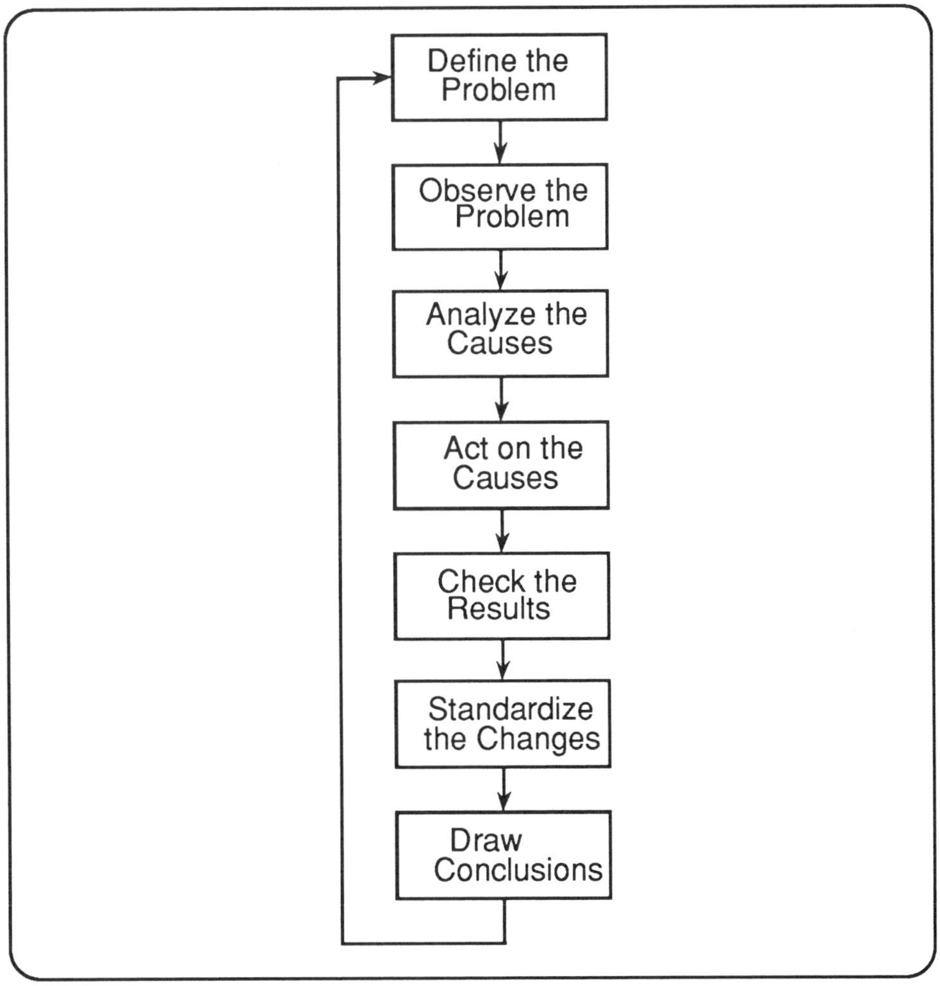

Symbols used in Flowcharting

Some of the more commonly used symbols appearing in flowcharts are illustrated below.

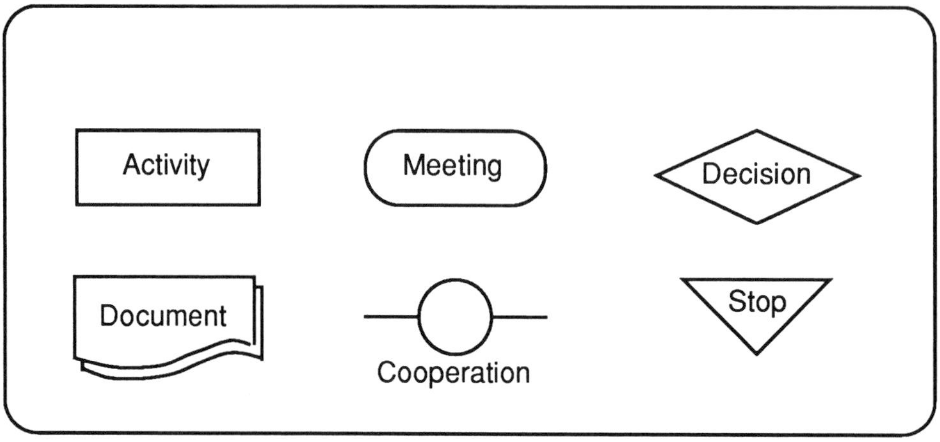

Before constructing a flowchart, determine what kind of information is required. This ensures that you are using the appropriate flowchart. The two most common types of flowcharts are *linear* and *integrated.* If information is sought regarding the flow of the process, as it passes from one organizational unit to another, construct an integrated flowchart.

Linear Flowcharts

Linear flowcharts provide a quick overview of a process. They display the sequence of steps or activities needed to produce a desired result. Each block can be expanded to provide more detail of how that activity is performed. An example is on the facing page.

Integrated Flowcharts

An integrated flowchart displays the process in relation to the responsible organizational unit to give a clear picture of how they interact. In the example on page 286, there are four units (in this case, persons) involved in the process of examining and diagnosing a patient. An analysis of this flowchart reveals how the different units relate to each other and who is responsible for what.

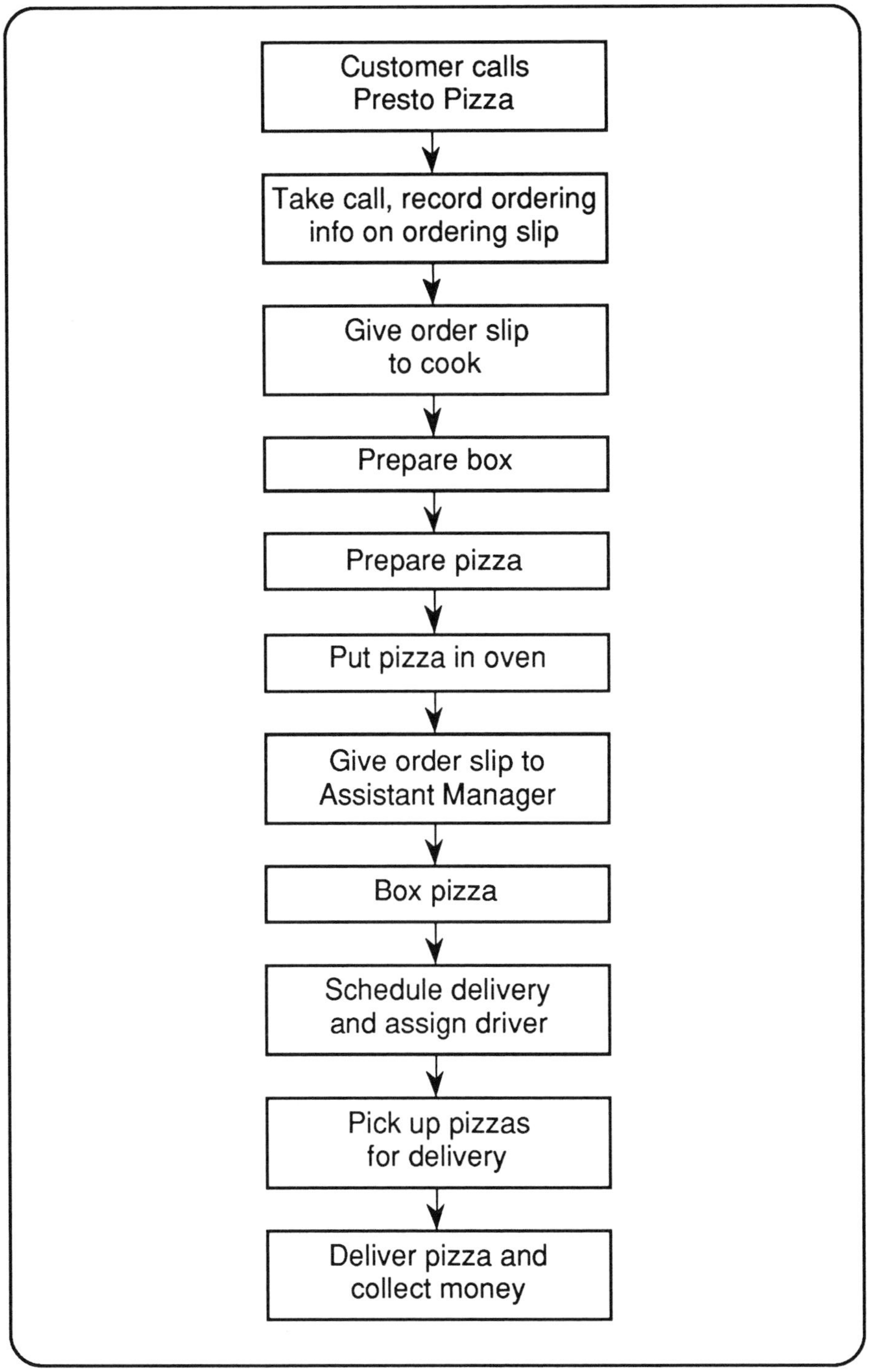

Example: Presto Pizza Linear Flowchart

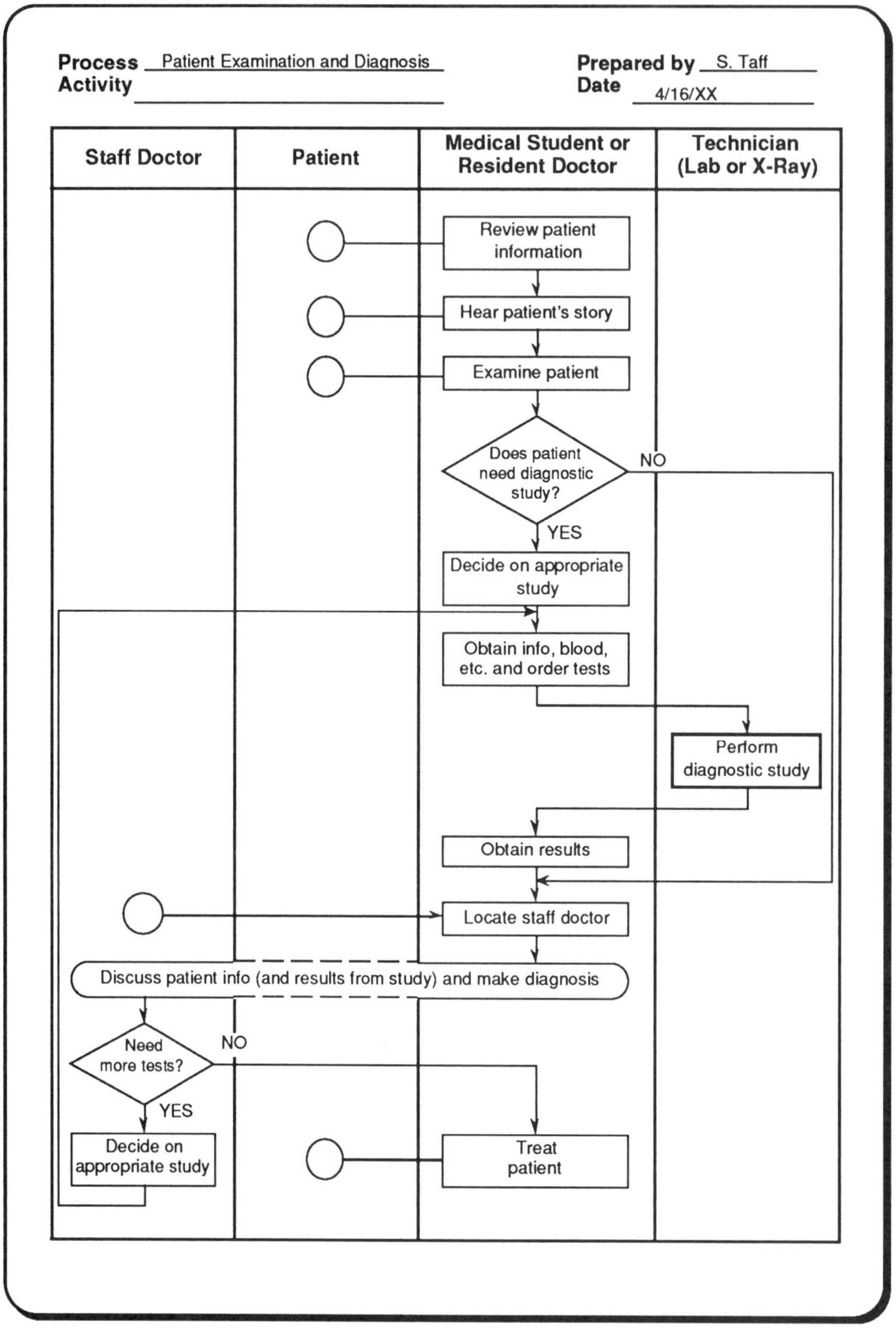
Process Patient Examination and Diagnosis
Activity
Prepared by S. Taff
Date 4/16/XX
Staff Doctor
Patient
Medical Student or Resident Doctor
Technician (Lab or X-Ray)
Review patient information
Hear patient's story
Examine patient
Does patient need diagnostic study?
NO
YES
Decide on appropriate study
Obtain info, blood, etc. and order tests
Perform diagnostic study
Obtain results
Locate staff doctor
Discuss patient info (and results from study) and make diagnosis
Need more tests?
NO
YES
Decide on appropriate study
Treat patient

An Example of an Integrated Flowchart

Appendix D–1

Two Sample Quality Manuals

THE MACHINE TOOL COMPANY QUALITY MANUAL

This Quality Manual is a statement of the organization, responsibility, procedures, and controls which have been implemented and maintained to conform with the requirements of the ISO 9001 Standard.

The requirements of this Quality Manual extend to all personnel who have been given responsibility for the implementation and maintenance of the procedures detailed or referenced in this manual.

The relationship between this manual, the above Standards, and the Company Procedure Manual is defined in Appendix I.

The contents of this manual are authorized and approved by the Chief Executive of the organization.

This manual is the property of The Machine Tool Company and must not be copied in whole or part without written authorization. It must be returned to the Company when requested.

___________*(signature)*___________

Chief Executive
April 1993

ISSUE: _____

MANUAL NO _____

THE MACHINE TOOL COMPANY QUALITY MANUAL

ISSUE: 1 **SHEET 1 OF 8**

CONTENTS

SCOPE: The marketing, design, manufacture, and servicing of machine tools and associated systems.

ORGANIZATION INFORMATION:

COMPANY NAME:	The Machine Tool Company
ADDRESS:	Anywhere Industrial Park, Anywhere
TELEPHONE NO:	00-000-000-0000
TELEX:	0000000000000000
FAX	00-000-000-0000

THE MACHINE TOOL COMPANY QUALITY MANUAL

ISSUE: 1 **SHEET 2 OF 8**

1.0 MANAGEMENT RESPONSIBILITY

1.1 QUALITY POLICY

The company management has developed and agreed on a policy for quality. This policy has been communicated to all employees and is displayed throughout the Company.

It is the quality policy of The Machine Tool Company to:

a. Achieve total quality performance, by understanding who the customers are, what their requirements are, and meeting these requirements without error, on time, every time.

b. Achieve the quality of product and service that meets the requirements and expectations of external and internal customers in a cost effective way.

c. Ensure, by third party assessment and internal quality audits, that the appropriate quality of goods and service are consistently achieved.

d. Work at all times, in the manner defined in the Company Documented Quality System, thus ensuring that the standards defined in ISO 9001 are being maintained.

1.2 ORGANIZATION

The overall responsibility for Quality in The Machine Tool Company rests with the Chief Executive. The detailed control of the Quality System is delegated to the Quality Coordinator who is the Management Representative for the organization and has full organizational freedom to identify Quality Assurance Problems and to initiate corrective actions which result in solutions to those problems.

THE MACHINE TOOL COMPANY QUALITY MANUAL

ISSUE: 1 **SHEET 3 OF 8**

Each member of the company management is responsible for ensuring that the part of the activities which they control is effectively operated in accordance with this Quality Manual and the associated Procedures Manual. The Quality System defines how employees contribute to the achievement of the Company's Quality Policy. It shows that the responsibility for Quality rests with all employees of the Company. These detailed responsibilities are defined in the procedures.

The Organization Structure of the Company defines the relationships between the members of the Company and shows how the authority to control quality is delegated. This structure is issued by the Personnel Department and a copy is in the Procedures Manual.

The detailed responsibilities for quality of the key members of the organization are defined in the Company Procedure Manual and are summarized below:

a. The Quality Coordinator has the organizational freedom and authority to initiate action to prevent the occurrence of product nonconformity.

b. All employees have the organizational freedom and authority to identify and record product quality problems in their own areas of work in accordance with the documented system.

c. All employees have the organizational freedom and authority to initiate, recommend, or provide solutions in their own areas of work through designated channels.

d. The Chief Executive, through the Quality Review Meeting, has the organizational freedom and authority to verify the implementation of solutions to quality problems.

e. The management, through the documented quality system, have the organizational freedom and authority, in their own functions, to control the further processing, delivery, or installation of nonconforming product until the deficiency or unsatisfactory condition has been corrected.

THE MACHINE TOOL COMPANY QUALITY MANUAL

ISSUE: 1 **SHEET 4 OF 8**

1.3 MANAGEMENT REVIEW

The Quality System is formally reviewed by the company management to ensure that it is suitable to meet the requirements of its customers. As the Company activities develop, training plans are implemented to support this development.

2.0 QUALITY SYSTEM

The Company has defined an effective Quality Assurance System which meets the requirements of ISO 9001 and this system is documented in this manual and in the associated Company Procedures Manual and Work Instructions and controlled through the Quality Review Meeting and other Management Meetings.

The System has been implemented and shown to be effective in the control of the quality of the Company's products and services. The procedures within the system provide the Quality Plan for the Company's activities and these are reviewed and updated as appropriate to take account of any changes in those activities.

3.0 CONTRACT REVIEW

The Company agrees with its customers on the details of the products and services that are to be supplied and this is confirmed in writing to the customer. Before accepting orders the requirements are reviewed to confirm that the Company has the capability to meet the requirements.

4.0 DESIGN CONTROL

The Company has established and maintains procedures that ensure the design and development of its products are planned, controlled, verified, and validated in order to confirm that the planned requirements are fully met. This activity includes the confirmation that all relevant legislative requirements are achieved.

THE MACHINE TOOL COMPANY QUALITY MANUAL

ISSUE: 1 **SHEET 5 OF 8**

5.0 DOCUMENT AND DATA CONTROL

All documents, records, and specifications used within the Company Quality System are formally authorized and controlled within the Quality Assurance Procedures. All issues and amendments are confirmed in writing to ensure that there is no danger of company personnel working with outdated information. Where applicable, outdated documents are withdrawn.

Where data is stored on computer media, security back-up copies are taken and securely stored in accordance with documented procedures.

6.0 PURCHASING

The Company places great emphasis on the selection and control of its suppliers. The Company does not specify that its suppliers are registered to ISO 9000, but its suppliers are committed to quality and have demonstrated their ability to supply goods and services to the required quality at the specified time.

The Company has agreed with these suppliers on specifications for the products purchased and only takes delivery of products that meet these requirements.

7.0 CONTROL OF CUSTOMER-SUPPLIED PRODUCT

The Company's activities do not normally involve the use of its customer's materials in the manufacture of its products.

Materials for trials are provided by customers and such materials are clearly marked and only used for the customer's products.

8.0 PRODUCT IDENTIFICATION AND TRACEABILITY

The Company makes use of labels and defined locations to maintain product identification in storage areas and its experienced staff have responsibility for the correct identification of sub-assemblies when these are not labeled.

Where a requirement for traceability is specified in a contract for a customer this is provided within the quality system.

THE MACHINE TOOL COMPANY QUALITY MANUAL

ISSUE: 1 SHEET 6 OF 8

9.0 PROCESS CONTROL

It is the policy of the company to ensure the quality of its services through control of its processes. This is achieved through operator-control of the processes and is facilitated by:

A work force having known training and experience.
Documented work instructions.
Operator inspection at all stages of the preparation process.
Approved processes and equipment.
Defined standards of workmanship.

As part of its manufacturing activities the Company heat-treats critical items. The control of this process is subject to special controls.

The Company has formal documented procedures to ensure that its equipment is maintained in a condition that ensures process capability.

10.0 INSPECTION AND TESTING

On receipt, all products are checked to confirm that the correct items have been delivered and that they are in a good condition.

During the production and assembly processes, employees are responsible for the inspection and control of the material being used. They have the responsibility for inspecting the work as it progresses and for identifying any material, parts, or products that are unsuitable for inclusion in the products.

Prior to packing, all products are inspected and tested to confirm that they are of a suitable standard for delivery to the customers. Records of these inspections and tests are maintained by the Company.

THE MACHINE TOOL COMPANY QUALITY MANUAL

ISSUE: 1 **SHEET 7 OF 8**

11.0 CONTROL OF INSPECTION, MEASURING, AND TEST EQUIPMENT

The Company places great emphasis on the accuracy of the measurements taken during the inspection and test of products. It has a comprehensive calibration system that covers all the measuring equipment used to demonstrate and product quality. This system provides traceability to national standards.

12.0 INSPECTION AND TEST STATUS

During the production processes, the Company relies on the skills and experience of its staff to identify and segregate any material, parts or products that are unsuitable.

13.0 CONTROL OF NONCONFORMING PRODUCT

At Goods Receiving and during production processes, material is identified as being unsuitable for specific operations. Once material is identified as unsuitable, it is recorded and such material may be reworked, used under concession, or disposed of.

14.0 CORRECTIVE AND PREVENTIVE ACTION

The quality system provides the means to identify where corrective action should be taken to eliminate the causes of nonconformity to specifications. The Company places great emphasis on corrective action as being the major benefit, for both the Company and its customers, to be gained from effective Control of Quality. The Company conducts formal reviews of all rejects, concessions, complaints, and returns to determine the need for corrective action and to confirm that the corrective actions taken have been effective.

15.0 HANDLING, STORAGE, PACKING, PRESERVATION, AND DELIVERY

The Company has appropriate handling equipment and trained staff for the movement material within the factory. It has defined storage areas appropriate to the material being stored.

The Company has defined appropriate packing specifications and delivery methods for its products.

THE MACHINE TOOL COMPANY QUALITY MANUAL

ISSUE: 1 **SHEET 8 OF 8**

16.0 QUALITY RECORDS

During the process the systems generate records of all the activities needed to provide products and service to specification. These records include the details of inspection and test results and are retained by the Company in case evidence is required of the activities carried out. Where records relating to the Quality System are generated on computers, back-up copies of critical files are regularly made and stored.

17.0 INTERNAL QUALITY AUDITS

The Company maintains the effectiveness of its control systems by conducting formal internal audits of all the procedures at planned intervals. These audits are carried out by the company audit team who has been trained in internal auditing techniques. The audits are used by the management as an indication of the effectiveness of the controls operating in the Company.

18.0 TRAINING

The Company considers that the control of quality by its staff to be the most effective way of controlling the quality of the products and the services it provides. It ensures this by employing appropriately skilled staff. The Company has a positive training program for all staff which builds on their existing education, training and experience. The training records of personnel are used for selection of employees for specific work.

19.0 SERVICING

The Company carries out the servicing of its products through a documented service control procedure. The service engineers are fully trained in the servicing of machines and are supported by technical staff.

20.0 STATISTICAL TECHNIQUES

The company has examined its processes to determine the need for the use of statistical techniques and uses such techniques where appropriate.

THE MACHINE TOOL COMPANY QUALITY MANUAL

APPENDIX I

ISSUE: 1 **SHEET 1 OF 2**

THE RELATIONSHIP BETWEEN THE QUALITY MANUAL AND PROCEDURES MANUAL

The following indicates the relationship between the Standard ISO 9001, the Quality Manual and the Procedures/Procedures Manual.

4.1 MANAGEMENT RESPONSIBILITY

4.1.1 QUALITY POLICY
Quality Manual.

4.1.2 ORGANIZATION
Quality Manual, Organization Chart, and the Responsibilities for Quality.

4.1.3 MANAGEMENT REVIEW
Procedure 3.

4.2 QUALITY SYSTEM
All procedures.

4.3 CONTRACT REVIEW
Procedures 5, 6, 7, 8, 9, 10, 11, 32.

4.4 DESIGN CONTROL
Procedure 6, 7, 9, 13.

4.5 DOCUMENT AND DATA CONTROL
Procedures 1, 10, 14, 15, 16, 17, 18, 34.

4.6 PURCHASING
Procedures 20, 21, 22.

4.7 CONTROL OF CUSTOMER-SUPPLIED PRODUCT
Procedure 12, 30, 32.

4.8 PRODUCT IDENTIFICATION AND TRACEABILITY
Procedures 8, 22, 23, 25, 26, 27, 28, 31.

4.9 PROCESS CONTROL
Procedures 8, 22, 23, 25, 26, 27, 28.

THE MACHINE TOOL COMPANY QUALITY MANUAL

ISSUE: 1 APPENDIX I **SHEET 2 OF 2**

RELATIONSHIP BETWEEN THE QUALITY MANUAL AND PROCEDURES MANUAL

4.10 INSPECTION AND TESTING
Procedures 8, 22, 23, 25, 26, 27, 28.

4.11 CONTROL OF INSPECTION, MEASURING, AND TEST EQUIPMENT
Procedure 33.

4.12 INSPECTION AND TEST STATUS
Procedures 8, 22, 23, 25, 26, 27, 28.

4.13 CONTROL OF NONCONFORMING PRODUCT
Procedures 8, 19, 22, 23, 25, 26, 27, 28, 29.

4.14 CORRECTIVE AND PREVENTIVE ACTION
Procedures 3, 19, 28, 29, 30.

4.15 HANDLING, STORAGE, PACKING, PRESERVATION AND DELIVERY
Procedures 8, 22, 23, 25, 26, 27, 28.

4.16 QUALITY RECORDS
All procedures and Record Summary

4.17 INTERNAL QUALITY AUDITS.
Procedure 2.

4.18 TRAINING
Procedure 4.

4.19 SERVICING
Procedure 32.

4.20 STATISTICAL TECHNIQUES
Procedures 3, 19, 28, 29, 30.

Optimum Systems for Quality Ltd.

Quality Manual

April 1993

ISSUE: 3
MANUAL NO 2

Optimum Systems for Quality Ltd.

ISSUE: 3 **SHEET 1 OF 5**

QUALITY MANUAL

CONTENTS

INTRODUCTION

This Quality Manual is a statement of the organization, responsibility, procedures and controls which have been implemented and maintained so as to conform with the requirements of ISO 9001.

The requirements of this Quality Manual extend to all personnel who have been given the responsibility for implementing and maintaining the procedures detailed or referenced in this manual.

The relationship between this manual, the above Standard, and the Company Procedure Manual is defined in Appendix I of this Manual.

The contents of this manual are authorized and approved by the Operations Director.

This manual is the Property of Optimum Systems for Quality Ltd. and must not be copied in whole or part without the written permission of the Chief Executive. It must be returned to the company when requested.

(signature)

Chief Executive
April 1993

SCOPE: Quality Management Consultancy

ORGANIZATION DETAILS:

NAME: OPTIMUM SYSTEMS FOR QUALITY LTD

ADDRESS: Simonstone Business Park, Simonstone, Lancashire, UK

TEL: (44)-282-77-9002 FAX: (44)-282-77-9099

Optimum Systems for Quality Ltd.

ISSUE: 3 **SHEET 2 OF 5**

1.0 MANAGEMENT RESPONSIBILITY

1.1 QUALITY POLICY

The management of Optimum Systems for Quality Ltd. has developed and agreed on a policy for quality. This policy has been communicated to all employees and is displayed throughout the Company. The policy is:

Every organization has a quality system. It is the route by which the organization identifies, defines and meets the requirements of its customers. All members of the organization are part of the quality system and hence the development of that system involves the development of all individuals.

The role of Optimum Systems for Quality Ltd. is to work with clients to improve their quality systems and hence improve the quality of the products and services they provide. The Company has demonstrated extensive expertise in improving the efficiency of clients' operations. This involves both system and people development provided by professional and experienced consultants using a proven approach to system design.

In carrying out this role it is the policy of the Company to control its own activities within a quality system which is externally accredited to international quality systems standards, to seek out ways to improve its operations and to continually strive to achieve the highest standard of service for its clients.

1.2 ORGANIZATION

The overall responsibility for Quality in Optimum Systems for Quality Ltd. rests with the Chief Executive who is responsible for the development and management of the Quality system. The Chief Executive is the Management Representative for Quality. He has full organizational freedom to identify Quality Assurance Problems, to initiate corrective action which results in solutions to those problems.

He is responsible for the issue and maintenance of the Company's Quality Assurance System and for ensuring that all employees conform to its requirements.

Each employee of Optimum Systems for Quality Ltd. is responsible for ensuring that the part of the activities which they control is effectively operated in accordance with this manual and the associated Procedure Manual. The Quality Assurance System defines how every member of staff contributes to the achievement of the Company's Quality Policy and shows that the responsibility for Quality rests with all employees of Optimum Systems for Quality Ltd. These detailed responsibilities are defined in the procedures.

The Organization Structure of the Company defines the relationships between the members of the Company and shows how the authority to control quality is delegated. This structure is in the Procedures Manual.

The detail responsibilities for quality of the key members of the organization are given in the Procedures Manual.

Optimum Systems for Quality Ltd.

ISSUE: 3 **SHEET 3 OF 5**

1.3 MANAGEMENT REVIEW

The Quality Assurance System of Optimum Systems for Quality Ltd. is formally reviewed by the management of the Company to ensure that it is suitable to meet the requirements of its clients. Records of these reviews are made and retained.

2.0 QUALITY SYSTEM

Optimum Systems for Quality Ltd. has defined an effective Quality Assurance System which meets the requirements of the International Standard, ISO 9001: these systems are documented in this manual and in the associated Company Procedures Manual.

These Systems have been implemented and shown to be effective in the control of the quality of Optimum Systems for Quality Ltd.'s services.

3.0 CONTRACT REVIEW

It is the policy of Optimum Systems for Quality Ltd. to ensure that on receipt, all inquiries are checked to confirm that the requirements are adequately defined and documented and that Optimum Systems for Quality Ltd. has suitable resources to enable any contract based on the inquiry to be satisfied.

Contracts based on proposals are formally developed by Optimum Systems for Quality Ltd. and are reviewed with the client to ensure that their requirements are met.

4.0 DESIGN CONTROL

Optimum Systems for Quality Ltd. believes that training courses have to be well designed for them to offer the client a real learning experience.

A design brief is generated for each course and this is agreed with the client where the course is client specific. During the design of a course the material generated is reviewed regularly, by a consultant not involved in the design, to verify that the brief is being met.

5.0 DOCUMENT AND DATA CONTROL

All documents, records, and specifications used within Optimum Systems for Quality Ltd. are formally authorized and controlled within the Quality Assurance Procedures. All issues and amendments are confirmed in writing to ensure that there is no danger of Optimum Systems for Quality Ltd. personnel working with outdated information. Where applicable outdated documents are withdrawn.

6.0 PURCHASING

Optimum Systems for Quality Ltd. Quality Assurance System is not directly involved in the purchase of products or services as part of the service it offers to its clients and hence this part of the Standard is not applicable.

Optimum Systems for Quality Ltd.

ISSUE: 3 **SHEET 4 OF 5**

7.0 CONTROL OF CUSTOMER-SUPPLIED PRODUCT

Optimum Systems for Quality Ltd.'s main activity is working with clients to develop, document, and implement quality systems that meet the requirements of external standards. This involves the consultants working on the projects in gaining access to confidential information, and the security of this information is maintained at all times.

8.0 PRODUCT IDENTIFICATION AND TRACEABILITY

The service provided by Optimum Systems for Quality Ltd. is regularly documented during the conduct of each project. This allows for the easy identification of the status of the project.

9.0 PROCESS CONTROL

It is the policy of Optimum Systems for Quality Ltd. to ensure that the quality of the services it provides through the use of professional staff of proven training and experience, appropriate controls throughout the delivery of the service and defined standards of workmanship.

10.0 INSPECTION AND TESTING

The service provided by Optimum Systems for Quality Ltd. is subjected to formal review assessment by the client at the end of the project. Throughout the project the conduct and progress of the project is monitored through the project files.

Participants in formal training courses are examined to confirm whether the objectives of the course have been met and asked to complete appraisal forms on the training they received.

11.0 CONTROL OF INSPECTION, MEASURING AND TEST EQUIPMENT

Optimum Systems for Quality Ltd. is not directly involved in inspection, measuring and testing and does not use inspection, measuring, or testing equipment during the provision of its service, and hence this part of the Standard is not applicable.

12.0 INSPECTION AND TEST STATUS

The current inspection and test status of projects is recorded in the Project Files.

13.0 CONTROL OF NONCONFORMING PRODUCT

When it is found that the consultancy service provided by the company falls short of the requirements, action is immediately taken to remedy the situation. This may involve additional work or the agreement of the client to change the objectives of the project. These actions are recorded in the Project File and are reviewed at the Management Review Meeting

The performance of the participants on training courses during the examination is used to confirm that the objectives have been achieved. Where the results show that there is a failure with respect to one or more objective, remedial work is undertaken to ensure that the objectives are met.

Optimum Systems for Quality Ltd.

ISSUE: 3 **SHEET 5 OF 5**

14.0 CORRECTIVE AND PREVENTIVE ACTION

The quality system provides the means to identify where corrective action should be taken to improve the service provided. Optimum Systems for Quality Ltd. places great emphasis on corrective action as being the major benefit, for both Optimum Systems for Quality Ltd. and its clients, to be gained from effective Control of Quality. The Company conducts formal reviews of all complaints and service appraisals to determine the need for corrective action and to confirm that the corrective actions taken have been effective.

15.0 HANDLING, STORAGE, PACKING, PRESERVATION, AND DELIVERY

Course materials are prepared and checked prior to the presentation of each training course. These are then stored in an appropriate container, transported to the course venue, and any unused materials are returned for future use.

16.0 QUALITY RECORDS

During the provision of the service the quality system generates records of all the activities needed to provide a service that meets the requirements of its clients. These records are retained by Optimum Systems for Quality Ltd. in case evidence is required of the activities carried out.

17.0 INTERNAL QUALITY AUDITS

Optimum Systems for Quality Ltd. maintains the effectiveness of its control systems by conducting formal audits of all the procedures at defined intervals. These audits are used by the management as an indication of the effectiveness of the controls operating in the Company.

18.0 TRAINING

Optimum Systems for Quality Ltd. is dedicated to the training of its personnel. It considers that the control of quality by professional staff to be the most effective way of controlling the quality of the services it provides. It believes that this requires a positive training program which builds on existing education, training and experience. The training records of personnel are used for selection of employees for specific work.

19.0 SERVICING

Optimum Systems for Quality does not currently offer servicing activities to its client.

20.0 STATISTICAL TECHNIQUES

Optimum Systems for Quality Ltd. use statistical techniques to analyze the client's perception of the performance of the service provided by the company.

ISSUE: 3

QUALITY MANUAL - APPENDIX I

SHEET 1 OF 1

MATRIX SHOWING RELATIONSHIP BETWEEN ISO 9001 AND PROCEDURES MANUAL

	ISO 9001 Standard Element																			
Quality System	1	2	3	4	5	6	7	8	9	10	11	12	13	14	15	16	17	18	19	20
Quality Manual	X	X	X	X	X	X	X	X	X	X		X	X	X		X	X	X		X
OrganizationalChart	X	X		X												X				
Records Summary		X														X				
Responsibilities	X	X														X				
Control of Manuals		X			X											X				
Internal Auditing		X														X	X			
Management Review	X	X											X	X		X	X			
Training		X														X		X		
Inquiries/Orders		X	X													X				
Consultancy Services		X				X	X	X	X	X		X				X				
Cont. of Specs		X			X				X							X				
Service Concerns		X											X	X		X				
Sortware Backup		X			X											X				
Office Procedures		X							X							X				X
Course Design		X		X												X				
Delivery of Courses		X							X							X				

Appendix D–2

Sample Procedures

INTRODUCTION:

These procedures are selected from organizations who have achieved registration. They are provided as examples of what has proved successful in *those* organizations. They are not intended to define optimum procedures for other organizations.

The use of these procedures should be limited to gaining an understanding of the format and general level of content appropriate in a procedure. They also illustrate the division of work processes into ISO 9000 procedures. It is not necessary to have one procedure for each procedure guide. The illustrations show how one procedure may cover the requirements of two or more procedure guides and also the case where several procedures have been used to cover the content of one procedure guide. The sections of this appendix are ordered to correspond to the order of the Procedure Guides in Chapter 9.

There is a brief profile of the organizations from which the examples have been taken. Do not just refer to examples from organizations with a similar profile as yours. You can learn from all of these examples, but do not make your process fit the example procedures. Every organization is unique and its procedures need to reflect that uniqueness.

Note: The Procedure Examples only include the basic seven sections of a procedure. Procedure appendices are noted, but not included. Some organizations use formats that identify who is responsible for the procedure and include a sign-off block. This is illustrated in the last example in this appendix, Section 25, Maintenance of Equipment.

Section 1. Inquiries / Orders...Example One

Organization profile : A designer and manufacturer of customized machine tools. The following two procedures were written by this organization to cover their inquiries and orders processing.

TITLE: QUOTATIONS PROCEDURE NO. 5
ISSUE: 4 SHEET 1 OF 3

1.0 OBJECTIVE

1.1 To record and control the preparation of quotations in response to enquiries for the Company's products and to ensure that the requirements are fully defined and are within the Company's capability.

2.0 SCOPE

2.1 All quotations prepared for the Company's machines and associated systems and products.

2.2 The processing of quotations for punches and dies are processed in accordance with the Receiving of Orders for Punches and Dies procedure.

3.0 RESPONSIBILITIES

3.1 The Sales Department are responsible for determining the customer's requirements, for liaison with the customer, for determining the selling price, delivery and the preparation of quotations.

3.2 The Engineering Department are responsible for determining the feasibility of non-standard features on machines and for determining the estimated costs of such features.

4.0 PROCEDURE

4.1 All enquiries from customers for the supply of machines are passed to the Sales Department, investigated and, if viable are recorded in the Quotations Log. If the details of the requirements are unclear or specific installation arrangements are required, the customer is contacted. The concerns are resolved and any proposed machine location drawings are sought from the customer. The dates of these contacts and details of the resolutions are recorded in the Log.

4.2 The details of the requirements are examined, in conjunction with the appropriate Chief Engineer if necessary. Then it is determined whether the enquiry can be met from the Company's standard range of products. Standard requirements are processed in accordance with paragraph 4.10.

4.3 If any special features are required, a check is made with the customer to confirm it is a real requirement. If the customer confirms the requirements a Special Feature Request (SFR) form is filled out giving all the details available on the requirements including any special lead times that may be identified by the Engineering Department. Details are entered into a log in the Sales Department and allocated a number from the log. The deadline for the information is entered onto the form and recorded in the log. The form is copied and the copy is filed in the quotation file. The original is passed to Technical Systems.

Section 1. Inquiries / Orders...Example One

TITLE: QUOTATIONS
ISSUE: 4

PROCEDURE NO. 5
SHEET 2 OF 3

4.4 The details of the SFR are discussed at a weekly meeting between the Sales Executive or his delegate and senior members of the Engineering Department. They decide whether the requirements on the special feature request is feasible and in line with the company's general product development policy. This decision is recorded on the Special Feature Request form by the Chief Engineer.

4.5 On receipt the details of the Special Feature Request are entered into a log in Technical Systems. The details of the request are examined and if the information required needs an input from a Chief Engineer, the form is passed to the appropriate Chief Engineer.

4.6 The details on the Special Feature Request are examined in detail and if there are any queries then these are resolved with the Sales Department. If the information requested cannot be provided by the date requested, the Sales Department are informed. This information is used for communications with the customer as considered appropriate by the Sales Department. If the special feature is accepted then the cost of providing it, and the associated design time, is determined and the details entered onto the form.

4.7 The Special Feature Request form is signed by the Chief Engineer and taken to the Engineering Executive for approval. The details of the request are discussed and if the request is approved it is signed by the Engineering Executive. If not approved, this is stated on the form. The form is passed to Technical Systems.

4.8 The date of completion of the form is entered into the log by Technical Systems. A copy of the completed form is retained. The original copy is passed to the Sales Department, via the Sales Executive who approves the price to be charged.

4.9 The receipt of the form is entered into the Sales Department Special Features Request Log, copied and the copy passed to the Sales Executive for filing. The original form is used by the Sales Department in the preparation of a quotation for the customer.

4.10 The delivery requirements are reviewed and if the previously identified delivery times are not acceptable to the customer, the Scheduling Manager is contacted and the position discussed. The earliest lead time is established and recorded by the Sales Controller. Any special commercial terms required by the customer are discussed with the Sales Executive. The terms to be offered are agreed upon and recorded.

4.11 From the information above, and the Contract Procedure Document, a quotation giving the full technical description of the proposed machine, with options, and the associated prices and terms, is prepared by the Sales Controller selecting standard wording for the Word Processor paragraph file and modifying this as necessary. The quotation is then typed and checked, signed by the Sales Controller and sent to the customer.

4.12 Two copies of the quotation are made and one copy is sent to the Salesman responsible for the customer and the other copy is filed by the Sales Controller, with any associated Special Feature Request forms and the original enquiry in the quotation file. This is recorded in the Quotation Log.

Section 1. Inquiries / Orders...Example One

TITLE: QUOTATIONS PROCEDURE NO. 5
ISSUE: 4 SHEET 3 OF 3

4.13 Periodically the Sales Controller progresses the status of outstanding quotes with the customer/agent and records this with the Quotation.

4.14 Every week the meeting described in 4.2 reviews the progress on Special Feature Requests and the priorities are established. Estimated times for processing the requests are given to the Sales Department and relayed to customers as required.

5.0 RELATED PROCEDURES

5.1	Order Entry	Procedure 6
5.2	Contract Procedure Document	Sales Work Instruction 1

6.0 DOCUMENTATION

6.1	Special Feature Request Form	Appendix 1
6.2	Quotation	Appendix 2
6.3	Enquiry Log	Appendix 3
6.4	Special Feature Request Log - Sales	Appendix 4
6.5	Special Feature Request Log - Engineering	Appendix 5

7.0 RECORDS

7.1 The quotation, Special Feature Requests and the original enquiry are filed by the Sales Department in the contracts file and retained at least three years. If an order is received relative to the quotation then the file is kept at least ten years after the delivery of the machine.

7.2 The copy of the Special Feature Request is filed by the Technical Systems and retained at least ten years.

Section 1. Inquiries / Orders...Example Two

TITLE: ORDER ENTRY OF MACHINES — PROCEDURE NO. 6
ISSUE: 5 — SHEET 1 OF 3

1.0 OBJECTIVE

1.1 To record and control the acceptance and processing of orders received by the company for machines.

2.0 SCOPE

2.1 All orders received for Company's machines, associated systems and products, and any retro fit assemblies to these products, including retro fit kits ordered as spares

2.2 This procedure does not cover the processing of orders for general spares, stills and punches and dies.

3.0 RESPONSIBILITIES

3.1 The Sales Department is responsible for the ensuring that the order specification meets the customers requirements and is the same as the quotation. They are responsible for liaison with the customers and/or agents. In following this procedure they are required to adhere to the Contract Acceptance Work Instruction.

3.2 The Spares Sales Department is responsible for retro fit kit spares as described in 3.1.

3.3 The Scheduling Department is responsible for establishing the planned delivery times associated with orders.

3.4 The Chief Engineers are responsible for confirming the technical feasibility of the orders for their range of products and for planning release dates of any new specifications.

3.5 The Chief Executive is responsible for the commercial acceptance of all orders.

4.0 PROCEDURE

4.1 When an order is received by the company it is passed to the Sales Department or in the case of a spares retro fit kit it is passed to the Spares Sales Department. The quotation relating to the order is taken from the quotation file and the details are compared with the order to confirm that the requirements are as quoted. If no quotation or current list price exists a quotation is prepared in accordance with the quotation procedure.

4.2 Any discrepancies are resolved with the customer and confirmed in writing or re-quoted as appropriate. If this resolution results in the need for a special feature then the order is held by the relevant Sales Department and a Special Feature Request is raised and processed in accordance with the Quotation procedure. If the Special Feature Request is accepted by Engineering then the order is processed. If it is declined the customer is contacted by the relevant Sales Department and it is either altered to an acceptable specification or the order is declined.

4.3 The details of the order are entered onto the appropriate Specification Sheets for the type of machine ordered. These are signed, with a copy filed in the customer contract file. If any special features are included on the order then the relevant Special Feature Request. If spares are included in the order, or if there is a request for external inspection or instructions of the machine, then this is noted on the Specification Sheets.

Section 1. Inquiries / Orders...Example Two

TITLE: ORDER ENTRY OF MACHINES — PROCEDURE NO. 6
ISSUE: 5 — SHEET 2 OF 3

4.4 A Machine Contract Control Sheet is completed by the relevant Sales Controller, signed by the Sales Manager or Sales Executive (in the case of a Spares retro fit kit it is signed by the Commercial/Spares Manager) and passed with a copy of the Specification Sheet to the Financial Controller and Chief Executive for commercial acceptance and signature. If acceptable, the documents are passed to the Scheduling Manager, if they are not acceptable, the order is held until details are commercially acceptable.

4.5 A Serial Number is allocated to the machine from reference to previous records and the Serial Number Formulation chart by the Scheduling Department and entered onto the Specification Sheets and the Machine Contract Control Sheet. The computer-generated sales order number is also noted on these documents. The details of the orders received are taken by the Scheduling Department and discussed with the Technical Engineer to establish the Engineering Release Date. The Machine Contract Control Sheet is passed to the Engineering Executive or Chief Engineer and signed.

4.6 The time to engineer any special feature requests and any non-engineered options is decided by the Chief Engineer and Technical Systems and entered onto the Engineering Forward Workload.

4.7 Once this Engineering Release Date is established, the Scheduling Manager calls a meeting between himself, the Operations Executive, Materials Manager and Production Manager to decide key dates of the production process. The Machine Contract Control Sheet is signed by the Operations Executive or Production Manager. From the discussions the customer acknowledgment date is noted, the kitting date, lay down date and completion dates are derived and entered onto the production program (contract tracking document).

4.8 The Sales Order Requirements for machines are entered into the computer system by the Scheduling Manager. The Machine Contract Control Document is returned to the relevant Sales Department.

4.9 The Specification Sheets are examined by Technical Systems to confirm the options selected are valid. If a Special Feature Request is quoted then the copy of the request is taken from the file. The receipt of the Specification Sheets is logged by Technical Systems. The Specification Sheets, and any Special Feature Request, are taken to the appropriate Chief Engineer. The validity of the chosen options is reviewed and, if invalid, is referred back to the customer via the Sales Department or Spares Sales Department as appropriate.

4.10 On receipt of the documents from the Scheduling Manager the relevant Sales Department add any requirements for spares or tooling to the order and print an order acknowledgment from the information compiled in Chameleon system. The white copy is sent to the customer as an acknowledgment for the order, the yellow copy is filed in the Sales Department or Spares Sales Department in the customer file, the green copy is sent to the company agent if one is relevant; if not, the green copy is destroyed, and the blue copy is passed to the Operations Executive.

4.11 If there are no special features then the Engineering Structure applicable to the machine is determined and entered onto the computer system by Technical Systems.

Section 1. Inquiries / Orders...Example Two

TITLE: ORDER ENTRY OF MACHINES | PROCEDURE NO. 6
ISSUE: 5 | SHEET 3 OF 3

4.12 Each two weeks a meeting between the Operations Executive, Materials Manager, Scheduling Manager, Sales & Marketing Executive, Machine Sales-Contracts Manager, Engineering Executive, Chief Engineers and Technical Engineers or their delegates is held and in conjunction with daily ongoing activities, all orders received from customers are examined to confirm that requirements have been accurately interpreted. Any concerns are resolved with the customers by the relevant Sales Department and confirmed in writing. The Material Managers Report (Control Tracking Document) is adjusted by the Materials Department to be in line with decision made at the meeting.

4.13 If at any stage after the issue of the Specification Sheet the customer requests a change to the details of the order, the request is reviewed with Engineering and Scheduling to confirm whether the change is acceptable and to determine any cost and delivery implications. These are communicated to the customer by Sales in writing. If instructions to proceed are received, an amended Specification Sheet is issued under an new issue number. This is then processed as above.

4.14 If a cancellation of an order is received by the Sales Department then the Operations Executive is immediately informed. The current build position is determined by the Operations Executive and reported to the other executives. A decision is made and recorded as to the action to be taken. If this involves a change of specification, the change is processed as in 4.10 above. The build of the machine is processed in accordance with standard procedures.

5.0 RELATED PROCEDURES

5.1	Quotations	Procedure 5
5.2	Requests for Change	Procedure 7
5.3	Contract Acceptance Work Instruction	Sales Work Instruction 2
5.4	Control of the Computer System	Procedure 23

6.0 DOCUMENTATION

6.1	Specification Sheet	Appendix 1
6.2	Order Acknowledgment	Appendix 2
6.3	Material Manager's Report	Appendix 3
6.4	Machine Contract Control Sheet	Appendix 4
6.5	Serial Number Formulation Chart	Appendix 5

7.0 RECORDS

7.1 Machine Contract Control Sheets are filed in the relevant Sales Department and kept for at least 10 years.

7.2 Tablet Press Specification Sheets are filed in the Engineering Department and kept for at least 10 years.

7.3 Spares retro fit kit Specification Sheets are filed in the Engineering Department and kept for at least 10 years.

Section 1. Inquiries / Orders...Example Three

Organization profile: A distributor of a range of standard cleaning chemicals which are sold direct to industrial customers by agents. The procedure covers the entire process of receiving the order and delivering the goods.

TITLE: ORDER PROCESSING — PROCEDURE NO. 4
ISSUE: 1 — SHEET 1 OF 3

1.0 OBJECTIVE

1.1 To control and record the processing of orders received by the Company for its products.

2.0 SCOPE

2.1 All orders received by the company are covered by this procedure. The products sold by the company are defined and described in the company's Product Data Sheets and Material Safety Data Sheets. All contracts accepted by the company are on the basis of this information.

3.0 RESPONSIBILITIES

3.1 The General Manager is overall responsible for the operation of this procedure.

3.2 The Office Manager has day to day responsibility for the administration of this procedure.

3.3 The Warehouse Supervisor is responsible for the marshaling of orders in accordance with this procedure.

3.4 The Company Agents are responsible for the accurate recording of the customer's orders in accordance with this procedure.

3.5 The Delivery Drivers are responsible for the delivery of orders in accordance with this procedure.

4.0 PROCEDURE

4.1 Orders are received by the company either verbally by the company's agents, or by telephone, Fax or post directly from the customer. In all cases the order is recorded onto a Company Order Form, stating the company's product names, the quantities and pack sizes required and any special instructions, either by the company agent or by the sales administrator. If the requirement is not clear then this is checked with the customer and resolved. In the case of verbal orders taken by the company agent the order is checked and signed by the customer or the agent. In the case of telephone orders the order is read back, confirmed by the customer and then signed by the sales administrator. If the customer gives the Agent a written order, or if a confirmation order is received, it is attached to the white copy of the Company Order Form and subsequently it remains with that copy.

4.2 The yellow copy of the order is given to the customer in the case of verbal orders. The pink copy is for the appropriate agent and the white copy is for the sales administrator. A check is made against a list held by the sales administrator to ascertain whether the customer is not on the Stop List. If they are on the list, the order is held in accordance with the credit control procedure. If the verbal order states "customer's order number to follow," a check is made as to whether the customer will accept delivery without the order number. If not, the order is held until an official order or order number is received.

Section 1. Inquiries / Orders...Example Three

TITLE: ORDER PROCESSING PROCEDURE NO. 4
ISSUE: 1 SHEET 2 OF 3

4.3 If the order is for a series of scheduled deliveries it is filed in the Blanket Order Clip. The Blanket Order Clip is checked by the Sales Administrator each week. When deliveries are scheduled, they are treated as a unique order and a note of the Delivery is made on the order.

4.4 Once the order is cleared it is listed in the Agent's Log Book by the Sales Administrator.

4.5 Two copies of a Delivery Note are typed detailing the products to be delivered and the delivery address (including any special requests by the customer). Material Safety Data Sheets for each of the products listed are stapled to the blue copy of the Delivery Note. These are paper-clipped to the respective white copy of the orders. These are placed in the appropriate one of the following files by the sales administrator:

a. Area Delivery File
b. Outside Carrier File
c. Next Month File
d. Direct Delivery from Supplier File
e. Delivery by Agent File

4.6 The Area Delivery Files are examined by the Sales Administrator and a decision is made when to deliver to the various areas. On the basis of this decision, the Delivery Notes and the White copies of the orders are separated. A check of the customer's delivery history is made and if any of the products on the order have not been sent to that particular customer, a Material Safety Data Sheet is sent to the customer's safety officer. The white copies of the orders are filed pending the return of the Delivery Notes. From the Delivery Notes a loading list is prepared by the Sales Administrator and passed to the Warehouse Supervisor. For those orders to be delivered by carriers, the Carrier's own paperwork is completed by the Sales Administrator. These are then clipped to the respective Delivery Notes and are passed to the Warehouse Supervisor.

4.7 The goods defined on the loading lists are marshaled by the Warehouse Supervisor, and when complete, the loading lists are signed and placed on the marshaled products. The Goods defined on the Carrier's Notes are marshaled by the Warehouse Supervisor. The blue copy of the Delivery Note, together with the Material Safety Data Sheets, is securely attached to one of the items on each order. When the marshaling is complete the paperwork relating to it is placed on the load.

4.8 When the delivery drivers are ready to take the goods, they are given the white and blue copies of the Delivery Notes, with the Material Safety Data Sheets attached to the blue copies, in the Drivers' Delivery Files. The contents of the files are examined and the sequence of delivery is decided by the Driver. The Delivery Van is loaded by the driver, taking account of the delivery order and the safety of the packed load. The goods are delivered to the customers by the drivers, and each customer is given the blue copy of the Delivery Note and the Material Safety Data Sheets and asked to sign the white copy of the Delivery Note to signify safe and correct delivery of the order. On the return to the Company the signed white copies of the Delivery Note are passed to the Sales Administrator and attached to the respective white copies of the Orders.

Section 1. Inquiries / Orders...Example Three

TITLE: ORDER PROCESSING — PROCEDURE NO. 4
ISSUE: 1 — SHEET 3 OF 3

4.9 When the Carrier arrives to pick up goods for delivery, the driver signs his sheets for each individual order to signify acceptance of the load. The appropriate copies of the Carrier's Notes are attached to the respective white copy of the Delivery Note. It is then passed to the Sales Administrator who attaches it to the respective white copy of the order.

4.10 Where the goods are to be delivered directly by the supplier the white and blue copies of the Delivery Note, with the appropriate Material Safety Data Sheets, are sent to the supplier with an order to deliver the products. The supplier asks the customer to sign the white copy of the Delivery Note and then returns this to the Sales Administrator.

4.11 The customer's account number and delivery address code is written on the order by the Sales Administrator. If there is an instruction to delay the invoicing of the products till the next month then the order is held in a Delay Invoice Clip until the required invoice time. The white copies of the Order with the white signed copies of the Delivery Note are passed to the Credit Controller who raises the necessary invoices, in duplicate on the computer.

4.12 The two copies of the Invoice together with the respective white copy of the Company Order Form and signed white copy of the Delivery Note are then returned to the Sales Administrator for checking. The Invoice Number and date is recorded on the white copy of the Company Order Form by the Stock Controller. The invoices are separated, the top copy being posted to the customer and the second copy is filed in numerical sequence in an Invoice File for future manual reference. The white copy of the Company Order Form together with the signed white copy of the Delivery Note is filed in the Customer file until payment is received.

4.13 After payment has been received the white copy of the Company Order Form together with the Delivery Note is filed in the Paid Accounts file in Date/Alphabetical sequence.

5.0 RELATED PROCEDURES

5.1	Purchasing, Stock Control and Goods Receiving	Procedure 6
5.2	Control of Company Specifications	Procedure 7

6.0 DOCUMENTATION

6.1	Company Order Form	Appendix A
6.2	Delivery Note	Appendix B
6.3	Loading List	Appendix C
6.4	Invoice	Appendix D

7.0 RECORDS

7.1 Copies of Invoices are filed in numerical sequence in an Invoice File and are retained for at least five years.

7.2 The white copies of the Company Order Form together with their respective Delivery Notes are filed in a Paid Accounts file in Date/Alphabetical sequence and retained for at least five years.

Section 2. Design Control...Example One

Organization profile: A designer and manufacturer of electronic equipment. The following two procedures cover the design of new products and the design validation using prototypes.

TITLE: DESIGN CONTROL PROCEDURE NO. 5
ISSUE: 1 SHEET 1 OF 2

1.0 OBJECTIVE

1.1 To control the research and development programs into the design of product undertaken by the Company.

2.0 SCOPE

2.1 All research and development formally undertaken by the Company into the design of products.

3.0 RESPONSIBILITIES

3.1 The Technical Executive has the responsibility for deciding the terms of reference for research and product development programs to be undertaken by the Company, and for reviewing the results of such programs. He is responsible for allocating resources to agreed research and development programs and for ensuring they are completed in accordance with the defined time scales.

3.2 The Technical Manager is responsible for the day to day management of the project, for identifying any significant problems and for maintaining the project file.

4.0 PROCEDURE

4.1 Every month a Product Strategy Meeting is held and it is attended by the Marketing Executive, Technical Executive, Financial Controller, and Production Executive. Additional meetings may be held as required.

4.2 The meeting decides on the strategy to be followed on existing product developments, new product developments and the relative priority of the work of the Technical Department. This meeting is responsible for agreeing on the overall product specification of any new product before design work commences. Minutes of the meetings with actions against the departments concerned are issued to all attendees.

4.3 A Project Specification for each new Product Development is developed by the Technical Executive and resources and a project number are allocated to the project. A Design Review Meeting is held every month by the Technical Executive, Technical Manager and members of the Technical Department as required. New Product Developments are discussed at the meeting. The progress on existing Product Developments is discussed and priorities defined in line with the decisions of the Product Strategy meeting. Minutes of these meetings with actions agreed are taken and issued to all attendees.

4.4 The engineers allocated to a project develop its design taking account of previous designs of similar products, the designs of the competition and marketing information. The design development may include mock-ups of the product for assessment. The progress of the project is recorded on a Project Program which is reviewed at the Design Review Meeting. All papers associated with the project are kept in the project file.

Section 2. Design Control...Example One

TITLE: DESIGN CONTROL — PROCEDURE NO. 5
ISSUE: 1 — SHEET 2 OF 2

4.5 The project is developed to the point where it is ready for Production Prototypes to be produced and a report on the Project Status is prepared by the team working on the project. This is presented to the Product Strategy Meeting which reviews the project and decides one of the following actions:

4.5.1 Allocate more resources to the project. If this decision is taken, an amendment to the Project Specification is drawn up for the additional work and it is then controlled in line with this procedure.

4.5.2 Close the study and do no more work.

4.5.3 Continue with the project through to Prototype manufacture. The manufacture of a prototype is controlled in accordance with the Prototype Manufacture Procedure.

The details of the decision made is minuted and entered into the Project file.

5.0 RELATED PROCEDURES

5.1 Prototype Manufacture — Procedure 4

6.0 DOCUMENTATION

6.1 Project Specification Sheet — Sheet 3

6.2 Project File Control Sheet — Sheet 4

7.0 RECORDS

7.1 Project Files are retained by the Technical Department for ten years.

Section 2. Design Control...Example Two

TITLE: PROTOTYPE MANUFACTURE — PROCEDURE NO. 4
ISSUE: 1 — SHEET 1 OF 2

1.0 OBJECTIVE

1.1 To control the manufacture of prototypes of the Company's products.

2.0 SCOPE

2.1 All prototypes manufactured by the Company as part of its Product Development Program.

3.0 RESPONSIBILITIES

3.1 The Technical Executive, is responsible for the allocation of resources to Prototype Manufacturing, and for deciding priorities.

3.2 The Technical Manager is responsible for developing Prototypes to meet the agreed objectives in accordance with this procedure.

4.0 PROCEDURE

4.1 When a design is cleared by the Design Control Procedure for product manufacture, or when decided by the Technical Executive, a full set of Project Specifications are approved by the Product Strategy Meeting. A Project Number is allocated and the project is recorded in the Project Register. If it is a project that has been through Design Control then the project number may be carried over.

4.2 The Project Specifications are recorded on a Project Specification Sheet and all the information defined on this sheet is supplied.

4.3 The Technical Manager responsible for the product development maintains a Project File for the project. This contains the Project Specification Sheet and Resource Allocation Plan. Any significant working papers and supplier quotations are kept in this file.

4.4 The team allocated to the project, design and build the prototypes in line with the Project Specifications and any relevant design codes of practice. A status report is prepared at the end of each month summarizing the work done and indicating any significant problems encountered. This is issued to the Design Review Meeting who reviews the content of the report and decides if any actions are needed to keep the project on schedule. A copy of this report is placed in the project file.

4.5 All drawings developed during prototype manufacture are produced as Sketches with numbers of the format SK**** or drawings with alpha issue levels. The sketches are registered in the Sketch Register, and the Drawings in the Drawing Register. Sketches and Drawings at alpha issue are not controlled and cannot be used for production purposes and remain the responsibility of the engineer raising them.

Section 2. Design Control...Example Two

TITLE: PROTOTYPE MANUFACTURE — PROCEDURE NO. 4
ISSUE: 1 — SHEET 2 OF 2

4.6 The status of each prototype development program is reported to the Product Strategy Meeting each month by the Technical Executive. The members of the meeting advise on how the program affects their own departments and report any plans they are making in anticipation of a subsequent new product being introduced into production. The Production Executive develops a manufacturing strategy for the product and reports this to the meeting as appropriate.

4.7 When the prototype build is complete the performance of the prototypes is reviewed by the Product Strategy Meeting. This review includes a comparison with previous models, detail estimates of material costs and build times and may include customer trials and reliability testing. Based on this review, modifications may be made to the design. The results of such modifications are subjected to the same reviewing process. The decisions made during these reviews are recorded in the Project File.

4.8 Once the design has been approved the Technical Manager arranges for full production drawings and specifications to be developed and the Production Director arranges for Process Sheets to be prepared as required and any special production equipment to be ordered. The Production Executive and the Technical Manager develop and document full test methods.

4.9 When the documentation defined above is complete it is reviewed by the Technical Executive, Production Executive, Production Supervisor, Technical Manager, and Buyer. If any changes are considered necessary, these are implemented and subject to subsequent review. During this review the buyer is responsible for involving potential supplier in the review and obtaining commitment from them to supply to specification. Once the documentation is considered to be complete then it is released for Production. The decisions made during these reviews are recorded in the Project File.

5.0 RELATED PROCEDURES

5.1	Design control	Procedure 6
5.2	Purchasing	Procedure 12
5.3	Drawing Control	Procedure 7
5.4	Production Planning and Control	Procedure 9

6.0 DOCUMENTATION

6.1	Project Specification Sheet	Sheet 3
6.2	Sketch Register	Sheet 4

7.0 RECORDS

7.1 The project file is maintained by the Technical Manager and contains all papers relevant to the development of the prototype. This file is kept for ten years after the completion of the project.

Section 3. Supplier Approval...Example One

Organization profile: A small chain of retail outlets.

TITLE: SUPPLIER APPROVAL PROCEDURE NO. 10
ISSUE: 2 SHEET 1 OF 2

1.0 OBJECTIVE

1.1 To ensure that all suppliers selected by the organization are capable of delivering materials, goods and services to the defined requirements within the agreed time scale at the most economical price.

2.0 SCOPE

2.1 All purchases of products and services used in the provision of the companies service.

2.2 Suppliers of ancillary supplies such as stationery, refreshments, etc., which do not form a substantive part of the service provided for clients, are excluded from this procedure.

3.0 RESPONSIBILITIES

3.1 The Chief Executive is directly responsible for the operation of this procedure.

4.0 PROCEDURE

4.1 A file of companies who are approved to supply materials, goods and services to the company is maintained by the Chief Executive. An Approved File has been developed on the basis of the past performance of suppliers and indicates the type of product each supplier is approved to supply. Approved suppliers are entered onto the Company Computer System.

4.2 Before a new supplier of materials, goods or services can be added to the Approved File they are required to provide evidence that they can operate in accordance with the Company's requirements. To achieve this, a sample of their products are examined, and tested as appropriate, by the responsible person as defined above. A trial order is placed with the potential supplier and the details are recorded on a Supplier Approval Form. When the goods or services are received they are closely monitored by the responsible person as defined above to confirm they are of the required standard and the results entered onto the Supplier Approval Form. If the results are satisfactory the supplier may be permanently added to the Approved File. The new supplier is added to the Company Computer System.

4.3 Any instance of delivery of material, goods or services from any supplier which is either not to specification or excessively late is reported to the responsible partner and the details are recorded on the Supplier Approval Form. At that time the number of such occurrences is reviewed. If it is considered they are excessive, the supplier is informed that unless the performance improves they will be removed from the Approved File. If the poor performance continues, the supplier is asked to submit a program of Corrective Action. If this proves to be ineffective, the supplier is removed from the Approved File and the company computer system marked accordingly.

Section 3. Supplier Approval...Example One

TITLE: SUPPLIER APPROVAL — PROCEDURE NO. 10
ISSUE: 2 — SHEET 2 OF 2

5.0 RELATED PROCEDURES

5.1 Purchasing — Procedure 11

6.0 DOCUMENTATION

6.1 Supplier Approval Form — Appendix A

7.0 RECORDS

7.1 The Supplier Approval Form is retained by the Chief Executive as a live file.

7.2 The Company Computer System is a live file of the Company and the data is backed up periodically.

Section 3. Supplier Approval...Example Two

Organization profile: A component supplier to the automotive industry.

TITLE: SUPPLIER APPROVAL PROCEDURE NO. 7
ISSUE: 2 SHEET 1 OF 2

1.0 OBJECTIVE

1.1 To ensure that all suppliers selected by the Company are capable of delivering materials, goods and services to the defined requirements within the agreed time scale at the most economic price.

2.0 SCOPE

2.1 The suppliers of all materials, goods and services which are incorporated into the Company's products or which are consumed during the manufacturing process.

3.0 RESPONSIBILITY

3.1 The Quality Manager is overall responsible for the operation of this procedure and for the approval and monitoring of all new suppliers.

4.0 PROCEDURE

4.1 The Quality Manager maintains a register of companies who are approved to supply materials, goods and services to the company. The register indicates the category of material, goods or services the supplier is considered capable of supplying. This register has been generated on the basis of historic data and designations of suppliers by customers. If a customer designates a supplier then that supplier is added to the register for orders relating to that customer. Such a supplier may be added to the full register only after full appraisal as defined below.

4.2 Before a new supplier can be added to the register, or an existing supplier can be used for a new category of material, goods or service, they are required to provide evidence that they can operate in accordance with the Company Supplier Quality Manual. To achieve this, they are required to provide information on their systems for controlling the quality of their work by returning a questionnaire giving information on their systems.

4.3 The information provided on the questionnaire is evaluated by the Quality Manager in relation to the type of material, goods or service to be provided and a decision is made as to whether the systems appear to be adequate. In cases where this decision is unclear, the supplier is visited and assessed in accordance with the Company Supplier Quality Manual.

4.4 All new suppliers are given a rating and if they achieve above the 70% minimum in all categories, they are asked to supply samples of their material, goods or service in accordance with the Initial Sample Procedure. If the sample proves to be satisfactory they are given a production schedule.

Section 3. Supplier Approval...Example Two

TITLE: SUPPLIER APPROVAL | PROCEDURE NO. 7
ISSUE: 2 | SHEET 2 OF 2

4.5 Any instance of delivery of materials, goods or services from the supplier which are either defective or excessively late are recorded by the Goods Inwards Storeman. At that time the number of such occurrences will be reviewed and if it is considered they are excessive then the Quality Manager is informed. The supplier is contacted and told that unless the performance improves their rating will be changed. If the poor performance continues then the supplier is visited to develop a program of Corrective Action. If this proves to be non-effective then the supplier's rating will be adjusted accordingly.

4.6 Where a supplier fails to achieve the minimum requirement in any vendor rating criteria, they are withdrawn from the Approved Supplier Register and placed on the Unapproved Supplier Register until such time as their corrective actions bring their rating above the required minimum in all categories. This corrective action must take place in a reasonable length of time agreed on by the Production Manager and Quality Manager.

4.7 All companies on the register are informed of their status and are given a copy of the Supplier Quality Manual. They are asked to confirm that they will allow the Company's representative access to confirm the quality of the materials, goods or services being supplied.

4.8 The Company recognizes that some of its suppliers are only stockers of materials and goods and therefore looks for evidence, when assessing such stockers, that they are exercising control over the quality of the goods they are purchasing.

4.9 In assessing suppliers, account is taken of any registration the supplier may have to meet, including National Standards or approvals by other parties. The Company encourages its suppliers to obtain such registration, but does not rely solely on such registration as to the supplier's suitability to have Approved status.

5.0 RELATED PROCEDURES

5.1 Purchasing of Stock Items — Procedure 12

6.0 DOCUMENTATION

6.1 Supplier Register — Appendix A

6.2 Supplier Questionnaire — Appendix B

6.3 Supplier Assessment Form — Appendix C

7.0 RECORDS

7.1 The Register of Approved Suppliers is maintained by the Customer Liaison Purchasing Administrator and is a permanent record maintained by the Company.

7.2 Any questionnaires and assessment reports are filed by the Quality Department and retained for at least five years.

Section 3. Supplier Approval...Example Two

SUPPLIER QUALITY QUESTIONNAIRE

Name
of Firm: ______________________________

Address: ______________________________

____

____

Telephone: ______________ Fax: ______________ Telex: ______________

Products: ______________________________

Contact Person for Quality: ______________________________

Chief Executive: ______________________________

Please answer all question either "YES" or "NO". If you wish to make any comments, please submit a separate sheet.

1. Is your Company registered to or approved by any of the following nationally recognized quality standards?

   a. ISO 9000
   b. Honda
   c. Rover
   d. Ford
   e. General Motors
   f. Toyota
   g. Nissan
   h. Other - (Please specify)

If "YES" please give full details including a copy of any certificate(s).

Section 3. Supplier Approval...Example Two

2. Is there an Organization Chart indicating the responsibility for Quality in the organization? If "YES" please enclose a copy.
3. Is there a senior manager/director in the organization with authority to resolve all matters relating to quality? If "YES" please give his position.
4. Is there a defined procedure for the selection and checking of the suppliers to the organization?
5. Are the quality arrangements of the organization's suppliers assessed?
6. Is there a defined system for the verification of all bought-out items and raw material used in manufacture or supplied to your customers?
7. Is the system defined for the storage and protection of all supplies?
8. If your organization is engaged in manufacture, are there written procedures for the processes to be used?
9. Do these procedures indicate the inspection and tests that are required to confirm the product/process quality?
10. Are all items the subject of appropriate inspection/tests prior to delivery to your customers?
11. Are these inspections and tests clearly defined?
12. Are records kept of the results of these inspections and tests?
13. Do you normally use SPC to control the process?
14. Are procedures defined to identify and segregate items which do not meet the requirements?
15. Is there a system for identifying the state of inspection of items prior to dispatch?
16. Is all inspection and test equipment used to confirm product quality or control processes regularly calibrated?
17. Is all inspection and test equipment used by personnel trained in its use?
18. Is all inspection and test equipment used in an appropriate environment?
19. Are the methods of packing and delivery planned to ensure that the product quality is maintained?
20. Is there a system for the return of defective goods from your customers?
21. Are the causes for defective goods reaching your customers analyzed and corrective actions taken to prevent recurrence?

If any of the above answers can be supported by examples of the systems used in the organization please enclose copies of such systems.

Signature: ______________________________

Chief Executive of the Organization

Section 4. Purchasing...Example One

Organization profile: The following two procedures cover the purchasing activities of a small injection molding company that purchases special inserts for inclusion in the moldings.

TITLE: BOUGHT OUT INITIAL SAMPLE APPROVAL PROCEDURE NO. 8
ISSUE: 1 SHEET 1 OF 2

1.0 OBJECTIVE

1.1 To ensure that the supplier is capable of producing items to the company's specification.

2.0 SCOPE

2.1 All new or modified items purchased by the company and existing items obtained from new tooling, locations or suppliers.

2.2 This procedure is not applied to materials defined by specification purchased from customer approved or designated suppliers.

3.0 RESPONSIBILITIES

3.1 The Quality Manager is overall responsible for the operation of this procedure.

3.2 It is the responsibility of the Materials Purchasing Administrator to ensure that the need for samples is defined in the purchase order and not to schedule bulk supplies until the sample has been approved in accordance with this procedure.

3.3 It is the responsibility of the Quality Engineer to ensure that all samples are verified to specification and that reports on the results of the validation are produced in a timely manner.

4.0 PROCEDURE

4.1 When the need for Initial Sample Approval is identified in the Purchasing of Stock Items procedure the Materials Purchasing Administrator in consultation with the Quality Engineer decides the number of samples, their size or quantity in the case of materials, and the sample due date. Current copies of specifications and a full set of Initial Sample Forms are sent to the supplier by the Materials Purchasing Administrator with the Order as defined in the above procedure.

4.2 When the samples are ready the supplier informs the Quality Engineer. It is then decided whether verification of the items or materials is to be witnessed at the suppliers and the supplier is informed accordingly. If the supplier has produced samples which do not meet the specification, but he considers they may be fit for purpose, he may apply through purchasing for a concession to supply the parts.

4.3 If the validation is to be done at the supplier, the Quality Engineer arranges for a visit to the supplier. The results on the Initial Sample Forms are examined and individual results are selected and confirmed as being correct. In making these confirmations the level of drawing or specifications is checked by the Quality Engineer. The selection of the results to be checked is based on the significant/critical features of the item or material. The Supplier's Control Plan for the future manufacture is assessed.

Section 4. Purchasing...Example One

TITLE: BOUGHT OUT INITIAL SAMPLE APPROVAL PROCEDURE NO. 8
ISSUE: 1 SHEET 2 OF 2

4.4 If the validation is done at the company, the supplier is instructed to send the samples and all the documentation defined in the Initial Sample Instruction to the Quality Manager who arranges for the Quality Engineer to examine the Initial Sample Forms. Individual results are selected and confirmed as correct. In making these checks, the level of drawing or specifications is checked by the Engineer. The selection of the results to be checked is based on the significant/critical features of the item or material. The Supplier's Control Plan for the future manufacture is assessed.

4.7 The results of the findings and the Engineer's recommendations are passed to the Materials Purchasing Administrator indicating the status of the samples. If the sample is approved, arrangements are made for the delivery of bulk supplies. If the sample is not approved, the supplier is asked to provide further samples which will be assessed in accordance with this procedure. Depending on the nature of the rejection, the Materials Purchasing Administrator may apply to the Technical Executive for a concession for initial supplies in accordance with the Concession procedure.

4.6 Two of the approved samples are labeled and signed as to their status. One sample is returned to the supplier as a workmanship standard and the other sample is retained by the Quality Department.

5.0 RELATED PROCEDURES

5.1 Purchasing of Stock Items — Procedure 12

5.2 Concessions — Procedure 28

6.0 DOCUMENTATION

6.1 Initial/Routine Sample Report — Appendix A

6.2 Initial Sample Report, Laboratory — Appendix B

6.3 Initial Sample Report, Dimensional — Appendix C

6.4 Initial Sample Instruction — Appendix D

6.5 Initial Sample Label — Appendix E

7.0 RECORDS

7.1 The Initial Sample Documentation is filed by the Purchase Department as per individual customer requirements or a minimum of five years.

Section 4. Purchasing...Example One

INITIAL SAMPLE INSTRUCTION

REQUIREMENTS

Prior to the delivery of production batches, the supplier shall submit samples from production tooling and processes for approval by the Quality Department at the company. New Sample approval is required in the following circumstances:

1. New Materials or Parts.
2. Existing materials or parts from new suppliers, new tooling, new processes or new locations.
3. After changes in design or specification.

INITIAL SAMPLE REQUIREMENTS

Samples submitted for approval must be clearly labeled with the Company Initial Sample Labels. If approval is to be at the company, they must be suitably packed and sent to the Quality Engineer. Prior to approval the supplier should have:

1. A detailed inspection and test report on the Company Initial Sample documentation providing the results of inspection and test results of all features specified on the drawing/ specification.
2. Evidence that the machines or processes that have produced the parts are capable of achieving the requirements consistently over a minimum of 200 manufactured units.

In some instances, the company may indicate the significant characteristics to be controlled, but irrespective of this, the supplier should establish criteria which are significant from their knowledge of the process. Evidence of conformity shall be established by any acceptable statistical analysis and tests on consecutively manufactured parts and for approval the +/- 4 standard deviations shall lie within the tolerance band.

If this level of capability cannot be demonstrated on any characteristics then the supplier shall introduce 100% inspection on those characteristics until control is achieved.

NOTIFICATION

The company will notify suppliers either of sample approval or rejection and the reason.

Resubmitted samples following sample rejection must be accompanied by full documentation as for initial samples and a statement of the corrective actions implemented in producing the new samples.

Production shall not commence until sample approval has been granted, or 100% inspection been introduced as above, or an official concession has been received from the company. It must be noted that any concession is of limited life and can be withdrawn, with no liability to the company, at any time.

Section 4. Purchasing...Example Two

TITLE: PURCHASING OF STOCK ITEMS PROCEDURE NO. 9
ISSUE: 2 SHEET 1 OF 2

1.0 OBJECTIVE

1.1 To ensure that the requirements of all materials, goods and services ordered by the company are adequately defined and meet the company's requirements, both with respect to quality and delivery, at the most economical cost.

2.0 SCOPE

2.1 All materials, parts and services ordered by the company for incorporation into the company's products or consumed during the Production Process. Throughout this procedure these materials, parts and services are referred to as items.

2.2 The purchase of capital equipment, office and factory sundries is specifically excluded from this procedure.

3.0 RESPONSIBILITIES

3.1 The Production Manager has overall responsibility for the operation of this procedure.

3.2 The Purchasing Administrator is responsible for selecting a supplier who is capable of meeting the company's requirements, both with respect to quality and delivery, at the most economical cost.

3.3 The Technical Manager is responsible for ensuring that all items ordered by the company are adequately defined to ensure that the company's requirements can be met.

4.0 PROCEDURE

4.1 When it is required for an item to be added to the current stock list, a "Bought Out Material Specification" is obtained by the person originating the request. The specification of the item, including details of all relevant drawings, is entered and agreed to with the Technical Manager, who signs the form in the appropriate place to indicate approval.

4.2 The "Bought Out Material Specification", together with any relevant information, is passed to the Purchasing Administrator and suitable suppliers are selected for enquiry purposes. In making that selection, note is taken of any customer recommendation.

4.3 The selected suppliers are sent a copy of the Quotation Request Form which clearly defines the requirements including, where applicable, the type class style, grade or other precise identification, and asked to indicate whether they are interested in supplying the item. If the selected supplier is not approved then the Supplier Approval Procedure is followed.

4.4 When the full responses are obtained from the potential suppliers the Purchasing Administrator selects the most suitable supplier. Where the requirement is for bought in components or special raw materials requiring color checks the Purchasing Administrator places orders for Initial Samples, which are dealt with in accordance with the Initial Sample Procedure.

Section 4. Purchasing...Example Two

TITLE: PURCHASING OF STOCK ITEMS PROCEDURE NO. 9
ISSUE: 2 SHEET 2 OF 2

4.5 When the samples have been approved in accordance with the Initial Sample Procedure the Purchasing Administrator raises four copies of a Purchase Order. The Purchase Order is circulated as below:

4.5.1 Top copy to the supplier.

4.5.2 Second copy is retained by the Purchasing Administrator.

4.5.3 Third copy to the Stock Controller.

4.5.4 Fourth copy to Finance.

4.6 On receipt of the Order an initial schedule for the item is raised in accordance with the Material Control Procedure by the Stock Controller.

4.7 If the decision is made to investigate the possibility of resourcing an existing supply then the procedure defined in 4.3 to 4.7 is followed.

5.0 RELATED PROCEDURES

5.1	Supplier Approval	Procedure 7
5.2	Material Control	Procedure 10
5.3	Bought Out Initial Sample Approval	Procedure 8

6.0 DOCUMENTATION

6.1	Bought Out Material Specification	Appendix A
6.2	Purchase Order	Appendix B
6.3	Quotation Request Form	Appendix C

7.0 RECORDS

7.1 The second copy of the Purchase Order is filed by the Purchasing Administrator and kept for seven years after the last delivery of parts to which it relates.

Section 5. Receiving and Inventory Control...Example

Organization profile: A manufacturing company with no computer control system for the material stocks.

TITLE: MATERIAL CONTROL PROCEDURE NO. 10
ISSUE: 2 SHEET 1 OF 2

1.0 OBJECTIVE

1.1 To record and control the scheduling, receiving, and storage of raw material and brought-in components used by the company in its manufacturing processes.

2.0 SCOPE

2.1 The scheduling, receiving, and storage of all raw materials and brought-in components used by the company in its manufacturing processes.

3.0 RESPONSIBILITIES

3.1 The Production Manager is overall responsible for the operation of the procedure and for deciding the quantities of material and components required to meet the manufacturing schedules.

3.2 The Stock Controller is responsible for scheduling, receiving and storing raw materials and brought-in components used by the company in accordance with this procedure.

3.3 The Quality Manager is responsible for verifying that all brought-in components are to the correct specification.

4.0 PROCEDURE

4.1 Each week the Production Manager and Stock Controller examine the current stocks of materials and the requirements to support the manufacturing program and decide on the quantities of raw material and brought-in components required. These are listed on an Order Due in List by the Stock Controller.

4.2 A Schedule is made out for each item indicating the requirements and referring to the Blanket for that item. This is signed by the Stock Controller or Production Manager and is sent by Fax to the supplier. The master of the Faxed Schedule is filed with the customer's order and the Order Due in List is used by the Stock Controller to progress the orders with the supplier.

4.3 When the material or brought-in component arrives at the company, the supplier's paperwork is checked to confirm that the items being delivered have been ordered. Any concerns are resolved with the supplier by the Stock Controller and the resolution recorded on the supplier's paperwork. If the resolution adversely effects the production requirements then the Production Manager is informed.

4.4 When the paperwork has been cleared the items are unloaded and moved into a suitable location in the Goods Inwards Stores. In the case of brought-in components the items are placed in a temporary location and labeled with a HOLD label and Quality are informed. The items are verified in accordance with the appropriate Quality Plan. If the items do not meet the requirements they are returned to the supplier. If they are accepted the Hold Label is signed by the Quality Engineer and the Stock Controller is informed.

Section 5. Receiving and Inventory Control...Example

TITLE: MATERIAL CONTROL — PROCEDURE NO. 10
ISSUE: 2 — SHEET 2 OF 2

4.5 The details of the delivery are recorded by the Stock Controller on a two-part Goods Receiving Note. The Goods Receiving Note number is written onto the supplier's paperwork and the top copy of the note is stapled to the paperwork and these are then passed to the Finance department by the Stock Controller.

4.6 The details of the items received are recorded on the Goods Inwards Stores Card for the item and the stock balance adjusted accordingly.

4.7 When material is required by Production the Stock Controller is informed and the material is issued and recorded on the Daily Material Issue Sheet. If the Storeman is not available then designated operators are authorized to take material and record the issue on the Issue Sheet.

4.8 The details recorded on the Daily Material Issue Sheet are transferred by the Stock Controller onto the Stock Record Card and the balances adjusted accordingly.

4.9 Each day the stock levels of at least eight items on which there has been movement during the previous day, is checked by the Stock Controller, or in his absence the Storeman. If any discrepancies are found between the physical stock and the Stock Card Balances, the balances are adjusted. If the differences are significant, the Production Manager is informed.

5.0 RELATED PROCEDURES

5.1 Purchasing of Stock Item — Procedure 9

6.0 DOCUMENTATION

6.1 Fax Sheet — Appendix A

6.2 Goods Receiving Note — Appendix B

6.3 Stock Card — Appendix C

6.4 Order Due In List — Appendix D

7.0 RECORDS

7.1 The Stock Cards are a permanent record maintained by the Stock Controller. As each Stock Card is filled it is replaced with a new Card.

7.2 The Top Copy of the Goods Received Note is filed in accounts and are retained for at least five years.

7.3 The book copy of the Goods Received Note is retained in the Goods Received Note Book by the Stock Controller. When the book is complete it is passed to accounts for retention.

Section 6. Process Planning...Example

Organization profile: A manufacturer of components for the automotive industry.

TITLE: ORDER ENTRY AND QUALITY PLANNING PROCEDURE NO. 5
ISSUE: 2 SHEET 1 OF 3

1.0 OBJECTIVE

1.1 To record and control the entry of orders for new products and the resulting pre-production planning.

2.0 SCOPE

2.1 All orders received by the Company for new products.

3.0 RESPONSIBILITIES

3.1 The Technical Executive is overall responsible for the operation of this procedure.

3.2 The Office Supervisor is responsible for receiving orders.

3.3 The Sales Managers are responsible for confirming that the details on the order are as quoted.

3.4 The Project Manager is responsible for the planning and control of the project to meet the agreed objectives.

3.5 The Quality Manager is responsible for identifying and planning the controls to be used during manufacture.

3.6 The Tooling Manager is responsible for the design and procurement of the tooling necessary to support the project.

3.7 The Day Supervisor is responsible for advising on and agreeing the process aspects of the project.

4.0 PROCEDURE

4.1 When an order for a new product is received by the company, it is passed to the Office Supervisor who copies the order, including any defined Terms and Conditions, and gives the copy to the appropriate Sales Manager. The original is filed by the Office Supervisor.

4.2 The details on the order, including the Terms and Conditions, are checked by the Sales Manager to confirm that they are as quoted. Any concerns are resolved with the customer. If a resolution is not achieved, the matter is discussed with the Chief Executive. Once the issues have been resolved and Order Acknowledgment is sent to the customer by the Sales Manager and copies for information are sent to the Chief Executive, Technical Executive, Tooling Manager, Project Manager, Production Manager, Office Supervisor and Quality Manager as appropriate.

4.3 The enquiry file becomes the order file through the inclusion of copies of the order and order acknowledgment by the Sales Manager. The appropriate entry in the enquiry register is over marked in green and the file is passed to the Project Manager. Unless being worked on, the order file is kept in the appropriate technical office cabinet.

Section 6. Process Planning...Example

TITLE: ORDER ENTRY AND QUALITY PLANNING — PROCEDURE NO. 5
ISSUE: 2 — SHEET 2 OF 3

4.4 If the order includes tooling, and an initial payment is to be made by the customer, an invoice raised for the initial tooling payment by the Office Supervisor is sent to the customer.

4.5 A Project Sheet is generated by the Project Manager and a Tool Number is obtained from the Tooling Manager for any tools included in the Project. Copies of the Project Sheet is sent to all Managers by the Project Manager.

4.6 An Advance Quality Planning Meeting is called by the Technical Manager and attended by the Project Team consisting of the Tooling Manager, Project Manager, Service Manager, Quality Engineer, Gauge Engineer and Day Supervisor. The meeting identifies the project requirements in terms of:

Key Timing Plan
Plant and Process Requirements
Basic Material Requirements
Ongoing Developments
Allocation of Project Resources

A detailed Project Timing Plan is agreed on by the members of the project team, this includes any customer specific Project Plans that may be requested, all the customer's and the company's specific timing and quality planning requirements, including FMEA, (also, where appropriate, requesting the Design FMEA from the customer), Controls Plans, Packaging or any other special features.

4.7 Regular meetings of the Project Team are held by the Technical Manager to progress and co-ordinate the team activities towards the achievement of the customer requirements. During these meetings any shortfalls are identified and action plans agreed to recover the situation. These are recorded by the Project Manager and circulated to the team members.

4.8 The individual team members conduct the activities of the project planning requirements in accordance with their individual responsibilities.

4.9 Each project continues until a full process capability study has achieved the requirements both with respect to specification and time standards and conducted in accordance with the Process Capability Study Procedure.

4.10 At the completion of the project the team hold a meeting under the chairmanship of the Technical Manager and all aspects of the project are evaluated and a report is prepared, indicating any areas for improvement, by the Technical Manager.

5.0 RELATED PROCEDURES

5.1 Enquiry — Procedure 4

5.2 Customer Initial Sample — Procedure 31

5.3 Preliminary Process Potential Capability — Procedure 32

Section 6. Process Planning...Example

TITLE: ORDER ENTRY AND QUALITY PLANNING	PROCEDURE NO. 5
ISSUE : 2	SHEET 3 OF 3

6.0	DOCUMENTATION	
6.1	Project Planning Program	Appendix A
6.2	Failure Mode and Effect Analysis Print Out	Appendix B
6.3	Control Plan Print Out	Appendix C
6.4	FMEA Instruction	Appendix D
6.5	Control Plan Instruction	Appendix E
6.6	Project Sheet	Appendix F
6.7	Advanced Quality Planning Review Sheet	Appendix G
6.8	Order Acknowledgment Form	Appendix H

7.0 RECORDS

7.1 All reports and plans are kept by the Technical Department as per individual customer requirements or for five years, whichever is the greater.

Section 7. Process Control...Example One

Organization profile: A manufacturing company producing welded steel products.

TITLE: MANUFACTURING CONTROL PROCEDURE NO. 7
ISSUE: 6 SHEET 1 OF 2

1.0 OBJECTIVE

1.1 To ensure that all manufacturing operations undertaken by the company are under control and that records are maintained that demonstrate this control.

2.0 SCOPE

2.1 All manufacturing activities undertaken by the company.

2.2 All manufacture of prototypes is excluded from this procedure.

3.0 RESPONSIBILITIES

3.1 The Planning Department is responsible for the issue of all manufacturing documentation and for filing of completed documentation in accordance with the Manufacturing Control Procedure.

3.2 The Works Foreman is responsible for ensuring that all production operators adhere to this procedure.

3.3 The Inspectors are responsible for inspecting the first off parts in accordance with this procedure. In their absence this may be done by the Works Foreman or Assistant Works Foreman.

4.0 PROCEDURE

4.1 All products which are manufactured by the company have a drawing, or customer's template, and a Route Card Master which are filed together in the Planning Office. The Route Card Master gives details of the operations required to manufacture the part, details of any Jigs and Templates used, and any special instructions on blank sizes etc.

4.2 When a Route Card Master does not exist, the card is sent to the Shop Floor with the manufacturing procedure entered. The blank sizes, Template and Jig Numbers are added as the Route Card is used to manufacture the first batch. The Route Card Master is produced from this information when the initial Route Card is returned to the Planning Department.

4.3 When a new Planning Sheet is issued, the drawing and the Route Card Master are extracted from the file and a copy of the Route Card is made. The details of the quantity are added and the Route Card and drawing is filed in the Works Files. The Route Card Master is replaced in the file.

4.4 When the Works Foreman receives his copy of the Planning Sheet the operations to manufacture the item are marked on the Planning Sheet. From the Planning Sheet a decision is made by the Works Foreman when it is necessary to start the job. The Route Card is issued to the operator who is to carry out the first operation.

Section 7. Process Control...Example One

TITLE: MANUFACTURING CONTROL PROCEDURE NO. 7
ISSUE: 6 SHEET 2 OF 2

4.4 The operator refers to the drawing, obtains the necessary material, sets the machine and makes one part to the specification. This part is checked by the operator and if adjustments to the machine are required, these are made until a part to specification is obtained. The card is taken to the Inspection Department with the part manufactured. Where the part is too large to be moved, the inspector is notified and the part is inspected by the machine. The operator continues to manufacture pending clearance from the inspector. The Route Card is signed by the Inspector to signify the part has been inspected and found to be to specification. If the part is not to specification then all the parts manufactured are checked and any defective parts are dealt with in accordance with the Control of Reject Material Procedure.

4.5 When the batch is complete the Route Card is signed by the operator to indicate the whole batch is to specification and it is placed with the parts. The Works Foreman is informed that the operation is complete and the operation is marked as complete on the Planning Sheet.

4.6 The Works Foreman decides when the next operation is to be done from the Planning Sheet and an operator is allocated to carry out the next operation. The next operator proceeds as in 4.3 above.

4.7 The above process is repeated until all the operations defined on the Route Cards have been completed and signed as being to specification.

4.8 The Inspection Department makes checks on all operations on new parts and signs the Route Card to signify they have been checked to specification. Additional checks may be made at the discretion of the Quality Department and the Route Card signed accordingly.

4.7 When the product is complete it is inspected in accordance with the Final Inspection Procedure.

5.0 RELATED PROCEDURES

5.1 Production Planning — Procedure 9

5.2 Final Inspection — Procedure 11

6.0 DOCUMENTATION

6.1 Route Card — Appendix A

7.0 RECORDS

7.1 The completed Route Cards are filed in the Quality Department Stores and kept for ten years.

Section 7. Process Control...Example Two

Organization profile: A supplier of components to the automotive industry.

TITLE: PROCESS POTENTIAL CAPABILITY PROCEDURE NO. 21
ISSUE: 2 SHEET 1 OF 2

1.0 OBJECTIVE

1.1 To ensure process capability is established on new products and processes where required.

1.2 To provide an assessment of the product/process in terms of meeting the specification.

2.0 SCOPE

2.1 All new products and processes required by the customer or deemed necessary by the Technical Manager.

3.0 RESPONSIBILITIES

3.1 It is the overall responsibility of the Technical Manager to control the operation of this procedure, for the initiation of Process Capability Studies on new and modified products and processes where required and to ensure that they are conducted in an efficient manner. The authority to carry out specific studies is delegated in accordance with this procedure.

3.2 It is the responsibility of the Project Manager to plan for Process Capability Studies to be done on new products, or processes, and to meet with the Quality Manager in order to ensure all significant and critical characteristics have been identified.

3.3 It is the responsibility of the Production Manager to allocate machines to allow Process Capability Studies to be conducted.

3.4 The Quality Manager is responsible for ensuring that parts produced during any studies under this procedure are monitored against the correct specifications in accordance with the control plan. It is the responsibility of the Quality Manager to agree with the customer all significant and critical characteristics.

4.0 PROCEDURE

4.1 The Process Capability study addresses significant and critical characteristics. The study covers a minimum production of 50 parts unless specifically agreed otherwise with the customer. The study is conducted during the manufacture of prototype or pre-production parts. The exact duration of the study is determined by the Quality Manager in agreement with the Technical Manager, and structured to allow the anticipated sources of variation to appear.

4.2 Prior to the study the process cycle and material are checked by the Quality Engineer to ensure they conform to the customers specifications.

4.3 Prior to the study the objectives are explained by the QE to the supervisor and operators by the Quality Engineer.

Section 7. Process Control...Example Two

TITLE: PROCESS POTENTIAL CAPABILITY — PROCEDURE NO. 21
ISSUE: 2 — SHEET 2 OF 2

4.4 The study is conducted under normal operating conditions.

4.5 Arrangements for checking jigs and any measuring equipment are made by the Quality Engineer who is also responsible for calculating the relevant indices from the results and recording them.

4.6 The study results are reviewed by the Technical Manager with the Quality Manager to decide if the process is capable and can be handed over for production.

4.7 If the results are unsatisfactory then the Technical Manager arranges for corrective actions to be taken and a further study conducted.

4.8 Studies are continued until the Technical Manager and Quality Manager are satisfied that capability has been achieved.

4.9 Once the study is complete the results are recorded on the Process Capability Assessment Sheet. This should in addition include comments regarding the study length and number of components.

5.0 RELATED PROCEDURES

5.1 Order Entry and Advanced Quality Planning — Procedure 5

5.2 Change Control — Procedure 12

5.3 Corrective Action and Management Review — Procedure no. 3

6.0 DOCUMENTATION

6.1 Process Capability Study Sheet — Appendix A

6.2 Process Capability Assessment Sheet — Appendix B

7.0 RECORDS

7.1 All the reports are filed by the Quality Department and retained as per individual customer requirements or for a minimum of five years.

NOTE: Further information on conducting Ppk studies is available by either consulting the Quality Engineer or by referring to the booklets available from the Quality Department, i.e. 'PLANNING FOR QUALITY'.

Section 7. Process Control...Example Three

Organization profile: A manufacturer of small tools.

TITLE: MANUFACTURING CONTROL — PROCEDURE NO. 23
ISSUE: 2 — SHEET 1 of 2

1.0 OBJECTIVE

1.1 To record and control the manufacture of Tools by the company.

2.0 SCOPE

2.1 All manufacturing activities associated with the production of Tools including the Masters for Tool production.

3.0 RESPONSIBILITIES

3.1 The Manager of Tool Production is overall responsible for the operation of this procedure.

3.2 The Tool Shop Superintendent is directly responsible for the planning and control of the work of the Tool Shop.

3.3 Individual members of the Tool Shop are responsible for the processing of orders in accordance with this procedure.

3.4 The Tool Inspector is responsible for inspecting the items manufactured at defined critical points in the manufacturing process. These are before heat treatment, after heat treatment and on completion.

4.0 PROCEDURE

4.1 When an order has been cleared from the Receiving of Orders procedure a file is created in the Tool Shop Production Control Office containing the copy of the Computer generated order, copy of the Order Acknowledgment, copy of the Tool Order Sheet plus all the drawings received from the Drawing Office.

4.2 The planning code for the Tools is determined and entered onto a Product Specification Sheet/Inspection Document with the details of the order. This information is entered into the Computer system and the necessary Route Cards and Job Cards are produced defining method of manufacture for the Tools.

4.3 A Product Specification / Inspection Document, the Route Card, Job Card and drawings are issued to the Manufacturing section. The operations defined on the Route Card are carried out and at defined critical points, the items are inspected.

4.4 Where Heat Treatment is defined on the Route Card this is carried out in accordance with the appropriate Heat Treatment Work Instruction. If the items are not to specification they are either scrapped or re-worked back to specification.

4.5 The times entered onto the Job Card as each operation is completed. The Job Card is returned to the Tool Shop Office and used for control purposes.

4.6 During the manufacture of Tools the required Master is located in the racks using the Master number which is etched onto the side of the Master. After use, the Master is inspected and any stress marks are removed by polishing and then replaced in the Master racks.

Section 7. Process Control...Example Three

TITLE: MANUFACTURING CONTROL PROCEDURE NO. 23
ISSUE: 2 SHEET 2 of 2

4.7 If no Master exists then the requirements are entered onto the computer system and a Route Card and Job Card set is produced. If the Master is to be manufactured using the "New Method" a Hobbing Blank First off Form is produced. The documentation plus a Master Blank is issued to the first operation on the Route Card.

4.8 The operations defined on the Route Card are carried out and at defined critical points the items are inspected by the Section Inspector.

4.9 If the items are not to specification they are either scrapped or re-worked back to specification. The times for each operation are entered onto the Job Card and the results of the inspections are recorded on the Product Specification Sheet/Inspection Document by the inspector.

4.10 Where Heat Treatment is defined on the Route Card, it is carried out in accordance with the appropriate Heat Treatment Work Instruction. The Job Card is returned to the Tool Shop office and used for control purposes. When the Master is complete, it is used to manufacture a trial tool.

4.11 The tool and the master are inspected and the results of the inspection recorded on the Inspection Document. If corrections are required then these are processed and the items reinspected.

4.12 When the total order is complete the items are protected from corrosion and packed in rust preventative media. Where the items are required for trials on a machine then they are passed to the Sales Department responsible for the trials.

4.13 Two copies of a Dispatch Note are printed in the Tool Shop office and the items are packed in accordance with the relevant Packing Instruction taking account of the method of dispatch and destination indicated on the Computer System.

5.0 RELATED PROCEDURES

5.1 Receiving of Orders Procedure 9

5.2 Heat Treatment Work Instruction

6.0 DOCUMENTATION

6.1 Hobbing Blank First Off Form Appendix B

6.2 Specification Sheet / Inspection Document

7.0 RECORDS

7.1 A file containing a copy of the computer-generated order, a copy of the Order Acknowledgment, the Tool Order Sheet, plus relevant drawings, is filed in the Tool Shop Office and retained for at least five years.

Section 7. Process Control...Example Four

Organization profile: A residential nursing home for the elderly.

TITLE: CONTROL OF NURSING CARE — PROCEDURE NO. 6
ISSUE: 3 — SHEET 1 OF 2

1.0 OBJECTIVE

1.1 To record and control the Nursing Care given to the residents of the Nursing Home.

2.0 SCOPE

2.1 All Nursing Care provided by the staff of the Nursing Home to its residents.

3.0 RESPONSIBILITIES

3.1 The Matron is overall responsible for the operation of this procedure.

3.2 The Nurse in Charge is responsible for the day to day operation of this procedure and for approving all Care Plans developed or changed during the shift of work for which they have responsibility.

3.3 All Nursing Staff are responsible for providing and recording Nursing Care in accordance with this procedure. At the front of the Card File is maintained a record of the names and qualifications of all personnel, whether permanent or temporary, who are employed as staff with respect to this procedure. This record also indicates the initials staff used when making entries into the record. When adding a new name to the list, care is taken to ensure that no confusion can arise between the initials used.

4.0 PROCEDURE

4.1 The Nursing Home operates a system of primary nursing and every resident has a named nurse, an associate nurse and key worker. This information is in the resident's room and on a file for the care team. All residents of the Nursing Home have a Care Plan which defines the nursing care considered to be appropriate for their needs. This plan is developed during the first two weeks of the resident's stay in the Home by a member of the Nursing Staff and is approved by the Nurse in Charge. This Care Plan is continually reviewed and adjusted as appropriate to cater for changes in the resident's condition, and all modifications are approved by the Nurse in Charge.

4.2 All residents of the home have a Nursing Record which is filed in a card alongside of the Care Plan. All actions relating to the day to day nursing care provided by the staff are recorded by them on the resident's Nursing Record. Any significant communications or specific instructions or requests received from the resident's relatives are also recorded on the Nursing Record. All entries to the Nursing Record are initialed by the member of staff making the entry.

4.3 The Nursing Records of all residents are reviewed by the two Nurses in Charge at shift change-over and any significant occurrences are discussed.

5.0 RELATED PROCEDURES

5.1 Control of Medication — Procedure 7

Section 7. Process Control...Example Four

TITLE: CONTROL OF NURSING CARE PROCEDURE NO. 6
ISSUE: 3 SHEET 2 OF 2

6.0 DOCUMENTATION

6.1 Care Plan Appendix A

6.2 Nursing Record Appendix B

7.0 RECORDS

7.1 All Care Plans and Nursing Records are maintained by the Matron. Completed Nursing Records are filed in date sequence for each resident and retained for at least seven years.

Section 8. Final Inspection and Test...Example

Organization profile: A designer and manufacturer of special purpose test equipment.

TITLE: FINAL INSPECTION AND TEST PROCEDURE NO. 19
ISSUE: 4 SHEET 1 OF 2

1.0 OBJECTIVE

1.1 To ensure that all systems and components manufactured by the company are inspected and tested to specification before dispatch to the customer.

2.0 SCOPE

2.1 All systems and components manufactured by the Company.

2.2 Proprietary items purchased from approved suppliers and sold with no work being done by the company are not tested or inspected unless it is a specific requirement of the order.

3.0 RESPONSIBILITIES

3.1 The Technical Manager is responsible for defining the tests to be done on specific systems and components.

3.2 The Works Manager is responsible for ensuring that the tests and inspections defined are carried out prior to the dispatch of all systems and components.

4.0 PROCEDURE

4.1 All standard systems and components requiring testing have test specifications defined. These are filed in the Technical Office. Special systems and components have test specifications defined by the Technical Manager in the Design Control procedure.

4.2 When a system or component is completed the Works Manager checks the Route Cards and confirms that all operations have been signed as being complete to specification. If the item requires testing the test specification for the system or component is obtained from the Technical Department. The details of the tests are entered onto a Test Report by the Works Manager.

4.3 The inspections indicated on the Test Specification are carried out by the Works Manager and the Test Report is signed indicating that it is to specification. The Test procedure is then followed and the results recorded on the Test Report. If the specification is not achieved then the Technical Manager is informed and action taken. A retest is then under taken.

4.4 Once the test has been completed and results within specification obtained the Test Report is signed by the Works Manager. If the tests are special they may be witnessed by the Technical Manager, the Chief Executive or the Area Sales Manager in which case the Test Report will also be signed by the above.

5.0 RELATED PROCEDURE

5.1 Design Control Procedure 5

5.2 Packing and Dispatch Procedure 18

Section 8. Final Inspection and Test...Example

TITLE: FINAL INSPECTION AND TEST PROCEDURE NO. 19
ISSUE: 4 SHEET 2 OF 2

6.0 DOCUMENTATION

6.1 Test Report. Appendix A

7.0 RECORDS

7.1 All test reports are filed by the Technical Manager in machine number sequence for at least ten years.

Section 9. Packaging and Shipping...Example

Organization profile: A manufacturer of capital equipment.

TITLE: PACKING AND DISPATCH PROCEDURE NO. 27
ISSUE: 2 SHEET 1 OF 2

1.0 OBJECTIVE

1.1 To record and control the packing and dispatch of products to customers.

2.0 SCOPE

2.1 The packing and dispatch of all machines, accessories and spare parts dispatched together is covered by this procedure.

3.0 RESPONSIBILITIES

3.1 The Materials Manager is overall responsible for the operation of this procedure.

3.2 The Scheduling Manager is responsible for the detail arrangements associated with the packing and dispatch of orders for machines and for the production of Export documentation for all orders.

3.3 The stores personnel are responsible for the in-house packing of products.

3.4 The Delivery Driver is responsible for the safe delivery to outside packers of products as appropriate.

3.5 The Chief Inspector is responsible for ensuring that all items included in the order are packed with the order.

4.0 PROCEDURE

4.1 When an order for a machine is cleared from audit, a Release Note is made out by the Auditor and a copy passed to both the Production Manager and the Scheduling Manager.

4.2 If it has been decided that the order may be dispatched with items outstanding then the details of the parts to be dispatched are closed off the computer system and a new order raised, at the same order number with a stroke.

4.3 Two copies of a Dispatch Note are raised on the Computer system and one copy, on completion of the Dispatch operations, is filed with customer/agent related documentation in the Sales Department, and the other copy is supplied for packing with the order.

4.4 The Delivery Driver and Chief Inspector identify the items to be included in the delivery and these are packed and/or protected by the Delivery Driver to minimize the chance of damage. In the case of export orders, the items are taken to an approved packer on suitable transport by the Delivery Driver and details of the order being packed are recorded on the Packers Job List by the Scheduling Manager. Home orders are taken directly to the customer with the Dispatch Note.

4.5 The parts making up the order are packed by the Approved Packer in accordance with the Company Packing Specification and the Scheduling Manager is notified when the packing is complete.

Section 9. Packaging and Shipping...Example

TITLE: PACKING AND DISPATCH	PROCEDURE NO. 27
ISSUE: 2	SHEET 2 OF 2

4.6 If the order is for export the Export Documentation appropriate to the destination is prepared by the Export Department and processed in accordance with appropriate regulations.

4.7 When any payments have been received, arrangements are made, using approved transporters, for the packed products to be taken to the next stage on route to the customer. The date of dispatch from the packer is recorded on the Packers Job List.

4.8 When the Invoice for packing is received from the packer the order number of the products packed is written on the invoice and a copy is taken. The original is passed to accounts for payment and the receipt of the invoice is recorded on the Packers Job List.

5.0 RELATED PROCEDURES

5.1 Order Entry — Procedure 10

5.2 Control of Assembly, Inspection and Test — Procedure 26

6.0 DOCUMENTATION

6.1 Dispatch Note — Appendix 1

6.2 Packers Job List — Appendix 2

6.3 Release Note — Appendix 3

7.0 RECORDS

7.1 The Release Note is filed with the Audit Report by the Auditor and retained for at least ten years.

7.2 A copy of the Dispatch Note is filed by the Scheduling Manager and retained for at least five years.

Section 10. Control of Reject Material...Example

Organization profile: A manufacturing company making complex assemblies.

TITLE: CONTROL OF NONCONFORMING ITEMS PROCEDURE NO. 28
ISSUE: 2 SHEET 1 OF 2

1.0 OBJECTIVE

1.1 To control and record all nonconforming items found.

2.0 SCOPE

2.1 All items found to be nonconforming at goods inwards, in stores or during assembly processes.

3.0 RESPONSIBILITIES

3.1 The Chief Inspector is overall responsible for the operation of this procedure. In the absence of the Chief Inspector the Quality Coordinator is overall responsible for this procedure.

3.2 The Purchasing Manager is responsible for the processing of nonconforming items which have been purchased by the Company.

3.3 The Engineering Department is responsible for approving all concessions in accordance with the concessions procedure.

4.0 PROCEDURE

4.1 When any items covered by this procedure are found by any employee not to conform to specification an Inspector is informed. An Inspection Report is made out by the Inspector giving full details of the nature of the defect and the items are labeled with a 'REJECTED' label giving details of the Inspection Report number, Part Number and Description, Quantity Rejected, Reason for Rejection and date by the Inspector. If possible the items are moved to a secure Quarantine Area otherwise they are marked to ensure that there is no danger of their inadvertent use.

4.2 Periodically, all such items are examined by the Chief Inspector and Production Supervision with one of the following decisions taken :

4.2.1 If the items are considered to be fit for the purpose for which they are being used then they may be accepted on a Concession. This is controlled in accordance with the control of concessions procedure.

4.2.2 If the items cannot be economically used, or are purchased and it is considered that their value is trivial, then they are scrapped.

4.2.3 If the items are purchased and are not of a trivial value then they are returned to the supplier.

4.2.4 If the items can be reworked to bring them totally to specification and it is economic or expedient to do so then the items may be rectified.

4.2.5 If the items can be reworked to bring them to a condition that might be acceptable but is not to specification then this may be done on a concession. This is controlled in accordance with the Control of Concessions procedure.

Section 10. Control of Reject Material...Example

TITLE: CONTROL OF NONCONFORMING ITEMS PROCEDURE NO. 28
ISSUE: 2 SHEET 2 OF 2

4.3 In cases 4.2.2 - 4.2.4 above, the decision taken is recorded on the appropriate part of the Inspection Report by the Chief Inspector. In cases 4.2.1 and 4.2.5 the Inspection Form is held pending a decision on whether a concession is granted. If it is refused then one of the other decisions need to be taken, if it is granted then the concession number is written on the Inspection Report and the items are released for use.

4.4 The inspection department retain the white copy of the report and pass the three colored copies to the Stores Office where stock or kit adjustments are made and stocked parts considered for further inspection as necessary.

4.5 The copies of the Inspection Report are passed to the Materials Office where they are examined for the inspection and/or Engineering salvage decision on any re-work possible or return of goods to suppliers.

4.6 If the goods are for re-work the blue copy of the Inspection Report is sent to Production Engineering and the work is progressed in accordance with the Control of Production Engineering Procedure and Job Cards are issued. The pink copy of the Inspection Report is destroyed and the green copy is retained by Material Control.

4.7 If the goods are to be returned to the supplier the blue copy is destroyed, the green copy is retained in Material Control and the pink copy is passed to the Purchasing Department where an Advice Note, pink, blue and white copies, is generated and the supplier is informed of the complaint. The set of Advice Notes are sent to the Stores Office.

4.8 Arrangements for return of goods are made by the dispatch department, in conjunction with the Purchasing Department, and the goods are dispatched to or collected by the supplier, together with the blue copy of the Advice Note. The white and pink copies of the Advice Note are signed by the delivery driver or marked with delivery details and returned to the Materials Office. Progress of goods to be returned to the customer is controlled through the Stores Office and the Purchasing Department to ensure efficiency.

4.9 The Inspection Reports are analyzed by the Quality Coordinator and reported in accordance with the Management Review and Corrective Action Procedure.

5.0 RELATED PROCEDURES

5.1	Management Review	Procedure 3
5.2	Goods Receiving and Stores Control	Procedure 22
5.3	Manufacturing Control	Procedure 23
5.4	Control of Assembly	Procedure 25
5.5	Final Inspection and Test	Procedure 26

6.0 DOCUMENTATION

6.1	Inspection Report	Appendix 1
6.2	Rejected Label	Appendix 2
6.3	Advice Note	Appendix 3

7.0 RECORDS

7.1 Inspection Reports are filed by the Inspection Department and kept for at least three years.

7.2 Concession request forms are filed by Engineering and retained for at least ten years.

Section 11. Customer Returns / Complaints...Example

Organization profile: A large car dealership.

TITLE: CUSTOMER COMPLAINTS PROCEDURE NO. 6
ISSUE: 1 SHEET 1 OF 2

1.0 OBJECTIVE.

1.1 To control and record the actions resulting from all customer complaints received by the company.

2.0 SCOPE

2.1 Any concern expressed by a customer with respect to the level of service provided by the company.

2.2 Any concern expressed by a customer with respect to the condition of any vehicle or part supplied by the company.

2.3 This procedure includes both internal and external customers within the definition of customer.

3.0 RESPONSIBILITIES

3.1 The Financial Controller is responsible for ensuring that all recorded complaints are processed in accordance with this procedure.

3.2 All employees receiving any complaints from customers covered by the scope of this procedure are required to record them in accordance with this procedure.

3.3 All Departmental Managers are responsible for dealing with Corrective Actions Forms passed to them in accordance with this procedure.

4.0 PROCEDURE

4.1 When a customer expresses a concern about the level of service, or the condition of a product or part, provided, then the details of the concern and the customer expressing the concern are recorded on a Corrective Action Form. Where applicable the details of the vehicle are recorded.

4.2 The two copies of the Corrective Action Form are passed to the Financial Controller who records the receipt of the form in the Corrective Action Register and allocates a sequential number to the form. The details of the concern are examined and a decision is made by the Financial Controller as to which Departmental Manager is responsible for the concern. This is recorded on both copies of the form and in the Register. The top copy of the Form is passed to the Departmental Manager responsible and the second copy is filed in the "Awaiting Investigation" file.

4.3 The Departmental Manager examines the details of the customer's concern and investigates the details and decides what remedial action is required to deal with the concern. The results of the investigation and the Remedial Action are entered onto the Form.

4.4 If the Departmental Manager can see a Corrective Action that can be taken to prevent recurrence of the concern then this is taken and recorded on the Form. If no Corrective Action is apparent at this stage then this is left blank.

Section 11. Customer Returns / Complaints...Example

TITLE: CUSTOMER COMPLAINTS	PROCEDURE NO. 6
ISSUE: 1	SHEET 2 OF 2

4.5 The Corrective Action Form is passed back to the Financial Controller who records it return in the Corrective Action Register. The second copy of the Corrective Action Form is removed from the 'Awaiting Investigation' file and destroyed and the top copy is filed in the 'Awaiting Resolution' file.

4.6 Each week the Corrective Action Registered is checked by the Financial Controller and any Departmental Managers with Corrective Action Forms outstanding for more than one week are contacted and appropriate action taken.

4.7 Each month the Corrective Action Forms in the 'Awaiting Resolution' file are analyzed by the Financial Controller and processed in accordance with the Management Review and Corrective Action Procedure.

4.8 Where it leads to greater efficiency or improved customer service the investigation and Remedial action may be taken and recorded by the Departmental Manager prior to the Corrective Action Form being passed to the Financial Controller.

5.0 RELATED PROCEDURES

5.1 All procedures in the Company's manuals

6.0 DOCUMENTATION

6.1	Corrective Action Form	Appendix A
6.2	Corrective Action Register	Appendix B

7.0 RECORDS

7.1 The Corrective Action Register is a permanent Register maintained by the Financial Controller and is retained for at least two years after its last entry.

7.2 The Corrective Action Forms, once processed through this procedure and the Management Review and Corrective action procedure, are filed by the Financial Controller and retained for at least five years.

Section 12. Servicing...Example

Organization profile: A servicer of fire protection systems.

TITLE: CONTROL OF SERVICE. PROCEDURE NO. 14
ISSUE: 3 SHEET 1 OF 1

1.0 OBJECTIVE

1.1 To record and control all service work carried out by the company.

2.0 SCOPE

2.1 All service work carried out by the Company.

3.0 RESPONSIBILITIES

3.1 The General Manager is responsible for the overall operation of this procedure.

4.0 PROCEDURE

4.1 When a service request is received a Service Agreement is drawn up and appropriate specification sheets detailing the work to be carried out are attached and a copy is sent to the customer for his acceptance. On receipt of his written acceptance the date of the service is recorded on the Service Planning Board. A copy of the Service Agreement signed by the company representative of Fire Protection Ltd. and the client is placed in the contract file and a copy is sent to the client.

4.2 When the service is due a Purchase Order is made out and given to the fitter/engineer who is to do the work.

4.3 The fitter/engineer visits the site and carries out the work defined on the Purchase Order. When the work has been completed a Clearance Certificate is signed by the client and the fitter/engineer and returned to the General Manager.

4.4 On receipt of the Clearance Certificate a service report on the equipment is issued to the client together with the invoice for the work.

5.0 RELATED PROCEDURES

5.1 Inquiries and Orders — Procedure 5

6.0 DOCUMENTATION

6.1 Service Agreement — Appendix A

6.2 Purchase Order — Appendix B

6.3 Service Planning Board — Appendix C

6.4 Clearance Certificate — Appendix D

7.0 RECORDS

7.1 The Service Agreement, Purchase Orders, Service Reports and Clearance Certificates are filed in the Service file by the General Manager and retained for at least ten years.

Section 13. Installation...Example

Organization profile: An installer of fire protection systems.

TITLE: INSTALLATION PROCEDURE NO. 12
ISSUE: 3 SHEET 1 OF 2

1.0 OBJECTIVE

1.1 To ensure that all the requirements of a contract associated with installation are identified and that the activities necessary to complete the contract to the customer's satisfaction are planned and controlled.

2.0 SCOPE

2.1 All installation work by the company.

3.0 RESPONSIBILITIES

3.1 The Installation Engineer allocated to the installation contract has overall responsibility for the management of the contract.

3.2 The General Manager is responsible for the overall control of all installation work.

3.3 The Site Foreman is responsible for the day to day activities associated with the installation of the contract.

4.0 PROCEDURE

4.1 When a contract is received which includes the installation of a system, once the drawings are released from the Design Control Procedure the drawings are passed to the Installation Engineer. Orders are placed in accordance with the Purchase Procedure for the items to complete the contract, and in the case of the Fabrication Contract the details of the requirements in the Contract File are studied by the General Manager and the activities required to complete the contract are entered onto the Contract Control Sheet. The timing on this sheet takes account of the customer's requirements, the availability of pipework and other supplies and the availability of resources. A copy of the Contract Control Sheet is placed in the Contract File which contains all documents relating to the Contract.

4.2 The General Manager examines contract details and the Contract Control Sheet and determines what site equipment will be needed for the contract. He contacts approved suppliers of the site equipment and determines the most suitable supplier for the contract. He places an order for the site equipment in accordance with the Purchasing Procedure. Copies of the orders are placed in the Contract File.

4.3 Arrangements are made to have the pipework delivered to the site and on receipt they are checked against the Cutting Sheets and Main Fabrication Sheets. Arrangements are made to have any pumps and tanks delivered to site.

4.4 The fire protection system is installed in accordance to the drawings and as each section is installed it is marked off on the site copy of the drawings. If during the installation major concerns are encountered with the routing of the pipework or the design of the system then the General Manager is informed. These concerns are discussed with the client, the designer or main contractor and resolved. The details of these discussions are recorded on a Meeting Pad and a copy is placed in the contract File and if necessary the details are confirmed to the Client/Contractor.

Section 13. Installation...Example

TITLE: INSTALLATION — PROCEDURE NO. 12
ISSUE: 3 — SHEET 2 OF 2

4.5 The General Manager or Design/Installation Engineer attends any site meetings with the client and records all decisions taken on a Meeting Pad. One copy is filed in the Contracts File. A second copy is given to the senior employee on site for information.

4.6 The General Manager determines the cost implications of all decisions recorded on the Meeting Pads and determines the possible price implications. If it is considered appropriate an amendment to contract is raised.

4.7 During visits to the site the General Manager or Design/Installation Engineer confirms that the installation is proceeding in accordance with the timing plan. The progress of the work is recorded on a Meeting Pad. One copy is filed in the Contracts File. The second copy is given to the senior employee on site for information.

4.8 As each phase of the work is completed the Installation Engineer visits the Site and carries out tests on the system as defined on the contract drawing. Any snags identified during these tests are recorded and corrected, and the client or his representative is contacted to witness the final sign off tests of the phase. This is repeated as each phase is completed. Test Certificates for all tests are completed and signed by the General Manager and the client's representative and a copy is given to the client and a copy is placed in the Contracts File.

4.9 When the installation is complete and commissioned the details of all the variations to the contract are summarized and costed by the General Manager and sent to the client. A detailed set of operating instructions defining the maintenance and operating requirements of the system is produced. This is sent to the customer with the final invoice for the contract.

5.0 RELATED PROCEDURES

5.1	Purchasing	Procedure 7
5.2	Design control	Procedure 3

6.0 DOCUMENTATION

6.1	System Pressure Test Certificate	Appendix A
6.2	Final Inspection Report	Appendix B
6.3	Sprinkler Completion Certificate	Appendix C

7.0 RECORDS

7.1 All the documents relating to the installation of the fire protection system are filed in the Contract File which is retained by the General Manager for at least ten years.

Section 14. Contract / Project Control...Example One

Organization Profile: An Architectural Firm. The two procedures cover the whole process and are divided into those activities before the placing a contract with the builder and control of the building contract.

TITLE: CONTROL OF PRE-TENDER SERVICES PROCEDURE NO. 6
ISSUE: 3 SHEET 1 OF 2

1.0 OBJECTIVE

1.1 To record and control the architectural services undertaken by the Partnership prior to the invitation of tenders.

2.0 SCOPE

2.1 All architectural design work and pre-tender documentation undertaken by the Partnership is covered by this procedure.

2.2 On appointments for partial services the Contract File is maintained in the Correspondence File.

3.0 RESPONSIBILITIES

3.1 The Partners are overall responsible for the operation of this procedure. Each Partner, and other members of the staff are responsible for working on designs and documentation allocated to them in accordance with this procedure.

4.0 PROCEDURE

4.1 When an appointment is obtained for architectural design services a Contract File is created and a Pre-Tender Control Sheet and a Drawing Control Sheet is placed in the front of the file. The details of the work are examined by the Partner responsible for the project and the activities relative to the project are indicated on the Pre-Tender Control Sheet. The planned completion date for each activity is indicated.

4.2 The client is contacted and a meeting is held to determine the details of the Design Brief. From the discussions at the meeting a draft Brief is prepared and sent to the client. This is then discussed and amended as necessary. When the Brief has been agreed this is recorded on the Pre-Tender Control Sheet and initialed by the Partner responsible.

4.3 The activities identified as necessary for the completion of the design are undertaken and as each activity is completed the date of completion is entered onto the Pre-Tender Control Sheet. If it becomes necessary to revise any of the planned dates then the Contract Controller is informed, new dates determined and entered on the Pre-Tender Control Sheet and the client informed. The reason for the delay is entered in the Comments Box.

4.4 As drawings are produced they are allocated numbers, but any prints produced are clearly marked with their status, *e.g.*, for quotation purposes. All drawings relating to the design are recorded and stored in accordance with the Control of Drawings procedure. As drawings and specifications are completed they are checked by another member of staff, reviewed by a Partner and signed.

Section 14. Contract / Project Control...Example One

TITLE: CONTROL OF PRE-TENDER SERVICES — PROCEDURE NO. 6
ISSUE: 3 — SHEET 2 OF 2

4.5 During the design process reference is made to relevant regulations, legislation, codes of practice, standards, and catalogues etc. As appropriate, members of staff are allocated to the various activities on the project and this allocation is recorded on the Sheet.

4.6 Where a Quantity Surveyor is being used the drawings are sent to the Quantity Surveyor for preparation of Bill of Quantities. As queries are received from the Quantity Surveyor these are answered, drawings altered as necessary and confirmed in writing. A copy of the query list and responses is kept in the contract file.

4.7 Where a Quantity Surveyor is not being used, a Specification of the Work is prepared and checked.

4.8 A Tender List is drawn up by the Partner responsible for the project and discussed with the client.

4.9 Where applicable Tender Documents are prepared and sent to the selected contractors with a request for them to submit tenders for completion of the work defined by a defined date. Any queries received from potential contractors with respect to the contract are answered.

5.0 RELATED PROCEDURES

5.1	Handling of Enquiries	Procedure 4
5.2	Control of Post-Tender Services	Procedure 7

6.0 DOCUMENTATION

6.1	Pre-Tender Control Sheet	Appendix A
6.2	Standard Form of Tender	Appendix B

7.0 RECORDS

7.1 All papers apart from drawings relating to the contract are filed in the Contract File. This file is kept for at least fifteen years after completion of the contract.

7.2 For appointments for partial services all the documents relating to the work are kept together in the Correspondence File. At the end of the contract the documents are removed from the file and placed in an envelope file with the drawings which related to the appointment. This file is retained for at least ten years.

Section 14. Contract / Project Control...Example Two

TITLE: CONTROL OF POST-TENDER SERVICES PROCEDURE NO. 7
ISSUE: 4 SHEET 1 OF 2

1.0 OBJECTIVE

1.1 To record and control the post-tender architectural services undertaken by the Partnership.

2.0 SCOPE

2.1 All post-tender architectural work undertaken by the Partnership is covered by this procedure.

3.0 RESPONSIBILITIES

3.1 The Partners are overall responsible for the operation of this procedure. Each Partner, and other members of the staff are responsible for working on contracts allocated to them in accordance with this procedure.

4.0 PROCEDURE

4.1 When an appointment for the provision of post-tender architectural services is received the Contract File from the Control of Pre-Tender Services procedure has a Post-Tender Contract Control Sheet placed in the front of the file. The details of the appointment are examined by the Partner responsible for the Contract and the activities relative to the project are indicated on the Post-Tender Control Sheet. The planned completion date for each activity is indicated.

4.2 When the tenders are received their contents are assessed, in conjunction with a Quantity Surveyor where one has been appointed. A priced Bill of Quantity/Specifications is requested from the lowest Tenderer. This is checked by the Quantity Surveyor/Partner as applicable. If any significant errors are found are reviewed in the light of the Code of Selected Tendering. Additional details may be requested from contractors. From this a Tender Report is prepared for the client making recommendations as to the most suitable contractor. Following approval by the client Contract Documents are prepared by the Partner or Quantity Surveyor and submitted to the selected contractor. Where the Contract Documents are prepared by the Partner they are checked for accuracy by another member of staff. If the contract is accepted then it is signed by the contractor and client. The unsuccessful tenders are informed of who was appointed and the agreed contract price.

4.3 The activities identified as necessary for the completion of the contract are undertaken and as each activity is completed the date of completion is entered onto the Post-Tender Control Sheet. The project is professionally managed in accordance with the terms of the contract and the procedures within the quality system. As appropriate members of staff are allocated to the various activities on the project and this allocation is recorded on the Sheet.

4.4 Any changes to the design are recorded on the drawings, approved and the revision level of the drawing is raised. Copies are sent to all concerned parties and these are clearly marked with their status e.g. for quotation purposes. All drawings relating to the design are recorded and stored in accordance with the Control of Drawings procedure.

4.5 Site meeting are attended as required by a Partner and minutes taken and issued to all interested parties. A copy of the minutes is filed in the Contract File.

Section 14. Contract / Project Control...Example Two

TITLE: CONTROL OF POST-TENDER SERVICES — PROCEDURE NO. 7
ISSUE: 4 — SHEET 2 OF 2

4.6 Stage payments are released to the contractor in line with the contract on the basis of assessments made of the work completed, in conjunction with the Quantity Surveyor where this is a contract requirement.

5.0 RELATED PROCEDURES

5.1	Handling of Enquiries	Procedure 4
5.2	Control of Pre-Tender Services	Procedure 6
5.3	Control of Drawings	Procedure 8
5.4	Control of Variations	Procedure 9
5.5	Control of Time Extensions	Procedure 10

6.0 DOCUMENTATION

6.1	Post-Tender Control Sheet	Appendix A

7.0 RECORDS

7.1 All papers apart from drawings relating to the contract are filed in the Contract File. This file is kept for at least fifteen years after completion of the contract.

Section 14. Contract / Project Control...Example Three

Organization profile: A small building contractor.

TITLE: CONTRACT CONTROL PROCEDURE NO. 9
ISSUE: 3 SHEET 1 OF 2

1.0 OBJECTIVE

1.1 To record and control the work undertaken on contracts for customers by the company.

2.0 SCOPE

2.1 All contracts undertaken by the company for clients.

3.0 RESPONSIBILITIES

3.1 The Managing Director is overall responsible for the operation of this procedure.

3.2 The Project Controller is responsible for the detail recording and control of the activities during a project in accordance with this procedure. The Project Controller is defined for each project of the Company and may be the Managing Director, the Contracts Manager, the Site Manager or may, on minor projects, be the employee carrying out the work.

4.0 PROCEDURE

4.1 When an order is received and cleared from the appropriate Enquiry procedure it is decided by the Managing Director or Contracts Manager whether the Contract is to be controlled as a minor or major contact. A Project Controller is selected by the Managing Director and allocated to the contract which is then controlled as below :

4.2 Minor Contracts

4.2.1 A Contract Sheet is made out stating the Job Number, clients name and a description of the work to be carried out. The Contract Control Sheet is filed in the Pending Minor Jobs envelope and the job is listed on the outside of the envelope.

4.2.2 If any items are required to be made in the Workshop then these are processed in accordance with the Workshop Control procedure and a copy of the Workshop Order is attached to the Contract Control Sheet.

4.2.3 Any material required for the project is ordered by the Project Controller in accordance with the Purchasing procedure and the copy of the Order or Delivery Note is attached to the Contract Control Sheet.

4.2.4 If the contract includes site work, when it is ready to start the site work, a copy of the Contract Control Sheet is made, indicating any free issue material to be used, and given to the employee who is to carry out the work. The work is carried out in accordance with the Description of work on the Contract Control Sheet. Any concerns are referred to the Project Controller. Instructions are obtained as necessary.

4.2.5 The progress of the work is periodically verified by the Project Controller as necessary and when the contract is finished it is inspected to confirm that it meets the requirements. The original of Contract Control Sheet is signed by the Project Controller and filed in the Minor Jobs Completed envelope and logged on the outside of the envelope, and the copy of the Contract Control Sheet is destroyed.

4.3 Major Contracts

4.3.1 The estimate for the contract is removed from the file and the details examined by the Project Controller. A Contract Envelope is started for the contract and the summary of the Contract work is entered onto the front of the envelope. All working papers for the contract are placed in the Envelope. The initial activities required for the project are listed on the front of

Section 14. Contract / Project Control...Example Three

TITLE: CONTRACT CONTROL — PROCEDURE NO. 9
ISSUE: 3 — SHEET 2 OF 2

(continued) the envelope. Where they are known the approximate planned start dates of each activity is entered. If the contents of the Envelope become excessive the contents are placed in a box file, but the Envelope is still used as the control document.

4.3.2 Work is carried out in accordance to the activities identified and the copies of drawings and/or other working papers from the Envelope. As further activities are identified these are entered onto the front of the Envelope.

4.3.3 The progress of the work is monitored and dates added. As each activity is completed it is initialed by the Project Controller and dated to signify that it has been verified as being to requirements.

4.3.4 At approximately weekly intervals meetings are held of the Managing Director, company Secretary, Contracts Manager and Site Manager. The position of the work on all current contracts is reviewed by the meeting and plans made as to the allocation of resources between contracts. The decisions taken at these meetings are recorded by the company Secretary.

4.3.5 When the contract requires regular meetings with the Client, these are attended by the Project Controller, who reports the progress. Actions arising from these meetings are taken as appropriate. If minutes of the meetings are issued they are filed in the Contract Envelope.

4.3.6 Where formal instructions are received from the client to modify the scope of the work of the contract then these are actioned. Where informal instructions are received from the client to modify the scope of the work of the contract these are recorded on a Job Authorization Sheet and the top copy is given to the client and the second copy is placed in the Contract Envelope. If these are accepted by the client they are actioned. The costs involved are recorded by the Project Controller.

4.3.7 On completion of the Contract work done is verified by the Project Controller and if additional work is identified then this is entered onto the front of the Envelope and carried out as above. When everything is considered satisfactory the date of completion is entered onto the front of the Envelope and it is signed to signify that the work has been verified and that the contract is considered to be complete.

5.0 RELATED PROCEDURES

5.1 Formal Enquiries and Orders — Procedure 4

5.2 Informal Enquiries and Orders — Procedure 5

5.3 Workshop Control Procedure 6

5.4 Purchasing — Procedure 7

6.0 DOCUMENTATION

6.1 Contract Envelope — Appendix A

6.2 Job Authorization Sheet — Appendix B

6.3 Contract Control Sheet — Appendix C

7.0 RECORD

7.1 At the end of a contract all the papers and drawings relating to the contract are filed in the Contract Envelope which is sealed and placed in the Completed Contracts File in Job Number sequence. These are retained for at least ten years.

Section 15. Product and Process Audits...Example

Organization Profile: An injection molding company.

TITLE: PROCESS AUDITS PROCEDURE NO. 20
ISSUE: 2 SHEET 1 OF 1

1.0 OBJECTIVE

1.1 To determine the level of conformance to specification of the Processes used by the Company.

2.0 SCOPE

2.1 All Processes used by the Company are covered by this procedure.

3.0 RESPONSIBILITIES

3.1 It is the responsibility of the Quality and Service Manager to plan the audits and to ensure that they are conducted in an efficient manner.

3.2 It is the responsibility of the Project Manager to carry out and record the results of process audits in accordance with this procedure.

4.0 PROCEDURE.

4.1 All molding machines are normally audited every month. This time interval is reduced when new machines are being introduced or when deficiencies have been found during previous audits and is increased when a process has been found, by several audits, to be totally conforming to specification.

4.2 An audit program is prepared by the Quality and Service Manager for a six month period indicating the time the audits are to be carried out in each month.

4.3 In accordance with the audit program the appropriate Machine Setting Sheet is obtained by the Project Manager. The machine settings are checked and the values of the process parameters being used are recorded on a Process Audit Report. The Specification Values are entered on the sheet and any instance of the process not being operated to specification is highlighted and appropriate action recorded and taken.

4.4 The completed Process Audit Reports are summarized into a report which is issued as part of the report to the Corrective action and Management Review meeting. The corrective actions are processed through that meeting.

5.0 RELATED PROCEDURES

5.1	Production Control	Procedure 17
5.2	Corrective Action	Procedure 26
5.3	Process Control	Procedure 19
5.4	Set up Control	Procedure 18
5.5	Concessions	Procedure 28

6.0 DOCUMENTATION

6.1	Process Audit Program	Appendix A
6.2	Process Audit Report	Appendix B

7.0 RECORDS

7.1 The Process Audit Program and Process Audit Reports are kept by the Quality and Service Manager in line with Customer requirements or for a minimum of five years.

Section 16. Control of Quality System Documentation...Example One

Organization profile: A small service company.

TITLE: CONTROL OF MANUALS PROCEDURE NO. 1
ISSUE: 2 SHEET 1 OF 2

1.0 OBJECTIVE

1.1 To ensure that the procedures contained in the Quality Manual and Procedure Manual are of the current issue.

2.0 SCOPE

2.1 All copies of the Company Manuals.

3.0 RESPONSIBILITIES

3.1 It is the responsibility of the General Manager to control the copies of the manuals.

3.2 It is the responsibility of all holders of 'Controlled' manuals to maintain them in accordance with this procedure.

3.3 It is the responsibility of all manual holders to advise the General Manager of all changes to the procedures which would improve the control of the Quality of the services provided. He is responsible for the contents of the manuals and for authorizing the content and issue of procedures.

4.0 PROCEDURE

4.1 UNCONTROLLED COPIES OF MANUALS

4.1.1 The General Manager may decide to issue a copy of the Quality Manual to an individual who does not fall under the control of the Company. In this case the Manual is marked "UNCONTROLLED COPY - WILL NOT BE UPDATED." The issue of these copies is recorded in the Quality Manual Register by the General Manager but these copies are not maintained in a current state.

4.2 CONTROLLED COPIES OF MANUALS

4.2.1 All controlled copies of the Company Manuals are numbered and a register maintained by the General Manager of the holder of these Manuals.

4.2.2 On issuing a manual the holder name, date and issue level is recorded in the register by the General Manager.

4.2.3 When a change to a procedure in any of the manuals is required then the General Manager is contacted and the details of the change discussed. A decision is made as to whether the change would reduce the level of control to below the requirements of the Quality Policy. If the change is acceptable then the Procedures concerned are re-issued at the next issue level and the necessary changes are made to the contents list, and the content list is signed by the General Manager to authorize the changes. The details of the modifications are recorded on a Detail of Modification Form, which is signed by the General Manager. All controlled manuals held within or outside of the Company are withdrawn by the General Manager. The old procedures are extracted from the manual and the new procedures are placed into the manual by the General Manager. All parties affected by the change are informed of the nature of the change by the General Manager. A record of this updating is made in the Manual Register.

Section 16. Control of Quality System Documentation...Example One

TITLE: CONTROL OF MANUALS — PROCEDURE NO. 1
ISSUE: 2 — SHEET 2 OF 2

4.2.4 Upon leaving the company or transferring to a position where the manual is nonessential, the holder must return his/her copy to the General Manager.

4.2.5 All copies of the manuals, both controlled and uncontrolled, remain the property of the company, and holders must return them when requested to do so by the General Manager.

4.2.6 The master copies of the old procedures are filed by the General Manager.

4.2.7 The Manuals are controlled documents and only the General Manager is authorized to copy them in whole or part. Any copy which is not made by the General Manager is an unauthorized copy and any one found which such copies will have them confiscated. If a copy of a part of the manual is required then an application is made to the General Manager who decides whether the copies are to be controlled or uncontrolled. If the copies are uncontrolled then they are marked as in paragraph 4.1.1 and they are governed by the contents of that paragraph. If the copies are controlled then they are recorded in the Manual Register and are subject to control under this procedure.

5.0 RELATED PROCEDURES

5.1 All procedures in the Company Manuals

6.0 DOCUMENTATION

6.1 Manual Register — Appendix A

6.2 Details of Modifications — Appendix B

7.0 RECORDS

7.1 The Registers of the Company manuals are kept permanently by the General Manager.

7.2 The master copies of the old procedures, and the Details of Modifications are filed by the General Manager and retained for at least ten years.

Section 16. Control of Quality System Documentation...Example Two

Organization Profile: A large manufacturing organization.

TITLE: CONTROL OF QUALITY SYSTEM PROCEDURE NO. 1
ISSUE: 3 SHEET 1 OF 2

1.0 OBJECTIVE

1.1 To ensure that the procedures contained in all controlled copies of the Company Quality Manual and Procedure Manual are of the current issue.

2.0 SCOPE

2.1 All copies of the Company's Manuals.

3.0 RESPONSIBILITY

3.1 It is the responsibility of the Quality Coordinator to maintain the manuals in a state that reflects the needs of the Company.

3.2 It is the responsibility of all holders of 'Controlled' manuals to maintain them in accordance with this procedure and to ensure that the manuals are available for reference by relevant personnel.

3.3 It is the responsibility of all manual holders to advise the Quality Coordinator of any changes to the procedures which would improve the control of the Quality of the products or services of the Company. The Quality Coordinator is responsible for the contents of the manuals and issue of procedures.

4.0 PROCEDURE

4.1 Uncontrolled Copies of Procedure and Quality Manuals

4.1.1 A copy of a Manual may be issued to an individual who does not fall under the control of the Company by the Quality Coordinator. In this case the Manual is marked UNCONTROLLED COPY. The issue of such copies is recorded in the Manual Register by the Quality Coordinator, but these copies are not maintained in a current state.

4.2 Controlled Copies of Manuals

4.2.1 All controlled copies of the Company Manuals are numbered and a register of Manual holders is maintained by the Quality Coordinator.

4.2.2 On issuing a manual the holder's title, date and issue level is recorded in the register by the Quality Coordinator and also on an procedure manual amendment sheet contained within each manual.

4.2.3 When a change to a procedure in either manual is required, the Quality Coordinator is contacted and the details of the change discussed. A decision is made as to whether the change would reduce the level of control to below the requirements of the Company's Quality Policy.

4.2.4 If the change is acceptable to the Quality Coordinator and all parties defined as responsible for the procedure then the Procedures concerned are re-issued at the next issue level and the necessary changes are made to the contents list which is signed by the Quality Coordinator to authorize the contents.

4.2.5 All controlled manuals held within or outside of the Company are withdrawn by the Quality Coordinator. The old procedures are extracted from the manual and the new procedures are inserted into the manual by the Quality Coordinator. A record of this updating is made in the Procedure Manual Amendment sheet and on the Manual Register. The details of the change are recorded on the Procedure Change Sheet.

Section 16. Control of Quality System Documentation...Example Two

TITLE: CONTROL OF QUALITY SYSTEM — PROCEDURE NO. 1
ISSUE: 3 — SHEET 2 OF 2

4.2.6 Upon leaving the Company or transferring to a position where the Quality or Procedure Manual is non-essential, the copy is returned to the Quality Coordinator.

4.2.7 All copies of the Quality or Procedure Manuals, both controlled and uncontrolled, remain the property of XXXX and holders must return them when requested to do so by the Quality Coordinator.

4.2.8 The master copies of the old procedures are filed by the Quality Coordinator.

4.2.9 The Quality and Procedure Manuals are controlled documents and only the Quality Coordinator is authorized to copy them in whole or part. If a copy of a part of the manual is required then an application is made to the Quality Coordinator who decides whether the copies are to be controlled or uncontrolled. If the copies are uncontrolled then they are marked as in paragraph 4.1.1 and they are governed by the contents of that paragraph. If the copies are controlled then they are recorded in the Manual Register and are subject to control under this procedure. Any copy which is not recorded in the Manual Register is deemed to be an unauthorized copy and any such copies are confiscated.

5.0 RELATED PROCEDURES

5.1 All procedures in the Company Manuals.

6.0 DOCUMENTATION

6.1	Quality Manual Register - Controlled Copies	Appendix 1
6.2.	Quality Manual Register - Uncontrolled Copies	Appendix 2
6.3	Procedure Manual Register - Controlled Copies	Appendix 3
6.4	Procedure Manual Register - Uncontrolled Copies	Appendix 4
6.5	Procedure Change Record	Appendix 5
6.6	Procedure Manual	
6.7	Quality Manual	
6.8	Quality Manual Amendment Sheet (Issue Level)	Appendix 6
6.9	Procedure Manual Amendment Sheet (Issue Level)	Appendix 7

7.0 RECORDS

7.1 The Registers of the Company Manuals and the Manual Change Sheets are kept permanently by the Quality Coordinator.

7.2 The master copies of the old procedures are filed by the Quality Coordinator and retained for at least ten years.

Section 17. Control of Product / Service Documentation...Example One

Organization Profile: A manufacturing and design company. The following four procedures were used to establish control over the range of documents used in the quality system.

TITLE: CONTROL OF ADVERTISING INFORMATION — PROCEDURE NO. 10
ISSUE: 3 — SHEET 1 of 1

1.0 OBJECTIVE

1.1 To record and control the production of the company advertising information and to ensure that the content of such information is technically correct and meaningful to the market.

2.0 SCOPE

2.1 All advertising and publicity brochures and information.

3.0 RESPONSIBILITY

3.1 It is the responsibility of the Sales Executive to ensure that all statements on publicity information are correct to the relevant specification for the advertised product and conform to policy.

3.2 It is the responsibility of the Engineering Executive to ensure that technical details of publicity information are correctly stated. This responsibility may be formally delegated to specific Chief Engineers as appropriate.

4.0 PROCEDURE

4.1 When the Sales Executive and/or other relevant sales personnel establishes that an advertising brochure or similar is required, a record is made, and the project is identified with a number.

4.2 The project is discussed with the Engineering Executive and Sales Managers and the main design criteria and key selling points are decided. A visual copy is produced.

4.3 The visual copy is considered by the Sales Executive and his delegates as required, and submitted to the Engineering Executive and the Field Sales Manager for comments and verbal approval prior to the production of the final documentation.

4.4 When advertising information is translated into a foreign language, copy approved by the Sales Executive, the Engineering Manager, and the Field Sales Manager is submitted to the Company's agent or an approved translator for translation.

5.0 RELATED PROCEDURES

5.1 Quotations — Procedure 5

6.0 DOCUMENTATION

6.1 Advertising Literature Register — Appendix 1

7.0 RECORDS

7.1 The Advertising Literature Register is maintained permanently in the Sales department.

Section 17. Control of Product / Service Documentation...Example Two

TITLE: CONTROL OF SPECIFICATIONS — PROCEDURE NO. 14
ISSUE: 4 — SHEET 1 OF 2

1.0 OBJECTIVE

1.1 To record and control the drawings produced by the company for the manufacture of its products.

2.0 SCOPE

2.1 All drawings, parts lists, machine specification sheets and product configurators produced by the Engineering Department. These documents are referred to as drawings within this procedure.

3.0 RESPONSIBILITIES

3.1 The Technical Engineer is overall responsible for the operation of this procedure.

3.2 The Print Room Staff are responsible for the day to day operation of this procedure.

3.3 All engineers issuing and altering drawings covered by this procedure are required to do so in accordance with this procedure.

4.0 PROCEDURE

4.1 All drawings covered by this procedure have a unique number. These numbers and a description of the drawing are kept on a series of registers.

4.2 When a new drawing is produced then it is allocated a number from the appropriate register and the title of the drawing is entered into the register by the appropriate drawing number. The number is entered onto the appropriate place on the drawing.

4.3 When a drawing is to be removed from the print room for reference or change, a drawing requisition is filled out, passed to the print room clerk and the drawing is retrieved from the file. Drawings returned to the print room are filed in the appropriate location, and the drawing requisition is destroyed.

4.4 When a drawing is changed the details of the change are entered onto the revision block on the drawing, the new revision level is entered onto the drawing and the details of the revision on Engineering Change Number is entered into the appropriate Register. If it is considered that the revision causes confusion on the original drawing then it is redrawn.

4.5 When prints of drawings are requested for manufacturing on a Works Order Operation Card or for Purchasing on a Drawing Requisition, then the Master Drawing is extracted from the file and a print made.

The print is stamped with its date and the Works Order Number or Purchase Order number for which it is issued is written onto the print. The print is given to the requisitioner and is valid for that order only. Prints, once issued, are updated in accordance with the Change Control procedure as necessary.

4.6 Any prints for other purposes are made and stamped "Uncontrolled Copy, will not be updated."

5.0 RELATED PROCEDURES

5.1 Project Control — Procedure 13

5.2 Change Control — Procedure 18

Section 17. Control of Product / Service Documentation...Example Two

TITLE: CONTROL OF SPECIFICATIONS — PROCEDURE NO. 14
ISSUE: 4 — SHEET 2 OF 2

6.0 DOCUMENTATION

6.1	Drawing Register	Appendix 1
6.2	Drawing Requisition	Appendix 2
6.3	Drawing Stamp for prints with order number	Appendix 3
6.4	Drawing Stamp for prints with no order number	Appendix 4

7.0 RECORDS

7.1 The Drawing Registers are permanent files kept by the Engineering Department.

7.2 The Master Drawings produced as hard copy are filed in the Engineering Department for at least ten years after the last supply of a product made in accordance with their designs.

7.3 Drawings produced on the CAD system are stored as data files on that system. A full copy of all files on the system is taken every two weeks on tape number one, and intermediate backups are taken as changes to drawings are made. At the end of two weeks this tape is stored and a full backup is made on tape number two. The above procedure is then followed alternating the two tapes. Drawings which are no longer associated with current design work are archived onto an archive system which is kept permanently.

Section 17. Control of Product / Service Documentation...Example Three

TITLE: CONTROL OF MICROFILMS | PROCEDURE NO. 15
ISSUE: 3 | SHEET 1 OF 1

1.0 OBJECTIVE

1.1 To control and record changes to drawings which have been microfilmed.

2.0 SCOPE

2.1 All master drawings except those produced by CAD are microfilmed for security reasons.

3.0 RESPONSIBILITIES

3.1 Design Engineers are responsible for informing Technical Systems via the Change Control procedure.

3.2 Technical Systems are responsible for ensuring update of microfilm.

4.0 PROCEDURE

4.1 When a change is made to a master drawing, the Engineering Change Note data base in Technical System is updated. Periodically, a report indicating drawing amendments is generated and is passed to the print room.

4.2 Upon receipt of the report, the original microfilm is removed and replaced with a blank microfilm card by the print room clerk. This denotes that the microfilm has been withdrawn for refilming.

4.3 The removed microfilm is then placed in a holding area until such a time as an economical batch is achieved to send to the microfilmer.

4.4 When a batch is achieved, the master drawings are removed from the file and replaced by a paper copy for security. The drawings are then sent for refilming.

4.5 When returned the drawings are checked to ensure they have been stamped with the date of refilm, and returned to the file and paper prints removed.

4.6 The new microfilms are then returned to microfilm library complete with the old microfilm which has been clearly stamped **"Obsolete"**. The card is removed.

4.7 The database for microfilms is updated by the Technical Systems Department.

5.0 RELATED PROCEDURES

5.1 Change Control — Procedure 18

6.0 DOCUMENTATION

6.1 Microfilm Card — Appendix 1

6.2 Amendment Report — Appendix 2

6.3 'Obsolete' Stamp — Appendix 4

7.0 RECORDS

7.1 The microfilm records are kept by Technical System indefinitely.

Section 17. Control of Product / Service Documentation...Example Four

TITLE: CONTROL OF STANDARDS PROCEDURE NO. 16
ISSUE: 3 SHEET 1 OF 1

1.0 OBJECTIVE

1.1 To record and control the National and International Standards used by the company in the design of its products.

2.0 SCOPE

2.1 All National and International Standards used by the company in the design of its products.

3.0 RESPONSIBILITIES

3.1 Technical Systems are responsible for the control of standards in accordance with this procedure.

3.2 All engineers who use standards during their work are required to do so in accordance with this procedure.

4.0 PROCEDURE

4.1 All standards covered by this procedure are listed on a standards register and kept in the standards library. The register is marked to record the issue level of each standard filed.

4.2 The company subscribes to an updating service with whom all of the standards held by the company are registered. When it is reported that one of the standards held by the company has been changed then either the standard is removed from the library or a copy of the updated standard is obtained by Technical Systems, filed in the library and the register is updated accordingly.

4.3 When an engineer wishes to refer to a standard, it is located in the library and either used there or is removed and logged out in the booking register. When it is returned, it is logged back in the booking register.

5.0 RELATED PROCEDURES

5.1 Project Control Procedure 13

5.2 Change Control Procedure 18

6.0 DOCUMENTATION

6.1 Standards Register Appendix 1

6.2 Booking Register Appendix 2

7.0 RECORDS

7.1 The Standards Register is a permanent record kept by the Engineering Department.

7.2 The current copies of the standards are kept in the standards library. Obsolete standards are marked as such and retained for at least ten years.

Section 18. Internal Auditing...Example

Organization Profile: A small service company.

TITLE: INTERNAL QUALITY AUDIT PROCEDURE NO. 2
ISSUE: 2 SHEET 1 OF 1

1.0 OBJECTIVE

1.1 To ensure that the procedures in the Quality and Procedure Manuals are being followed and to determine the effectiveness of the above procedures in controlling the quality of the service provided.

2.0 SCOPE

2.1 All procedures in the Company's Manuals are covered by this procedure.

3.0 RESPONSIBILITY

3.1 It is the responsibility of the Management Representative for Quality to initiate the audits and to ensure that they are conducted in an efficient manner. The authority to carry out specific audits is delegated to members of the audit team in accordance with this procedure.

4.0 PROCEDURE

4.1 All procedures are normally audited every six months. This time interval is reduced when new procedures are being introduced or when deficiencies have been found during previous audits and is increased when a procedure has been found, by several audits, to be functioning efficiently. The maximum interval between audits is twelve months.

4.2 An audit program for a six month period is prepared by the Management Representative for Quality and auditors selected for the audits defined. The auditor is independent from the function being audited and has been trained in internal auditing techniques.

4.3 Prior to each audit the auditor of the procedures to be audited is briefed by the Management Representative for Quality and the scope of the audit and any previous noncompliancies are discussed.

4.4 The auditor studies the procedures to be audited and follows a selection of "transactions" through the procedure and ensures that the procedure has been followed. During the audit the auditor completes a copy of the Quality Systems Audit Report recording the details of the documents checked, personnel interviewed and clearly identifying any deficiencies found.

4.5 On completion of the audit the Quality Systems Audit Report is given to the Management Representative for Quality who discusses the findings with the auditor and any staff responsible for the procedures audited. Corrective actions are agreed and entered onto the audit report. Based on the report the date of the next audit is decided by the Management Representative for Quality.

4.6 The corrective actions agreed are monitored by the Management Review Meeting and when they have proved to be effective and this is recorded on the Quality Systems Audit Report which is then filed.

5.0 RELATED PROCEDURES

5.1 All procedures in the Company Manuals.

6.0 DOCUMENTATION

6.1 Quality Systems Audit Report Appendix A

6.2 Audit Plan Appendix B

7.0 RECORDS

7.1 All Quality Audit Reports are filed by the Secretary and retained for at least ten years.

Section 19. Management Review...Example

Organization profile: A small manufacturer of precision components.

TITLE: MANAGEMENT REVIEW PROCEDURE NO. 3
ISSUE : 1 SHEET 1 OF 1

1.0 OBJECTIVE

1.1 To confirm that the company is fulfilling the commitments made in the Company Quality Policy.

2.0 SCOPE

2.1 All aspects of the company's activities which effect the quality of the Company's products and services.

3.0 RESPONSIBILITIES

3.1 The Managing Director, as chief executive, is responsible for conducting this review.

4.0 PROCEDURE

4.1 Every three months, the Company Directors and the Quality Manager meet.

4.2 Prior to this meeting, a report is prepared by the Quality Manager which summarizes the Quality Audit Reports and the minutes of the Corrective Action meetings.

4.3 The meeting considers this report, together with any reports from the assessment authority, and decides what actions, if any, the company needs to take to ensure that the commitments in the Policy are totally met. The future plans of the company are discussed at the meeting and considered against the Quality Policy. The training implications of any changes in the Company's activities are considered and training plans developed as appropriate.

4.4 Minutes of these meetings are issued and reviewed at each meeting to ensure that timely action is taken on the issues agreed.

5.0 RELATED PROCEDURES

5.1 All the procedures in the company's manuals.

6.0 DOCUMENTATION

6.1 The minutes of the meeting are the only formal documentation that are generated by this procedure.

7.0 RECORDS

7.1 The minutes of the meetings will be kept for at least ten years by the Managing Director.

Section 20. Deviations / Waivers / Concessions...Example

Organization profile: A supplier of precision parts to the automotive industry.

TITLE: CONCESSIONS PROCEDURE NO. 18
ISSUE: 2 SHEET 1 OF 2

1.0 OBJECTIVE

1.1 To record and control the use of items which do not conform to specification.

2.0 SCOPE

2.1 All products, materials, parts and processes for which authorization is required to deviate from specification.

3.0 RESPONSIBILITIES

3.1 The Technical Manager is overall responsible for the operation of this procedure.

3.2 The Quality Manager is responsible for seeking authorization for concessions for finished products from customers and for granting concessions which do not affect the final product in accordance with this procedure.

3.3 The Production Manager is responsible for seeking concessions from the Quality Manager to use parts and materials not defined in the product or process specification.

3.4 The Sales Department are responsible for passing any requests for deviations to specification received from customers to the Technical Manager.

4.0 PROCEDURE

4.1 When it is decided in the Nonconforming Material procedure that it is appropriate to seek a concession, or when it is necessary to use alternative parts or materials in the manufacturing process, a Concession Request Form is prepared and passed to the Quality Manager for approval.

4.2 The details on the Concession Request Forms are examined by the Quality Manager and a decision is made as to whether the request is justifiable. If this decision involves the state of the tooling then it is discussed with the Technical Manager. A decision is made by the Quality Manager as to whether the concession is technically feasible and if not, the material is classified nonconforming Quality Manager.

4.3 If it is not nonconforming a decision is made by the Quality Manager as to whether the deviation from specification is of a nature which requires clearance from the customer. If it is decided that customer approval is required the relevant customer concession procedure is followed by the Quality Manager.

4.4 If the application is approved through the customers-defined procedure, or if it is a concession which does not require customer clearance, the Concession Request is approved by the Quality Manager. Once approved the Concession Request Form is completed by the Quality Manager indicating the limitations on the concession with respect to time or numbers and the corrective action that is to be taken. The form is copied and a copy sent to the originator and the original filed in the Quality Department with the written evidence of the customer's acceptance where applicable. The approval of the Concession is noted in the Concession Log in the Quality Department and the date of the expiration of the concession is noted.

Section 20. Deviations / Waivers / Concessions...Example

TITLE: CONCESSIONS PROCEDURE NO. 18
ISSUE: 2 SHEET 2 OF 2

4.5 The Concessions Log is checked by the Quality Engineer each week and when the expiration date of the concession arrives the Production Manager is informed. The Production Manager reviews the position and either applies for a extension to the concession or ensures that the products are being produced to specification.

5.0 RELATED PROCEDURES

5.1 Control of Nonconforming Material — Procedure 16

5.2 Control of Production — Procedure 14

5.3 Specification Control — Procedure 11

6.0 DOCUMENTATION

6.1 Concession Request Form — Appendix A

7.0 RECORDS

7.1 The Quality Department are responsible for filing their copy of the Concession Request Form, with the written customer evidence where applicable. These are retained in line with the individual customer requirements or for a minimum of five years.

Section 21. Training...Example One

Organization profile : A large manufacturing company that produces and sells machine tools.

TITLE: TRAINING PROCEDURE NO. 4
ISSUE: 3 SHEET 1 OF 1

1.0 OBJECTIVE

1.1 To ensure that all employees are adequately trained in the company's systems and have the manufacturing skill necessary to ensure that the company's products and services meet the customers' requirements.

2.0 SCOPE

2.1 All employees in the Company.

3.0 RESPONSIBILITIES

3.1 The Chief Executive is overall responsible for the operation of this procedure.

3.2 Each Head of Department is responsible for the operation of this procedure within their own departments.

3.3 The Personnel Officer is responsible for the maintenance of the Training Records in line with this procedure.

4.0 PROCEDURE

4.1 The Chief Executive and each Head of Department identify the minimum experience, training and qualification for each of the positions in the Department and records this as a Job Summary for each position.

4.2 The existing experience, skills and training of each employee is recorded on a Personnel Training Record by the Head of Department. These are updated whenever training is formally given. The experience of the employees is updated each year as appropriate. When an employee has undergone training that employee's training record is updated accordingly.

4.3 The information defined above is obtained for all applicants for positions in the Company and compared with the Job Description of the post. If an applicant who does not have the defined requirements is employed, a training program is developed and implemented. In all cases, new employees undergo induction training in accordance with the Induction Training Program and this is recorded on their Training Record.

4.4 When an existing employee is considered for another position in the company then the policy defined in 4.3 is followed.

4.5 Care is taken not to allocate work which is outside the skill level of the employee.

5.0 RELATED PROCEDURES

5.1 None.

6.0 DOCUMENTATION

6.1 Personnel Training Record. Appendix 1

6.2 Job Summary. Appendix 2

6.3 Induction Training Program Appendix 3

7.0 RECORDS

7.1 The Personnel Training Record is filed by the Personnel Officer and is kept for at least ten years after the employee leaves the service of the Company.

Section 21. Training...Example Two

Organization profile : An automotive distributor.

TITLE: TRAINING — PROCEDURE NO. 4
ISSUE: 1 — SHEET 1 OF 1

1.0 OBJECTIVE

1.1 To ensure that all employees are adequately trained in the company's systems and have the knowledge and skill necessary to ensure that the company's products and services meet the Customers' requirements.

2.0 SCOPE

2.1 All employees in the Company whose work is directly related to the quality of the product or the service provided to the customers.

3.0 RESPONSIBILITIES

3.1 The Chief Executive is responsible for ensuring that this procedure is carried out every year or whenever there is a change in the workforce or the systems which effect quality.

3.2 The Customer Care Coordinator is responsible for the maintenance of the training records for all employees in accordance with this procedure.

4.0 PROCEDURE

4.1 The Chief Executive, in association with the Line Manager, determines the minimum experience, training and qualifications for each of the positions in the Company. This is recorded on a Job Description for each position.

4.2 The existing experience, skills, training and qualifications of each employee is recorded on a Training Record Form. This form is originated when the employee joins the Company and is updated by the Customer Care Coordinator whenever training takes place.

4.3 The work done and an assessment of the performance of all employees is recorded on a Training Needs Analysis each year by the employee's Line Manager. At that time the requirements of each job is compared with the training record of each employee and any deficiencies are identified. Suitable programs of training are identified to eliminate these deficiencies. These programs are implemented during the following year and records of the training is maintained by the Customer Care Coordinator.

5.0 RELATED PROCEDURES

5.1 None.

6.0 DOCUMENTATION

6.1 Training Record Form. — Appendix A

6.2 Job Description Form. — Appendix B

6.3 Training Needs Analysis. — Appendix C

7.0 RECORDS

7.1 The Training Record Forms, Training Needs Analysis and Job Description Forms are filed by the Customer Care Coordinator and are retained for at least two years after the employee leaves the service of the Company.

Section 22. Corrective and Preventive Action...Example

Organization profile: A manufacturer of precision steel rollers for the printing industry.

TITLE: CORRECTIVE AND PREVENTIVE ACTION PROCEDURE NO. 17
ISSUE: 1 SHEET 1 OF 1

1.0 OBJECTIVE

1.1 The Company recognizes that an essential feature of Quality is to ensure that quality concerns, wherever located in the manufacturing cycle, are not just remedied but that knowledge of the source of the problem is gained and action is taken to prevent recurrence. In this way the Company aims to improve product quality, reduce the cost of manufacturing, and improve its service to its customers.

2.0 SCOPE

2.1 This procedure covers all areas of a Company's operations.

3.0 RESPONSIBILITIES

3.1 The Quality Manager is responsible for ensuring that all data pertaining to product quality are analyses to determine the causes of the concerns and corrective action is taken to prevent recurrence. He is responsible for analyzing all data pertaining to product quality.

4.0 PROCEDURE

4.1 At the end of each month all Reject/Complaint Notes and the results of Quality Audits are analyzed by the Quality Manager. A report is prepared and issued to the Works Director, Works Manager and Fabrication Foreman.

4.2 A meeting is held between the recipients of the report when the report is considered and plans of corrective and preventive action agreed.

4.3 The plans of corrective and preventive actions made at previous meetings are reviewed to determine the extent to which the objectives have been met. Further actions may be agreed as appropriate.

5.0 RELATED PROCEDURES

5.1 All procedures in the Company manuals.

6.0 DOCUMENTATION

6.1 No formal documentation is used during this procedure, but minutes of the meetings are recorded by the Quality Manager.

7.0 RECORDS

7.1 The reports and minutes are filed for ten years by the Quality Manager.

Section 23. Calibration...Example

Organization profile: A precision injection molding company which has a large number of special gauges to control critical dimensions on its products.

TITLE: CALIBRATION PROCEDURE NO. 13
ISSUE: 2 SHEET 1 OF 2

1.0 OBJECTIVE

1.1 To ensure that the results of all measurements and tests taken to confirm product quality are of known accuracy, and can be related to National Standards or Physical Standards.

2.0 SCOPE

2.1 All inspection, measuring and test equipment used by the Company to control the quality of its products, processes and services.

2.2 Inspection and test equipment owned by employees can only be used to confirm product quality if it is controlled under this procedure.

3.0 RESPONSIBILITIES

3.1 The Quality Manager is overall responsible for the operation of this procedure.

3.2 The Gauge Engineer arranging the calibration of the equipment as required and for maintaining records of the calibration.

4.0 PROCEDURE

4.1 Each item of inspection and test equipment is given a serial number and for each item there is a Gauge Record Card and a record of the Gauge on the Computer based Calibration Record System. The details on the manual and computer based system are identical. The Gauge Number is marked on the gauge.

4.2 The Gauge Record defines the measurement capability of the gauge, frequency of calibration and location of the item. If the item is calibrated in-house then the relevant Calibration Instruction is indicated.

4.3 The Gauge Engineer prior to the start of a calibration period produces from the computer system a list of the Gauges that require to be calibrated during the next period. This is based on the dates and re-calibration frequencies defined on the records.

4.4 The items are calibrated in accordance with the requirements defined on the list either by the Gauge Engineer or by an approved outside calibration service. The actual results obtained, the date of calibration and for outside calibrations the calibration certificate number on the records. Inspection and test equipment is marked with a label to indicate calibration status. Wherever possible, wax is used to integrate controls to prevent unauthorized adjustments.

4.5 The re-calibration period is set to avoid measuring equipment coming out of specification before the end of that period when used normally and correctly. The recalibration period is reviewed after each calibration by the Gauge Engineer to achieve this objective.

4.6 If an item of measuring equipment is found to be out of specification then the measurements taken with the item since it was last calibrated are reviewed by the Gauge Engineer and the Quality Manager and a decision is taken and recorded on the records as to whether action needs to be taken. The gauge is either withdrawn from use, refurbished and/or re-calibrated.

Section 23. Calibration...Example

TITLE: CALIBRATION — PROCEDURE NO. 13
ISSUE: 2 — SHEET 2 OF 2

5.0	RELATED PROCEDURES	
5.1	Customer Initial Sample Approval	Procedure 6
5.2	Bought Out Initial Sample Approval	Procedure 9
5.3	Process Audits	Procedure 20
5.4	Control of Production	Procedure 14
6.0	DOCUMENTATION	
6.1	Calibration Record Card	Appendix A
6.2	Computer Calibration Record	Appendix B
6.3	Calibration Program	Appendix C

7.0 RECORDS

7.1 All calibration records and the relevant calibration certificates are kept in line with individual customer requirements or for a minimum of five years after their last entry. These records are maintained by the Quality Department. The Records on the Computer Calibration System are backed up after each usage and the back-up disc is kept remote from the computer.

Section 24. Control of Software Systems...Example

Organization profile: A manufacturing company that uses a standard computer system for production planning, material procurement and stock control.

TITLE: CONTROL OF THE COMPUTER SYSTEM — PROCEDURE NO. 35
ISSUE: 1 — SHEET 1 OF 2

1.0 OBJECTIVE

1.1 To ensure that the Computer Production Control system is efficiently maintained and controlled.

2.0 SCOPE

2.1 All aspects of the Computer Production Control system are covered by this procedure.

2.2 The operation of the Computer System itself is fully described in the Systems Manuals which are of the same issue as the issue of the software used by the Company. Copies of these manuals are registered by the Commercial Manager-Spares and are available to all users as necessary and they describe the various transactions of the system.

3.0 RESPONSIBILITIES

3.1 The Commercial Manager - Spares is responsible for the control of the Computer System in accordance with this procedure. In his absence the Systems Accountant carries out these responsibilities.

4.0 PROCEDURE

4.1 Access to all menus, options and transactions on the Computer System are password protected. The access to each option is controlled by the Commercial Manager and is dependent on the responsibilities of the password holders.

4.2 At 3 a.m. each day except Sunday a back-up copy of all data files, binary files and defined parts of the operating system is automatically made on a Tape Streamer. The tape produced is placed in a fire proof safe, recorded on a register which is dated and signed by the person storing the copy. These back up copies are retained for ten working days and are then used for the eleventh back up copy.

4.3 At the end of each 4 to 5 week accounting period, the tape in place is removed from the 10 day cycle and retained for at least seven years in a fire proof safe. The vacant position in the cycle is filled with a new tape.

5.0 RELATED PROCEDURES

5.1	Order Entry of Machines	Procedure 6
5.2	Supplier Approval	Procedure 20
5.3	Purchasing	Procedure 21
5.4	Goods Receiving and Stores Control	Procedure 22
5.5	Control of Manufacture	Procedure 25
5.6	Control of Assembly, Inspection and Test	Procedure 26

Section 24. Control of Software Systems...Example

TITLE: CONTROL OF THE COMPUTER SYSTEM — PROCEDURE NO. 35
ISSUE: 1 — SHEET 2 OF 2

5.7	Packing and Dispatch	Procedure 27
5.8	Control of Nonconforming	Procedure 28
5.9	Customer Returns	Procedure 30
6.0	DOCUMENTATION	
6.1	Register of Back-ups	Appendix 1
6.2	Systems Manual	
7.0	RECORDS	
7.1	The Registers of Back-ups are retained by the Commercial Manager for a period of at least one year.	
7.2	The period end back-up tapes are retained for at least seven years in the fire-proof safe.	

Section 25. Maintenance of Equipment...Example One

Organization profile: A chemical processing company.

TITLE: PLANT MAINTENANCE PROCEDURE NO. 23
ISSUE: 3 SHEET 1 OF 2

1.0 OBJECTIVE

1.1 To ensure that the plant used by the company is maintained in a condition suitable for efficient manufacture and plant life.

2.0 SCOPE

2.1 All items of plant and equipment used by the company. This includes the main operating plant, the material handling equipment and the delivery vehicles used by the company.

3.0 RESPONSIBILITIES

3.1 The Plant Engineer is overall responsible for the operation of this procedure.

3.2 Individual electricians and mechanics are responsible for carrying out maintenance duties in accordance with this procedure.

3.3 Production Staff are responsible for reporting any faults with plant and equipment in accordance with this procedure.

4.0 PROCEDURE

4.1 Each item of plant and equipment covered by this procedure has a plant number, a plant file and a computer record. The plant file holds all the literature from the manufacturer or supplier on the item. From this information, and knowledge of the operation of the plant a Maintenance Schedule is drawn up by the Plant Engineer defining the maintenance activities to be carried out and the frequency of the activities. The outline of the Maintenance Schedule is entered onto the computer system.

4.2 Each month a printout of the maintenance to be carried out during the next month is produced by the Plant Engineer. A meeting is held with the Production Manager and the detail timing of the maintenance is agreed and entered onto a Monthly Maintenance Plan. Copies of this are issued to the Production Manager, Production Controller and all Production Superintendents.

4.3 Special Materials and Parts required for the Monthly Maintenance Plan are determined from the Plant Files and ordered in accordance with the Purchasing procedure. If any items are not expected to be available to support the plan then adjustments are made and all holders of the plan are informed.

4.4 Resources are allocated to the Monthly Maintenance Plan by the Plant Engineer, and it is issued to the Maintenance Electricians and Mechanics.

4.5 At the times indicated on the Monthly Maintenance Plan the Electricians and Mechanics liaise with Production Management to confirm the release of the plant and equipment and carry out the maintenance activities indicated on the Monthly Maintenance Plan. Reference is made to the information in the Plant File as necessary and a Maintenance Report is filled out.

Section 25. Maintenance of Equipment...Example One

TITLE: PLANT MAINTENANCE	PROCEDURE NO. 23
ISSUE: 3	SHEET 2 OF 2

4.6 If any concerns are identified during the maintenance the Plant Engineer is informed and the concern is investigated. If additional activities are required then these are authorized. If the additional activities would result in the plant or equipment not being returned to Production on time then the issue is discussed with Production Management and agreement reached. This may result in the additional activities being done at a later date. This is all recorded on the Maintenance Record.

4.7 On completion of the maintenance the performance of the plant or equipment is tested by the Electricians or Mechanics, and the Production Staff as necessary. The efficient running of the plant or equipment is established before hand-over, and this is recorded on the Maintenance Record.

4.8 If a concern with an item of Plant or Equipment is identified by a member of Production Staff then a Production Superintendent is informed. The matter is investigated and if it is found that maintenance action is required a three part Request for Maintenance Form is filled out and the top two copies are given to the Plant Engineer. The concern is investigated and the relative priority decided. In line with this decision an electrician or mechanic is allocated to investigate and carry out the maintenance required. The top copy of the Request for Maintenance Form is given to the Electrician or Fitter and the second copy is retained by the Plant Engineer. If special parts or materials are required these are ordered in accordance with the Purchasing procedure. On completion of the maintenance, the details of the activities and materials used are entered onto the Request for Maintenance Form, and it is returned to the Plant Engineer.

4.9 The Plant Superintendent originating the Request for Maintenance Form is contacted by the Plant Engineer then together, the item of Plant or Equipment is checked. The results are verified and recorded on the Request for Maintenance Form. The down time is agreed and recorded and the Request for Maintenance Forms are filed in the Plant File.

5.0 RELATED PROCEDURES

5.1	Process Control	Procedure 7
5.2	Purchasing	Procedure 9
5.3	Delivery	Procedure 17

6.0 DOCUMENTATION

6.1	Maintenance Schedule	Appendix A
6.2	Monthly Maintenance Plan	Appendix B
6.3	Request for Maintenance	Appendix C
6.4	Computer Printout	Appendix D

7.0 RECORDS

7.1 All records for each item of Plant and Equipment are filed in the Plant File and retained for at least the life of the Plant.

Section 25. Maintenance of Equipment...Example Two

Earth, Inc.
North American Division

Procedure No.: 17
Effective Date: 9/21/92
Revision Date: 3/14/93

MAINTENANCE

Approved By:

Procedure Owner__________________________________Date_______________

Production Supervisor______________________________Date_______________

Management Representative for Quality__________________

Date______________________

Section 25. Maintenance of Equipment...Example Two

Earth, Inc.	Procedure No.: 17
North American Division	Effective Date: 9/21/92
	Revision Date: 3/14/93

1.0 PURPOSE

To provide suitable maintenance of equipment to ensure continuing process capability and a safe environment.

2.0 SCOPE

2.1 All production and lab equipment that impacts product quality and requires maintenance.

2.2 Delivery trucks are not covered by this procedure.

3.0 RESPONSIBILITIES

3.1 The Production Supervisor is responsible for the Maintenance Program.

4.0 PROCEDURE

4.1 Scheduled Maintenance

4.1.1 Production Supervisor does an annual maintenance schedule for all equipment. Each machine and equipment record shows what is to be done and how often or when.

4.1.2 Maintenance is performed using work instructions for machine/equipment type.

4.1.3 Completed maintenance work is recorded in the Maintenance Log and acknowledged by the operator performing the maintenance.

4.2 Breakdowns

4.2.1 All breakdowns are recorded in the breakdown log indicating the problem, the solution, date, time and duration.

4.2.2 If necessary, the Lab verifies quality of products produced prior to and during breakdown.

5.0 RELATED PROCEDURES

5.1	Process Control	Procedure 4
5.2	Process Control - Disposable	Procedure 5
5.3	Handling Nonconforming Products	Procedure 7

6.0 DOCUMENTATION

6.1	Annual Maintenance Schedule	
6.2	Maintenance Log	Appendix A
6.3	Maintenance Work Instruction	
6.4	Breakdown Log	Appendix B

7.0 RECORDS

7.1 Annual Maintenance Schedule and Maintenance Log are filed by the Production Supervisor for at least 7 years.

7.2 The Breakdown Log is kept by the Production Supervisor for at least 10 years.

Appendix D–3

Responsibilities for Quality

A Section of the Procedure Manual as Discussed in Chapter 11

Organization Profile: A Leisure Complex.

TITLE: RESPONSIBILITIES FOR QUALITY
ISSUE: 1 SHEET 1 OF 2

TITLE: LEISURE MANAGER

REPORTS TO: COMMERCIAL MANAGER

DEPUTY: DEPUTY LEISURE MANAGER

GENERAL

The efficient, safe, and profitable management of the leisure facilities operated by the Company.

QUALITY RESPONSIBLITIES

The specific responsibilities with respect to the Quality System are defined in the procedures in the Procedure Manual. These are summarized below:

PROCEDURE NO 1: CONTROL OF MANUALS

It is the responsibility of all holders of 'Controlled' manuals to maintain them in accordance with this procedure.

It is the responsibility of all manual holders to advise the Commercial Manager of all changes to the procedures which would improve the control of the Quality of the services provided. He is responsible for the contents of the manuals and for authorizing the content and issue of procedures.

PROCEDURE NO 4: TRAINING

The Leisure Manager is overall responsible for the operation of this procedure and for ensuring the training standards of all Leisure staff.

PROCEDURE NO 5: CLIENT CONTRACT REVIEW

The Commercial Manager, Leisure Manager and Deputy Leisure Manager are responsible for preparing the details of any proposals prepared under this procedure.

PROCEDURE NO 6: CONTROL OF BLOCK BOOKINGS

The Leisure Manager is overall responsible for the operation of this procedure.

The Leisure Manager or Deputy Leisure Manager is responsible for approving all bookings for Leisure Facilities. For bookings with no special safety aspects this responsibility may be delegated to the Leisure Administrator.

PROCEDURE NO 7: CONTROL OF ONE-TIME BOOKINGS

The Leisure Manager is overall responsible for the operation of this procedure.

The Leisure Manager or Deputy Leisure Manager is responsible for approving all bookings for Leisure Facilities. For booking with no special safety aspects this responsibility may be delegated to the Leisure Administrator.

TITLE: RESPONSIBILITIES FOR QUALITY
ISSUE: 1 SHEET 2 OF 2

TITLE: LEISURE MANAGER

PROCEDURE NO 8: PROGRAMMING OF LEISURE FACILITIES

The Leisure Manager is overall responsible for the operation of this procedure.

PROCEDURE NO 9: CONTROL OF LEISURE FACILITIES

The Leisure Manager is overall responsible for the operation of this procedure.

PROCEDURE NO 10: PROVISION OF CATERING FACILITIES

The Leisure Manager is responsible for the day to day control of the Catering Contract.

PROCEDURE NO 11: SUPPLIER APPROVAL

The Leisure Manager is responsible for the maintenance of a records of Approved Suppliers, for the approval of new suppliers and for the monitoring of such suppliers.

PROCEDURE NO 13: CONTROL OF CASUAL STAFF

The Leisure Manager is overall responsible for the operation of this procedure.

The Leisure Manager or Assistant Leisure Manager is responsible for the approval of casual staff as being suitable for their duties.

PROCEDURE NO 14: CONTROL OF CLEANING SERVICES

The Leisure Manager is overall responsible for the operation of this procedure.

PROCEDURE NO 15: CONTROL OF MAINTENANCE

The Leisure Manager is overall responsible for the operation of this procedure.

PROCEDURE NO 16: CONTROL OF COMPLAINTS

All employees who receive serious complaints are required to report such instances to the Commercial Manager in accordance with this procedure.

PROCEDURE NO 17: CALIBRATION

The Leisure Manager is responsible for ensuring that the calibration procedure is followed by all employees taking measurements and tests.

All employees who use measuring test equipment during the provision of the service to residents are responsible for ensuring that it has been calibrated in accordance with this calibration procedure.

The Leisure Manager is responsible for arranging for a sub-contractor to calibrate the equipment as required and for maintaining records of the calibration.

PROCEDURE NO 18: CONTROL OF THE USE OF THE CONDITIONING EQUIPMENT

The Leisure Manager is overall responsible for the operation of this procedure.

Appendix D–4

Quality Records

A Section of the Procedure Manual as Discussed in Chapter 11

Organization Profile: A Leisure Complex.

TITLE: RECORDS SUMMARY
ISSUE: 1 SHEET 1 OF 2

The quality records associated with each procedure are defined at the end of the procedures. The following is a summary of these records.

PROCEDURE NO 1: CONTROL OF MANUALS

The Register of the Company manuals is kept permanently by the Commercial Manager.

The master copies of the old procedures are filed by the Commercial Manager and retained for at least ten years.

PROCEDURE NO 2: QUALITY SYSTEMS AUDIT

All Quality Audit Reports are filed by the Commercial Manager and retained for at least ten years.

PROCEDURE NO 3: CORRECTIVE ACTION AND MANAGEMENT REVIEW

Notes of the Management Review Meeting are kept by the Commercial Manager for at least ten years.

PROCEDURE NO 4: TRAINING

The Job Descriptions and Training Record Forms are filed in a binder in the General Office.

PROCEDURE NO 5: CLIENT CONTRACT REVIEW

The tender, Specification and all correspondence, including modification to the agreement, is filed by the Works Manager and retained for at least ten years after the expiration of the agreement.

PROCEDURE NO 6: CONTROL OF BLOCK BOOKINGS

The Club Membership Application Forms and Club Booking Sheets are filed by the Administrator in Club Membership Number Sequence and are retained for at least one year after the end year of validity.

The Master Daily Booking Sheet is retained by the Administrator and kept for at least one year after the end of the period to which it refers.

The School Block Booking Forms are filed by the Administrator in a Schools File and retained for at least one year after the end of the period to which they refer.

PROCEDURE NO 7: CONTROL OF ONE-TIME BOOKINGS

The Application Forms are filed by the Administrator in date order of the booking and are retained for at least six months after the booking.

The Daily Booking Sheets is retained by the Administrator and kept for at least one year after the end of the period to which it refers.

TITLE: RECORDS SUMMARY
ISSUE: 1 SHEET 2 OF 2

PROCEDURE NO 8: PROGRAMMING OF LEISURE FACILITIES

The Booking Sheets are retained by the Administrator and kept for at least one year after the end of the period to which it refers.

PROCEDURE NO 9: CONTROL OF LEISURE FACILITIES

The Daily Staffing Rota, Daily Change Over Sheets and Weekly Staffing Rotas are filed by the Assistant Leisure Manager and retained for at least six months.

PROCEDURE NO 10: PROVISION OF CATERING FACILITIES

All documents relating to the Catering Services are filed by the Works Department and copies kept by the Leisure Manager.

PROCEDURE NO 11: SUPPLIER APPROVAL

The current copies of the Approved Supplier Forms are maintained by the Leisure Manager and form a current record.

PROCEDURE NO 12: PURCHASING

Copies of the orders are filed by the Administrator and retained for at least six months.

PROCEDURE NO 13: CONTROL OF CASUAL STAFF

The file of approved Casual Staff is maintained by the Leisure Manager and is a current file. A copy of the file relating to non-specialist casual staff is maintained by the Senior Attendant at the Reception Desk.

PROCEDURE NO 14: CONTROL OF CLEANING SERVICES

The Cleaning Audit Reports are filed by the Duty Officer in date order and are retained for at least one year.

PROCEDURE NO 15: CONTROL OF MAINTENANCE

The company copy of the Stores Requisition is retained in the Requisition book and then filed and retained for at least two years.

The Maintenance Audit Reports are filed in date order by the Duty Officer and retained for at least two years.

PROCEDURE NO 16: CONTROL OF COMPLAINTS

The Complaints Book is a permanent record kept by the Leisure Manager and retained for at least ten years.

PROCEDURE NO 17: CALIBRATION

All Calibration Record Sheets are kept for a period of ten years after their last entry and all calibration certificates are kept for ten years by the Leisure Manager.

PROCEDURE NO 18: CONTROL OF THE USE OF THE CONDITIONING EQUIPMENT

The Application Forms and the Training Records are filed in the General Office and are retained permanently.

Appendix D–5

Document Summary

A Section of the Procedure Manual as Discussed in Chapter 11

Organization Profile: A Leisure Complex

TITLE: DOCUMENT SUMMARY	PREFACE III
ISSUE: 1	SHEET 1 OF 2

The documentation records associated with each procedure are listed in the procedures and samples are provided as appendices. These documents are at their first issue level unless otherwise stated. If any of the documents are revised they will be reissued with the revision level indicated on them. If the previous issue of the document becomes invalid they will be withdrawn and replaced with the new issue. If either document may be used, the stocks will be used up before replacement.

The following is a summary of the current documents showing their current revision status:

PROCEDURE NO 1: CONTROL OF MANUALS

Manual Register	First Issue
Details of Modifications	Revision Number 1

PROCEDURE NO 2: QUALITY SYSTEMS AUDIT

Quality Systems Audit Report	First Issue
Audit Plan	First Issue

PROCEDURE NO 3: CORRECTIVE ACTION AND MANAGEMENT REVIEW

No additional formal documentation is used during this procedure.

PROCEDURE NO 4: TRAINING

Job Description	Revision Number 2
Training Record Form	Revision Number 1
Induction/Skills Training Record Form	First Issue

PROCEDURE NO 5: CLIENT CONTRACT REVIEW

No specific documentation is used in this procedure.

PROCEDURE NO 6: CONTROL OF BLOCK BOOKINGS

Club Membership Application Form	Revision Number 4
Club Booking sheet	Revision Number 1
Master Daily Booking sheet	First Issue
General Conditions of Entry	First Issue
Conditions of Hire Facilities	First Issue
School Block Booking Form	Revision Number 2

PROCEDURE NO. 7: CONTROL OF ONE-TIME BOOKINGS

Application Form for Hire of Facilities	First Issue
Application Form - Soft Play Birthday Party	First Issue
Application Form for Children's Birthday Party	First Issue
Daily Booking Sheet	Revision Number 3

PROCEDURE NO 8: PROGRAMMING OF LEISURE FACILITIES

Sports Center Master Daily Booking sheet	First Issue
Sports Center Daily Booking Sheet	First Issue
Sports Center Sauna Booking Sheet	First Issue

TITLE: DOCUMENT SUMMARY ISSUE: 1	PREFACE III SHEET 2 OF 2
Leisure Center Master Weekly Booking Sheet	First Issue
Leisure Center Weekly Booking Sheet	First Issue
PROCEDURE NO 9: CONTROL OF LEISURE FACILITIES	
Daily Staffing Rota	Revision Number 5
Daily Change Over Sheet	Revision Number 2
Weekly Staffing Rota	Revision Number 3
Safety Requirements	First Issue
Duty Officer's Log	First Issue
PROCEDURE NO 10: PROVISION OF CATERING FACILITIES	
Catering Contract	First Issue
PROCEDURE NO 11: SUPPLIER APPROVAL	
Approved supplier Form	First Issue
PROCEDURE NO 12: PURCHASING	
Order	First Issue
Requisition	First Issue
PROCEDURE NO 13: CONTROL OF CASUAL STAFF	
Casual Staff Form	Revision Number 2
PROCEDURE NO 14: CONTROL OF CLEANING SERVICES	
Cleaning Audit Report - Sports Center	Revision Number 2
Cleaning audit Report - Leisure Center	Revision Number 2
PROCEDURE NO 15: CONTROL OF MAINTENANCE	
Stores Requisition	First Issue
Building Maintenance Request Form	First Issue
Maintenance Audit Report - Sports Center	Revision Number 2
Maintenance Audit Report - Leisure Center	Revision Number 2
Building Maintenance Instructions	First Issue
PROCEDURE NO 16: CONTROL OF COMPLAINTS	
Complaints Book	First Issue
Comments/Suggestions Care	First Issue
PROCEDURE NO 17: CALIBRATION	
Calibration Record Sheet	First Issue
PROCEDURE NO 18: CONTROL OF THE USE OF THE CONDITIONING EQUIPMENT	
Application Form	First Issue
Training Record	First Issue
Membership Card	First Issue

Appendix D–6

Work Instructions

Sixteen examples of work instructions follow; all come from organizations registered to ISO 9000. They describe processes used to carry out tasks. Note that they are all different in style, content, and formality as discussed in Chapter 12. Regardless, they have all proved adequate to their application. They are included as examples of the types of documents used to provide detail instructions to those who carry out tasks.

It is interesting to note that the Work Instruction on the calibration of micrometers (Work Instruction – Example 5) was acceptable for its application in a workshop. If the micrometer was being used elsewhere and was calibrated by a calibration service, this simple method would not be used. Instead checks on the flatness and parallelism of the faces would likely be part of the calibration. The Standard clearly states that the accuracy of the measuring equipment should relate to the tolerances of the dimensions being measured. For high accuracy work a more complex device and calibration is required.

As one of the more time consuming tasks in achieving registration in manufacturing involves calibration, a number of calibration instructions have been included. These need to be viewed in light of the comments above. The forms for data recording are not included with the Work Instructions.

Work Instruction – Example 1 (Food Processor)

PROCESS INSTRUCTION NO. 10
RECEIVING CHECKS

ISSUE: 1 JANUARY 24, 1991

1. When a delivery arrives the following checks have to be made:
   a. Is the delivery vehicle clean and fit for carrying foodstuffs?
   b. Is the delivery driver hygienically dressed?

   If the answer to either of these questions is no, the Production Director should be informed and meat should not be accepted.

   c. Is the delivery as per the order?

   If there are any discrepancies then the Production Director should be informed. The supplier name and description of the goods should be recorded on the Goods Received Sheet.
2. If delivery is meat, check the temperature and record on the Goods Inwards Sheet.
   a. For Fresh meat if temp. is above 5 degrees Celsius then inform Production Director. If temperature is above 8 degrees Celsius then do not accept delivery.
   b. For frozen meat, if the temperature is above -18 degrees Celsius then the Production Director should be informed.
3. The supplier's paperwork should be handed to the Office Staff who check the delivery against the original order. A signed copy of the Delivery Note should then be given to the driver.
4. A date of delivery label must then be located on the bottom of each pallet.
5. The product must then be stored in the appropriate storage area, i.e.
   a. Frozen Meat - Finished Goods Coldstore
   b. Fresh Meat - Raw Meat Chiller
   c. Pudding & Gravy Ingredients - Slicing Storage Area
   d. Packing and other Materials - a designated storage area

Work Instruction – Example 2

METAL PLATING LTD.

TITLE: Hard Chrome Plating on Cast Iron

PROCESS NO 1
ISSUE: 2 SHEET 1 OF 1

1. Degrease with Trichloroethylene 111.
2. Place/fix to suitable jig.
3. Grit blast to dull finish all over.
4. Place in hard chrome vat and adjust rheostat to RED 'STRIKE' mark immediately. Leave for up to 1 min. Lower rheostat to BLACK 'PLATE' mark and leave until sufficient chrome has been deposited.
5. Check size/thickness of deposit.
6. Swill with cold running water.
7. Remove from jig.
8. Dry.
9. Inspect.
10. Wrap/pack.

Work Instruction – Example 3

LABORATORY INSTRUCTION 1
ANALYSIS OF CHROMIUM TANKS FOR CHROMIC ACID.

FREQUENCY: Once per week

METHOD:

1. Instruct the plating operator to top up the tank with water and agitate the tank to mix.
2. Take a sample of about 250 ml from the tank in a beaker.
3. Select a 5 ml pipette and check for damage.
4. Fill the pipette to the 5 ml mark and drain into a 100 ml Volumetric Flask.
5. Make up to 100 mls with de-ionized water.
6. Place stopper in the flask and shake.
7. Extract 5 mls with pipette and drain into a 250 ml beaker.
8. Add 5 ml of concentrated Hydrochloric Acid.
9. Add 100 ml of de-ionized water.
10. Add a spatula of Potassium Iodide.
11. Leave for at least 1 minute.
12. Titrate with N/10 Sodium Thiosulphate until liquid is straw yellow. Add Thyodene or equivalent Iodine indicator. Solution turns black.
13. Continue titration to a lime green end point.
14. Record volume of Sodium Thiosulphate.
15. Volume of Sodium Thiosulphate X 13.5 = gm/liter of CrO_3
16. Subtract concentration from specified concentration.
17. Multiply shortage by Volume of the VAT and determine additions to be made.
18. Record results and recommended action in the VAT book.

Work Instruction – Example 4

PRODUCTION TRAINING

1.0 SCOPE:
Work instructions for Technician training.

2.0 RESPONSIBILITIES:
Individual department managers are responsible for providing training for their technicians.

3.0 PROCEDURE:
3.1 Pre-Employment
3.1.1 Applicants are screened to determine general abilities in electrical insight and learning.
3.2 Employment
3.2.1 Shift Supervisor introduces new employee to management and other personnel.
3.2.2 New employee is issued necessary safety clothing and locker. Orientation includes safety, quality, organization and product modules.
3.2.3 Administrative Assistant informs employee of benefits, safety rules, and regulations.
3.2.4 Specific training begins in the work area assigned. At this time, process and associated safety factors are reviewed.
3.2.5 Trainee is given Standard Operating Manual, along with process flow sheets to review.
3.2.6 A training schedule is set up to address all aspects of job function.
3.2.7 Two week instruction period is established and includes:
- Review and question period at end of each day.
- Brief test given at the end of the training period, to ensure that the individual has comprehended information given. Test is prepared by area representative.
- A score of 85% must be attained. A score less than 85% requires additional review until individual achieves a passing score.

3.3 Shift Assignment
3.3.1 Once a technician is assigned on-the-job training begins immediately under the supervision of the Shift Supervisor.
3.3.2 The Shift Supervisor outlines job description, routine duties and area of responsibility.
3.4 Special Training
3.4.1 On-going evaluations through employee presentation of various sections of operations to management.
3.4.2 Monthly safety meetings
3.4.3 Refresher sessions on specific operational tasks as specified by management
3.4.4 Quality control training
- Statistical tools

3.4.5 Quarterly ISO 9000 refresher course
3.4.6 Quarterly quality audit review

Effective Date: 2/93	Rev. No: A	Rev. Date: 4/93
Approved By: PMM	Page 1 of 2	Type: Work Instructions

Work Instruction – Example 4 (continued)

3.5 Operating Personnel

3.5.1 Shift Supervisor – managed plant operations for several years and is familiar with every aspect of plant operations. Assisted with writing or modifying Standard Operating Procedures.

3.5.2 Production Manager/Process Chemical Engineer – qualified through college background and professional seminars.

4.0 DOCUMENTATION:

4.1 All training records are kept in employee training file maintained by the Quality Officer.

Effective Date: 2/93	Rev. No: A	Rev. Date: 4/93
Approved By: PMM	Page 2 of 2	Type: Work Instructions

Work Instruction – Example 5

CALIBRATION WORK INSTRUCTION

TITLE: MICROMETERS
ISSUE: 1

INSTRUCTION NO 1
SHEET 1 OF 1

1.0 PROCEDURE

1.1 Examine micrometer for any signs of damage or wear and check seal for integrity. Check function of ratchet. Record findings on calibration record.

1.2 Set micrometer to zero and record the reading. If not zero adjust to zero.

1.3 Select a series of five sizes which require measurements at different places on the barrel of the micrometer and which cover the whole of the measuring scale.

1.4 Make stack of slip gauges up to the sizes selected and measure the stack with the micrometer. Record readings on the calibration record.

1.5 Assess the readings obtained and compare with the required accuracy of the micrometer.

1.6 If the readings indicate that the micrometer is achieving the required accuracy then mark the micrometer accordingly, seal the adjusters and return to use. Record this on the calibration record.

1.7 If the readings indicate that the micrometer is *not* achieving the required accuracy then remove the micrometer from service and inform the Chief Inspector. Record this on the calibration record.

Work Instruction – Example 6

CALIBRATION WORK INSTRUCTION

TITLE: VERNIER / DIGITAL CALIPERS — INSTRUCTION NO 2
ISSUE: 1 — SHEET 1 OF 1

1.0 PROCEDURE

1.1 Examine caliper for any signs of damage or wear and check seal for integrity. Close the jaws completely and check the squareness of the jaws. If daylight can be seen then check with slip gauge across the jaws. Record findings on calibration record.

1.2 Set caliper to zero and record the reading. If not zero adjust to zero.

1.3 Select a series of five sizes which require measurements at different places along the length of the caliper. If the caliper uses a vernier then the points should be selected which require different points on the vernier scale to record them.

1.4 Make stack of slip gauges up to the sizes selected and measure the stack with the caliper. Record readings on the calibration record.

1.5 Assess the readings obtained and compare with the required accuracy of the caliper.

1.6 If the readings indicate that the caliper is achieving the required accuracy, mark the caliper accordingly and return to use. Record this on the calibration record.

1.7 If the readings indicate that the caliper is *not* achieving the required accuracy then remove the caliper from service and inform the Chief Inspector. Record this on the calibration record.

Work Instruction – Example 7

CALIBRATION WORK INSTRUCTION

TITLE: HEIGHT GAUGES | INSTRUCTION NO 3
ISSUE: 1 | SHEET 1 OF 1

1.0 PROCEDURE

1.1 Examine height gauge for any signs of damage or wear and check seal for integrity. Record findings on calibration record.

1.2 Fix a calibrated clock gauge in the moving arm of the height gauge with the pointer horizontal and at right angles to the measuring scale. Place on a calibrated surface table and place a calibrated square adjacent to the height gauge. Use the square to check the squareness of the height gauge with the calibrated clock. Adjust as necessary. If it is not possible to adjust the height gauge square to within the required accuracy then report to the Chief Inspector.

1.3 Repeat 1.2 above with the calibrated clock parallel to the measuring scale.

1.4 Place a calibrated clock gauge in the moving arm of the height gauge and place on a calibrated surface table. If the clock can come down to the table then set to zero on the table and record the reading. If it is not possible to set to zero on the table. place a suitable size of slip gauge on the table to allow the clock to be set to zero.

1.5 Select a series of five sizes which require measurements at different places on the height gauge.

1.6 Make stack of slip gauges up to the sizes selected and measure each stack with the height gauge. Record readings on the calibration record.

1.7 Assess the readings obtained and compare with the required accuracy of the height gauge.

1.8 If the readings indicate that the height gauge is achieving the required accuracy, mark the height gauge accordingly, seal the adjusters and return to use. Record this on the calibration record.

1.9 If the readings indicate that the height gauge is *not* achieving the required accuracy then remove the height gauge from service and inform the Chief Inspector. Record this on the calibration record.

Work Instruction – Example 8

CALIBRATION WORK INSTRUCTION

TITLE: WORKSHOP SLIP GAUGES INSTRUCTION NO 4
ISSUE: 1 SHEET 1 OF 1

NOTE 1 Only workshop slip gauges are to be calibrated in-house; higher standards of slip gauge must be calibrated at nationally-approved laboratories.

NOTE 2 Slip gauges should only be handled with tweezers during calibration to minimize the expansion of the gauges due to heat from hands. Where it is necessary to ring gauges together to obtain the correct values, the gauges should be rung together and then left for their temperature to settle on the surface plate for at least six hours.

1.0 PROCEDURE

1.1 At least twenty four hours before the start of calibration the slip gauges are brought into the calibration room and individually laid out on a surface table adjacent to the calibrated set of slip gauges, placing each workshop gauge adjacent to its size equivalent.

1.2 Each calibrated slip gauge is lifted off the surface table and placed under a calibrated clock gauge which is zeroed on the surface of the center of the calibrated slip.

1.3 The calibrated slip gauge is removed from under the calibrated clock gauge without altering the setting. The equivalent workshop slip gauge to this placed under the clock gauge and measured at the center and at each corner. The readings obtained are recorded.

1.4 The size of the workshop slip gauge is determined from the average of the readings taken and the known size of the calibrated slip gauge as recorded on the calibration certificate for the slip gauges.

1.5 The size determined is entered onto the calibration certificate for the workshop gauge and recorded on the calibration record.

1.6 The level of uncertainty for the calibration of the set of slip gauges is written onto the Calibration Certificate. This value is determined from the accuracy of the calibrated clock gauge and the level of uncertainty of the calibrated slip gauges.

Work Instruction – Example 9

CALIBRATION WORK INSTRUCTION

TITLE: PLUG GAUGES INSTRUCTION NO 5
ISSUE: 1 SHEET 1 OF 1

1.0 PROCEDURE

1.1 Examine plug gauge for any signs of damage or wear. Record findings on calibration record.

1.2 Select slip gauges to the size of the 'go' end of the plug gauge and place under a comparator. Set the comparator to the set of slips.

1.3 Place the 'go' end of the plug gauge under the comparator and check the diameter in at least three positions and record the findings.

1.4 Repeat above procedure for the 'no go' end of the gauge.

1.5 If the readings indicate that both ends of the gauge are achieving the required accuracy then mark the gauge accordingly and return to use. Record this on the calibration record.

1.6 If the readings indicate that either end of the gauge is *not* achieving the required accuracy then remove the gauge from service and inform the Chief Inspector. Record this on the calibration record.

Work Instruction – Example 10

CALIBRATION WORK INSTRUCTION

TITLE: GAP GAUGES — INSTRUCTION NO 6
ISSUE: 1 — SHEET 1 OF 1

1.0 PROCEDURE

1.1 Examine gap gauge for any signs of damage or wear and check integrity of any wax seals. Record findings on calibration record.

1.2 Measure the 'go' end of the gap gauge with a set of slip gauges and record the size found on the calibration record card. If this size is not the required size and the gap gauge can be adjusted then adjust the gap to the required size.

1.3 Repeat step 1.2 above for the 'no go' end of the gap gauge.

1.4 If the gap gauge is non adjustable and the readings indicate that both ends of the gauge is achieving the required accuracy then mark the gauge accordingly and return to use. Record this on the calibration record.

1.5 If the gauge is adjustable and after the adjustments both ends are achieving the required accuracy then mark the gauge accordingly and return to use. Record this on the calibration record.

1.6 If the gauge is not adjustable and the readings indicate that either end of the gauge is *not* achieving the required accuracy then remove the gauge from service and inform the Chief Inspector. Record this on the calibration record.

1.7 If the gauge is adjustable and initially either end of the gauge was *not* achieving the required accuracy then inform the Chief Inspector. Record this on the calibration record.

Work Instruction – Example 11

CALIBRATION WORK INSTRUCTION

TITLE: THREADED GAUGES — INSTRUCTION NO 7
ISSUE: 1 — SHEET 1 OF 1

1.0 PROCEDURE

1.1 Examine thread gauge for any signs of damage or wear. Record findings on calibration record.

1.2 Place 'go' end of the thread gauge in jaws of a thread micrometer and place the appropriate wires in the holders. Using the wires check the effective diameter of the thread gauge in at least three positions and record the findings.

1.3 Repeat above procedure for the 'no go' end of the gauge.

1.4 Place the 'go' end of the thread gauge onto the centers of the shadow graph and examine the form of the thread using overlays. Record the findings.

1.5 Repeat above procedure for the 'no go' end of the gauge.

1.6 If the readings indicate that both ends of the gauge are achieving the required accuracy then mark the gauge accordingly and return to use. Record this on the calibration record.

1.7 If the readings indicate that either end of the gauge is *not* achieving the required accuracy then remove the gauge from service and inform the Chief Inspector. Record this on the calibration record.

Work Instruction – Example 12

CALIBRATION WORK INSTRUCTION

TITLE: THREAD GAP GAUGES — INSTRUCTION NO 8
ISSUE: 1 — SHEET 1 OF 1

1.0 PROCEDURE

1.1 Examine gap gauge for any signs of damage or wear and check integrity of any wax seals. Record findings on calibration record.

1.2 Measure the 'go' end of the gap gauge with a calibrated thread gauge of the correct size. Record the finding on the calibration record card. If this size is not the required size then adjust the thread gap to the required size.

1.3 Repeat step 1.2 above for the 'no go' end of the gap gauge.

1.4 If after any adjustments both ends are achieving the required accuracy then mark the gauge accordingly and return to use. Record this on the calibration record.

1.5 If after adjustments the readings indicate that either end of the gauge is *not* achieving the required accuracy then remove the gauge from service and inform the Chief Inspector. Record this on the calibration record.

1.6 If initially either end of the gauge was *not* achieving the required accuracy then inform the Chief Inspector. Record this on the calibration record.

Work Instruction – Example 13

CALIBRATION WORK INSTRUCTION

TITLE: DEPTH MICROMETERS — INSTRUCTION NO 9
ISSUE: 1 — SHEET 1 OF 1

1.0 PROCEDURE

1.1 Examine micrometer for any signs of damage or wear and check seal for integrity. Check function of ratchet. Record findings on calibration record.

1.2 Set micrometer to zero and record the reading. If not zero adjust to zero.

1.3 Select a series of five sizes which require measurements at different places on the barrel of the micrometer and which cover the whole of the measuring scale.

1.4 Make two stacks of slip gauges up to the sizes selected. Place the two stacks close to each other on a surface plate and place the depth micrometer on top of the two stacks. Measure the depth of the gap between the two stacks with the micrometer. Record readings on the calibration record.

1.5 Assess the readings obtained and compare with the required accuracy of the micrometer.

1.6 If the readings indicate that the micrometer is achieving the required accuracy then mark the micrometer accordingly, seal the adjusters and return to use. Record this on the calibration record.

1.7 If the readings indicate that the micrometer is *not* achieving the required accuracy then remove the micrometer from service and inform the Chief Inspector. Record this on the calibration record.

Work Instruction – Example 14

CALIBRATION WORK INSTRUCTION

TITLE: COMPARATORS INSTRUCTION NO 10
ISSUE: 1 SHEET 1 OF 1

1.0 PROCEDURE

1.1 Examine comparator for any signs of damage or wear and check smooth function and even movement of pointer. Record findings on calibration record.

1.2 Set comparator to zero on a slip gauge.

1.3 Select a series of five sizes which require measurements at different places on the scale of the comparator and which cover the whole of the measuring scale.

1.4 Make stacks of slip gauges up to the sizes selected. Place the two stacks close to each other on a surface plate and measure with the comparator. Record readings on the calibration record.

1.5 Assess the readings obtained and compare with the required accuracy of the comparator.

1.6 If the readings indicate that the comparator is achieving the required accuracy then mark the comparator accordingly, and return to use. Record this on the calibration record.

1.7 If the readings indicate that the micrometer is *not* achieving the required accuracy then remove the comparator from service and inform the Chief Inspector. Record this on the calibration record.

Work Instruction – Example 15

CALIBRATION WORK INSTRUCTION

TITLE: SQUARES INSTRUCTION NO 11
ISSUE: 1 SHEET 1 OF 1

1.0 PROCEDURE

1.1 Clamp the square to be calibrated on a surface plate.

1.2 Set a master calibrated square next to the square with the gap between the calibrated square and the master square at the bottom of the blades adjusted to the size of calibrated slip gauge. Clamp the master square to the surface plate.

1.3 Measure the gap between the blades along the length of the blade in approximately five positions along the length of the blade. Record the readings obtained.

1.4 Assess the readings obtained and compare with the required accuracy of the square.

1.6 If the readings indicate that the square is achieving the required accuracy then mark the square accordingly, and return to use. Record this on the calibration record.

1.7 If the readings indicate that the square is *not* achieving the required accuracy then remove the square from service and inform the Chief Inspector. Record this on the calibration record.

Work Instruction – Example 16

PROCESS INSTRUCTION NO. 1 - PRODUCTION OF MEAT LOGS

ISSUE: 1

1. Collect Meat from store taking care to choose oldest stock first.
2. Put meat into Hobart Mixer. Weigh meat as it comes out of mixer into a 100kg batch.
4. Make up Ingredient batch as follows :
   a. Salt 1.5 Kg
   b. Phosphate 0.5 Kg
   c. Flour 9.0 Kg
   d Water 15 Liters
5. a. Put meat into Z-Blade mixer sprinkle in salt and add half the water.
   b. Add phosphate to remaining water and mix well and then add to mixer.
6. Close lid on mixer and mix for 15 minutes. Check mix, and if it is not thoroughly mixed continuing mixing until mixed properly.
7. Gradually add flour to mix while mixer running until all added and then mix for a further 5 minutes. Check mix. If it is not thoroughly mixed, continuing mixing until mixed properly.
8. Empty mix into tote bin and then feed into VF20.
9. Fill sausage bag with mix and clip end. Place sausage onto cooking rack.
10. When rack full place in cooker and cook for 5 hours on timer.
11. After 5 hours of cooking the core temperature of three logs are taken: bottom of rack, middle of rack and top of rack. If any are under 72 degrees Celsius then the product is left in oven for further cooking. When the product has reached its core temperature, the temperatures are recorded on the Temperature Control Sheet.
12. The rack is removed from the oven and chilled using water shower. MEAT NOT REACHING CORE TEMPERATURE MUST NOT BE REMOVED FROM AN OVEN.
13. Product is to be chilled for at least two hours under the shower before being labeled up with meat type and date cooked. The product is then located in the Cooked Meat Chiller.

Appendix D–7

Sample Forms

The ISO 9000 Standards do not specifically mention "forms." They do, however, require quality records to "demonstrate conformance to specified requirements and the effective operation of the quality system." All organizations use forms which, when completed, become a part of the organization's quality records. Forms are best designed specifically for the intended purpose, but generic purchased forms are also usable. Forms must have a date or revision level so that document control is possible.

This appendix includes sample forms used by ISO 9000 registered companies. They were done on a personal computer. Hand generated forms can also be used. The samples are intended to indicate the main requirement for forms—that is utility.

NEW PRODUCT CONTROL SHEET		NO.
PRODUCT NAME:		
FULL FUNCTIONAL SPECIFICATION		
TITLE	SIGNATURE	DATE
GENERAL MANAGER		
GROUP Q. C.		
MATERIAL SAFETY DATA SHEETS RECEIVED		
1ST SAMPLE RECEIVED		
COMMENTS		
2ND SAMPLE RECEIVED		
COMMENTS		
3RD SAMPLE RECEIVED		
COMMENTS		

APPROVED BY	DATE	
GENERAL MANAGER	GROUP Q.C.	

Rev. A 10/06/89

<table>
<tr><td colspan="6">CUSTOMER INQUIRY FORM</td></tr>
<tr><td colspan="3">CUSTOMER</td><td>PHONE</td><td colspan="2"></td></tr>
<tr><td colspan="3">ADDRESS</td><td>FAX</td><td colspan="2"></td></tr>
<tr><td colspan="3"></td><td>POST CODE</td><td colspan="2"></td></tr>
<tr><td>CONTACT NAME</td><td colspan="2"></td><td colspan="2">CONTACT POSITION</td><td></td></tr>
<tr><td colspan="6">TYPE OF BUSINESS</td></tr>
<tr><td>NO. OF EMPLOYEES</td><td colspan="2"></td><td colspan="2">APPROX TURNOVER</td><td></td></tr>
<tr><td colspan="6">SCOPE OF PROJECT</td></tr>
<tr><td colspan="6">COMMENTS</td></tr>
<tr><td colspan="6">FOLLOW-UP ACTION</td></tr>
<tr><td>ORIGINATOR</td><td></td><td>DATE</td><td></td><td>COM. DIR.</td><td></td></tr>
</table>

3/14/90

CHECKLIST FOR DISCHARGE

RESIDENT		DATE	

REASON FOR DISCHARGE:

PROPOSED DATE OF DISCHARGE:

DESTINATION

CONTACT NAME: ADDRESS:

TELEPHONE NO.:

	DATE	CONFIRM
GENERAL PRACTITIONER INFORMED		
SUPPORT SERVICES NOTIFIED		
1.		
2.		
3.		
INFORMATION GIVEN TO DESTINATION CONTACT		
1. CURRENT MEDICATION		
2. CURRENT CARE REQUIRED		
3.		
FUNDING AGENCY INFORMED		
ACTUAL DATE OF DISCHARGE		
PENSION BOOK RETURNED TO DSS		
BELONGINGS BOOKED OUT		
MEDICATION HANDED OVER		

MISCELLANEOUS:

REVIEWED	MANAGER	
SIGNED	RESIDENT OR REPRESENTATIVE	

Rev. A 2/17/89

SUMMARY OF SUPPLIER CORRECTIVE ACTIONS REPORT

SUPPLIER				DATE	
ADDRESS				PHONE	
				FAX	
				POST CODE	
CONTACT		APPROVED BY		DATE	
APPROVAL BASIS					
TYPE OF PRODUCT OR SERVICE					

CONCERN	ACTION	CORRECTIVE ACTION	CLEARED BY	DATE

Rev. B 1/07/93 JPM

PROJECT DAILY REPORT					
CLIENT		DATE		CONSULTANT	

CONTACTS
ACTIVITIES

CONSULTANT ACTIVITIES BEFORE NEXT VISIT	COMPLETED

CLIENT ACTIVITIES BEFORE NEXT VISIT	COMPLETED

DATE OF NEXT VISIT		REVIEWED		DATE	

10/31/91 MLM

Corrective Action for Suppliers

Name of Supplier: ______________________________

Contact Name: ______________________________

Street Address: ______________________________

____

City: ______________ State: ________ Zip Code: __________

Phone Number: ____________________

Description of Discrepancy: ______________________________

____

____

____

____

Corrective Action: ______________________________

____

____

____

____

Action Completed? ☐ Yes ☐ No Date: __________

Prepared By: ____________________ Date: __________

Copy to Office Manager ***Copy to Purchasing Officer***

RJR 4/5/93

Appendix E:

Where to Go for Help

For Consulting, Training Assistance, Speeches, Case Studies, and Other Information:

The authors provide consultancy assistance, training materials, and training courses in North America and Europe. The rest of the world is covered by affiliates. You may call or write to the Authors.

In North America	Peter M. Malkovich Process Management International 7801 Eash Bush Lake Road, Suite 360 Minneapolis, Minnesota 55439-3115 Phone: 800-258-0313 Fax: 612-893-0502
In Europe	Dr. Bryn Owen Optimum Systems for Quality, Ltd. Simonstone Business Park Simonstone, Lancs. BB12 7NJ U. K. Phone: 0282 779002 Fax: 0282 779099

For Speeches and Case Studies:

Mr. Thomas Cothran
Cothran PR
3948 West 50th Street
Minneapolis, Minnesota 55424
Phone: 612-925-9473

To Obtain Copies of the ISO 9000 Standards:

In the United States	ASQC Quality Press Customer Service Department P.O. Box 3066 Milwaukee, WI 53201-3066 Phone: 800-248-1946 Fax: 414-272-1734

In Canada	Standards Council of Canada (SCC) 45 O'Connor Street, Suite 1200 Ottawa, Ontario K1P 6N7 Phone: 613-238-3222 Fax: 613-995-4564
In the United Kingdom	British Standards Institute P. O. Box 375 Milton Keynes MK14 6LL, UK Phone: 0908-22908 Fax: 0908-220671
In Europe	Swiss Association for Standardization Muhlebachstrasse 54 CH-8008 Zurich Phone: +41 1 254 54 54 Fax: +41 1 254 54 74

General Information:

CEEM of Fairfax, Virginia publishes a monthly newsletter on ISO 9000. It includes case studies of companies who have achieved ISO 9000 registration, information on the standards and their interpretation, and news on what is happening in the International Organization for Standardization and other groups and industries. They also publish the names of registration achievers, training availability, and a directory of U.S. and Canadian registrations.

CEEM
P.O. Box 200
Fairfax Station, Virginia 22039-0200
Phone: 800-745-5565 or 703-250-5900
Fax: 703-250-5313

Appendix F

Glossary

The authors have worked on three continents and in a wide variety of industries, and even though everyone uses a common Standard, terminology varies by country, industry, and publication. This short glossary defines selected terms that have different meanings in some areas.

ISO: The International Organization for Standardization:

This body is based in Geneva, Switzerland, and is governed by representatives from all industrial nations. Its objective is to promote international trade through the development and issue of standards for a wide range of products and services.

ISO 9000:

A series of standards addressing the systems used by organizations to control the quality of the products and services they provide.

Chief Executive:

The person having overall responsibility for the organization being registered. This may be the Plant Manager, General Manager, Managing Director, Senior Partner or many other titles.

Executive Management:

Members of management reporting directly to the Chief Executive and having the authority to make decisions regarding their function, on behalf of the organization.

Management Representative for Quality:

The member of the executive management who takes responsibility for quality, and for the development and operation of the quality system.

Registrar:

An organization carrying out audits of quality systems against the requirements of ISO 9000; also referred to as third-party auditor.

ISO 9000 Audit:

The assessment of an organization's quality system to determine whether it meets the requirements of the appropriate ISO 9000 Standard.

ISO 9000 Registration:

The outcome of a successful ISO 9000 Audit of the quality system, conducted by a Registrar.

ISO 9000 Auditors:

The employees of Registrars who actually carry out the audits. The training and qualifications of ISO 9000 Auditors are defined by the ISO. There are three levels of ISO auditors. Based on their qualifications and experience, auditors are designated as provisional auditors, auditors, or lead auditors. A lead auditor is responsible for an audit and may be assisted by provisional auditors and auditors.

Internal Audit:

An examination of the quality activities of an organization to confirm that they are aligned with the documented quality system.

Internal Auditors:

Members of an organization who have been trained to carry out internal audits of the quality system.